THE MAJOR WORKS
OF ALEXANDER POPE

A Digireads.com Book
Digireads.com Publishing

The Major Works of Alexander Pope
By Alexander Pope
ISBN 10: 1-4209-3915-7
ISBN 13: 978-1-4209-3915-6

Please visit *www.digireads.com*

CONTENTS

4

PASTORALS

SPRING
THE
FIRST PASTORAL
OR
DAMON
To Sir William Trumbull

First in these fields I try the sylvan strains,
Nor blush to sport on Windsor's blissful plains:
Fair Thames, flow gently from thy sacred spring,
While on thy banks Sicilian Muses sing;
Let vernal airs through trembling osiers play,
And Albion's cliffs resound the rural lay.
   You that, too wise for pride, too good for power,
Enjoy the glory to be great no more,
And, carrying with you all the world can boast,
To all the world illustriously are lost!
Oh, let my Muse her slender reed inspire,
Till in your native shades you tune the lyre:
So when the nightingale to rest removes,
The thrush may chant to the forsaken groves,
But, charmed to silence, listens while she sings,
And all th' aërial audience clap their wings.
   Soon as the flocks shook off the nightly dews,
Two swains, whom Love kept wakeful, and the Muse,
Poured over the whitening vale their fleecy care,
Fresh as the morn, and as the season fair:
The dawn now blushing on the mountain's side,
Thus Daphnis spoke, and Strephon thus replied.

DAPHNIS.

   Hear how the birds, on every bloomy spray,
With joyous music wake the dawning day!
Why sit we mute when early linnets sing,
When warbling Philomel salutes the spring?
Why sit we sad, when Phosphor shines so clear,
And lavish Nature paints the purple year?

STREPHON.

   Sing then, and Damon shall attend the strain,
While yon slow oxen turn the furrowed plain.
Here the bright crocus and blue violet glow;
Here western winds on breathing roses blow.

I'll stake yon lamb, that near the fountain plays,
And from the brink his dancing shade surveys.

DAPHNIS.

And I this bowl, where wanton ivy twines,
And swelling clusters bend the curling vines:
Four Figures rising from the work appear,
The various Seasons of the rolling year;
And what is that, which binds the radiant sky,
Where twelve fair signs in beauteous order lie?

DAMON.

Then sing by turns, by turns the Muses sing;
Now hawthorns blossom, now the daisies spring;
Now leaves the trees, and flowers adorn the ground:
Begin, the vales shall every note rebound.

STREPHON.

Inspire me, Phoebus, in my Delia's praise,
With Waller's strains, or Granville's moving lays!
A milk-white bull shall at your altars stand,
That threats a fight, and spurns the rising sand.

DAPHNIS.

O Love! for Sylvia let me gain the prize,
And make my tongue victorious as her eyes;
No lambs or sheep for victims I'll impart,
Thy victim, Love, shall be the shepherd's heart.

STREPHON.

Me gentle Delia beckons from the plain,
Then hid in shades, eludes her eager swain;
But feigns a laugh, to see me search around,
And by that laugh the willing fair is found.

DAPHNIS.

The sprightly Sylvia trips along the green,
She runs, but hopes she does not run unseen;
While a kind glance at her pursuer flies,
How much at variance are her feet and eyes!

STREPHON.

O'er golden sands let rich Pactolus flow,
And trees weep amber on the banks of Po;
Blessed Thames's shores the brightest beauties yield,
Feed here, my lambs, I'll seek no distant field.

DAPHNIS.

Celestial Venus haunts Idalia's groves;
Diana Cynthus, Ceres Hybla loves;
If Windsor-shades delight the matchless maid,
Cynthus and Hybla yield to Windsor-shade.

STREPHON.

All nature mourns, the skies relent in showers,
Hushed are the birds, and closed the drooping flowers;
If Delia smile, the flowers begin to spring,
The skies to brighten, and the birds to sing.

DAPHNIS.

All nature laughs, the groves are fresh and fair,
The sun's mild lustre warms the vital air;
If Sylvia smiles, new glories gild the shore,
And vanquished Nature seems to charm no more.

STREPHON.

In spring the fields, in autumn hills I love,
At morn the plains, at noon the shady grove,
But Delia always; absent from her sight,
Nor plains at morn, nor groves at noon delight.

DAPHNIS.

Sylvia's like autumn ripe, yet mild as May,
More bright than noon, yet fresh as early day;
Even spring displeases, when she shines not here;
But, blessed with her, 'tis spring throughout the year.

STREPHON.

Say, Daphnis, say, in what glad soil appears,
A wondrous tree that sacred monarchs bears?
Tell me but this, and I'll disclaim the prize,
And give the conquest to thy Sylvia's eyes.

DAPHNIS.

Nay, tell me first, in what more happy fields
The thistle springs, to which the lily yields?
And then a nobler prize I will resign;
For Sylvia, charming Sylvia shall be thine.

DAMON.

Cease to contend, for, Daphnis, I decree,
The bowl to Strephon, and the lamb to thee:
Blessed swains, whose nymphs in every grace excel;
Blessed nymphs, whose swains those graces sing so well!
Now rise, and haste to yonder woodbine bowers,
A soft retreat from sudden vernal showers;
The turf with rural dainties shall be crowned.
While opening blooms diffuse their sweets around.
For see! the gathering flocks to shelter tend,
And from the Pleiades fruitful showers descend.

SUMMER
THE
SECOND PASTORAL
OR
ALEXIS
To Dr Garth

A shepherd's boy (he seeks no better name)
Led forth his flocks along the silver Thame,
Where dancing sunbeams on the waters played,
And verdant alders formed a quivering shade.
Soft as he mourned, the streams forgot to flow,
The flocks around a dumb compassion show:
The Naiads wept in every watery bower,
And Jove consented in a silent shower.
Accept, O GARTH, the Muse's early lays,
That adds this wreath of ivy to thy bays;
Hear what from love unpractised hearts endure:
From love, the sole disease thou canst not cure.
'Ye shady beeches, and ye cooling streams,

Defence from Phoebus', not from Cupid's beams,
To you I mourn, nor to the deaf I sing,
The woods shall answer, and their echo ring.'
The hills and rocks attend my doleful lay;
Why art thou prouder and more hard than they?
The bleating sheep with my complaints agree,
They parched with heat, and I inflamed by thee.
The sultry Sirius burns the thirsty plains,
While in thy heart eternal winter reigns.
    Where stray ye, Muses, in what lawn or grove,
While your Alexis pines in hopeless love?
In those fair fields where sacred Isis glides,
Or else where Cam his winding vales divides?
As in the crystal spring I view my face,
Fresh rising blushes paint the watery glass;
But since those graces please thy eyes no more,
I shun the fountains which I sought before.
Once I was skilled in every herb that grew,
And every plant that drinks the morning dew;
Ah, wretched shepherd, what avails thy art,
To cure thy lambs, but not to heal thy heart!
    Let other swains attend the rural care,
Feed fairer flocks, or richer fleeces shear:
But nigh yon mountain let me tune my lays,
Embrace my love, and bind my brows with bays.
That flute is mine which Colin's tuneful breath
Inspired when living, and bequeathed in death;
He said, 'Alexis, take this pipe--the same
That taught the groves my Rosalinda's name':
But now the reeds shall hang on yonder tree,
For ever silent, since despised by thee.
Oh! were I made by some transforming power
The captive bird that sings within thy bower!
Then might my voice thy listening ears employ,
And I those kisses he receives, enjoy.
    And yet my numbers please the rural throng,
Rough Satyrs dance, and Pan applauds the song:
The Nymphs, forsaking every cave and spring,
Their early fruit, and milk-white turtles bring;
Each amorous nymph prefers her gifts in vain.
On you their gifts are all bestowed again.
For you the swains the fairest flowers design,
And in one garland all their beauties join;
Accept the wreath which you deserve alone,
In whom all beauties are comprised in one.
    See what delights in sylvan scenes appear!
Descending gods have found Elysium here.
In woods bright Venus with Adonis strayed,

And chaste Diana haunts the forest shade.
Come, lovely nymph, and bless the silent hours,
When swains from shearing seek their nightly bowers,
When weary reapers quit the sultry field,
And crowned with corn their thanks to Ceres yield;
This harmless grove no lurking viper hides,
But in my breast the serpent love abides.
Here bees from blossoms sip the rosy dew,
But your Alexis knows no sweets but you.
Oh, deign to visit our forsaken seats,
The mossy fountains, and the green retreats!
Where'er you walk, cool gales shall fan the glade,
Trees, where you sit, shall crowd into a shade:
Where'er you tread, the blushing flowers shall rise,
And all things flourish where you turn your eyes.
Oh, how I long with you to pass my days,
Invoke the Muses, and resound your praise!
Your praise the birds shall chant in every grove,
And winds shall waft it to the Powers above.
But would you sing, and rival Orpheus' strain,
The wondering forests soon should dance again,
The moving mountains hear the powerful call,
And headlong streams hang listening in their fall!
    But see, the shepherds shun the noonday heat,
The lowing herds to murmuring brooks retreat,
To closer shades the panting flocks remove;
Ye gods! and is there no relief for love?
But soon the sun with milder rays descends
To the cool ocean, where his journey ends:
On me Love's fiercer flames for ever prey,
By night he scorches, as he burns by day.'

AUTUMN
THE
THIRD PASTORAL
OR
HYLAS AND AEGON
To Mr. Wycherley

Beneath the shade a spreading Beech displays,
Hylas and Aegon sung their rural lays,
This mourned a faithless, that an absent Love,
And Delia's name and Doris' filled the Grove.
Ye Mantuan nymphs, your sacred succour bring;
Hylas and Aegon's rural lays I sing.
    Thou, whom the Nine with Plautus' wit inspire,
The art of Terence, and Menander's fire;
Whose sense instructs us, and whose humour charms,

Whose judgment sways us, and whose spirit warms!
Oh, skilled in Nature! see the hearts of Swains,
Their artless passions, and their tender pains.
Now setting Phoebus shone serenely bright,
And fleecy clouds were streaked with purple light;
When tuneful Hylas with melodious moan,
Taught rocks to weep, and made the mountains groan.
    'Go, gentle gales, and bear my sighs away!
To Delia's ear, the tender notes convey.
As some sad turtle his lost love deplores,
And with deep murmurs fills the sounding shores;
Thus, far from Delia, to the winds I mourn,
Alike unheard, unpitied, and forlorn.
    Go, gentle gales, and bear my sighs along!
For her, the feathered quires neglect their song;
For her, the limes their pleasing shades deny;
For her, the lilies hang their heads and die.
Ye flowers that droop, forsaken by the spring,
Ye birds that, left by summer, cease to sing,
Ye trees that fade when autumn-heats remove,
Say, is not absence death to those who love?
    Go, gentle gales, and bear my sighs away!
Cursed be the fields that cause my Delia's stay;
Fade every blossom, wither every tree,
Die every flower, and perish all, but she.
What have I said? where'er my Delia flies,
Let spring attend, and sudden flowers arise;
Let opening roses knotted oaks adorn,
And liquid amber drop from every thorn.
    Go, gentle gales, and bear my sighs along!
The birds shall cease to tune their evening song,
The winds to breathe, the waving woods to move,
And streams to murmur, e'er I cease to love.
Not bubbling fountains to the thirsty swain,
Not balmy sleep to labourers faint with pain,
Not showers to larks, nor sun-shine to the bee,
Are half so charming as thy sight to me.
    Go, gentle gales, and bear my sighs away!
Come, Delia, come; ah, why this long delay?
Through rocks and caves the name of Delia sounds,
Delia, each cave and echoing rock rebounds.
Ye powers, what pleasing frenzy sooths my mind!
Do lovers dream, or is my Delia kind?
She comes, my Delia comes!—Now cease my lay,
And cease, ye gales, to bear my sighs away!'
    Next Aegon sung, while Windsor groves admired;
Rehearse, ye Muses, what yourselves inspired.
    'Resound, ye hills, resound my mournful strain!

12

Of perjured Doris, dying I complain:
Here where the mountains lessening as they rise
Lose the low vales, and steal into the skies:
While labouring oxen, spent with toil and heat,
In their loose traces from the field retreat:
While curling smokes from village-tops are seen,
And the fleet shades glide o'er the dusky green.
   Resound, ye hills, resound my mournful lay!
Beneath yon poplar oft we past the day:
Oft on the rind I carved her amorous vows,
While she with garlands hung the bending boughs:
The garlands fade, the vows are worn away;
So dies her love, and so my hopes decay.
   Resound ye hills, resound my mournful strain!
Now bright Arcturus glads the teeming grain,
Now golden fruits on loaded branches shine,
And grateful clusters swell with floods of wine;
Now blushing berries paint the yellow grove;
Just Gods! shall all things yield returns but love?
   Resound, ye hills, resound my mournful lay!
The shepherds cry, 'Thy flocks are left a prey—'
Ah! what avails it me, the flocks to keep,
Who lost my heart, while I preserved my sheep.
Pan came, and asked, what magic caused my smart,
Or what ill eyes malignant glances dart?
What eyes but hers, alas, have power to move!
And is here magic but what dwells in love?
   Resound, ye hills, resound my mournful strains!
I'll fly from shepherds, flocks, and flowery plains.
From shepherds, flocks, and plains, I may remove,
Forsake mankind, and all the world but love!
I know thee, Love! on foreign Mountains bred,
Wolves gave thee suck, and savage Tigers fed.
Thou wert from Etna's burning entrails torn,
Got by fierce whirlwinds, and in thunder born!
   Resound, ye hills, resound my mournful lay!
Farewell, ye woods! adieu the light of day!
One leap from yonder cliff shall end my pains,
No more, ye hills, no more resound my strains!
   Thus sung the shepherds till th' approach of night,
The skies yet blushing with departing light,
When falling dews with spangles decked the glade,
And the low sun had lengthened every shade.

WINTER THE FOURTH PASTORAL
OR
DAPHNE
To the memory of Mrs. Tempest

LYCIDAS.

Thyrsis, the music of that murmuring spring,
Is not so mournful as the strains you sing.
Nor rivers winding through the vales below,
So sweetly warble, or so smoothly flow.
Now sleeping flocks on their soft fleeces lie,
The moon, serene in glory, mounts the sky,
While silent birds forget their tuneful lays,
Oh sing of Daphne's fate, and Daphne's praise!

THYRSIS.

Behold the groves that shine with silver frost,
Their beauty withered, and their verdure lost.
Here shall I try the sweet Alexis' strain,
That called the listening Dryads to the plain?
Thames heard the numbers as he flowed along,
And bade his willows learn the moving song.

LYCIDAS.

So may kind rains their vital moisture yield,
And swell the future harvest of the field.
Begin; this charge the dying Daphne gave,
And said; 'Ye shepherds, sing around my grave!
Sing, while beside the shaded tomb I mourn,
And with fresh bays her rural shrine adorn.'

THYRSIS.

Ye gentle Muses, leave your crystal spring,
Let Nymphs and sylvans cypress garlands bring;
Ye weeping Loves, the stream with myrtles hide,
And break your vows, as when Adonis died;
And with your golden darts, now useless grown,
Inscribe a verse on this relenting stone:
'Let nature change, let heaven and earth deplore,
Fair Daphne's dead, and love is now no more!'
'Tis done, and nature's various charms decay,
See gloomy clouds obscure the cheerful day!
Now hung with pearls the dropping trees appear,

14

Their faded honours scattered on her bier.
See, where on earth the flowery glories lie,
With her they flourished, and with her they die.
Ah what avail the beauties nature wore?
Fair Daphne's dead, and beauty is no more!
   For her the flocks refuse their verdant food,
The thirsty heifers seek the gliding flood.
The silver swans her hapless fate bemoan,
In notes more sad than when they sing their own;
In hollow caves sweet Echo silent lies,
Silent, or only to her name replies;
Her name with pleasure once she taught the shore,
Now Daphne's dead, and pleasure is no more!
   No grateful dews descend from evening skies,
Nor morning odours from the flowers arise;
No rich perfumes refresh the fruitful field,
Nor fragrant herbs their native incense yield.
The balmy zephyrs, silent since her death,
Lament the ceasing of a sweeter breath;
Th' industrious bees neglect their golden store;
Fair Daphne's dead, and sweetness is no more!
No more the mounting larks, while Daphne sings,
Shall listening in mid air suspend their wings;
No more the birds shall imitate her lays,
Or hushed with wonder, hearken from the sprays;
No more the streams their murmur shall forbear,
A sweeter music than their own to hear,
But tell the reeds, and tell the vocal shore,
Fair Daphne's dead, and music is no more!
   Her fate is whispered by the gentle breeze,
And told in sighs to all the trembling trees;
The trembling trees, in every plain and wood,
Her fate remurmur to the silver flood;
The silver flood, so lately calm, appears
Swelled with new passion, and o'erflows with tears;
The winds and trees and floods her death deplore,
Daphne, our grief! our glory now no more!
   But see! where Daphne wondering mounts on high
Above the clouds, above the starry sky!
Eternal beauties grace the shining scene,
Fields ever fresh, and groves for ever green!
There while you rest in Amaranthine bowers,
Or from those meads select unfading flowers,
Behold us kindly, who your name implore,
Daphne, our Goddess, and our grief no more!

LYCIDAS.

How all things listen, while thy Muse complains!
Such silence waits on Philomela's strains,
In some still evening, when the whispering breeze
Pants on the leaves, and dies upon the trees.
To thee, bright goddess, oft a lamb shall bleed,
If teeming ewes increase my fleecy breed.
While plants their shade, or flowers their odours give,
Thy name, thy honour, and thy praise shall live!

THYRSIS.

But see, Orion sheds unwholesome dews,
Arise, the pines a noxious shade diffuse;
Sharp Boreas blows, and Nature feels decay,
Time conquers all, and we must Time obey.
Adieu, ye vales, ye mountains, streams and groves,
Adieu, ye shepherd's rural lays and loves;
Adieu, my flocks, farewell ye sylvan crew,
Daphne, farewell, and all the world adieu!

AN
ESSAY
ON
CRITICISM
Written in the Year MDCCIX

CONTENTS

PART I

PART II. Ver. 203, etc.

Causes hindering a true judgment. 1. Pride, v. 208. 2. Imperfect learning, v. 215. 3. *Judging by* parts, *and not by the* whole, v. 233 *to* 288. *Critics in* wit, language, versification, *only*, v. 288. 305. 399, *etc.* 4. *Being too hard to please, or too apt to admire*, v. 384. 5. Partiality — *too much love to a* sect, — *to the* Ancients *or* Moderns, v. 394. 6. Prejudice *or* Prevention, v. 408. 7. Singularity, v. 424. 8. Inconstancy, v. 430. 9. Party Spirit, v. 452 etc. 10. Envy, v. 466. *Against envy, and in praise of good nature,* v. 508, *etc. When severity is chiefly to be used by critics,* v. 526, *etc.*

PART III. v. 560, etc.

Rules for the conduct *of* manners *in a critic,* 1. Candour, v. 563. Modesty, v. 566. Good breeding, v. 572. Sincerity, *and* freedom *of advice,* v. 578. 2. *When one's counsel is to be restrained,* v. 584. *Character of an* incorrigible poet, v. 600. *And of an* impertinent critic, v. 610, *etc. Character of a* good critic, v. 629. *The* history *of* criticism, and characters of the best critics, Aristotle, v. 645. Horace, v. 653. Dionysius, v. 665. Petronius, v. 667. Quintilian, v. 670. Longinus, v. 675. *Of the decay of criticism, and its revival.* Erasmus, v. 693. Vida, v. 705. Boileau, v. 714. Lord Roscommon, *etc.* v. 725. *Conclusion.*

—Si quid novisti rectius istis,
Candidus imperti; si non, his utere mecum.
HORACE.

'Tis hard to say if greater want of skill
Appear in writing or in judging ill;
But of the two, less dangerous is th' offence
To tire our patience, than mislead our sense.
Some few in that, but numbers err in this,
Ten censure wrong for one who writes amiss;
A fool might once himself alone expose,
Now one in verse makes many more in prose.
    'Tis with our judgments as our watches, none
Go just alike, yet each believes his own.
In poets as true genius is but rare,
True taste as seldom is the critic share;
Both must alike from Heaven derive their light,
These born to judge as well as those to write.
Let such teach others who themselves excel,
And censure freely, who have written well.
Authors are partial to their wit, 'tis true,
But are not critics to their judgment too?
    Yet if we look more closely, we shall find
Most have the seeds of judgment in their mind:
Nature affords at least a glimmering light;
The lines, though touched but faintly, are drawn right.
But as the slightest sketch, if justly traced,

Is by ill-colouring but the more disgraced,
So by false learning is good sense defaced:
Some are bewildered in the maze of schools,
And some made coxcombs nature meant but fools.
In search of wit these lose their common sense,
And then turn critics in their own defence:
Each burns alike, who can, or cannot write,
Or with a rival's, or an eunuch's spite.
All fools have still an itching to deride,
And fain would be upon the laughing side.
If Maevius scribble in Apollo's spite,
There are, who judge still worse than he can write.

   Some have at first for wits, then poets passed
Turned critics next, and proved plain fools at last.
Some neither can for wits nor critics pass,
As heavy mules are neither horse nor ass.
Those half-learned witlings, numerous in our isle,
As half-formed insects on the banks of Nile;
Unfinished things, one knows not what to call,
Their generation's so equivocal:
To tell 'em, would a hundred tongues require,
Or one vain wit's, that might a hundred tire.

   But you who seek to give and merit fame,
And justly bear a critic's noble name,
Be sure yourself and your own reach to know,
How far your genius, taste, and learning go;
Launch not beyond your depth, but be discreet,
And mark that point where sense and dullness meet.

   Nature to all things fixed the limits fit
And wisely curbed proud man's pretending wit.
As on the land while here the ocean gains,
In other parts it leaves wide sandy plains;
Thus in the soul while memory prevails,
The solid power of understanding fails;
Where beams of warm imagination play,
The memory's soft figures melt away.
One science only will one genius fit;
So vast is art, so narrow human wit:
Not only bounded to peculiar arts,
But oft in those confined to single parts.
Like kings we lose the conquests gained before,
By vain ambition still to make them more;
Each might his several province well command,
Would all but stoop to what they understand.

   First follow *Nature,* and your judgment frame
By her just standard, which is still the same:
Unerring NATURE, still divinely bright,
One clear, unchanged, and universal light,

Life, force, and beauty, must to all impart,
At once the source, and end, and test of art.
Art from that fund each just supply provides,
Works without show, and without pomp presides:
In some fair body thus th' informing soul
With spirits feeds, with vigor fills the whole,
Each motion guides, and every nerve sustains;
Itself unseen, but in the effects remains.
Some, to whom Heaven in wit has been profuse,
Want as much more, to turn it to its use;
For wit and judgment often are at strife,
Though meant each other's aid, like man and wife.
'Tis more to guide, than spur the Muse's steed,
Restrain his fury, than provoke his speed;
The winged courser, like a generous horse,
Shows most true mettle when you check his course.

    Those RULES, of old discovered, not devised,
Are nature still, but nature methodized;
Nature, like liberty, is but restrained
By the same laws which first herself ordained.

    Hear how learned Greece her useful rules indites,
When to repress, and when indulge our flights:
High on Parnassus' top her sons she showed,
And pointed out those arduous paths they trod;
Held from afar, aloft, th' immortal prize,
And urged the rest by equal steps to rise.
Just precepts thus from great examples given,
She drew from them what they derived from Heaven.
The generous critic fanned the poet's fire,
And taught the world with reason to admire.
Then criticism the Muse's handmaid proved,
To dress her charms, and make her more beloved:
But following wits from that intention strayed,
Who could not win the mistress, wooed the maid;
Against the poets their own arms they turned,
Sure to hate most the men from whom they learned.
So modern 'pothecaries taught the art
By doctors bills to play the doctor's part,
Bold in the practice of mistaken rules,
Prescribe, apply, and call their masters fools.
Some on the leaves of ancient authors prey,
Nor time nor moths e'er spoil so much as they.
Some drily plain, without invention's aid,
Write dull receipts how poems may be made.
These leave the sense, their learning to display,
And those explain the meaning quite away.

    You then, whose judgment the right course would steer,
Know well each ANCIENT'S proper character;

His fable, subject, scope in every page;
Religion, country, genius of his age:
Without all these at once before your eyes,
Cavil you may, but never criticize.
Be Homer's works your study, and delight,
Read them by day, and meditate by night;
Thence form your judgment, thence your maxims bring,
And trace the muses upward to their spring.
Still with itself compared, his text peruse;
And let your comment be the Mantuan Muse.
    When first young Maro in his boundless mind
A work t'outlast immortal Rome designed,
Perhaps he seemed above the critic's law,
And but from nature's fountain scorned to draw:
But when t'examine every part he came
Nature and Homer were, he found, the same.
Convinced, amazed, he checks the bold design;
And rules as strict his labored work confine,
As if the Stagyrite o'erlooked each line
Learn hence for ancient rules a just esteem,
To copy nature is to copy them.
    Some beauties yet no precepts can declare,
For there's a happiness as well as care.
Music resembles poetry, in each
Are nameless graces which no methods teach,
And which a master-hand alone can reach.
If, where the rules not far enough extend,
(Since rules were made but to promote their end)
Some lucky license answer to the full
Th'intent proposed, that license is a rule.
Thus Pegasus, a nearer way to take,
May boldly deviate from the common track.
Great wits sometimes may gloriously offend,
And rise to faults true critics dare not mend;
From vulgar bounds with brave disorder part,
And snatch a grace beyond the reach of art,
Which without passing through the judgment, gains
The heart, and all its end at once attains.
In prospects thus, some objects please our eyes,
Which out of nature's common order rise,
The shapeless rock, or hanging precipice.
But though the ancients thus their rules invade,
(As kings dispense with laws themselves have made)
Moderns, beware! or if you must offend
Against the precept, ne'er transgress its end;
Let it be seldom, and compelled by need;
And have, at least, their precedent to plead.
The critic else proceeds without remorse,

Seizes your fame, and puts his laws in force.
   I know there are, to whose presumptuous thoughts
Those freer beauties, even in them, seem faults.
Some figures monstrous and misshaped appear,
Considered singly, or beheld too near,
Which, but proportioned to their light, or place,
Due distance reconciles to form and grace.
A prudent chief not always must display
His powers in equal ranks, and fair array,
But with th'occasion and the place comply.
Conceal his force, nay seem sometimes to fly.
Those oft are stratagems which errors seem,
Nor is it Homer nods, but we that dream.
   Still green with bays each ancient altar stands,
Above the reach of sacrilegious hands;
Secure from flames, from envy's fiercer rage,
Destructive war, and all-involving age.
See, from each clime the learned their incense bring!
Hear, in all tongues consenting paeans ring!
In praise so just let every voice be joined,
And fill the general chorus of mankind.
Hail, bards triumphant! born in happier days;
Immortal heirs of universal praise!
Whose honors with increase of ages grow,
As streams roll down, enlarging as they flow;
Nations unborn your mighty names shall sound,
And worlds applaud that must not yet be found!
Oh may some spark of your celestial fire,
The last, the meanest of your sons inspire,
(That on weak wings, from far pursues your flights;
Glows while he reads, but trembles as he writes),
To teach vain wits a science little known,
T'admire superior sense, and doubt their own!

   Of all the causes which conspire to blind
Man's erring judgment, and misguide the mind
What the weak head with strongest bias rules,
Is *pride*, the never-failing vice of fools.
Whatever nature has in worth denied,
She gives in large recruits of needful pride;
For as in bodies, thus in souls, we find
What wants in blood and spirits, swelled with wind:
Pride, where wit fails, steps in to our defence,
And fills up all the mighty void of sense.
If once right reason drives that cloud away,
Truth breaks upon us with resistless day.
Trust not yourself; but your defects to know,
Make use of every friend—and every foe.

A *little learning* is a dangerous thing;
Drink deep, or taste not the Pierian spring:
There shallow draughts intoxicate the brain,
And drinking largely sobers us again.
Fired at first sight with what the muse imparts,
In fearless youth we tempt the heights of arts,
While from the bounded level of our mind,
Short views we take, nor see the lengths behind;
But, more advanced, behold with strange surprise
New distant scenes of endless science rise!
So pleased at first the towering Alps we try,
Mount o'er the vales, and seem to tread the sky,
Th' eternal snows appear already past,
And the first clouds and mountains seem the last:
But, those attained, we tremble to survey
The growing labors of the lengthened way,
Th' increasing prospect tires our wandering eyes,
Hills peep o'er hills and Alps on Alps arise!

A perfect judge will read each work of wit
With the same spirit that its author writ
Survey the WHOLE nor seek slight faults to find
Where nature moves and rapture warms the mind,
Nor lose for that malignant dull delight
The generous pleasure to be charmed with wit
But in such lays as neither ebb nor flow,
Correctly cold, and regularly low,
That shunning faults, one quiet tenor keep;
We cannot blame indeed—but we may sleep.
In wit, as nature, what affects our hearts
Is not th' exactness of peculiar parts;
'Tis not a lip, or eye, we beauty call,
But the joint force and full result of all.
Thus, when we view some well-proportioned dome
(The worlds just wonder, and even thine, O Rome!),
No single parts unequally surprise,
All comes united to the admiring eyes;
No monstrous height, or breadth, or length appear;
The whole at once is bold, and regular.
Whoever thinks a faultless piece to see,
Thinks what ne'er was, nor is, nor e'er shall be.
In every work regard the writer's end,
Since none can compass more than they intend;
And if the means be just, the conduct true,
Applause, in spite of trivial faults, is due.
As men of breeding, sometimes men of wit,
T' avoid great errors, must the less commit:
Neglect the rules each verbal critic lays,

For not to know some trifles is a praise.
Most critics, fond of some subservient art,
Still make the whole depend upon a part:
They talk of principles, but notions prize,
And all to one loved folly sacrifice.
  Once on a time La Mancha's knight, they say,
A certain bard encountering on the way,
Discoursed in terms as just, with looks as sage,
As e'er could Dennis, of the Grecian stage;
Concluding all were desperate sots and fools,
Who durst depart from Aristotle's rules.
Our author, happy in a judge so nice,
Produced his play, and begged the knight's advice;
Made him observe the subject, and the plot,
The manners, passions, unities; what not?
All which, exact to rule, were brought about,
Were but a combat in the lists left out.
'What! leave the combat out?' exclaims the knight;
Yes, or we must renounce the Stagyrite.
'Not so, by heaven!' (he answers in a rage)
'Knights, squires, and steeds must enter on the stage.'
So vast a throng the stage can ne'er contain.
'Then build a new, or act it in a plain.'
  Thus critics of less judgment than caprice,
Curious, not knowing, not exact, but nice,
Form short ideas; and offend in arts
(As most in manners) by a love to parts.
  Some to *conceit* alone their taste confine,
And glittering thoughts struck out at every line;
Pleased with a work where nothing's just or fit;
One glaring chaos and wild heap of wit.
Poets like painters, thus, unskilled to trace
The naked nature and the living grace,
With gold and jewels cover every part,
And hide with ornaments their want of art.
True wit is nature to advantage dressed,
What oft was thought, but ne'er so well expressed;
Something, whose truth convinced at sight we find,
That gives us back the image of our mind.
As shades more sweetly recommend the light,
So modest plainness sets off sprightly wit.
For works may have more wit than does 'em good,
As bodies perish through excess of blood.
  Others for *language* all their care express,
And value books, as women men, for dress:
Their praise is still,—the style is excellent:
The sense they humbly take upon content.
Words are like leaves; and where they most abound

Much fruit of sense beneath is rarely found.
False eloquence, like the prismatic glass.
Its gaudy colours spreads on every place;
The face of nature we no more survey,
All glares alike without distinction gay:
But true expression, like th' unchanging sun,
Clears, and improves whate'er it shines upon;
It gilds all objects, but it alters none.
Expression is the dress of thought, and still
Appears more decent, as more suitable;
A vile conceit in pompous words expressed,
Is like a clown in regal purple dressed:
For different styles with different subjects sort,
As several garbs with country, town, and court.
Some by old words to fame have made pretense,
Ancients in phrase, mere moderns in their sense:
Such labored nothings, in so strange a style,
Amaze th' unlearned, and make the learned smile.
Unlucky, as Fungoso in the play,
These sparks with awkward vanity display
What the fine gentleman wore yesterday;
And but so mimic ancient wits at best,
As apes our grandsires, in their doublets dressed.
In words, as fashions, the same rule will hold;
Alike fantastic, if too new, or old;
Be not the first by whom the new are tried,
Nor yet the last to lay the old aside.
   But most by numbers judge a poet's song,
And smooth or rough, with them, is right or wrong;
In the bright Muse though thousand charms conspire,
Her voice is all these tuneful fools admire;
Who haunt Parnassus but to please their ear,
Not mend their minds; as some to church repair,
Not for the doctrine, but the music there.
These equal syllables alone require,
Though oft the ear the open vowels tire;
While expletives their feeble aid do join;
And ten low words oft creep in one dull line;
While they ring round the same unvaried chimes,
With sure returns of still expected rhymes.
Where'er you find 'the cooling western breeze,'
In the next line it 'whispers through the trees;'
If crystal streams 'with pleasing murmurs creep'
The reader's threatened (not in vain) with 'sleep.'
Then, at the last and only couplet fraught
With some unmeaning thing they call a thought,
A needless Alexandrine ends the song
That, like a wounded snake, drags its slow length along.

Leave such to tune their own dull rhymes, and know
What's roundly smooth, or languishingly slow;
And praise the easy vigor of a line,
Where Denham's strength, and Waller's sweetness join.
True ease in writing comes from art, not chance,
As those move easiest who have learned to dance
'Tis not enough no harshness gives offence,
The sound must seem an echo to the sense:
Soft is the strain when Zephyr gently blows,
And the smooth stream in smoother numbers flows;
But when loud surges lash the sounding shore,
The hoarse, rough verse should like the torrent roar.
When Ajax strives, some rock's vast weight to throw,
The line too labors, and the words move slow;
Not so, when swift Camilla scours the plain,
Flies o'er th' unbending corn, and skims along the main.
Hear how Timotheus varied lays surprise,
And bid alternate passions fall and rise!
While, at each change, the son of Libyan Jove
Now burns with glory, and then melts with love;
Now his fierce eyes with sparkling fury glow,
Now sighs steal out, and tears begin to flow:
Persians and Greeks like turns of nature found,
And the world's victor stood subdued by sound!
The power of music all our hearts allow,
And what Timotheus was, is DRYDEN now.

   Avoid *extremes*, and shun the fault of such,
Who still are pleased too little or too much.
At every trifle scorn to take offence,
That always shows great pride, or little sense;
Those heads, as stomachs, are not sure the best,
Which nauseate all, and nothing can digest.
Yet let not each gay turn thy rapture move,
For fools admire, but men of sense approve:
As things seem large which we through mist descry,
Dullness is ever apt to magnify.

   Some foreign writers, some our own despise;
The ancients only, or the Moderns prize.
Thus wit, like faith, by each man is applied
To one small sect, and all are damned beside.
Meanly they seek the blessing to confine,
And force that sun but on a part to shine,
Which not alone the southern wit sublimes,
But ripens spirits in cold northern climes;
Which from the first has shone on ages past,
Enlights the present, and shall warm the last:
Though each may feel increases and decays,
And see now clearer and now darker days.

Regard not then if wit be old or new,
But blame the false, and value still the true.
   Some ne'er advance a judgment of their own,
But catch the spreading notion of the town;
They reason and conclude by precedent,
And own stale nonsense which they ne'er invent.
Some judge of authors' names, not works, and then
Nor praise nor blame the writing, but the men.
Of all this servile herd, the worst is he
That in proud dullness joins with quality.
A constant critic at the great man's board,
To fetch and carry nonsense for my Lord.
What woeful stuff this madrigal would be,
In some starved hackney sonneteer, or me!
But let a lord once own the happy lines,
How the wit brightens! how the style refines!
Before his sacred name flies every fault,
And each exalted stanza teems with thought!
   The vulgar thus through imitation err;
As oft the learned by being singular;
So much they scorn the crowd, that if the throng
By chance go right, they purposely go wrong:
So schismatics the plain believers quit,
And are but damned for having too much wit.
   Some praise at morning what they blame at night;
But always think the last opinion right.
A Muse by these is like a mistress used,
This hour she's idolized, the next abused;
While their weak heads, like towns unfortified,
'Twixt sense and nonsense daily change their side.
Ask them the cause; they're wiser still, they say;
And still tomorrow's wiser than to-day.
We think our fathers fools, so wise we grow;
Our wiser sons, no doubt, will think us so.
Once school-divines this zealous isle o'er-spread;
Who knew most sentences, was deepest read;
Faith, gospel, all, seemed made to be disputed,
And none had sense enough to be confuted:
Scotists and Thomists, now in peace remain,
Amidst their kindred cobwebs in Duck Lane.
If faith itself has different dresses worn,
What wonder modes in wit should take their turn?
Oft, leaving what is natural and fit,
The current folly proves the ready wit;
And authors think their reputation safe,
Which lives as long as fools are pleased to laugh.
   Some valuing those of their own side or mind,
Still make themselves the measure of mankind:

Fondly we think we honor merit then,
When we but praise ourselves in other men.
Parties in wit attend on those of state,
And public faction doubles private hate.
Pride, Malice, Folly against Dryden rose,
In various shapes of parsons, critics, beaux;
But sense survived, when merry jests were past;
For rising merit will buoy up at last.
Might he return, and bless once more our eyes,
New Blackmores and new Millbourns must arise:
Nay, should great Homer lift his awful head,
Zoilus again would start up from the dead
Envy will merit, as its shade, pursue;
But like a shadow, proves the substance true;
For envied wit, like Sol eclipsed, makes known
Th' opposing body's grossness, not its own.
When first that sun too powerful beams displays,
It draws up vapors which obscure its rays;
But even those clouds at last adorn its way,
Reflect new glories and augment the day.
    Be thou the first true merit to befriend;
His praise is lost, who stays till all commend.
Short is the date, alas, of modern rhymes,
And 'tis but just to let them live betimes.
No longer now that golden age appears,
When patriarch-wits survived a thousand years:
Now length of fame (our second life) is lost,
And bare threescore is all even that can boast;
Our sons their fathers failing language see,
And such as Chaucer is, shall Dryden be.
So when the faithful pencil has designed
Some bright idea of the master's mind,
Where a new world leaps out at his command,
And ready nature waits upon his hand;
When the ripe colours soften and unite,
And sweetly melt into just shade and light,
When mellowing years their full perfection give,
And each bold figure just begins to live;
The treacherous colours the fair art betray,
And all the bright creation fades away!
    Unhappy wit, like most mistaken things,
Atones not for that envy which it brings.
In youth alone its empty praise we boast,
But soon the short-lived vanity is lost:
Like some fair flower the early spring supplies,
That gaily blooms, but even in blooming dies.
What is this wit, which must our cares employ?
The owner's wife that other men enjoy;

Then most our trouble still when most admired,
And still the more we give, the more required;
Whose fame with pains we guard, but lose with ease,
Sure some to vex, but never all to please;
'Tis what the vicious fear, the virtuous shun,
By fools 'tis hated, and by knaves undone!
   If wit so much from ignorance undergo,
Ah let not learning too commence its foe!
Of old, those met rewards who could excel,
And such were praised who but endeavored well:
Though triumphs were to generals only due,
Crowns were reserved to grace the soldiers too.
Now, they who reach Parnassus' lofty crown,
Employ their pains to spurn some others down;
And, while self-love each jealous writer rules,
Contending wits become the sport of fools:
But still the worst with most regret commend,
For each ill author is as bad a friend.
To what base ends, and by what abject ways,
Are mortals urged through sacred lust of praise!
Ah, ne'er so dire a thirst of glory boast,
Nor in the critic let the man be lost
Good-nature and good sense must ever join;
To err is human, to forgive, divine.
   But if in noble minds some dregs remain,
Not yet purged off, of spleen and sour disdain;
Discharge that rage on more provoking crimes,
Nor fear a dearth in these flagitious times.
No pardon vile obscenity should find,
Though wit and art conspire to move your mind;
But dullness with obscenity must prove
As shameful sure as impotence in love.
In the fat age of pleasure, wealth, and ease,
Sprung the rank weed, and thrived with large increase;
When love was all an easy monarch's care;
Seldom at council, never in a war:
Jilts ruled the state, and statesmen farces writ;
Nay wits had pensions, and young lords had wit:
The fair sate panting at a courtier's play,
And not a mask went unimproved away:
The modest fan was lifted up no more,
And virgins smiled at what they blushed before.
The following license of a foreign reign
Did all the dregs of bold Socinus drain;
Then unbelieving priests reformed the nation,
And taught more pleasant methods of salvation;
Where Heaven's free subjects might their rights dispute,
Lest God himself should seem too absolute:

Pulpits their sacred satire learned to spare,
And vice admired to find a flatterer there!
Encouraged thus, wit's Titans braved the skies,
And the press groaned with licensed blasphemies.
These monsters, critics! with your darts engage,
Here point your thunder, and exhaust your rage!
Yet shun their fault, who, scandalously nice,
Will needs mistake an author into vice;
All seems infected that th' infected spy,
As all looks yellow to the jaundiced eye.
    LEARN, then, what MORALS critics ought to show,
For 'tis but half a judge's task, to know.
'Tis not enough, taste, judgment, learning, join;
In all you speak, let truth and candor shine:
That not alone what to your sense is due
All may allow; but seek your friendship too.
    Be silent always, when you doubt your sense;
And speak, though sure, with seeming diffidence:
Some positive, persisting fops we know,
Who, if once wrong, will needs be always so;
But you, with pleasure own your errors past,
And make each day a critique on the last.
    'Tis not enough your counsel still be true;
Blunt truths more mischief than nice falsehoods do;
Men must be taught as if you taught them not,
And things unknown proposed as things forgot.
Without good breeding truth is disapproved;
That only makes superior sense beloved.
    Be niggards of advice on no pretense;
For the worst avarice is that of sense.
With mean complacence, ne'er betray your trust,
Nor be so civil as to prove unjust.
Fear not the anger of the wise to raise;
Those best can bear reproof, who merit praise.
    'Twere well might critics still this freedom take,
But Appius reddens at each word you speak,
And stares, tremendous, with a threatening eye,
Like some fierce tyrant in old tapestry.
Fear most to tax an honorable fool,
Whose right it is, uncensured to be dull;
Such, without wit, are poets when they please,
As without learning they can take degrees.
Leave dangerous truths to unsuccessful satires,
And flattery to fulsome dedicators,
Whom, when they praise, the world believes no more,
Than when they promise to give scribbling o'er.
'Tis best sometimes your censure to restrain,
And charitably let the dull be vain:

Your silence there is better than your spite,
For who can rail so long as they can write?
Still humming on, their drowsy course they keep,
And lashed so long, like tops, are lashed asleep.
False steps but help them to renew the race,
As, after stumbling, jades will mend their pace.
What crowds of these, impenitently bold,
In sounds and jingling syllables grown old,
Still run on poets, in a raging vein,
Even to the dregs and squeezing of the brain,
Strain out the last dull droppings of their sense,
And rhyme with all the rage of impotence.
    Such shameless bards we have, and yet, 'tis true,
There are as mad, abandoned critics too.
The bookful blockhead, ignorantly read,
With loads of learnèd lumber in his head,
With his own tongue still edifies his ears,
And always listening to himself appears.
All books he reads, and all he reads assails,
From Dryden's fables down to Durfey's tales
With him most authors steal their works, or buy;
Garth did not write his own *Dispensary*.
Name a new play, and he's the poets friend,
Nay showed his faults—but when would poets mend?
No place so sacred from such fops is barred,
Nor is Paul's Church more safe than Paul's church yard:
Nay, fly to altars; there they'll talk you dead:
For fools rush in where angels fear to tread.
Distrustful sense with modest caution speaks,
It still looks home, and short excursions makes;
But rattling nonsense in full volleys breaks,
And never shocked, and never turned aside,
Bursts out, resistless, with a thundering tide.
    But where's the man who counsel can bestow,
Still pleased to teach, and yet not proud to know?
Unbiased, or by favor, or by spite,
Not dully prepossessed, nor blindly right;
Though learned, well-bred; and though well-bred, sincere;
Modestly bold, and humanly severe:
Who to a friend his faults can freely show,
And gladly praise the merit of a foe?
Blessed with a taste exact, yet unconfined;
A knowledge both of books and human kind;
Generous converse; a soul exempt from pride;
And love to praise, with reason on his side?
    Such once were critics such the happy few,
Athens and Rome in better ages knew.
The mighty Stagyrite first left the shore,

Spread all his sails, and durst the deeps explore;
He steered securely, and discovered far,
Led by the light of the Maeonian star.
Poets, a race long unconfined, and free,
Still fond and proud of savage liberty,
Received his laws; and stood convinced 'twas fit,
Who conquered nature, should preside o'er wit.

Horace still charms with graceful negligence,
And without method talks us into sense,
Will, like a friend, familiarly convey
The truest notions in the easiest way.
He, who supreme in judgment, as in wit,
Might boldly censure, as he boldly writ,
Yet judged with coolness, though he sung with fire,
His precepts teach but what his works inspire.
Our critics take a contrary extreme,
They judge with fury, but they write with phlegm.
Nor suffers Horace more in wrong translations
By wits than critics in as wrong quotations.

See Dionysius Homer's thoughts refine,
And call new beauties forth from every line!

Fancy and art in gay Petronius please,
The scholar's learning with the courtier's ease.

In grave Quintilian's copious work we find
The justest rules and clearest method joined:
Thus useful arms in magazines we place,
All ranged in order, and disposed with grace,
But less to please the eye, than arm the hand,
Still fit for use, and ready at command.

Thee, bold Longinus! all the Nine inspire,
And bless their critic with a poet's fire.
An ardent judge, who, zealous in his trust,
With warmth gives sentence, yet is always just:
Whose own example strengthens all his laws;
And is himself that great sublime he draws.

Thus long succeeding critics justly reigned,
License repressed, and useful laws ordained.
Learning and Rome alike in empire grew;
And arts still followed where her eagles flew:
From the same foes at last, both felt their doom,
And the same age saw learning fall, and Rome.
With tyranny, then superstition joined,
As that the body, this enslaved the mind;
Much was believed, but little understood,
And to be dull was construed to be good;
A second deluge learning thus o'er-run,
And the monks finished what the Goths begun.

At length Erasmus, that great injured name

(The glory of the priesthood and the shame!)
Stemmed the wild torrent of a barbarous age,
And drove those holy Vandals off the stage.
   But see! each muse, in LEO'S golden days,
Starts from her trance and trims her withered bays!
Rome's ancient genius o'er its ruins spread
Shakes off the dust, and rears his reverent head
Then sculpture and her sister-arts revive,
Stones leaped to form, and rocks began to live;
With sweeter notes each rising temple rung;
A Raphael painted, and a Vida sung.
Immortal Vida: on whose honored brow
The poet's bays and critics ivy grow:
Cremona now shall ever boast thy name,
As next in place to Mantua, next in fame!
   But soon by impious arms from Latium chased,
Their ancient bounds the banished Muses passed;
Thence arts o'er all the northern world advance,
But critic-learning flourished most in France:
The rules a nation born to serve, obeys;
And Boileau still in right of Horace sways.
But we, brave Britons, foreign laws despised,
And kept unconquered and uncivilized;
Fierce for the liberties of wit and bold,
We still defied the Romans, as of old.
Yet some there were, among the sounder few
Of those who less presumed, and better knew,
Who durst assert the juster ancient cause,
And here restored wit's fundamental laws.
Such was the muse, whose rule and practice tell,
'Nature's chief masterpiece is writing well.'
Such was Roscommon, not more learned than good,
With manners generous as his noble blood;
To him the wit of Greece and Rome was known,
And every author's merit, but his own.
Such late was Walsh—the Muse's judge and friend,
Who justly knew to blame or to commend;
To failings mild, but zealous for desert;
The clearest head, and the sincerest heart.
This humble praise, lamented shade! receive,
This praise at least a grateful Muse may give:
The Muse whose early voice you taught to sing
Prescribed her heights, and pruned her tender wing,
(Her guide now lost) no more attempts to rise,
But in low numbers short excursions tries:
Content, if hence th' unlearned their wants may view,
The learned reflect on what before they knew:
Careless of censure, nor too fond of fame;

Still pleased to praise, yet not afraid to blame;
Averse alike to flatter, or offend;
Not free from faults, nor yet too vain to mend.

SAPPHO TO PHAON

Say, lovely youth, that dost my heart command,
Can Phaon's eyes forget his Sappho's hand?
Must then her name the wretched writer prove,
To thy remembrance lost, as to thy love?
Ask not the cause that I new numbers choose,
The lute neglected, and the lyric muse;
Love taught my tears in sadder notes to flow,
And tuned my heart to elegies of woe.
I burn, I burn, as when through ripened corn
By driving winds the spreading flames are borne!
Phaon to Aetna's scorching fields retires,
While I consume with more than Etna's fires!
No more my soul a charm in music finds,
Music has charms alone for peaceful minds.
Soft scenes of solitude no more can please,
Love enters there, and I'm my own disease.
No more the Lesbian dames my passion move,
Once the dear objects of my guilty love;
All other loves are lost in only thine,
Ah youth ungrateful to a flame like mine!
Whom would not all those blooming charms surprise,
Those heavenly looks, and dear deluding eyes?
The harp and bow would you like Phoebus bear,
A brighter Phoebus Phaon might appear;
Would you with ivy wreath your flowing hair,
Not Bacchus' self with Phaon could compare:
Yet Phoebus loved, and Bacchus felt the flame,
One Daphne warmed, and one the Cretan dame,
Nymphs that in verse no more could rival me,
That even those Gods contend in charms with thee.
The Muses teach me all their softest lays,
And the wide world resounds with Sappho's praise.
Though great Alcaeus more sublimely sings,
And strikes with bolder rage the sounding strings,
No less renown attends the moving lyre,
Which Venus tunes, and all her loves inspire;
To me what nature has in charms denied,
Is well by wit's more lasting flames supplied.
Though short my stature, yet my name extends
To heaven itself, and earth's remotest ends.
Brown as I am, an Ethiopian dame
Inspired young Perseus with a generous flame;

Turtles and doves of differing hues unite,
And glossy jet is paired with shining white.
If to no charms thou wilt thy heart resign,
But such as merit, such as equal thine,
By none, alas! by none thou canst be moved,
Phaon alone by Phaon must be loved!
Yet once thy Sappho could thy cares employ,
Once in her arms you centered all your joy:
No time the dear remembrance can remove,
For oh! how vast a memory has love!
My music, then, you could for ever hear,
And all my words were music to your ear.
You stopped with kisses my enchanting tongue,
And found my kisses sweeter than my song.
In all I pleased, but most in what was best;
And the last joy was dearer than the rest.
Then with each word, each glance, each motion fired,
You still enjoyed, and yet you still desired,
Till all dissolving in the trance we lay,
And in tumultuous raptures died away.
The fair Sicilians now thy soul inflame;
Why was I born, ye Gods, a Lesbian dame?
But ah beware, Sicilian nymphs! nor boast
That wandering heart which I so lately lost;
Nor be with all those tempting words abused,
Those tempting words were all to Sappho used.
And you that rule Sicilia's happy plains,
Have pity, Venus, on your poet's pains!
Shall fortune still in one sad tenor run,
And still increase the woes so soon begun?
Inured to sorrow from my tender years,
My parent's ashes drank my early tears:
My brother next, neglecting wealth and fame,
Ignobly burned in a destructive flame:
An infant daughter late my griefs increased,
And all a mother's cares distract my breast.
Alas, what more could fate itself impose,
But thee, the last and greatest of my woes?
No more my robes in waving purple flow,
Nor on my hand the sparkling diamonds glow;
No more my locks in ringlets curled diffuse
The costly sweetness of Arabian dews,
Nor braids of gold the varied tresses bind,
That fly disordered with the wanton wind:
For whom should Sappho use such arts as these?
He's gone, whom only she desired to please!
Cupid's light darts my tender bosom move,
Still is there cause for Sappho still to love:

So from my birth the sisters fixed my doom,
And gave to Venus all my life to come;
Or while my Muse in melting notes complains,
My yielding heart keeps measure to my strains.
By charms like thine which all my soul have won,
Who might not— ah! who would not be undone?
For those Aurora Cephalus might scorn,
And with fresh blushes paint the conscious morn.
For those might Cynthia lengthen Phaon's sleep,
And bit Endymion nightly tend his sheep.
Venus for those had rapt thee to the skies,
But Mars on thee might look with Venus' eyes.
O scarce a youth, yet scarce a tender boy!
O useful time for lovers to employ!
Pride of thy age, and glory of thy race,
Come to these arms, and melt in this embrace!
The vows you never will return, receive;
And take at least the love you will not give.
See, while I write, my words are lost in tears;
The less my sense, the more my love appears.
Sure 'twas not much to bid one kind adieu,
(At least to feign was never hard to you)
'Farewell, my Lesbian love', you might have said,
Or coldly thus, 'Farewell, oh Lesbian maid!'
No tear did you, no parting kiss receive,
Nor knew I then how much I was to grieve.
No lover's gift your Sappho could confer,
And wrongs and woes were all you left with her.
No charge I gave you, and no charge could give,
But this, 'Be mindful of our loves, and live.'
Now by the Nine, those powers adored by me,
And Love, the God that ever waits on thee,
When first I heard (from whom I hardly knew)
That you were fled, and all my joys with you,
Like some sad statue, speechless, pale, I stood,
Grief chilled my breast, and stopped my freezing blood;
No sigh to rise, no tear had power to flow,
Fixed in a stupid lethargy of woe:
But when its way th' impetuous passion found,
I rend my tresses, and my breast I wound,
I rave, then weep, I curse, and then complain,
Now swell to rage, no melt in tears again.
Not fiercer pangs distract the mournful dame,
Whose first-born infant feeds the funeral flame.
My scornful brother with a smile appears,
Insults my woes, and triumphs in my tears;
His hated image ever haunts my eyes,
'And why this grief? thy daughter lives', he cries.

Stung with my love, and furious with despair,
All torn my garments, and my bosom bare,
My woes, thy crimes, I to the world proclaim;
Such inconsistent things are love and shame!
'Tis thou art all my care and my delight,
My daily longing, and my dream by night:
Oh night more pleasing than the brightest day,
When fancy gives what absence takes away,
And, dressed in all its visionary charms,
Restores my fair deserter to my arms!
Then round your neck in wanton wreaths I twine,
Then you, methinks, as fondly circle mine:
A thousand tender words, I hear and speak;
A thousand melting kisses, give, and take:
Then fiercer joys, I blush to mention these,
Yet while I blush, confess how much they please.
But when, with day, the sweet delusions fly,
And all things wake to life and joy, but I,
As if once more forsaken, I complain,
And close my eyes, to dream of you again;
Then frantic rise, and like some Fury rove
Through lonely plains, and through the silent grove,
As if the silent grove, and lonely plains,
That knew my pleasures, could relieve my pains.
I view the grotto, once the scene of love,
The rocks around, the hanging roofs above,
That charmed me more, with native moss o'ergrown,
Than Phyrgian marble, or the Parian stone.
I find the shades that veiled our joys before;
But, Phaon gone, those shades delight no more.
Here the pressed herbs with bending tops betray
Where oft entwined in amorous folds we lay;
I kiss that earth which once was pressed by you,
And all with tears the withering herbs bedew.
For thee the fading trees appear to mourn,
And birds defer their songs till thy return:
Night shades the groves, and all in silence lie,
All but the mournful Philomel and I:
With mournful Philomel I join my strain,
Of Tereus she, of Phaeon I complain.
   A spring there is, whose silver waters show,
Clear as a glass, the shining sands below:
A flowery lotus spreads its arms above,
Shades all the banks, and seems itself a grove;
Eternal greens the mossy margin grace,
Watched by the sylvan Genius of the place.
Here as I lay, and swelled with tears the flood,
Before my sight a watery Virgin stood:

She stood and cried, 'O you that love in vain!
Fly hence, and seek the fair Leucadian main;
There stands a rock, from whose impending steep
Apollo's fane surveys the rolling deep;
There injured lovers, leaping from above,
Their flames extinguish, and forget to love.
Deucalion once, with hopeless fury burned,
In vain he loved, relentless Pyrrha scorned;
But when from hence he plunged into the main,
Deucalion scorned, and Pyrrha loved in vain.
Haste, Sappho, haste, from high Leucadia throw
The wretched weight, nor dread the deeps below!'
She spoke, and vanished with the voice–I rise,
And silent tears fall trickling from my eyes.
I go, ye nymphs! those rocks and seas to prove;
How much I fear, but ah, how much I love!
I go, ye nymphs! where furious love inspires;
Let female fears submit to female fires.
To rocks and seas I fly from Phaon's hate,
And hope from seas and rocks a milder fate.
Ye gentle gales, beneath my body blow,
And softly lay me on the waves below!
And thou, kind Love, my sinking limbs sustain,
Spread thy soft wings, and waft me o'er the main,
Nor let a Lover's death the guiltless flood profane!
On Phoebus' shrine my harp I'll then bestow,
And this Inscription shall be placed below.
'Here she who sung, to him that did inspire,
Sappho to Phoebus consecrates her lyre:
What suits with Sappho, Phoebus, suits with thee;
The gift, the giver, and the god agree.'
    But why, alas, relentless youth, ah why
To distant seas must tender Sappho fly?
Thy charms than those may far more powerful be,
And Phoebus' self is less a God to me.
Ah! canst thou doom me to the rocks and sea,
O far more faithless and more hard than they?
Ah! canst thou rather see this tender breast
Dashed on these rocks than to thy bosom pressed?
This breast which once, in vain! you liked so well;
Where Loves played, and where the Muses dwell.
Alas! the Muses now no more inspire,
Untuned my lute, and silent is my lyre,
My languid numbers have forgot to flow,
And fancy sinks beneath a weight of woe.
Ye Lesbian virgins, and ye Lesbian dames,
Themes of my verse, and objects of my flames,
No more your groves with my glad songs shall ring,

No more these hands shall touch the trembling string:
My Phaon's fled, and I those arts resign
(Wretch that I am, to call that Phaon mine!)
Return, fair youth, return, and bring along
Joy to my soul, and vigour to my song:
Absent from thee, the Poet's flame expires;
But ah! how fiercely burn the lover's fires!
Gods! can no prayers, no sighs, no numbers move
One savage heart, or teach it how to love?
The winds my prayers, my sighs, my numbers bear,
The flying winds have lost them all in air!
Oh when, alas! shall more auspicious gales
To these fond eyes restore thy welcome sails?
If you return—ah why these long delays?
Poor Sappho dies while careless Phaon stays.
O launch thy bark, secure of prosperous gales;
Cupid for thee shall spread the swelling gales;
I you will fly—(yet ah! what cause can be,
Too cruel youth, that you should fly from me?)
If not from Phaon I must hope for ease,
Ah let me seek it from the raging seas:
To raging seas unpitied I'll remove,
And either cease to live, or cease to love!

EPISTLE
TO MISS BLOUNT,
WITH THE WORKS OF VOITURE

In these gay thoughts the Loves and Graces shine,
And all the writer lives in every line;
His easy art may happy nature seem,
Trifles themselves are elegant in him.
Sure, to charm all was his peculiar fate,
Who without flattery pleased the fair and great;
Still with esteem no less conversed than read;
With wit well-natured, and with books well-bred:
His heart, his mistress, and his friend did share,
His time, the Muse, the witty, and the fair.
Thus wisely careless, innocently gay,
Cheerful he played the trifle, life, away;
Till Fate scarce felt his gentle breath suppressed,
As smiling infants sport themselves to rest.
Even rival wits did Voiture's death deplore,
And the gay mourned who never mourned before;
The truest hearts for Voiture heaved with sighs,
Voiture was wept by all the brightest eyes:
The smiles and loves had died in Voiture's death,
But that for ever in his lines they breathe.

Let the strict life of graver mortals be
A long, exact, and serious comedy;
In every scene some moral let it teach,
And if it can, at once both please and preach.
Let mine an innocent gay farce appear,
And more diverting still than regular,
Have humour, wit, a native ease and grace,
Though not too strictly bound to time and place:
Critics in wit, or life, are hard to please,
Few write to those, and none can live to these.

Too much your sex is by their forms confined,
Severe to all, but most to womankind;
Custom, grown blind with age, must be your guide;
Your pleasure is a vice, but not your pride;
By nature yielding, stubborn but for fame;
Made slaves by honour, and made fools by shame.
Marriage may all those petty tyrants chase,
But sets up one, a greater, in their place;
Well might you wish for change, by those accursed,
But the last tyrant ever proves the worst.
Still in constraint your suffering sex remains,
Or bound in formal, or in real chains:
Whole years neglected, for some months adored,
The fawning servant turns a haughty lord.
Ah quit not the free innocence of life,
For the dull glory of a virtuous wife;
Nor let false shows, or empty titles please:
Aim not at joy, but rest content with ease.

The gods, to curse Pamela with her prayers,
Gave the gilt coach and dappled Flanders mares,
The shining robes, rich jewels, beds of state,
And, to complete her bliss, a fool for mate.
She glares in balls, front boxes, and the Ring,
A vain, unquiet, glittering, wretched thing!
Pride, pomp, and state but reach her outward part;
She sighs, and is no duchess at her heart.

But, Madam, if the Fates withstand, and you
Are destined Hymen's willing victim too;
Trust not too much your now resistless charms,
Those, age or sickness, soon or late, disarms:
Good humour only teaches charms to last,
Still makes new conquests, and maintains the past;
Love, raised on beauty, will like that decay,
Our hearts may bear its slender chain a day;
As flowery bands in wantonness are worn,
A morning's pleasure, and at evening torn;
This binds in ties more easy, yet more strong,
The willing heart, and only holds it long.

Thus [1] Voiture's early care still shone the same,
And Monthausier was only changed in name:
By this, even now they live, even now they charm,
Their wit still sparkling, and their flames still warm.
　　Now crowned with myrtle, on th' Elysian coast,
Amid those lovers, joys his gentle ghost:
Pleased, while with smiles his happy lines you view,
And finds a fairer Rambouillet in you.
The brightest eyes of France inspired his Muse;
The brightest eyes of Britain now peruse;
And dead, as living, 'tis our author's pride
Still to charm those who charm the world beside.

[1] Mademoiselle Paulet.

WINDSOR FOREST
TO THE RIGHT HONOURABLE
GEORGE LORD LANSDOWNE

　　Non injussa cano: Te nostrae, *Vare*, myricae
Te *Nemus* omne canet; nec Phoebo gratior ulla est
Quam sibi quae *Vari* praescripsit pagina nomen.
VIRGIL.

Thy forests, Windsor! and thy green retreats,
At once the Monarch's and the Muse's seats,
Invite my lays. Be present, sylvan maids!
Unlock your springs, and open all your shades.
GRANVILLE commands; your aid O Muses bring!
What Muse for GRANVILLE can refuse to sing?
　　The groves of Eden, vanished now so long,
Live in description, and look green in song:
These, were my breast inspired with equal flame,
Like them in beauty, should be like in fame.
Here hills and vales, the woodland and the plain,
Here earth and water, seem to strive again,
Not chaos-like together crushed and bruised,
But as the world, harmoniously confused:
Where order in variety we see,
And where, though all things differ, all agree.
Here waving groves a chequered scene display,
And part admit, and part exclude the day;
As some coy nymph her lover's warm address
Nor quite indulges, nor can quite repress.
There, interspersed in lawns and opening glades,
Thin trees arise that shun each other's shades.
Here in full light the russet plains extend:

There wrapped in clouds the blueish hills ascend.
Even the wild heath displays her purple dyes,
And 'midst the desert fruitful fields arise,
That crowned with tufted trees and springing corn,
Like verdant isles the sable waste adorn.
Let India boast her plants, nor envy we
The weeping amber or the balmy tree,
While by our oaks the precious loads are borne,
And realms commanded which those trees adorn.
Not proud Olympus yields a nobler sight,
Though Gods assembled grace his towering height,
Than what more humble mountains offer here,
Where, in their blessings, all those Gods appear.
See Pan with flocks, with fruits Pomona crowned,
Here blushing Flora paints th'enameled ground,
Here Ceres' gifts in waving prospect stand,
And nodding tempt the joyful reaper's hand;
Rich Industry sits smiling on the plains,
And peace and plenty tell, a STUART reigns.
    Not thus the land appeared in ages past,
A dreary desert and a gloomy waste,
To savage beasts and savage laws a prey,
And kings more furious and severe than they;
Who claimed the skies, dispeopled air and floods,
The lonely lords of empty wilds and woods:
Cities laid waste, they stormed the dens and caves,
(For wiser brutes were backward to be slaves):
What could be free, when lawless beasts obeyed,
And even the elements a tyrant swayed?
In vain kind seasons swelled the teeming grain,
Soft showers distilled, and suns grew warm in vain;
The swain with tears his frustrate labour yields,
And famished dies amidst his ripened fields.
What wonder then, a beast or subject slain
Were equal crimes in a despotic reign?
Both doomed alike, for sportive tyrants bled,
But while the subject starved, the beast was fed.
Proud Nimrod first the bloody chase began,
A mighty hunter, and his prey was man:
Our haughty Norman boasts that barbarous name,
And makes his trembling slaves the royal game.
The fields are ravished from th'industrious swains,
From men their cities, and from Gods their fanes:
The levelled towns with weeds lie covered o'er;
The hollow winds through naked temples roar;
Round broken columns clasping ivy twined;
O'er heaps of ruin stalked the stately hind;
The fox obscene to gaping tombs retires,

And savage howlings fill the sacred quires.
Awed by his nobles, by his commons curst,
Th'oppressor ruled tyrannic where he durst,
Stretched o'er the poor and church his iron rod,
And served alike his vassals and his God.
Whom even the Saxon spared and bloody Dane,
The wanton victims of his sport remain.
But see, the man who spacious regions gave
A waste for beasts, himself denied a grave!
Stretched on the lawn, his second hope survey,
At once the chaser, and at once the prey:
Lo Rufus, tugging at the deadly dart,
Bleeds in the forest, like a wounded hart.
Succeeding Monarchs heard the subjects cries,
Nor saw displeased the peaceful cottage rise.
Then gathering flocks on unknown mountains fed,
O'er sandy wilds were yellow harvests spread,
The forests wondered at th' unusual grain,
And secret transport touched the conscious swain.
Fair Liberty, Britannia's Goddess, rears
Her cheerful head, and leads the golden years.
    Ye vigorous swains! while youth ferments your blood,
And purer spirits swell the sprightly flood,
Now range the hills, the thickest woods beset,
Wind the shrill horn, or spread the waving net.
When milder autumn summer's heat succeeds,
And in the new-shorn field the partridge feeds,
Before his lord the ready spaniel bounds,
Panting with hope, he tries the furrowed grounds;
But when the tainted gales the game betray,
Couched close he lies, and meditates the prey:
Secure they trust th' unfaithful field, beset,
Till hovering o'er 'em sweeps the swelling net.
Thus (if small things we may with great compare)
When Albion sends her eager sons to war,
Some thoughtless town, with ease and plenty blessed,
Near, and more near, the closing lines invest;
Sudden they seize th' amazed, defenceless prize,
And high in air Britannia's standard flies.
    See! from the brake the whirring pheasant springs,
And mounts exulting on triumphant wings:
Short is his joy; he feels the fiery wound,
Flutters in blood, and panting beats the ground.
Ah! what avail his glossy, varying dyes,
His purple crest, and scarlet-circled eyes,
The vivid green his shining plumes unfold,
His painted wings, and breast that flames with gold?
    Nor yet, when moist Arcturus clouds the sky,

The woods and fields their pleasing toils deny.
To plains with well-breathed beagles we repair,
And trace the mazes of the circling hare:
(Beasts, urged by us, their fellow-beasts pursue,
And learn of man each other to undo.)
With slaughtering guns th' unwearied fowler roves,
When frosts have whitened all the naked groves;
Where doves in flocks the leafless trees o'ershade,
And lonely woodcocks haunt the watery glade.
He lifts the tube, and levels with his eye;
Straight a short thunder breaks the frozen sky.
Oft, as in airy rings they skim the heath,
The clamorous plovers feel the leaden death:
Oft', as the mounting larks their notes prepare,
They fall, and leave their little lives in air.
    In genial spring, beneath the quivering shade,
Where cooling vapours breathe along the mead,
The patient fisher takes his silent stand,
Intent, his angle trembling in his hand;
With looks unmoved, he hopes the scaly breed,
And eyes the dancing cork, and bending reed.
Our plenteous streams a various race supply,
The bright-eyed perch with fins of Tyrian dye,
The silver eel, in shining volumes rolled,
The yellow carp, in scales bedropped with gold,
Swift trouts, diversified with crimson stains,
And pikes, the tyrants of the watery plains.
    Now Cancer glows with Phoebus' fiery car;
The youth rush eager to the sylvan war,
Swarm o'er the lawns, the forest walks surround,
Rouse the fleet hart, and cheer the opening hound.
Th' impatient courser pants in every vein,
And pawing, seems to beat the distant plain;
Hills, vales, and floods appear already crossed,
And e'er he starts, a thousand steps are lost.
See! the bold youth strain up the threatening steep,
Rush through the thickets, down the valleys sweep,
Hang o'er their coursers heads with eager speed,
And earth rolls back beneath the flying steed.
Let old Arcadia boast her ample plain,
Th' immortal huntress, and her virgin-train;
Nor envy, Windsor! since thy shades have seen
As bright a Goddess, and as chaste a QUEEN;
Whose care, like hers, protects the sylvan reign,
The earth's fair light, and Empress of the main.
    Here too, 'tis sung, of old Diana strayed,
And Cynthus' top forsook for Windsor shade;
Here was she seen over airy wastes to rove

Seek the clear spring, or haunt the pathless grove;
Here armed with silver bows, in early dawn,
Her buskined virgins traced the dewy lawn.
   Above the rest a rural nymph was famed,
Thy offspring, Thames! the fair Lodona named;
(Lodona's fate, in long oblivion cast,
The Muse shall sing, and what she sings shall last.)
Scarce could the Goddess from her nymph be known,
But by the crescent and the golden zone:
She scorned the praise of beauty, and the care;
A belt her waist, a fillet binds her hair;
A painted quiver on her shoulder sounds,
And with her dart the flying deer she wounds.
It chanced, as eager of the chase, the maid
Beyond the forest's verdant limits strayed,
Pan saw and loved, and burning with desire
Pursued her flight, her flight increased his fire.
Not half so swift the trembling doves can fly,
When the fierce eagle cleaves the liquid sky;
Not half so swiftly the fierce eagle moves,
When through the clouds he drives the trembling doves;
As from the God she flew with furious pace,
Or as the God, more furious, urged the chase.
Now fainting, sinking, pale, the nymph appears;
Now close behind, his sounding steps she hears;
And now his shadow reached her as she run,
(His shadow lengthened by the setting sun)
And now his shorter breath, with sultry air,
Pants on her neck, and fans her parting hair.
In vain on father Thames she called for aid,
Nor could Diana help her injured maid.
Faint, breathless, thus she prayed, nor prayed in vain;
'Ah Cynthia! ah—though banished from thy train,
Let me, O let me, to the shades repair,
My native shades—there weep, and murmur there.'
She said, and melting as in tears she lay,
In a soft, silver stream dissolved away.
The silver stream her virgin coldness keeps,
For ever murmurs, and for ever weeps;
Still bears the name the hapless virgin bore,
And bathes the forest where she ranged before.
In her chaste current oft' the Goddess laves,
And with celestial tears augments the waves.
Oft in her glass the musing shepherd spies
The headlong mountains and the downward skies.
The watery landskip of the pendant woods,
And absent trees that tremble in the floods;
In the clear azure gleam the flocks are seen,

And floating forests paint the waves with green.
Through the fair scene roll slow the lingering streams,
Then foaming pour along, and rush into the Thames.
 Thou too, great father of the British floods!
With joyful pride surveyst our lofty woods;
Where towering oaks their spreading honours rear,
And future navies on thy shores appear.
Not Neptune's self from all his streams receives
A wealthier tribute, than to thine he gives.
No seas so rich, so gay no banks appear,
No lake so gentle, and no spring so clear.
Not fabled Po more swells the poet's lays,
While Through the skies his shining current strays,
As thine, which visits Windsor's famed abodes,
To grace the mansion of our earthly Gods:
Nor all his stars a brighter lustre show,
Like the bright beauties on thy side below:
Where Jove, subdued by mortal passion still,
Might change Olympus for a nobler hill.
 Happy the man whom this bright Court approves,
His sovereign favours, and his country loves:
Happy next him, who to these shades retires,
Whom nature charms, and whom the Muse inspires:
Whom humbler joys of home-felt quiet please,
Successive study, exercise, and ease.
He gathers health from herbs the forest yields,
And of their fragrant physic spoils the fields:
With chymic art exalts the mineral powers,
And draws the aromatic souls of flowers:
Now marks the course of rolling orbs on high;
O'er figured worlds now travels with his eye:
Of ancient writ unlocks the learned store,
Consults the dead, and lives past ages o'er:
Or wandering thoughtful in the silent wood,
Attends the duties of the wise and good,
T'observe a mean, be to himself a friend,
To follow nature, and regard his end;
Or looks on heaven with more than mortal eyes,
Bids his free soul expatiate in the skies,
Amid her kindred stars familiar roam,
Survey the region, and confess her home!
Such was the life great Scipio once admired,
Thus Atticus, and TRUMBULL thus retired.
 Ye sacred Nine! that all my soul possess,
Whose raptures fire me, and whose visions bless,
Bear me, oh bear me to sequestered scenes,
The bowery mazes, and surrounding greens:
To Thames's banks which fragrant breezes fill,

Or where ye Muses sport on COOPER'S HILL.
(On COOPER'S HILL eternal wreaths shall grow,
While lasts the mountain, or while Thames shall flow)
I seem through consecrated walks to rove,
I hear soft music die along the grove:
Led by the sound, I roam from shade to shade,
By god-like Poets venerable made:
Here his first lays majestic DENHAM sung;
There the last numbers flowed from COWLEY'S tongue.
O early lost! what tears the river shed,
When the sad pomp along his banks was led?
His drooping swans on every note expire,
And on his willows hung each Muse's lyre.
    Since fate relentless stopped their heavenly voice,
No more the forests ring, or groves rejoice;
Who now shall charm the shades, where COWLEY strung
His living harp, and lofty DENHAM sung?
But hark! the groves rejoice, the forest rings!
Are these revived? or is it GRANVILLE sings?
'Tis yours, my Lord, to bless our soft retreats,
And call the Muses to their ancient seats;
To paint anew the flowery sylvan scenes,
To crown the forests with immortal greens,
Make Windsor-hills in lofty numbers rise,
And lift her turrets nearer to the skies;
To sing those honours you deserve to wear,
And add new lustre to her silver star.
    Here noble SURREY felt the sacred rage,
SURREY, the GRANVILLE of a former age:
Matchless his pen, victorious was his lance,
Bold in the lists, and graceful in the dance:
In the same shades the Cupids tuned his lyre,
To the same notes, of love, and soft desire:
Fair Geraldine, bright object of his vow,
Then filled the groves, as heavenly Myra now.
    Oh wouldst thou sing what Heroes Windsor bore,
What Kings first breathed upon her winding shore,
Or raise old warriors, whose adored remains
In weeping vaults her hallowed earth contains!
With Edward's acts adorn the shining page,
Stretch his long triumphs down through every age,
Draw Monarchs chained, and Cressi's glorious field,
The lilies blazing on the regal shield:
Then, from her roofs when Verrio's colours fall,
And leave inanimate the naked wall,
Still in thy song should vanquished France appear,
And bleed for ever under Britain's spear.
    Let softer strains ill-fated Henry mourn,

And palms eternal flourish round his urn,
Here o'er the Martyr-King the marble weeps,
And fast beside him, once-feared Edward sleeps:
Whom not th' extended Albion could contain,
From old Belerium to the northern main,
The grave unites; where even the great find rest,
And blended lie th' oppressor and th' oppressed!
    Make sacred Charles's tomb for ever known,
(Obscure the place, and un-inscribed the stone)
Oh fact accursed! what tears has Albion shed,
Heavens, what new wounds! and how her old have bled?
She saw her sons with purple deaths expire,
Her sacred domes involved in rolling fire,
A dreadful series of intestine wars,
Inglorious triumphs, and dishonest scars.
At length great ANNA said—'Let Discord cease!'
She said, the world obeyed, and all was peace!
    In that blessed moment, from his oozy bed
Old father Thames advanced his reverend head.
His tresses dropped with dews, and o'er the stream
His shining horns diffused a golden gleam:
Graved on his urn appeared the moon, that guides
His swelling waters, and alternate tides;
The figured streams in waves of silver rolled,
And on their banks Augusta rose in gold.
Around his throne the sea-born brothers stood,
Who swell with tributary urns his flood;
First the famed authors of his ancient name,
The winding Isis and the fruitful Thame:
The Kennet swift, for silver eels renowned;
The Loddon slow, with verdant alders crowned;
Cole, whose clear streams his flowery islands lave;
And chalky Wey, that rolls a milky wave:
The blue, transparent Vandalis appears;
The gulphy Lee his sedgy tresses rears;
And sullen Mole, that hides his diving flood;
And silent Darent, stained with Danish blood.
    High in the midst, upon his urn reclined,
(His sea-green mantle waving with the wind)
The God appeared: he turned his azure eyes
Where Windsor-domes and pompous turrets rise;
Then bowed and spoke; the winds forget to roar,
And the hushed waves glide softly to the shore.
    Hail, sacred Peace! hail long-expected days,
That Thames's glory to the stars shall raise!
Though Tiber's streams immortal Rome behold,
Though foaming Hermus swells with tides of gold,
From heaven itself though seven-fold Nilus flows,

And harvests on a hundred realms bestows;
These now no more shall be the Muse's themes,
Lost in my fame, as in the sea their streams.
Let Volga's banks with iron squadrons shine,
And groves of lances glitter on the Rhine,
Let barbarous Ganges arm a servile train;
Be mine the blessings of a peaceful reign.
No more my sons shall dye with British blood
Red Iber's sands, or Ister's foaming flood:
Safe on my shore each unmolested swain
Shall tend the flocks, or reap the bearded grain;
The shady empire shall retain no trace
Of war or blood, but in the sylvan chase;
The trumpet sleep, while cheerful horns are blown,
And arms employed on birds and beasts alone.
Behold! th' ascending Villa's on my side,
Project long shadows o'er the crystal tide.
Behold! Augusta's glittering spires increase,
And temples rise, the beauteous works of peace.
I see, I see where two fair cities bend
Their ample bow, a new Whitehall ascend!
There mighty nations shall enquire their doom,
The world's great oracle in times to come;
There kings shall sue, and suppliant States be seen
Once more to bend before a BRITISH QUEEN.
    Thy trees, fair Windsor! now shall leave their woods,
And half thy forests rush into my floods,
Bear Britain's thunder, and her cross display,
To the bright regions of the rising day;
Tempt icy seas, where scarce the waters roll,
Where clearer flames glow round the frozen pole;
Or under southern skies exalt their sails,
Led by new stars, and borne by spicy gales!
For me the balm shall bleed, and amber flow,
The coral redden, and the ruby glow,
The pearly shell its lucid globe enfold,
And Phoebus warm the ripening ore to gold.
The time shall come, when free as seas or wind
Unbounded Thames shall flow for all mankind,
Whole nations enter with each swelling tide,
And seas but join the regions they divide;
Earth's distant ends our glory shall behold,
And the new world launch forth to seek the old.
Then ships of uncouth form shall stem the tide,
And feathered people crowd my wealthy side,
And naked youths and painted chiefs admire
Our speech, our colour, and our strange attire!
Oh stretch thy reign, fair Peace! from shore to shore,

48

Till Conquest cease, and slavery be no more;
Till the freed Indians in their native groves
Reap their own fruits, and woo their sable loves,
Peru once more a race of kings behold,
And other Mexicos be roofed with gold.
Exiled by thee from earth to deepest hell,
In brazen bonds shall barbarous Discord dwell;
Gigantic Pride, pale Terror, gloomy Care,
And mad Ambition, shall attend her there:
There purple Vengeance bathed in gore retires,
Her weapons blunted, and extinct her fires:
There hateful Envy her own snakes shall feel,
And Persecution mourn her broken wheel:
There Faction roar, Rebellion bite her chain,
And gasping Furies thirst for blood in vain.
    Here cease thy flight, nor with unhallowed lays
Touch the fair fame of Albion's golden days:
The thoughts of Gods let GRANVILLE'S verse recite,
And bring the scenes of opening fate to light.
My humble Muse, in unambitious strains,
Paints the green forests and the flowery plains,
Where Peace descending bids her olives spring,
And scatters blessings from her dove-like wing.
Even I more sweetly pass my careless days,
Pleased in the silent shade with empty praise;
Enough for me, that to the listening swains
First in these fields I sung the sylvan strains.

THE GUARDIAN, NO. 173
TUESDAY, 29 SEPTEMBER 1713

—Nec sera comantem
Narcissum, aut flexi tacuissem Vimen Acanthi,
Pallentesque Haederas, & amantes littoral myrtos.
VIRGIL.

ON GARDENS

    I lately took a particular Friend of mine to my house in the country, not without some apprehension that it could afford little entertainment to a man of his polite taste, particularly in architecture and gardening, who had so long been conversant with all that is beautiful and great in either. But it was a pleasant Surprise to me, to hear him often declare, he had found in my little retirement that beauty which he always thought wanting in the most celebrated seats, or if you will villa's, of the nation. This he described to me in those verses with which Martial begins one of his epigrams:

Baiana nostri Villa, Basse, Faustini,
Non otiosis ordinata myrtetis,
Viduaque platano, tonsilique buxeto,
Ingrata lati spatia detinet campi,
Sed rure vero, barbaroque *laetatur.*

There is certainly something in the amiable simplicity of unadorned nature that spreads over the mind a more noble sort of tranquility, and a loftier sensation of pleasure, than can be raised from the nicer scenes of art.

This was the taste of the ancients in their gardens, as we may discover from the descriptions are extant of them. The two most celebrated wits of the world have each of them left us a particular picture of a garden; wherein those great masters, being wholly unconfined, and painting at pleasure, may be thought to have given a full idea of what they esteemed most excellent in this way. These (one may observe) consist entirely of the useful part of horticulture, fruit trees, herbs, water, etc. The pieces I am speaking of are Virgil's account of the garden of the old Corycian, and Homer's of that of Alcinous. The first of these is already known to the English Reader, by the excellent Versions of Mr. Dryden and Mr. Addison. The other having never been attempted in our language with any elegance, and being the most beautiful plan of this sort that can be imagined, I shall here present the reader with a translation of it.

The Gardens of Alcinous, from Homer's *Odyss.* 7.

Close to the gates a spacious garden lies,
From storms defended and inclement skies:
Four acres was th' allotted space of ground,
Fenced with a green enclosure all around.
Tall thriving trees confessed the fruitful mold;
The reddening apple ripens here to gold,
Here the blue fig with luscious juice o'erflows,
With deeper red the full pomegranate glows,
The branch here bends beneath the weighty pear,
And verdant olives flourish round the year.
The balmy spirit of the western gale
Eternal breaths on fruits untaught to fail:
Each dropping pear a following pear supplies,
On apples apples, figs on figs arise:
The same mild Season gives the blooms to blow,
The buds to harden, and the fruits to grow.
*   Here ordered vines in equal ranks appear,*
With all th' united labours of the year.
Some to unload the fertile branches run,
Some dry the blackening clusters in the sun,
Others to tread the liquid harvest join,
The groaning presses foam with floods of wine.
Here are the vines in early flower descried,
Here grapes discoloured on the sunny side,

> *And there in Autumn's richest Purple dyed.*
>   *Beds of all various Herbs, forever green,*
> *In beauteous order terminate the scene.*
> *Two plenteous fountains the whole prospect crowned;*
> *This through the gardens leads its streams around,*
> *Visits each plant, and waters all the ground:*
> *While that in pipes beneath the palace flows,*
> *And thence its current on the town bestows;*
> *To various use their various streams they bring,*
> *The people one, and one supplies the king.*

Sir William Temple has remarked, that this description contains all the justest rules and provisions which can go toward composing the best gardens. Its extent was four acres, which in those times of simplicity was looked upon as a large one, even for a prince: it was enclosed all round for defence; and, for conveniency joined close to the gates of the palace.

He mentions next the trees which were standards, and suffered to grow to their full height. The fine description of the fruits that never failed, and the eternal zephyrs, is only a more noble and poetical way of expressing the continual succession of one fruit after another throughout the year.

The *vineyard* seems to have been a plantation distinct from the *garden*; as also the *beds of greens* mentioned afterwards at the extremity of the enclosure, in the nature and usual place of our *kitchen gardens*.

The two fountains are disposed very remarkably. They rose within the enclosure, and were brought by conduits, or ducts; one of them to water all pans of the gardens, and the other underneath the pak.ee into the town for the service of the public.

How contrary to this simplicity is the modern practice of gardening; we seem to make it our study to recede from nature, not only in the various tonsure of greens into the most jugular and formal shapes, but even in monstrous attempts beyond the reach of the art itself. We run into sculpture; and are yet better pleased to have our trees in the most awkward figures of men and animals, than in the most regular of their own.

> *Hinc & nexilibus videas e frondibus hortos,*
> *Implexos late muros, & Moenia circum*
> *Porrigere, & latas e ramis surgere turres;*
> *Deflexam & Myrtum in Puppes, atque aerea rostra:*
> *In buxisque undare fretum, atque e rore rudentes.*
> *Parte aliâ frondere suis tentoria Castris;*
> *Scutaque, spiculaque & jaculantia citria Vallos.*

I believe it is no wrong observation that persons of genius, and those who are most capable of art, are always most fond of nature; as such are chiefly sensible, that all art consists in the imitation and study of nature. On the contrary, people of the common level of understanding are principally delighted with the little niceties and fantastical operations of art, and constantly think that *finest* which is least natural. A citizen is no sooner proprietor of a couple of yews, but he entertains thoughts of erecting them into giants, like those of Guildhall. I know an eminent cook, who beautified his country seat with a coronation dinner in greens; where you see the Champion flourishing on horseback at one end of the table, and the Queen in perpetual youth at the other.

For the benefit of all my loving countrymen of this curious taste, I shall here publish a catalogue of greens to be disposed of by an eminent town-gardener, who has lately applied to me upon this head. He represents, that for the advancement of a politer sort of ornament in the villas and gardens adjacent to this great city, and in order to distinguish, those places from the mere barbarous countries of gross nature, the world stands much in need of a virtuoso gardener who has a turn to sculpture, and is thereby capable of improving upon the ancients of his profession in the imagery of evergreens. My correspondent is arrived to such perfection, that he cuts family pieces of men, women, or children. Any ladies that please may have their own effigies in myrtle, or their husbands in hornbeam. He is a puritan wag, and never fails, when he shows his garden, to repeat that passage in the Psalms, *Thy wife shall be as the fruitful vine, and thy children as olive branches round thy table.* I shall proceed to his catalogue, as he sent it for my recommendation.

Adam and Eve in yew; Adam a little shattered by the fall of the tree of knowledge in the Great Storm; Eve and the serpent very flourishing.

The Tower of Babel, not yet-finished.

St. George in box; his arm scarce long enough, but will be in a condition to stick the dragon by next April.

A green dragon of the same, with a tail of ground-ivy for the present.

N.B. *These two not to be sold separately.*

Edward the Black Prince in cypress.

A Laurustine bear in blossom, with a juniper hunter in berries.

A pair of giants, *stunted*, to be sold cheap.

A Queen Elizabeth in phylyraea, a little inclining to the green sickness, but of full growth.

Another Queen Elizabeth in myrtle, which was very forward, but miscarried by being too near a savin.

An old maid of honour in wormwood.

A topping Ben Jonson in laurel.

Divers eminent modern poets in bays, somewhat blighted, to be disposed of, a pennyworth.

A quick-set hog shot up into a porcupine, by it's being forgot a week in rainy weather.

A lavender pig with sage growing in his belly.

Noah's ark in holly, standing on the mount; the ribs a little damaged for want of water.

A pair of Maidenheads in fir, in great forwardness.

THE WIFE OF BATH
FROM CHAUCER

Behold the woes of matrimonial life,
And hear with reverence an experienced wife!
To dear-bought wisdom give the credit due,
And think, for once, a woman tells you true.
In all these trials I have borne a part,
I was myself the scourge that caused the smart;
For, since fifteen, in triumph have I led
Five captive husbands from the church to bed.

    Christ saw a wedding once, the scripture says,
And saw but one, 'tis thought, in all his days;
Whence some infer, whose conscience is too nice,
No pious Christian ought to marry twice.

    But let them read, and solve me, if they can,
The words addressed to the Samaritan:
Five times in lawful wedlock she was joined;
And sure the certain stint was ne'er defined.

    'Increase and multiply,' was heaven's command,
And that's a text I clearly understand:
This too, 'Let men their sires and mothers leave,
And to their dearer wives for ever cleave.'
More wives than one by Solomon were tried,
Or else the wisest of mankind's belied.
I've had myself full many a merry fit,
And trust in Heaven I may have many yet;
For when my transitory spouse, unkind,
Shall die, and leave his woeful wife behind,
I'll take the next good Christian I can find.

    Paul, knowing one could never serve our turn,
Declared 'twas better far to wed than burn.
There's danger in assembling fire and tow;
I grant 'em that; and what it means you know.
The same apostle, too, has elsewhere owned
No precept for virginity he found:
'Tis but a counsel—and we women still
Take which we like, the counsel or our will.

    I envy not their bliss, if he or she
Think fit to live in perfect chastity;
Pure let them be, and free from taint of vice;
I, for a few slight spots, am not so nice.
Heaven calls us different ways; on these bestows
One proper gift, another grants to those:
Not every man's obliged to sell his store,
And give up all his substance to the poor;
Such as are perfect, may, I can't deny;

But, by your leave, Divines, so am not I.
Full many a saint, since first the world began,
Lived an unspotted maid in spite of man:
Let such (a-God's name) with fine wheat be fed,
And let us honest wives eat barley bread.
For me, I'll keep the post assigned by heaven,
And use the copious talent it has given:
Let my good spouse pay tribute, do me right,
And keep an equal reckoning every night;
His proper body is not his, but mine;
For so said Paul, and Paul's a sound divine.
Know then, of those five husbands I have had,
Three were just tolerable, two were bad.
The three were old, but rich and fond beside,
And toiled most piteously to please their bride:
But since their wealth (the best they had) was mine,
The rest, without much loss, I could resign:
Sure to be loved, I took no pains to please,
Yet had more pleasure far than they had ease.
Presents flowed in apace: with showers of gold,
They made their court, like Jupiter of old.
If I but smiled, a sudden youth they found,
And a new palsy seized them when I frowned.
Ye sovereign wives! give ear, and understand;
Thus shall ye speak, and exercise command;
For never was it given to mortal man,
To lie so boldly as we women can:
Forswear the fact, though seen with both his eyes,
And call your maids to witness how he lies.
'Hark, old Sir Paul!' ('twas thus I used to say)
'Whence is our neighbour's wife so rich and gay?
Treated, caressed, where'er she's pleased to roam—
I sit in tatters, and immured at home.
Why to her house dost thou so oft repair?
Art thou so amorous? and is she so fair?
If I but see a cousin or a friend,
Lord! how you swell and rage like any fiend!
But you reel home, a drunken beastly bear,
Then preach till midnight in your easy chair;
Cry, wives are false, and every woman evil,
And give up all that's female to the devil.
If poor (you say), she drains her husband's purse;
If rich, she keeps her priest, or something worse;
If highly born, intolerably vain;
Vapours and pride by turns possess her brain:
Now gaily mad, now sourly splenetic,
Freakish when well, and fretful when she's sick.
If fair, then chaste she cannot long abide,

By pressing youth attacked on every side.
If foul, her wealth the lusty lover lures,
Or else her wit some fool-gallant procures,
Or else she dances with becoming grace,
Or shape excuses the defects of face.
There swims no goose so grey, but soon or late,
She finds some honest gander for her mate.

   Horses (thou sayst) and asses, men may try,
And ring suspected vessels ere they buy:
But wives, a random choice, untried they take,
They dream in courtship, but in wedlock wake;
Then, nor till then, the veil's removed away,
And all the woman glares in open day.

   You tell me, to preserve your wife's good grace,
Your eyes must always languish on my face,
Your tongue with constant flatteries feed my ear,
And tag each sentence with 'My life! my dear!'
If by strange chance a modest blush be raised,
Be sure my fine complexion must be praised:
My garments always must be new and gay,
And feasts still kept upon my wedding-day.
Then must my nurse be pleased, and favourite maid;
And endless treats, and endless visits paid,
To a long train of kindred, friends, allies;
All this thou sayst, and all thou sayst are lies.

   On Jenkin, too, you cast a squinting eye:
What! can your 'prentice raise your jealousy?
Fresh are his ruddy cheeks, his forehead fair,
And like the burnished gold his curling hair.
But clear thy wrinkled brow, and quit thy sorrow,
I'd scorn your prentice, should you die tomorrow.

   Why are thy chests all locked? on what design?
Are not thy worldly goods and treasure mine?
Sir, I'm no fool: nor shall you, by St. John,
Have goods and body to yourself alone.
One you shall quit, in spite of both your eyes—
I heed not, I, the bolts, the locks, the spies.
If you had wit, you 'd say, 'Go where you will,
Dear spouse, I credit not the tales they tell:
Take all the freedoms of a married life;
I know thee for a virtuous, faithful wife.'

   Lord! when you have enough, what need you care
How merrily soever others fare?
Though all the day I give and take delight,
Doubt not, sufficient will be left at night.
'Tis but a just and rational desire
To light a taper at a neighbour's fire.

   There's danger too, you think, in rich array,

And none can long be modest that are gay.
The cat, if you but singe her tabby skin,
The chimney keeps, and sits content within;
But once grown sleek, will from her corner run,
Sport with her tail, and wanton in the sun;
She licks her fair round face, and frisks abroad,
To show her fur, and to be catterwawed.'
   Lo thus, my friends, I wrought to my desires
These three right ancient venerable sires.
I told 'em, 'Thus you say, and thus you do'—
And told 'em false, but Jenkin swore 'twas true.
I, like a dog, could bite as well as whine,
And first complained, whene'er the guilt was mine.
I taxed them oft with wenching and amours,
When their weak legs scarce dragged 'em out of doors;
And swore the rambles that I took by night,
Were all to spy what damsels they bedight.
That colour brought me many hours of mirth;
For all this wit is given us from our birth.
Heaven gave to woman the peculiar grace
To spin, to weep, and cully human race.
By this nice conduct, and this prudent course,
By murmuring, wheedling, stratagem, and force,
I still prevailed, and would be in the right;
Or curtain-lectures made a restless night.
If once my husband's arm was o'er my side,
'What! so familiar with your spouse?' I cried:
I levied first a tax upon his need,
Then let him—'twas a nicety indeed!
Let all mankind this certain maxim hold,
Marry who will, our sex is to be sold!
With empty hands no tassels you can lure,
But fulsome love for gain we can endure;
For gold we love the impotent and old,
And heave, and pant, and kiss, and cling, for gold.
Yet with embraces curses oft I mixed,
Then kissed again, and chid and railed betwixt.
Well, I may make my will in peace, and die,
For not one word in man's arrears am I.
To drop a dear dispute I was unable,
Ev'n though the Pope himself had sat at table;
But when my point was gained, then thus I spoke:
'Billy, my dear, how sheepishly you look!
Approach, my spouse, and let me kiss thy cheek;
Thou shouldst be always thus, resigned and meek!
Of Job's great patience since so oft you preach,
Well should you practise who so well can teach.
'Tis difficult to do, I must allow,

But I, my dearest, will instruct you how.
Great is the blessing of a prudent wife,
Who puts a period to domestic strife.
One of us two must rule, and one obey;
And since in man right Reason bears the sway,
Let that frail thing, weak woman, have her way.
The wives of all my family have ruled
Their tender husbands, and their passions cooled.
Fie! 'tis unmanly thus to sigh and groan;
What! would you have me to yourself alone?
Why, take me, love! take all and every part!
Here's your revenge! you love it at your heart.
Would I vouchsafe to sell what nature gave,
You little think what custom I could have.
But see! I'm all your own—nay hold—for shame!
What means my dear—indeed—you are to blame.'
    Thus with my first three lords I passed my life,
A very woman and a very wife.
What sums from these old spouses I could raise,
Procured young husbands in my riper days.
Though past my bloom, not yet decayed was I,
Wanton and wild, and chattered like a pie.
In country dances still I bore the bell,
And sung as sweet as evening Philomel.
To clear my quail-pipe, and refresh my soul,
Full oft I drained the spicy nut-brown bowl;
Rich luscious wines, that youthful blood improve,
And warm the swelling veins to feats of love:
For 'tis as sure as cold engenders hail,
A liquorish mouth must have a lecherous tail;
Wine lets no lover unrewarded go,
As all true gamesters by experience know.
    But oh, good Gods! whene'er a thought I cast
On all the joys of youth and beauty past,
To find in pleasures I have had my part,
Still warms me to the bottom of my heart.
This wicked world was once my dear delight;
Now all my conquests, all my charms, good night!
The flour consumed, the best that now I can,
Is even to make my market of the bran.
    My fourth dear spouse was not exceeding true;
He kept, 'twas thought, a private miss or two;
But all that score I paid—as how? you 'll say:
Not with my body, in a filthy way;
But I so dressed, and danced, and drank, and dined;
And viewed a friend with eyes so very kind,
As stung his heart, and made his marrow fry,
With burning rage, and frantic jealousy.

His soul, I hope, enjoys eternal glory,
For here on earth I was his purgatory.
Oft, when his shoe the most severely wrung,
He put on careless airs, and sat and sung.
How sore I galled him only Heaven could know,
And he that felt, and I that caused the woe.
He died when last from pilgrimage I came,
With other gossips, from Jerusalem;
And now lies buried underneath a rood,
Fair to be seen, and reared of honest wood:
A tomb, indeed, with fewer sculptures graced,
Than that Mausolus' pious widow placed,
Or where enshrined the great Darius lay;
But cost on graves is merely thrown away.
The pit filled up, with turf we covered o'er;
So bless the good man's soul, I say no more.
    Now for my fifth loved lord, the last and best;
(Kind heaven afford him everlasting rest)
Full hearty was his love, and I can show
The tokens on my ribs, in black and blue;
Yet, with a knack, my heart he could have won,
While yet the smart was shooting in the bone.
How quaint an appetite in women reigns!
Free gifts we scorn, and love what costs us pains:
Let men avoid us, and on them we leap;
A glutted market makes provision cheap.
    In pure good will I took this jovial spark,
Of Oxford he, a most egregious clerk.
He boarded with a widow in the town,
A trusty gossip, one dame Alison.
Full well the secrets of my soul she knew,
Better than e'er our parish priest could do.
To her I told whatever could befall:
Had but my husband pissed against a wall,
Or done a thing that might have cost his life,
She—and my niece—and one more worthy wife,
Had known it all: what most he would conceal,
To these I made no scruple to reveal.
Oft has he blushed from ear to ear for shame,
That e'er he told a secret to his dame.
    It so befell, in holy time of Lent,
That oft a day I to this gossip went;
(My husband, thank my stars, was out of town)
From house to house we rambled up and down,
This clerk, myself, and my good neighbour Alice,
To see, be seen, to tell, and gather tales.
Visits to every church we daily paid,
And marched in every holy masquerade,

The stations duly and the vigils kept;
Not much we fasted, but scarce ever slept.
At sermons, too, I shone in scarlet gay,
The wasting moth ne'er spoiled my best array;
The cause was this, I wore it every day.
   'Twas when fresh May her early blossoms yields,
This clerk and I were walking in the fields.
We grew so intimate, I can't tell how,
I pawned my honour, and engaged my vow,
If e'er I laid my husband in his urn,
That he, and only he, should serve my turn.
We straight struck hands, the bargain was agreed;
I still have shifts against a time of need.
The mouse that always trusts to one poor hole,
Can never be a mouse of any soul.
   I vowed I scarce could sleep since first I knew him,
And durst be sworn he had bewitched me to him;
If e'er I slept I dreamed of him alone,
And dreams foretell, as learned men have shown:
All this I said; but dreams, sirs, I had none:
I followed but my crafty crony's lore,
Who bid me tell this lie—and twenty more.
   Thus day by day, and month by month we past;
It pleased the Lord to take my spouse at last.
I tore my gown, I soiled my locks with dust,
And beat my breasts, as wretched widows—must.
Before my face my handkerchief I spread,
To hide the flood of tears I—did not shed.
The good man's coffin to the church was borne;
Around, the neighbours, and my clerk, too, mourn.
But as he marched, good Gods! he showed a pair
Of legs and feet, so clean, so strong, so fair!
Of twenty winters' age he seemed to be;
I (to say truth) was twenty more than he;
But vigorous still, a lively buxom dame;
And had a wondrous gift to quench a flame.
A conjurer once, that deeply could divine,
Assured me, Mars in Taurus was my sign.
As the stars ordered, such my life has been:
Alas, alas! that ever love was sin!
Fair Venus gave me fire, and sprightly grace,
And Mars assurance, and a dauntless face.
By virtue of this powerful constellation,
I followed always my own inclination.
   But to my tale: A month scarce passed away,
With dance and song we kept the nuptial day.
All I possessed I gave to his command,
My goods and chattels, money, house, and land:

But oft repented, and repent it still;
He proved a rebel to my sovereign will:
Nay once by heaven he struck me on the face;
Hear but the fact, and judge yourselves the case.
    Stubborn as any lioness was I;
And knew full well to raise my voice on high;
As true a rambler as I was before,
And would be so, in spite of all he swore.
He, against this, right sagely would advise,
And old examples set before my eyes;
Tell how the Roman matrons led their life,
Of Gracchus' mother, and Duilius' wife;
And close the sermon, as beseemed his wit,
With some grave sentence out of holy writ.
Oft would he say, who builds his house on sands,
Pricks his blind horse across the fallow lands,
Or lets his wife abroad with pilgrims roam,
Deserves a fool's cap and long ears at home.'
All this availed not; for whoe'er he be
That tells my faults, I hate him mortally:
And so do numbers more, I'll boldly say,
Men, women, clergy, regular and lay.
    My spouse (who was, you know, to learning bred)
A certain treatise oft at evening read,
Where divers authors (whom the devil confound
For all their lies) were in one volume bound.
Valerius, whole; and of St. Jerome, part;
Chrysippus and Tertullian, Ovid's Art,
Solomon's Proverbs, Eloïsa's loves;
And many more than sure the church approves.
More legends were there here, of wicked wives,
Than good, in all the Bible and saints' lives.
Who drew the lion vanquished? 'Twas a man.
But could we women write as scholars can,
Men should stand marked with far more wickedness,
Than all the sons of Adam could redress.
Love seldom haunts the breast where learning lies,
And Venus sets ere Mercury can rise.
Those play the scholars who can't play the men,
And use that weapon which they have, their pen;
When old, and past the relish of delight,
Then down they sit, and in their dotage write,
That not one woman keeps her marriage-vow.
(This by the way, but to my purpose now.)
    It chanced my husband, on a winter's night,
Read in this book, aloud, with strange delight,
How the first female (as the scriptures show)
Brought her own spouse and all his race to woe.

How Samson fell; and he whom Dejanire
Wrapped in th' envenomed shirt, and set on fire.
How cursed Eryphile her lord betrayed,
And the dire ambush Clytemnestra laid.
But what most pleased him was the Cretan dame,
And husband-bull—oh, monstrous! fie, for shame!
   He had by heart the whole detail of woe
Xantippe made her good man undergo;
How oft she scolded in a day, he knew,
How many piss-pots on the sage she threw;
Who took it patiently, and wiped his head;
Rain follows thunder, that was all he said.
   He read how Arius to his friend complained
A fatal tree was growing in his land.
On which three wives successively had twined
A sliding noose, and wavered in the wind.
'Where grows this plant,' replied the friend, 'oh where?'
For better fruit did never orchard bear:
Give me some slip of this most blissful tree,
And in my garden planted it shall be.'
   Then how two wives their lords' destruction prove,
Through hatred one, and one through too much love;
That for her husband mixed a poisonous draught,
And this for lust an amorous philtre bought:
The nimble juice soon seized his giddy head,
Frantic at night, and in the morning dead.
   How some with swords their sleeping lords have slain,
And some have hammered nails into their brain,
And some have drenched them with a deadly potion;
All this he read, and read with great devotion.
   Long time I heard, and swelled, and blushed, and frowned;
But when no end of these vile tales I found,
When still he read, and laughed, and read again,
And half the night was thus consumed in vain;
Provoked to vengeance, three large leaves I tore
And with one buffet felled him on the floor.
With that my husband in a fury rose,
And down he settled me with hearty blows.
I groaned, and lay extended on my side;
'Oh! thou hast slain me for my wealth,' I cried,
'Yet I forgive thee—take my last embrace—'
He wept, kind soul! and stooped to kiss my face;
I took him such a box as turned him blue,
Then sighed and cried, 'Adieu, my dear, adieu!'
   But after many a hearty struggle past,
I condescended to be pleased at last.
Soon as he said, 'My mistress and my wife!
Do what you list the term of all your life';

I took to heart the merits of the cause,
And stood content to rule by wholesome laws;
Received the reins of absolute command,
With all the government of house and land;
And empire o'er his tongue, and o'er his hand.
As for the volume that reviled the dames,
'Twas torn to fragments, and condemned to flames.
   Now Heaven on all my husbands gone, bestow
Pleasures above for tortures felt below:
That rest they wished for, grant them in the grave,
And bless those souls my conduct helped to save!

THE
RAPE OF THE LOCK
AN
HEROI-COMICAL
POEM

Written in the Year MDCCXII

To Mrs. Arabella Fermor

Madam,
It will be in vain to deny that I have some regard for this piece, since I dedicate it to you. Yet you may bear me witness, it was intended only to divert a few young ladies, who have good sense and good humour enough to laugh not only at their sex's little unguarded follies, but at their own. But as it was communicated with the air of a secret, it soon found its way into the world. An imperfect copy having been offered to a bookseller, you had the good-nature for my sake to consent to the publication of one more correct: this I was forced to, before I had executed half my design, for the machinery was entirely wanting to complete it.

The machinery, Madam, is a term invented by the critics, to signify that part which the deities, angels, or daemons are made to act in a poem: for the ancient poets are in one respect like many modern ladies; let an action be never so trivial in itself, they always make it appear of the utmost importance. These machines I determined to raise on a very new and odd foundation, the Rosicrucian doctrine of spirits.

I know how disagreeable it is to make use of hard words before a lady; but 'tis so much the concern of a poet to have his works understood, and particularly by your sex, that you must give me leave to explain two or three difficult terms.

The Rosicrucians are a people I must bring you acquainted with. The best account I know of them is in a French book called *Le Comte de Gabalis*, which both in its title and size is so like a novel, that many of the fair sex have read it for one by mistake. According to these Gentlemen, the four Elements are inhabited by Spirits, which they call sylphs, gnomes, nymphs, and salamanders. The gnomes or daemons of earth delight in mischief; but the sylphs whose habitation is in the air, are the best conditioned creatures imaginable. For they say, any mortals may enjoy the most intimate familiarities with these gentle spirits, upon a condition very easy to all true adepts, an inviolate preservation of Chastity.

As to the following cantos, all the passages of them are as fabulous, as the vision at the beginning, or the transformation at the end (except the loss of your Hair, which I always mention with reverence). The human persons are as fictitious as the airy ones; and the character of Belinda, as it is now managed, resembles you in nothing but in beauty.

If this poem had as many graces as there are in your person, or in your mind, yet I could never hope it should pass through the world half so uncensured as you have done. But let its fortune be what it will, mine is happy enough, to have given me this occasion of assuring you that I am, with the truest esteem,

MADAM,

Your most obedient, humble servant,

A. POPE.

Nolueram, Belinda, tuos violare capillos;
Sed juvat, hoc precibus me tribuisse tuis.
MARTIAL.

CANTO I

What dire offence from amorous causes springs,
What mighty contests rise from trivial things,
I sing — This verse to CARYLL, Muse! is due:
This, even Belinda may vouchsafe to view:
Slight is the subject, but not so the praise,
If She inspire, and He approve my lays.
  Say what strange motive, Goddess! could compel
A well-bred Lord t'assault a gentle Belle?
Oh say what stranger cause, yet unexplored,
Could make a gentle belle reject a lord?
In tasks so bold, can little men engage,
And in soft bosoms dwells such mighty rage?
  Sol through white curtains shot a timorous ray,
And oped those eyes that must eclipse the day:
Now lap-dogs give themselves the rousing shake,
And sleepless lovers, just at twelve, awake:
Thrice rung the bell, the slipper knocked the ground,
And the pressed watch returned a silver sound.
Belinda still her downy pillow pressed,
Her guardian SYLPH prolonged the balmy rest:
'Twas He had summoned to her silent bed
The morning-dream that hovered o'er her head.
A youth more glittering than a birth-night Beau,
(That even in slumber caused her cheek to glow)
Seemed to her ear his winning lips to lay,
And thus in whispers said, or seemed to say:
  'Fairest of mortals, thou distinguished care
Of thousand bright inhabitants of air!
If e'er one vision touched thy infant thought,
Of all the Nurse and all the Priest have taught;

Of airy elves by moonlight shadows seen,
The silver token, and the circled green,
Or virgins visited by angel-powers,
With golden crowns and wreaths of heavenly flowers;
Hear and believe! thy own importance know,
Nor bound thy narrow views to things below.
Some secret truths, from learned pride concealed,
To maids alone and children are revealed:
What though no credit doubting wits may give?
The fair and innocent shall still believe.
Know, then, unnumbered spirits round thee fly,
The light militia of the lower sky;
These, though unseen, are ever on the wing,
Hang o'er the Box, and hover round the ring.
Think what an equipage thou hast in air,
And view with scorn two pages and a chair.
As now your own, our beings were of old,
And once enclosed in woman's beauteous mould;
Thence, by a soft transition, we repair
From earthly Vehicles to these of air.
Think not, when woman's transient breath is fled,
That all her vanities at once are dead;
Succeeding vanities she still regards,
And though she plays no more, o'erlooks the cards.
Her joy in gilded chariots, when alive,
And love of ombre, after death survive.
For when the fair in all their pride expire,
To their first elements their souls retire:
The sprites of fiery termagants in flame
Mount up, and take a salamander's name.
Soft yielding minds to water glide away,
And sip, with nymphs, their elemental tea.
The graver prude sinks downward to a gnome,
In search of mischief still on earth to roam.
The light coquettes in sylphs aloft repair,
And sport and flutter in the fields of air.
    Know further yet; whoever fair and chaste
Rejects mankind, is by some sylph embraced:
For spirits, freed from mortal laws, with ease
Assume what sexes and what shapes they please.
What guards the purity of melting maids,
In courtly balls, and midnight masquerades,
Safe from the treacherous friend, the daring spark,
The glance by day, the whisper in the dark,
When kind occasion prompts their warm desires,
When music softens, and when dancing fires?
'Tis but their sylph, the wise celestials know,
Though honour is the word with men below.

Some nymphs there are, too conscious of their face,
For life predestined to the gnomes' embrace.
These swell their prospects and exalt their pride,
When offers are disdained, and love denied:
Then gay ideas crowd the vacant brain,
While peers, and dukes, and all their sweeping train,
And garters, stars, and coronets appear,
And in soft sounds, 'Your Grace' salutes their ear.
'tis these that early taint the female soul,
Instruct the eyes of young coquettes to roll,
Teach infant-cheeks a bidden blush to know,
And little hearts to flutter at a beau.
Oft, when the world imagine women stray,
The sylphs through mystic mazes guide their way,
Through all the giddy circle they pursue,
And old impertinence expel by new.
What tender maid but must a victim fall
To one man's treat, but for another's ball?
When Florio speaks, what virgin could withstand,
If gentle Damon did not squeeze her hand?
With varying vanities, from every part,
They shift the moving toyshop of their heart;
Where wigs with wigs, with sword-knots sword-knots strive,
Beaux banish beaux, and coaches coaches drive.
This erring mortals levity may call;
Oh blind to truth! the sylphs contrive it all.
Of these am I, who thy protection claim,
A watchful sprite, and Ariel is my name.
Late, as I ranged the crystal wilds of air,
In the clear mirror of thy ruling star
I saw, alas! some dread event impend,
Ere to the main this morning sun descend,
But heaven reveals not what, or how, or where:
Warned by the sylph, oh pious maid, beware!
This to disclose is all thy guardian can:
Beware of all, but most beware of Man!'
He said; when Shock, who thought she slept too long,
Leaped up, and waked his mistress with his tongue.
'twas then, Belinda, if report say true,
Thy eyes first opened on a billet-doux;
Wounds, charms, and ardors were no sooner read,
But all the vision vanished from thy head.
And now, unveiled, the Toilet stands displayed,
Each silver vase in mystic order laid.
First, robed in white, the nymph intent adores,
With head uncovered, the cosmetic powers.
A heavenly image in the glass appears,
To that she bends, to that her eyes she rears;

Th' inferior priestess, at her altar's side,
Trembling, begins the sacred rites of pride.
Unnumbered treasures ope at once, and here
The various offerings of the world appear;
From each she nicely culls with curious toil,
And decks the Goddess with the glittering spoil.
This casket India's glowing gems unlocks,
And all Arabia breathes from yonder box.
The tortoise here and elephant unite,
Transformed to combs, the speckled, and the white.
Here files of pins extend their shining rows,
Puffs, powders, patches, bibles, billet-doux.
Now awful beauty puts on all its arms;
The fair each moment rises in her charms,
Repairs her smiles, awakens every grace,
And calls forth all the wonders of her face;
Sees by degrees a purer blush arise,
And keener lightnings quicken in her eyes.
The busy sylphs surround their darling care,
These set the head, and those divide the hair,
Some fold the sleeve, whilst others plait the gown;
And Betty's praised for labours not her own.

CANTO II

Not with more glories, in th' ethereal plain,
The sun first rises o'er the purpled main,
Than, issuing forth, the rival of his beams
Launched on the bosom of the silver Thames.
Fair nymphs, and well-dressed youths around her shone.
But every eye was fixed on her alone.
On her white breast a sparkling cross she wore,
Which Jews might kiss, and infidels adore.
Her lively looks a sprightly mind disclose,
Quick as her eyes, and as unfixed as those:
Favours to none, to all she smiles extends;
Oft she rejects, but never once offends.
Bright as the sun, her eyes the gazers strike,
And, like the sun, they shine on all alike.
Yet graceful ease, and sweetness void of pride
Might hide her faults, if belles had faults to hide:
If to her share some female errors fall,
Look on her face, and you'll forget 'em all.
    This nymph, to the destruction of mankind,
Nourished two locks, which graceful hung behind
In equal curls, and well conspired to deck
With shining ringlets her smooth ivory neck.
Love in these labyrinths his slaves detains,

And mighty hearts are held in slender chains.
With hairy springes we the birds betray,
Slight lines of hair surprise the finny prey,
Fair tresses man's imperial race ensnare,
And beauty draws us with a single hair.

    Th' adventurous Baron the bright locks admired;
He saw, he wished, and to the prize aspired.
Resolved to win, he meditates the way,
By force to ravish, or by fraud betray;
For when success a lover's toil attends,
Few ask, if fraud or force attained his ends.

    For this, ere Phoebus rose, he had implored
Propitious heaven, and every power adored,
But chiefly love—to love an altar built,
Of twelve vast French romances, neatly gilt.
There lay three garters, half a pair of gloves;
And all the trophies of his former loves;
With tender billet-doux he lights the pyre,
And breathes three amorous sighs to raise the fire.
Then prostrate falls, and begs with ardent eyes
Soon to obtain, and long possess the prize:
The powers gave ear, and granted half his prayer,
The rest, the winds dispersed in empty air.

    But now secure the painted vessel glides,
The sunbeams trembling on the floating tides;
While melting music steals upon the sky,
And softened sounds along the waters die;
Smooth flow the waves, the zephyrs gently play,
Belinda smiled, and all the world was gay.
All but the sylph— with careful thoughts oppressed,
Th' impending woe sat heavy on his breast.
He summons strait his denizens of air;
The lucid squadrons round the sails repair:
Soft o'er the shrouds aërial whispers breathe,
That seemed but zephyrs to the train beneath.
Some to the sun their insect-wings unfold,
Waft on the breeze, or sink in clouds of gold;
Transparent forms, too fine for mortal sight,
Their fluid bodies half dissolved in light,
Loose to the wind their airy garments flew,
Thin glittering textures of the filmy dew,
Dipped in the richest tincture of the skies,
Where light disports in ever-mingling dyes,
While every beam new transient colours flings,
Colours that change whene'er they wave their wings.
Amid the circle, on the gilded mast,
Superior by the head, was Ariel placed;
His purple pinions opening to the sun,

He raised his azure wand, and thus begun:
   'Ye sylphs and sylphids, to your chief give ear,
Fays, fairies, genii, elves, and daemons, hear!
Ye know the spheres and various talks assigned
By laws eternal to th' aërial kind.
Some in the fields of purest ether play,
And bask and whiten in the blaze of day.
Some guide the course of wandering orbs on high,
Or roll the planets through the boundless sky.
Some less refined, beneath the moon's pale light
Pursue the stars that shoot athwart the night,
Or suck the mists in grosser air below,
Or dip their pinions in the painted bow,
Or brew fierce tempests on the wintry main,
Or o'er the glebe distil the kindly rain.
Others on earth o'er human race preside,
Watch all their ways, and all their actions guide:
Of these the chief the care of Nations own,
And guard with arms divine the British throne.
   Our humbler province is to tend the fair,
Not a less pleasing, though less glorious care;
To save the powder from too rude a gale,
Nor let th' imprisoned-essences exhale;
To draw fresh colours from the vernal flowers;
To steal from rainbows e'er they drop in showers
A brighter wash; to curl their waving hairs,
Assist their blushes, and inspire their airs;
Nay oft, in dreams, invention we bestow,
To change a flounce, or add a furbelow.
   This day, black omens threat the brightest fair,
That e'er deserved a watchful spirit's care;
Some dire disaster, or by force, or slight;
But what, or where, the fates have wrapped in night.
Whether the nymph shall break Diana's law,
Or some frail china jar receive a flaw;
Or stain her honour or her new brocade;
Forget her prayers, or miss a masquerade;
Or lose her heart, or necklace, at a ball;
Or whether Heaven has doomed that Shock must fall.
Haste, then, ye spirits! to your charge repair:
The fluttering fan be Zephyretta's care;
The drops to thee, Brillante, we consign;
And, Momentilla, let the watch be thine;
Do thou, Crispissa, tend her favourite lock;
Ariel himself shall be the guard of Shock.
   To fifty chosen sylphs, of special note,
We trust th' important charge, the petticoat:
Oft have we known that seven-fold fence to fail,

Though stiff with hoops, and armed with ribs of whale;
Form a strong line about the silver bound,
And guard the wide circumference around.
   Whatever spirit, careless of his charge,
His post neglects, or leaves the fair at large,
Shall feel sharp vengeance soon o'ertake his sins,
Be stopped in vials, or transfixed with pins;
Or plunged in lakes of bitter washes lie,
Or wedged whole ages in a bodkin's eye:
Gums and pomatums shall his flight restrain,
While clogged he beats his silken wings in vain;
Or alum styptics with contracting power
Shrink his thin essence like a rivelled flower:
Or, as Ixion fixed, the wretch shall feel
The giddy motion of the whirling mill,
In fumes of burning chocolate shall glow,
And tremble at the sea that froths below!'
   He spoke; the spirits from the sails descend;
Some, orb in orb, around the nymph extend,
Some thread the mazy ringlets of her hair,
Some hang upon the pendants of her ear;
With beating hearts the dire event they wait,
Anxious, and trembling for the birth of fate.

CANTO III

Close by those meads, for ever crowned with flowers,
Where Thames with pride surveys his rising towers,
There stands a structure of majestic frame,
Which from the neighbouring Hampton takes its name.
Here Britain's statesmen oft the fall foredoom
Of foreign tyrants and of nymphs at home;
Here thou, great ANNA! whom three realms obey,
Dost sometimes counsel take— and sometimes tea.
   Hither the heroes and the nymphs resort,
To taste awhile the pleasures of a court;
In various talk th' instructive hours they passed,
Who gave the ball, or paid the visit last:
One speaks the glory of the British Queen,
And one describes a charming Indian screen;
A third interprets motions, looks, and eyes;
At every word a reputation dies.
Snuff, or the fan, supply each pause of chat,
With singing, laughing, ogling, and all that.
   Meanwhile, declining from the noon of day,
The sun obliquely shoots his burning ray;
The hungry judges soon the sentence sign,
And wretches hang that jurymen may dine;

The merchant from th'Exchange returns in peace,
And the long labours of the toilet cease.
Belinda now, whom thirst of fame invites,
Burns to encounter two adventurous knights,
At ombre singly to decide their doom;
And swells her breast with conquests yet to come.
Straight the three bands prepare in arms to join,
Each band the number of the sacred nine.
Soon as she spreads her hand, th' aërial guard
Descend, and sit on each important card:
First Ariel perched upon a matadore,
Then each, according to the rank they bore;
For sylphs, yet mindful of their ancient race,
Are, as when women, wondrous fond of place.
    Behold, four Kings in majesty revered,
With hoary whiskers and a forky beard;
And four fair queens whose hands sustain a flower,
Th' expressive emblem of their softer power;
Four knaves in garbs succinct, a trusty band,
Caps on their heads, and halberts in their hand;
And particoloured troops, a shining train,
Draw forth to combat on the velvet plain.
    The skilful nymph reviews her force with care:
'Let Spades be trumps!' she said, and trumps they were.
    Now move to war her sable matadores,
In show like leaders of the swarthy Moors.
Spadillio first, unconquerable lord!
Led off two captive trumps, and swept the board.
As many more Manillio forced to yield,
And marched a victor from the verdant field.
Him Basto followed, but his fate more hard
Gained but one trump and one plebeian card.
With his broad sabre next, a chief in years,
The hoary majesty of spades appears,
Puts forth one manly leg, to sight revealed,
The rest, his many-coloured robe concealed.
The rebel knave, who dares his prince engage,
Proves the just victim of his royal rage.
Even mighty Pam, that kings and queens o'erthrew
And mowed down armies in the fights of lu,
Sad chance of war! now destitute of aid,
Falls undistinguished by the victor spade!
    Thus far both armies to Belinda yield;
Now to the Baron fate inclines the field.
His warlike Amazon her host invades,
Th' imperial consort of the crown of spades.
The club's black tyrant first her victim died,
Spite of his haughty mien, and barbarous pride:

What boots the regal circle on his head,
His giant limbs, in state unwieldy spread;
That long behind he trails his pompous robe,
And, of all monarchs, only grasps the globe?
   The Baron now his diamonds pours apace;
Th' embroidered king who shows but half his face,
And his refulgent queen, with powers combined
Of broken troops an easy conquest find.
Clubs, diamonds, hearts, in wild disorder seen,
With throngs promiscuous strow the level green.
Thus when dispersed a routed army runs,
Of Asia's troops, and Afric's sable sons,
With like confusion different nations fly,
Of various habit, and of various dye,
The pierced battalions disunited fall,
In heaps on heaps; one fate o'erwhelms them all.
   The knave of diamonds tries his wily arts,
And wins (oh shameful chance!) the queen of hearts.
At this, the blood the virgin's cheek forsook,
A livid paleness spreads o'er all her look;
She sees, and trembles at th' approaching ill,
Just in the jaws of ruin, and codille.
And now (as oft in some distempered state)
On one nice trick depends the general fate.
An ace of hearts steps forth: The king unseen
Lurked in her hand, and mourned his captive queen:
He springs to vengeance with an eager pace,
And falls like thunder on the prostrate ace.
The nymph exulting fills with shouts the sky;
The walls, the woods, and long canals reply.
   Oh thoughtless mortals! ever blind to fate,
Too soon dejected, and too soon elate.
Sudden, these honours shall be snatched away,
And cursed for ever this victorious day.
   For lo! the board with cups and spoons is crowned,
The berries crackle, and the mill turns round;
On shining altars of Japan they raise
The silver lamp; the fiery spirits blaze:
From silver spouts the grateful liquors glide,
While China's earth receives the smoking tide:
At once they gratify their scent and taste,
And frequent cups prolong the rich repast.
Straight hover round the fair her airy band;
Some, as she sipped, the fuming liquor fanned,
Some o'er her lap their careful plumes displayed,
Trembling, and conscious of the rich brocade.
Coffee (which makes the politician wise,
And see through all things with his half-shut eyes)

Sent up in vapours to the Baron's brain
New stratagems, the radiant Lock to gain.
Ah cease, rash youth! desist ere 'tis too late,
Fear the just Gods, and think of Scylla's fate!
Changed to a bird, and sent to flit in air,
She dearly pays for Nisus' injured hair!
   But when to mischief mortals bend their will,
How soon they find fit instruments of ill!
Just then, Clarissa drew with tempting grace
A two-edged weapon from her shining case:
So Ladies in romance assist their knight,
Present the spear, and arm him for the fight.
He takes the gift with reverence, and extends
The little engine on his fingers' ends;
This just behind Belinda's neck he spread,
As o'er the fragrant steams she bends her head.
Swift to the lock a thousand sprites repair,
A thousand wings, by turns, blow back the hair;
And thrice they twitched the diamond in her ear;
Thrice she looked back, and thrice the foe drew near.
Just in that instant, anxious Ariel sought
The close recesses of the virgin's thought;
As on the nosegay in her breast reclined,
He watched th' ideas rising in her mind,
Sudden he viewed, in spite of all her art,
An earthly lover lurking at her heart.
Amazed, confused, he found his power expired,
Resigned to fate, and with a sigh retired.
   The peer now spreads the glittering forfex wide,
T' enclose the lock; now joins it, to divide.
Even then, before the fatal engine closed,
A wretched sylph too fondly interposed;
Fate urged the shears, and cut the sylph in twain,
(But airy substance soon unites again)
The meeting points the sacred hair dissever
From the fair head, for ever, and for ever!
   Then flashed the living lightning from her eyes,
And screams of horror rend th' affrighted skies.
Not louder shrieks to pitying heaven are cast,
When husbands, or when lapdogs breathe their last,
Or when rich china vessels fallen from high,
In glittering dust and painted fragments lie!
   'Let wreaths of triumph now my temples twine,'
The victor cried, 'the glorious prize is mine!
While fish in streams, or birds delight in air,
Or in a coach and six the British Fair,
As long as *Atalantis* shall be read,
Or the small pillow grace a Lady's bed,

While visits shall be paid on solemn days,
When numerous wax-lights in bright order blaze,
While nymphs take treats, or assignations give,
So long my honour, name, and praise shall live!
What time would spare, from steel receives its date,
And monuments, like men, submit to fate!
Steel could the labour of the Gods destroy,
And strike to dust th' imperial towers of Troy;
Steel could the works of mortal pride confound,
And hew triumphal arches to the ground.
What wonder then, fair nymph! thy hairs should feel
The conquering force of unresisted steel?

CANTO IV

But anxious cares the pensive nymph oppressed,
And secret passions laboured in her breast.
Not youthful kings in battle seized alive,
Not scornful virgins who their charms survive,
Not ardent lovers robbed of all their bliss,
Not ancient ladies when refused a kiss,
Not tyrants fierce that unrepenting die,
Not Cynthia when her manteau's pinned awry,
E'er felt such rage, resentment, and despair,
As thou, sad Virgin! for thy ravished hair.
   For, that sad moment, when the sylphs withdrew
And Ariel weeping from Belinda flew,
Umbriel, a dusky, melancholy sprite,
As ever sullied the fair face of light,
Down to the central earth, his proper scene,
Repaired to search the gloomy Cave of Spleen.
   Swift on his sooty pinions flits the Gnome,
And in a vapour reached the dismal dome.
No cheerful breeze this sullen region knows,
The dreaded East is all the wind that blows.
Here in a grotto, sheltered close from air,
And screened in shades from day's detested glare,
She sighs for ever on her pensive bed,
Pain at her side, and megrim at her head.
   Two handmaids wait the throne: alike in place,
But differing far in figure and in face.
Here stood Ill-nature like an ancient maid,
Her wrinkled form in black and white arrayed;
With store of prayers, for mornings, nights, and noons,
Her hand is filled; her bosom with lampoons.
   There Affectation, with a sickly mien,
Shows in her cheek the roses of eighteen,
Practised to lisp, and hang the head aside.

Faints into airs, and languishes with pride,
On the rich quilt sinks with becoming woe,
Wrapped in a gown, for sickness, and for show.
The fair ones feel such maladies as these,
When each new night-dress gives a new disease.
    A constant vapour o'er the palace flies;
Strange phantoms rising as the mists arise;
Dreadful, as hermit's dreams in haunted shades,
Or bright, as visions of expiring maids.
Now glaring fiends, and snakes on rolling spires,
Pale spectres, gaping tombs, and purple fires:
Now lakes of liquid gold, Elysian scenes,
And crystal domes, and angels in machines.
    Unnumbered throngs on every side are seen,
Of bodies changed to various forms by spleen.
Here living teapots stand, one arm held out,
One bent; the handle this, and that the spout:
A Pipkin there, like Homer's tripod walks;
Here sighs a jar, and there a goose-pie talks;
Men prove with child, as powerful fancy works,
And maids turned bottles, call aloud for corks.
    Safe passed the gnome through this fantastic band,
A branch of healing spleenwort in his hand.
Then thus addressed the power: 'Hail, wayward Queen!
Who rule the sex to fifty from fifteen;
Parent of vapours and of female wit,
Who give th' hysteric, or poetic fit,
On various tempers act by various ways,
Make some take physic, others scribble plays;
Who cause the proud their visits to delay,
And send the godly in a pet to pray.
A nymph there is, that all thy power disdains,
And thousands more in equal mirth maintains.
But oh! if e'er thy Gnome could spoil a grace,
Or raise a pimple on a beauteous face,
Like citron-waters matrons cheeks inflame,
Or change complexions at a losing game;
If e'er with airy horns I planted heads,
Or rumpled petticoats, or tumbled beds,
Or caused suspicion when no soul was rude,
Or discomposed the head-dress of a prude,
Or e'er to costive lap-dog gave disease,
Which not the tears of brightest eyes could ease:
Hear me, and touch Belinda with chagrin,
That single act gives half the world the spleen.'
    The Goddess with a discontented air
Seems to reject him, though she grants his prayer.
A wondrous bag with both her hands she binds,

Like that where once Ulysses held the winds;
There she collects the force of female lungs,
Sighs, sobs, and passions, and the war of tongues.
A vial next she fills with fainting fears,
Soft sorrows, melting griefs, and flowing tears.
The gnome rejoicing bears her gifts away,
Spreads his black wings, and slowly mounts to day.
  Sunk in Thalestris' arms the nymph he found,
Her eyes dejected and her hair unbound.
Full o'er their heads the swelling bag he rent,
And all the Furies issued at the vent.
Belinda burns with more than mortal ire,
And fierce Thalestris fans the rising fire.
'O wretched maid!' she spread her hands, and cried,
(While Hampton's echoes, 'wretched maid!' replied)
'Was it for this you took such constant care
The bodkin, comb, and essence to prepare?
For this your locks in paper durance bound,
For this with torturing irons wreathed around?
For this with fillets strained your tender head,
And bravely bore the double loads of lead?
Gods! shall the ravisher display your hair,
While the fops envy, and the ladies stare!
Honour forbid! at whose unrivalled shrine
Ease, pleasure, virtue, all, our sex resign.
Methinks already I your tears survey,
Already hear the horrid things they say,
Already see you a degraded toast,
And all your honour in a whisper lost!
How shall I, then, your helpless fame defend?
'Twill then be infamy to seem your friend!
And shall this prize, th' inestimable prize,
Exposed through crystal to the gazing eyes,
And heightened by the diamond's circling rays,
On that rapacious hand for ever blaze?
Sooner shall grass in Hyde-park Circus grow,
And wits take lodgings in the sound of Bow;
Sooner let earth, air, sea, to chaos fall,
Men, monkeys, lap-dogs, parrots, perish all!'
  She said; then raging to Sir Plume repairs,
And bids her beau demand the precious hairs:
(Sir Plume of amber snuff-box justly vain,
And the nice conduct of a clouded cane)
With earnest eyes, and round unthinking face,
He first the snuff-box opened, then the case,
And thus broke out—'My Lord, why, what the devil?
Z—ds! damn the lock! 'fore Gad, you must be civil!
Plague on't! 'tis past a jest— nay prithee, pox!

Give her the hair'— he spoke, and rapped his box.
'It grieves me much,' replied the peer again,
'Who speaks so well should ever speak in vain.
But by this lock, this sacred lock I swear,
(Which never more shall join its parted hair;
Which never more its honours shall renew,
Clipped from the lovely head where late it grew)
That while my nostrils draw the vital air,
This hand, which won it, shall for ever wear.'
He spoke, and speaking, in proud triumph spread
The long-contended honours of her head.
    But Umbriel, hateful gnome! forbears not so;
He breaks the vial whence the sorrows flow.
Then see! the nymph in beauteous grief appears,
Her eyes half-languishing, half-drowned in tears;
On her heaved bosom hung her drooping head,
Which, with a sigh, she raised; and thus she said:
    'For ever cursed be this detested day,
Which snatched my best, my favourite curl away!
Happy! ah ten times happy had I been,
If Hampton-Court these eyes had never seen!
Yet am not I the first mistaken maid,
By love of courts to numerous ills betrayed.
Oh had I rather un-admired remained
In some lone isle, or distant northern land;
Where the gilt chariot never marks the way,
Where none learn ombre, none e'er taste bohea!
There kept my charms concealed from mortal eye,
Like roses, that in deserts bloom and die.
What moved my mind with youthful lords to roam?
Oh had I stayed, and said my prayers at home!
'Twas this, the morning omens seemed to tell;
Thrice from my trembling hand the patch-box fell;
The tottering china shook without a wind,
Nay Poll sat mute, and Shock was most unkind!
A sylph too warned me of the threats of fate,
In mystic visions, now believed too late!
See the poor remnants of these slighted hairs!
My hands shall rend what even thy rapine spares:
These in two sable ringlets taught to break
Once gave new beauties to the snowy neck;
The sister-lock now sits uncouth, alone,
And in its fellow's fate foresees its own;
Uncurled it hangs, the fatal shears demands,
And tempts once more thy sacrilegious hands.
Oh hadst thou, cruel! been content to seize
Hairs less in sight, or any hairs but these!'

CANTO V

She said: the pitying audience melt in tears.
But Fate and Jove had stopped the Baron's ears.
In vain Thalestris with reproach assails,
For who can move when fair Belinda fails?
Not half so fixed the Trojan could remain,
While Anna begged and Dido ragged in vain.
Then grave Clarissa graceful waved her fan;
Silence ensued, and thus the nymph began:
    'Say why are beauties praised and honoured most,
The wise man's passion, and the vain man's toast?
Why decked with all that land and sea afford,
Why Angels called, and Angel-like adored?
Why round our coaches crowd the white-gloved beaux,
Why bows the side-box from its inmost rows?
How vain are all these glories, all our pains,
Unless good sense preserve what beauty gains:
That men may say, when we the front-box grace,
Behold the first in virtue as in face!
Oh! if to dance all night, and dress all day,
Charmed the small-pox, or chased old age away;
Who would not scorn what housewife's cares produce,
Or who would learn one earthly thing of use?
To patch, nay ogle, might become a saint,
Nor could it sure be such a sin to paint.
But since, alas! frail beauty must decay,
Curled or uncurled, since locks will turn to grey;
Since painted, or not painted, all shall fade,
And she who scorns a man, must die a maid;
What then remains but well our power to use,
And keep good-humour still whate'er we lose?
And trust me, dear! good-humour can prevail,
When airs, and flights, and screams, and scolding fail.
Beauties in vain their pretty eyes may roll;
Charms strike the sight, but merit wins the soul.'
    So spoke the dame, but no applause ensued;
Belinda frowned, Thalestris called her prude.
'To arms, to arms!' the fierce virago cries,
And swift as lightning to the combat flies.
All side in parties, and begin th' attack;
Fans clap, silks rustle, and tough whalebones crack;
Heroes' and heroines' shouts confusedly rise,
And bass and treble voices strike the skies.
No common weapons in their hands are found,
Like gods they fight, nor dread a mortal wound.
    So when bold Homer makes the Gods engage,

And heavenly breasts with human passions rage;
'Gainst Pallas, Mars; Latona, Hermes arms;
And all Olympus rings with loud alarms:
Jove's thunder roars, heaven trembles all around,
Blue Neptune storms, the bellowing deeps resound:
Earth shakes her nodding towers, the ground gives way,
And the pale ghosts start at the flash of day!
    Triumphant Umbriel on a sconce's height
Clapped his glad wings, and sate to view the fight:
Propped on the bodkin spears, the sprites survey
The growing combat, or assist the fray.
    While through the press enraged Thalestris flies,
And scatters death around from both her eyes,
A beau and witling perished in the throng,
One died in metaphor, and one in song.
'O cruel nymph! a living death I bear,'
Cried Dapperwit, and sunk beside his chair.
A mournful glance Sir Fopling upwards cast,
'Those eyes are made so killing'—was his last.
Thus on Maeander's flowery margin lies
Th' expiring Swan, and as he sings he dies.
    When bold Sir Plume had drawn Clarissa down,
Cloe stepped in, and killed him with a frown;
She smiled to see the doughty hero slain,
But, at her smile, the Beau revived again.
    Now Jove suspends his golden scales in air,
Weighs the men's wits against the lady's hair;
The doubtful beam long nods from side to side;
At length the wits mount up, the hairs subside.
    See, fierce Belinda on the Baron flies,
With more than usual lightning in her eyes:
Nor feared the chief th' unequal fight to try,
Who sought no more than on his foe to die.
But this bold lord with manly strength endued,
She with one finger and a thumb subdued:
Just where the breath of life his nostrils drew,
A charge of snuff the wily virgin threw;
The gnomes direct, to every atom just,
The pungent grains of titillating dust.
Sudden, with starting tears each eye o'erflows,
And the high dome re-echoes to his nose.
    'Now meet thy fate,' incensed Belinda cried,
And drew a deadly bodkin from her side.
(The same, his ancient personage to deck,
Her great great grandsire wore about his neck
In three seal-rings; which after, melted down,
Formed a vast buckle for his widow's gown:
Her infant grandame's whistle next it grew,

The bells she jingled, and the whistle blew;
Then in a bodkin graced her mother's hairs,
Which long she wore, and now Belinda wears.)
   'Boast not my fall,' (he cried) 'insulting foe!
Thou by some other shalt be laid as low.
Nor think, to die dejects my lofty mind:
All that I dread is leaving you behind!
Rather than so, ah let me still survive,
And burn in Cupid's flames,—but burn alive.'
   'Restore the Lock!' she cries; and all around
'Restore the Lock!' the vaulted roofs rebound.
Not fierce Othello in so loud a strain
Roared for the handkerchief that caused his pain.
But see how oft ambitious aims are crossed,
And chiefs contend 'till all the prize is lost!
The lock, obtained with guilt, and kept with pain,
In every place is sought, but sought in vain:
With such a prize no mortal must be blessed,
So heaven decrees! with heaven who can contest?
   Some thought it mounted to the lunar sphere,
Since all things lost on earth are treasured there.
There heroes' wits are kept in ponderous vases,
And beaux' in snuff-boxes and tweezer-cases.
There broken vows, and death-bed alms are found,
And lovers' hearts with ends of ribband bound,
The courtier's promises, and sick man's prayers,
The smiles of harlots, and the tears of heirs,
Cages for gnats, and chains to yoke a flea,
Dried butterflies, and tomes of casuistry.
   But trust the Muse—she saw it upward rise,
Though marked by none but quick, poetic eyes:
(So Rome's great founder to the heavens withdrew,
To Proculus alone confessed in view)
A sudden star, it shot through liquid air,
And drew behind a radiant trail of hair.
Not Berenice's locks first rose so bright,
The heavens bespangling with dishevelled light.
The sylphs behold it kindling as it flies,
And pleased pursue its progress through the skies.
   This the beau monde shall from the Mall survey,
And hail with music its propitious ray.
This the blessed Lover shall for Venus take,
And send up vows from Rosamonda's lake.
This Partridge soon shall view in cloudless skies,
When next he looks Through Galileo's eyes;
And hence th' egregious wizard shall foredoom
The fate of Louis, and the fall of Rome.
   Then cease, bright nymph! to mourn thy ravished hair,

Which adds new glory to the shining sphere!
Not all the tresses that fair head can boast,
Shall draw such envy as the lock you lost.
For, after all the murders of your eye,
When, after millions slain, yourself shall die;
When those fair suns shall set, as set they must,
And all those tresses shall be laid in dust;
This lock, the Muse shall consecrate to fame,
And 'midst the stars inscribe Belinda's name.

TO BELINDA ON THE RAPE OF THE LOCK

Pleased in these lines, Belinda, you may view
How things are prized, which once belonged to you:
If on some meaner head this lock had grown,
The nymph despised, the rape had been unknown.
But what concerns the valiant and the fair,
The Muse asserts as her peculiar care.
Thus Helens rape and Menelaus' wrong
Became the subject of great Homer's song;
And, lost in ancient times, the golden fleece
Was raised to fame by all the wits of Greece.
    Had fate decreed, propitious to your prayers,
To give their utmost date to all your hairs;
This lock, of which late ages now shall tell,
Had dropped like fruit, neglected, when it fell.
    Nature to your undoing arms mankind
With strength of body, artifice of mind;
But gives your feeble sex, made up of fears,
No guard but virtue, no redress but tears.
Yet custom (seldom to your favour gained)
Absolves the virgin when by force constrained.
Thus Lucrece lives unblemished in her fame,
A bright example of young Tarquin's shame.
Such praise is yours—and such shall you possess,
Your virtue equal, though your loss be less.
Then smile Belinda at reproachful tongues,
Still warm our hearts, and still inspire our songs.
But would your charms to distant times extend,
Let Jervas paint them, and let Pope commend.
Who censure most, more precious hairs would lose,
To have the *Rape* recorded by his Muse.

POPE TO MARTHA BLOUNT.

November 1714

Most Divine!—'Tis some proof of my sincerity towards you that I write when I am prepared by drinking to speak truth, and sure a letter after twelve at night must abound with that noble ingredient. That heart must have abundance of flames which is at once warmed by wine and you; wine awakens and refreshes the lurking passions of the mind, as does the colours that are sunk in a picture, and brings them out in all their natural glowings. My good qualities have been so frozen and locked up in a dull constitution at all my former sober hours, that it is very astonishing to me, now I am drunk, to find so much virtue in me.

In these overflowings of my heart I pay you my thanks for those two obliging letters you favoured me with of the 18th and 24th instant. That which begins with 'Dear Creature', and 'my charming Mr. Pope' was a delight to me beyond all expression. You have at last entirely gained the conquest over your fair sister; 'tis true you are not handsome, for you are a woman, and think you are not; but this good humour and tenderness for me has a charm that cannot be resisted. That face must needs be irresistible, which was adorned with smiles even when it could not see the Coronation.

I must own I have long been shocked at your sister on several accounts, but above all things at her prudery: I am resolved to break with her for ever; and therefore tell her I shall take the first opportunity of sending back all her letters.

I do suppose you will not show this epistle out of vanity, as I doubt not your sister does all I writ to her. Indeed to correspond with Mr. Pope, may make anyone proud who lives under a dejection of heart in the country. Every one values Mr. Pope, but every one for a different reason. One for his adherence to the Catholic faith, another for his neglect of Popish superstition, one for his grave behaviour, another for his whimsicalness. Mr. Tidcombe for his pretty atheistical jests, Mr. Caryll for his moral and Christian sentences, Mrs. Teresa, for his reflections on Mrs. Patty, and Mrs. Patty, for his reflections on Mrs. Teresa.

My acquaintance runs so much in an anti-Catholic channel, that it was but t'other day I heard of Mrs. Fermor's being actually, directly, and consummatively, married. I wonder how the guilty couple and their accessories at Whiteknights look, stare, or simper, since that grand secret came out which they so well concealed before. They concealed it was well as a barber does his utensils when he goes to trim upon a Sunday and his towels hand out all the way: or as well as a friar concealed a little wench, whom he was carrying under his habit to Mr. Colingwood's convent; 'Pray, Father', said one in the street to him, 'what's that under your arm?' 'A saddle for one of the brothers to ride with', quoth the friar. 'Then Father', criend he, 'take care and shorten the stirrups'—For the girl's legs hung out—

You know your doctor is gone the way of all his patients, and was hard put to it how to dispose of an estate miserably unwieldy, and splendidly unuseful to him. Sir Sam. Garth says, that for Radcliffe to leave a library was as if an eunuch should found a seraglio. Dr. Shadwell lately told a lady he wondered she could be alive after him; she made answer she wondered at it too, both because Dr. Radcliffe was dead, and because Dr. Shadwell was alive.

Poor Parnell is now on the briny ocean which he increases with his briny tears for the loss of you etc. Pray for him, if you please, but not for me. Don't so much as hope I may go to Heaven: 'tis a place I am not very fond of, I hear no great good of it. All the descriptions I ever heard of it amount to no more than just this: it is eternal singing, and piping, and sitting in sunshine. Much good may it do the saints; and those who intend to be saints. For my part I am better than a saint, for I am, Madam, Your most faithful admirer, friend, servant, anything.

I send you Gay's poem on the Princess. She is very fat. God keep her husband.

THE TEMPLE OF FAME

Advertisement

The hint of the following piece was taken from Chaucer's *House of Fame*. The design is in a manner entirely altered, the descriptions and most of the particular thoughts my own: yet I could not suffer it to be printed without this acknowledgment. The reader who would compare this with Chaucer, may begin with his third book of *Fame*, there being nothing in the two first books that answers to their title: wherever any hint is taken from him, the passage itself is set down in the marginal notes.

> In that soft season, when descending showers
> Call forth the greens, and wake the rising flowers;
> When opening buds salute the welcome day,
> And earth relenting feels the genial ray;
> As balmy sleep had charmed my cares to rest,
> And love itself was banished from my breast,
> (What time the morn mysterious visions brings,
> While purer slumbers spread their golden wings)
> A train of phantoms in wild order rose,
> And, joined, this intellectual scene compose.
>   I stood, methought, betwixt earth, seas, and skies;
> The whole creation open to my eyes;
> In air self-balanced hung the globe below,
> Where mountains rise and circling oceans flow;
> Here naked rocks, and empty wastes were seen;
> There towery cities, and the forests green:
> Here sailing ships delight the wandering eyes:
> There trees, and intermingled temples rise;
> Now a clear sun the shining scene displays,
> The transient landscape now in clouds decays.
>   O'er the wide prospect as I gazed around,
> Sudden I heard a wild promiscuous sound,
> Like broken thunders that at distance roar,
> Or billows murmuring on the hollow shore:
> Then gazing up, a glorious pile beheld,
> Whose towering summit ambient clouds concealed.
> High on a rock of ice the structure lay,
> Steep its ascent, and slippery was the way;

The wondrous rock like Parian marble shone,
And seemed, to distant sight, of solid stone.
Inscriptions here of various names I viewed,
The greater part by hostile time subdued;
Yet wide was spread their fame in ages past,
And poets once had promised they should last.
Some fresh engraved appeared of wits renowned;
I looked again, nor could their trace be found.
Critics I saw, that other names deface,
And fix their own, with labour, in their place:
Their own, like others, soon their place resigned,
Or disappeared and left the first behind.
Nor was the work impaired by storms alone,
But felt th' approaches of too warm a sun;
For Fame, impatient of extremes, decays
Not more by envy than excess of praise.
Yet part no injuries of heaven could feel,
Like crystal faithful to the graving steel:
The rock's high summit, in the temple's shade,
Nor heat could melt, nor beating storm invade.
There names inscribed unnumbered ages past
From time's first birth, with time itself shall last;
These ever new, nor subject to decays,
Spread, and grow brighter with the length of days.

   So Zembla's rocks (the beauteous work of frost)
Rise white in air, and glitter o'er the coast;
Pale suns, unfelt, at distance roll away,
And on th' impassive ice the lightnings play;
Eternal snows the growing mass supply,
Till the bright mountains prop th' incumbent sky:
As Atlas fixed, each hoary pile appears,
The gathered winter of a thousand years.

   On this foundation Fame's high temple stands;
Stupendous pile! not reared by mortal hands.
Whate'er proud Rome or artful Greece beheld,
Or elder Babylon, its frame excelled.
Four faces had the dome, and every face
Of various structure, but of equal grace:
Four brazen gates, on columns lifted high,
Salute the different quarters of the sky.
Here fabled chiefs in darker ages born,
Or worthies old, whom arms or arts adorn,
Who cities raised, or tamed a monstrous race;
The walls in venerable order grace:
Heroes in animated marble frown,
And legislators seem to think in stone.

   Westward, a sumptuous frontispiece appeared,
On Doric pillars of white marble reared,

Crowned with an architrave of antique mold,
And sculpture rising on the roughened gold.
In shaggy spoils here Theseus was beheld,
And Perseus dreadful with Minerva's shield:
There great Alcides , stooping with his toil,
Rests on his club, and holds th' Hesperian spoil.
Here Orpheus sings; trees moving to the sound
Start from their roots, and form a shade around:
Amphion there the loud creating lyre
Strikes, and beholds a sudden Thebes aspire!
Cythaeron's echoes answer to his call,
And half the mountain rolls into a wall:
There might you see the lengthening spires ascend,
The domes swell up, and widening arches bend,
The growing towers, like exhalations rise,
And the huge columns heave into the skies.
　　The eastern front was glorious to behold,
With diamond flaming, and barbaric gold.
There Ninus shone, who spread th'Assyrian fame,
And the great founder of the Persian name;
There in long robes the royal Magi stand,
Grave Zoroaster waves the circling wand;
The sage Chaldeans robed in white appeared,
And Brahmans, deep in desert woods revered.
These stopped the moon, and call' th' unbodied shades
To midnight banquets in the glimmering glades;
Made visionary fabrics round them rise,
And airy spectres skim before their eyes;
Of talismans and sigils knew the power,
And careful watched the planetary hour.
Superior, and alone, Confucius stood,
Who taught that useful science, to be good.
　　But on the south, a long majestic race
Of Egypt's priests the gilded niches grace,
Who measured earth, described the starry spheres,
And traced the long records of lunar years.
High on his car Sesostris struck my view,
Whom sceptered slaves in golden harness drew:
His hands a bow and pointed javelin hold;
His giant limbs are armed in scales of gold.
Between the statues obelisks were placed,
And the learned walls with hieroglyphics graced.
　　Of Gothic structure was the northern side,
O'erwrought with ornaments of barbarous pride.
There huge colosses rose, with trophies crowned,
And runic characters were graved around.
There sat Zamolxis with erected eyes,
And Odin here in mimic trances dies.

There on rude iron columns, smeared with blood,
The horrid forms of Scythian Heroes stood,
Druids and bards (their once loud harps unstrung)
And youths that died to be by poets sung.
These and a thousand more of doubtful fame,
To whom old fables gave a lasting name,
In ranks adorned the temple's outward face;
The wall in lustre and effect like glass,
Which o'er each object casting various dyes,
Enlarges some, and others multiplies:
Nor void of emblem was the mystic wall,
For thus romantic Fame increases all.
   The temple shakes, the sounding gates unfold,
Wide vaults appear, and roofs of fretted gold:
Raised on a thousand pillars, wreathed around
With laurel-foliage, and with eagles crowned:
Of bright, transparent beryl were the walls,
The friezes gold, and gold the capitals:
As heaven with stars, the roof with jewels glows,
And ever-living lamps depend in rows.
Full in the passage of each spacious gate,
The sage historians in white garments wait;
Graved o'er their seats the form of Time was found,
His scythe reversed, and both his pinions bound.
Within stood Heroes, who through loud alarms
In bloody fields pursued renown in arms.
High on a throne, with trophies charged, I viewed
The youth that all things but himself subdued;
His feet on sceptres and tiaras trod,
And his horned head belied the Libyan God,
There Caesar, graced with both Minervas, shone;
Caesar, the world's great master, and his own;
Unmoved, superior still in every state,
And scarce detested in his country's fate.
But chief were those, who not for empire fought,
But with their toils their people's safety bought:
High o'er the rest Epaminondas stood;
Timoleon, glorious in his brother's blood;
Bold Scipio, saviour of the Roman state;
Great in his triumphs, in retirement great;
And wise Aurelius, in whose well-taught mind
With boundless power unbounded virtue joined,
His own strict judge, and patron of mankind.
   Much-suffering heroes next their honours claim,
Those of less noisy, and less guilty fame,
Fair Virtue's silent train: supreme of these
Here ever shines the godlike Socrates:
He whom ungrateful Athens could expel,

At all times just, but when he signed the shell:
Here his abode the martyred Phocion claims,
With Agis, not the last of Spartan names:
Unconquered Cato shows the wound he tore,
And Brutus his ill genius meets no more.
    But in the centre of the hallowed choir,
Six pompous columns o'er the rest aspire;
Around the shrine itself of Fame they stand;
Hold the chief honours, and the fane command.
High on the first, the mighty Homer shone;
Eternal adamant composed his throne;
Father of verse! in holy fillets dressed,
His silver beard waved gently o'er his breast;
Though blind, a boldness in his looks appears;
In years he seemed, but not impaired by years.
The wars of Troy were round the pillar seen:
Here fierce Tydides wounds the Cyprian Queen;
Here Hector, glorious from Patroclus' fall,
Here, dragged in triumph round the Trojan wall.
Motion and life did every part inspire,
Bold was the work, and proved the master's fire:
A strong expression most he seemed t'affect,
And here and there disclosed a brave neglect.
    A golden column next in rank appeared,
On which a shrine of purest gold was reared;
Finished the whole, and laboured every part,
With patient touches of unwearied art:
The Mantuan there in sober triumph sate,
Composed his posture, and his look sedate;
On Homer still he fixed a reverend eye,
Great without pride, in modest majesty.
In living sculpture on the sides were spread
The Latian wars, and haughty Turnus dead;
Eliza stretched upon the funeral pyre,
Aeneas bending with his aged sire:
Troy flamed in burning gold, and o'er the throne
ARMS AND THE MAN in golden ciphers shone.
    Four swans sustain a car of silver bright,
With heads advanced, and pinions stretched for flight:
Here, like some furious prophet, Pindar rode,
And seemed to labour with th'inspiring god.
Across the harp a careless hand he flings,
And boldly sinks into the sounding strings.
The figured games of Greece the column grace,
Neptune and Jove survey the rapid race:
The youths hang o'er the chariots as they run;
The fiery steeds seem starting from the stone;
The champions in distorted postures threat;

And all appeared irregularly great.
   Here happy Horace tuned th' Ausonian lyre
To sweeter sounds, and tempered Pindar's fire:
Pleased with Alcaeus' manly rage t' infuse
The softer spirit of the Sapphic Muse.
The polished pillar different sculptures grace;
A work outlasting monumental brass.
Here smiling Loves and Bacchanals appear,
The Julian star, and great Augustus here.
The doves, that round the infant poet spread
Myrtles and bays, hung hovering o'er his head.
   Here, in a shrine that cast a dazzling light,
Sate fixed in thought the mighty Stagyrite;
His sacred head a radiant Zodiac crowned,
And various animals his sides surround;
His piercing eyes, erect, appear to view
Superior worlds, and look all Nature through.
   With equal rays immortal Tully shone,
The Roman rostra decked the consul's throne:
Gathering his flowing robe, he seemed to stand
In act to speak, and graceful stretched his hand.
Behind, Rome's Genius waits with civic crowns,
And the great father of his country owns.
   These massy columns in a circle rise,
O'er which a pompous dome invades the skies:
Scarce to the top I stretched my aching sight,
So large it spread, and Swelled to such a height.
Full in the midst proud Fame's imperial seat
With jewels blazed, magnificently great;
The vivid emeralds there revive the eye,
The flaming rubies show their sanguine dye,
Bright azure rays from lively sapphires stream,
And lucid amber casts a golden gleam.
With various-coloured light the pavement shone,
And all on fire appeared the glowing throne;
The dome's high arch reflects the mingled blaze,
And forms a rainbow of alternate rays.
When on the Goddess first I cast my sight,
Scarce seemed her stature of a cubit's height,
But Swelled to larger size, the more I gazed,
Till to the roof her towering front she raised.
With her, the temple every moment grew,
And ampler vistas opened to my view:
Upward the columns shoot, the roofs ascend,
And arches widen, and long aisles extend.
Such was her form as ancient bards have told;
Wings raise her arms, and wings her feet enfold;
A thousand busy tongues the Goddess bears,

A thousand open eyes, and thousand listening ears.
Beneath, in order ranged, the tuneful Nine
(Her virgin handmaids) still attend the shrine:
With eyes on Fame for ever fixed, they sing;
For Fame they raise the voice, and tune the string.
With time's first birth began the heavenly lays,
And last, eternal, through the length of days.
   Around these wonders as I cast a look,
The trumpet sounded, and the temple shook,
And all the nations summoned at the call,
From different quarters fill the crowded hall:
Of various tongues the mingled sounds were heard;
In various garbs promiscuous throngs appeared;
Thick as the bees, that with the spring renew
Their flowery toils, and sip the fragrant dew,
When the winged colonies first tempt the sky,
O'er dusky fields and shaded waters fly,
Or settling, seize the sweets the blossoms yield,
And a low murmur runs along the field.
Millions of suppliant crowds the shrine attend,
And all degrees before the Goddess bend;
The poor, the rich, the valiant, and the sage,
And boasting youth, and narrative old-age.
Their pleas were different, their request the same:
For good and bad alike are fond of Fame.
Some she disgraced and some with honours crowned;
Unlike successes equal merits found.
Thus her blind sister, fickle Fortune, reigns,
And, undiscerning, scatters crowns and chains.
   First at the shrine the learnéd world appear,
And to the Goddess thus prefer their prayer:
'Long have we sought t' instruct and please mankind,
With studies pale, with midnight-vigils blind;
But thanked by few, rewarded yet by none,
We here appeal to thy superior throne:
On wit and learning the just prize bestow,
For Fame is all we must expect below.'
   The Goddess heard, and bade the Muses raise
The golden trumpet of eternal praise:
From pole to pole the winds diffuse the sound,
That fills the circuit of the world around;
Not all at once, as thunder breaks the cloud;
The notes at first were rather sweet than loud:
By just degrees they every moment rise,
Fill the wide earth, and gain upon the skies.
At every breath were balmy odours shed,
Which still grew sweeter as they wider spread;
Less fragrant scents th' unfolding rose exhales,

Or spices breathing in Arabian gales.
   Next these the good and just, an awful train,
Thus on their knees address the sacred fane.
'Since living virtue is with envy cursed,
And the best men are treated like the worst,
Do thou, just Goddess, call our merits forth,
And give each deed th' exact intrinsic worth.'
'Not with bare justice shall your act be crowned'
Said Fame, 'but high above desert renowned:
Let fuller notes th' applauding world amaze,
And the loud clarion labour in your praise.'
   This band dismissed, behold another crowd
Preferred the same request, and lowly bowed;
The constant tenor of whose well-spent days
No less deserved a just return of praise.
But straight the direful trump of slander sounds;
Through the big dome the doubling thunder bounds;
Loud as the burst of cannon rends the skies,
The dire report Through every region flies:
In every ear incessant rumours rung,
And gathering scandals grew on every tongue.
From the black trumpet's rusty concave broke
Sulphureous flames, and clouds of rolling smoke:
The poisonous vapour blots the purple skies,
And withers all before it as it flies.
   A troop came next, who crowns and armour wore,
And proud defiance in their looks they bore:
'For thee' (they cried) 'amidst alarms and strife,
We sailed in tempests down the stream of life;
For thee whole nations filled with flames and blood,
And swam to empire through the purple flood.
Those ills we dared, thy inspiration own,
What virtue seemed, was done for thee alone.'
'Ambitious fools!' (the Queen replied, and frowned)
'Be all your acts in dark oblivion drowned;
There sleep forgot, with mighty tyrants gone,
Your statues mouldered, and your names unknown!'
A sudden cloud straight snatched them from my sight,
And each majestic phantom sunk in night.
   Then came the smallest tribe I yet had seen;
Plain was their dress, and modest was their mien:
'Great Idol of mankind! we neither claim
The praise of merit, nor aspire to fame!
But safe in deserts from th' applause of men,
Would die unheard of, as we lived unseen;
'Tis all we beg thee, to conceal from sight
Those acts of goodness, which themselves requite.
O let us still the secret joy partake,

To follow virtue even for virtue's sake.'
    'And live there men who slight immortal fame?
Who then with incense shall adore our name?
But, mortals! know, 'tis still our greatest pride
To blaze those virtues which the good would hide.
Rise! Muses, rise, add all your tuneful breath,
These must not sleep in darkness and in death.'
She said: in air the trembling music floats,
And on the winds triumphant swell the notes;
So soft, though high, so loud, and yet so clear,
Even listening angels leaned from Heaven to hear:
To farthest shores th' ambrosial spirit flies,
Sweet to the world, and grateful to the skies.
    Next these a youthful train their vows expressed,
With feathers crowned, with gay embroidery dressed:
'Hither' they cried 'direct your eyes, and see
The men of pleasure, dress, and gallantry;
Ours is the place at banquets, balls, and plays;
Sprightly our nights, polite are all our days;
Courts we frequent, where 'tis our pleasing care
To pay due visits, and address the fair:
In fact, 'tis true, no nymph we could persuade,
But still in fancy vanquished every maid;
Of unknown duchesses lewd tales we tell,
Yet, would the world believe us, all were well.
The joy let others have, and we the name,
And what we want in pleasure, grant in fame.'
    The Queen assents, the trumpet rends the skies,
And at each blast a lady's honour dies.
    Pleased with the strange success, vast numbers pressed
Around the shrine, and made the same request:
'What you' (she cried) 'unlearned in arts to please,
Slaves to yourselves, and even fatigued with ease,
Who lose a length of undeserving days,
Would you usurp the lover's dear-bought praise?
To just contempt, ye vain pretenders, fall,
The people's fable, and the scorn of all.'
Straight the black clarion sends a horrid sound,
Loud laughs burst out, and bitter scoffs fly round,
Whispers are heard, with taunts reviling loud,
And scornful hisses run through all the crowd.
    Last, those who boast of mighty mischiefs done,
Enslave their country, or usurp a throne;
Or who their glory's dire foundation laid
On sovereigns ruined, or on friends betrayed;
Calm, thinking villains, whom no faith could fix,
Of crooked counsels and dark politics;
Of these a gloomy tribe surround the throne,

And beg to make th' immortal treasons known.
The trumpet roars, long flaky flames expire,
With sparks that seemed to set the world on fire.
At the dread sound pale mortals stood aghast,
And startled nature trembled with the blast.
   This having heard and seen, some power unknown
Straight changed the scene, and snatched me from the throne.
Before my view appeared a structure fair,
Its site uncertain, if in earth or air;
With rapid motion turned the mansion round;
With ceaseless noise the ringing walls resound:
Not less in number were the spacious doors,
Than leaves on trees, or sands upon the shores;
Which still unfolded stand, by night, by day,
Previous to winds, and open every way.
As flames by nature to the skies ascend,
As weighty bodies to the centre tend,
As to the sea returning rivers roll,
And the touched needle trembles to the pole:
Hither, as to their proper place, arise
All various sounds from earth, and seas, and skies,
Or spoke aloud, or whispered in the ear;
Nor ever silence, rest, or peace is here.
As on the smooth expanse of crystal lakes
The sinking stone at first a circle makes;
The trembling surface by the motion stirred,
Spreads in a second circle, then a third;
Wide, and more wide, the floating rings advance,
Fill all the watery plain, and to the margin dance:
Thus every voice and sound, when first they break,
On neighbouring air a soft impression make;
Another ambient circle then they move;
That, in its turn, impels the next above;
Through undulating air the sounds are sent,
And spread o'er all the fluid element.
   There various news I heard of love and strife,
Of peace and war, health, sickness, death, and life,
Of loss and gain, of famine and of store,
Of storms at sea, and travels on the shore,
Of prodigies, and portents seen in air,
Of fires and plagues, and stars with blazing hair,
Of turns of fortune, changes in the state,
The fall of favourites, projects of the great,
Of old mismanagements, taxations new:
All neither wholly false, nor wholly true.
   Above, below, without, within, around,
Confused, unnumbered multitudes are found,
Who pass, repass, advance, and glide away,

Hosts raised by fear, and phantoms of a day:
Astrologers, that future fates foreshow,
Projectors, quacks, and lawyers not a few;
And priests, and party-zealots, numerous bands,
With home-born lies or tales from foreign lands;
Each talked aloud, or in some secret place,
And wild impatience stared in every face.
The flying rumours gathered as they rolled.
Scarce any tale was sooner heard than told;
And all who told it added something new,
And all who heard it made enlargements too,
In every ear it spread, on every tongue it grew.
Thus flying east and west, and north and south,
News travelled with increase from mouth to mouth.
So from a spark that, kindled first by chance,
With gathering force the quickening flames advance;
Till to the clouds their curling heads aspire,
And towers and temples sink in floods of fire.
    When thus ripe lies are to perfection sprung,
Full grown, and fit to grace a mortal tongue,
Through thousand vents, impatient forth they flow,
And rush in millions on the world below.
Fame sits aloft, and points them out their course,
Their date determines, and prescribes their force:
Some to remain, and some to perish soon;
Or wane and wax alternate like the moon.
Around, a thousand winged wonders fly,
Borne by the trumpet's blast, and scattered through the sky.
    There, at one passage, oft you might survey
A lie and truth contending for the way;
And long 'twas doubtful, both so closely pent,
Which first should issue Through the narrow vent:
At last agreed, together out they fly,
Inseparable now the truth and lie;
The strict companions are for ever joined,
And this or that unmixed, no mortal e'er shall find.
    While thus I stood, intent to see and hear,
One came, methought, and whispered in my ear:
'What could thus high thy rash ambition raise?
Art thou, fond youth, a candidate for praise?'
    "Tis true,' said I, 'not void of hopes I came,
For who so fond as youthful bards of Fame?
But few, alas! the casual blessing boast,
So hard to gain, so easy to be lost.
How vain that second life in others' breath,
Th' estate which wits inherit after death!
Ease, health, and life for this they must resign,
(Unsure the tenure, but how vast the fine!)

The great man's curse, without the gains, endure,
Be envied, wretched; and be flattered, poor;
All luckless wits their enemies professed,
And all successful, jealous friends at best.
Nor Fame I slight, nor for her favours call;
She comes unlooked for, if she comes at all.
But if the purchase costs so dear a price,
As soothing Folly, or exalting Vice:
Oh! if the Muse must flatter lawless sway,
And follow still where fortune leads the way;
Or if no basis bear my rising name,
But the fallen ruins of another's fame;
Then teach me, heaven! to scorn the guilty bays,
Drive from my breast that wretched lust of praise,
Unblemished let me live or die unknown;
Oh, grant an honest fame, or grant me none!'

A FAREWELL TO LONDON
IN THE YEAR 1715

Dear, damned, distracting town, farewell!
   Thy fools no more I'll tease:
This year in peace, ye critics, dwell,
   Ye harlots, sleep at ease!

Soft Bethel and rough Craggs, adieu!
   Earl Warwick, make your moan,
The lively Hinchinbrook and you
   May knock up whores alone.

To drink and droll be Rowe allowed
   Till the third watchman's toll;
Let Jervas gratis paint, and Frowde
   Save threepence and his soul.

Farewell Arbuthnot's raillery
   On every learned sot;
And Garth, the best good Christian he,
   Although he knows it not.

Lintot, farewell! thy bard must go;
   Farewell, unhappy Tonson!
Heaven gives thee for thy loss of Rowe,
   Lean Philips, and fat Johnson.

Why should I stay? Both parties rage;
  My vixen mistress squalls;
The wits in envious feuds engage:
  And Homer (damn him) calls.

The love of arts lies cold and dead
  In Halifax's urn;
And not one muse of all he fed,
  Has yet the grace to mourn.

My friends, by turns, my friends confound,
Betray, and are betrayed:
Poor Younger's sold for fifty pounds,
  And Bicknell is a jade.

Why make I friendships with the great,
  When I no favour seek?
Or follow girls seven hours in eight?—
  I need but once a week.

Still idle, with a busy air,
  Deep whimsies to contrive;
The gayest valetudinaire,
  Most thinking rake alive.

Solicitous for others' ends,
  Though fond of dear repose;
Careless or drowsy with my friends,
  And frolic with my foes.

Luxurious lobster-nights, farewell,
  For sober, studious days;
And Burlington's delicious meal,
  For salads, tarts, and pease.

Adieu to all but Gay alone,
  Whose soul sincere and free,
Loves all mankind but flatters none,
  And so may starve with me.

EPISTLE TO MR. JERVAS
WITH DRYDEN'S TRANSLATION OF FRESNOY'S
ART OF PAINTING

This verse be thine, my friend, nor thou refuse
This from no venal or ungrateful Muse.
Whether thy hand strike out some free design,
Where life awakes, and dawns at every line;
Or blend in beauteous tints the coloured mass,
And from the canvas call the mimic face:
Read these instructive leaves, in which conspire
Fresnoy's close art, and Dryden's native fire:
And reading wish, like theirs, our fate and fame,
So mixed our studies, and so joined our name;
Like them to shine through long succeeding age,
So just thy skill, so regular my rage.

   Smit with the love of sister-arts we came,
And met congenial, mingling flame with flame;
Like friendly colours found them both unite,
And each from each contract new strength and light.
How oft in pleasing tasks we wear the day,
While summer-suns roll unperceived away!
How oft our slowly-growing works impart,
While images reflect from art to art?
How oft review; each finding, like a friend
Something to blame, and something to commend?

   What flattering scenes our wandering fancy wrought,
Rome's pompous glories rising to our thought!
Together o'er the Alps methinks we fly,
Fired with ideas of fair Italy.
With thee on Raphael's monument I mourn,
Or wait inspiring dreams at Maro's urn:
With thee repose, where Tully once was laid,
Or seek some ruin's formidable shade:
While fancy brings the vanished piles to view,
And builds imaginary Rome anew,
Here thy well-studied marbles fix our eye;
A fading fresco here demands a sigh:
Each heavenly piece unwearied we compare,
Match Raphael's grace with thy loved Guido's air,
Carracci's strength, Correggio's softer line,
Paulo's free stroke, and Titian's warmth divine.

   How finished with illustrious toil appears
This small, well-polished gem, the [2] work of years!
Yet still how faint by precept is expressed
The living image in the painter's breast?
Thence endless streams of fair ideas flow,

Strike in the sketch, or in the picture glow;
Thence beauty, waking all her forms, supplies
An angel's sweetness, or Bridgewater's eyes.
   Muse! at that name thy sacred sorrows shed,
Those tears eternal that embalm the dead:
Call round her tomb each object of desire,
Each purer frame informed with purer fire:
Bid her be all that cheers or softens life,
The tender sister, daughter, friend, and wife:
Bid her be all that makes mankind adore;
Then view this marble, and be vain no more!
   Yet still her charms in breathing paint engage;
Her modest cheek shall warm a future age.
Beauty, frail flower, that every season fears,
Blooms in thy colours for a thousand years.
Thus Churchill's race shall other hearts surprise,
And other beauties envy Worsley's eyes;
Each pleasing Blount shall endless smiles bestow,
And soft Belinda's blush for ever glow.
   Oh lasting as those colours may they shine,
Free as thy stroke, yet faultless as thy line;
New graces yearly like thy works display,
Soft without weakness, without glaring gay;
Led by some rule that guides, but not constrains;
And finished more through happiness than pains.
The kindred arts shall in their praise conspire,
One dip the pencil, and one string the lyre.
Yet should the Graces all thy figures place,
And breathe an air divine on every face;
Yet should the Muses bid my numbers roll
Strong as their charms, and gentle as their soul;
With Zeuxis' Helen thy Bridgewater vie,
And these be sung till Granville's Myra die:
Alas! how little from the grave we claim!
Thou but preserv'st a face and I a name!

[2] Fresnoy employed above twenty years in finishing his poem.

EPISTLE TO MISS BLOUNT
ON HER LEAVING THE TOWN AFTER THE CORONATION

As some fond virgin, whom her mother's care
Drags from the town to wholesome country air,
Just when she learns to roll a melting eye,
And hear a spark, yet think no danger nigh;
From the dear man unwilling she must sever,
Yet takes one kiss before she parts for ever:
Thus from the world fair Zephalinda flew,

Saw others happy, and with sighs withdrew;
Not that their pleasures caused her discontent,
She sighed not that they stayed, but that She went.
   She went, to plain-work, and to purling brooks,
Old-fashioned halls, dull aunts, and croaking rooks:
She went from opera, park, assembly, play,
To morning-walks, and prayers three hours a day;
To part her time 'twixt reading and bohea,
To muse, and spill her solitary tea,
Or o'er cold coffee trifle with the spoon,
Count the slow clock, and dine exact at noon;
Divert her eyes with pictures in the fire,
Hum half a tune, tell stories to the squire;
Up to her godly garret after seven,
There starve and pray, for that's the way to heaven.
   Some squire, perhaps, you take delight to rack;
Whose game is whist, whose treat a toast in sack;
Who visits with a gun, presents you birds,
Then gives a smacking buss, and cries,—'No words!'
Or with his hound comes hollowing from the stable,
Makes love with nods, and knees beneath a table;
Whose laughs are hearty, though his jests are coarse,
And loves you best of all things—but his horse.
   In some fair evening, on your elbow laid,
You dream of triumphs in the rural shade;
In pensive thought recall the fancied scene,
See coronations rise on every green;
Before you pass th' imaginary sights
Of Lords and Earls and Dukes and gartered knights,
While the spread fan o'ershades your closing eyes;
Then gives one flirt, and all the vision flies.
Thus vanish sceptres, coronets, and balls,
And leave you in lone woods, or empty walls!
   So when your slave, at some dear idle time,
(Not plagued with head-aches or the want of rhyme)
Stands in the streets, abstracted from the crew,
And while he seems to study, thinks of you;
Just when his fancy paints your sprightly eyes,
Or sees the blush of soft Parthenia rise,
Gay pats my shoulder, and you vanish quite,
Streets, chairs, and coxcombs rush upon my sight;
Vexed to be still in town, I knit my brow,
Look sour, and hum a tune, as you may now.

A FULL AND TRUE ACCOUNT OF
A HORRID AND BARBAROUS REVENGE
BY POISON,
ON THE BODY OF
MR. EDMUND CURLL,
BOOKSELLER;
WITH A FAITHFUL COPY OF
HIS LAST WILL AND TESTAMENT
PUBLISHED BY AN EYEWITNESS

So when Curll's stomach the strong drench o'ercame,
(Infused in vengeance of insulted fame)
Th' avenger sees, with a delighted eye,
His long jaws open, and his colour fly;
And while his guts the keen emetics urge,
Smiles on the vomit, and enjoys the purge.

History furnishes us with examples of many satirical authors, who have fallen sacrifices to revenge, but not of any booksellers, that I know of, except the unfortunate subject of the following papers. I mean Mr. Edmund Curll, at the Bible and Dial in Fleet Street, who was yesterday poisoned by Mr. Pope, after having lived many years an instance of the mild temper of the British nation.

Everybody knows that the said Mr. Edmund Curll, on Monday the 26th instant, published a satirical piece, entitled *Court Poems*, in the preface whereof they were attributed to a Lady of Quality, Mr. Pope, or Mr. Gay; by which indiscreet method, though he had escaped one revenge, there were still two behind in reserve.

Now on the Wednesday ensuing, between the hours of ten and eleven, Mr. I.intot, a neighbouring bookseller, desired a conference with Mr. Curll about settling a title page of *Wiquefort's Ambassador*, inviting him at the same time to take a whet together. Mr. Pope, (who is not the only instance how persons of bright parts may be carried away by the instigation of the devil) found means to convey himself into the same room under pretence of business with Mr. Lintot, who, it seems, is the printer of his *Homer*. This gentleman with a seeming coolness reprimanded Mr. Curll for wrongfully ascribing to him the aforesaid poems. He excused himself by declaring, that one of his authors (Mr. Oldmixon by name) gave the copies to the press, and wrote the Preface. Upon this Mr. Pope (being to all appearance reconciled) very civilly drank a glass of sack to Mr. Curll, which he as civilly pledged; and though the liquor in colour and taste differed not from common sack, yet was it plain by the pangs this unhappy stationer felt soon after, that some poisonous drug had been secretly infused therein.

About eleven o'clock he went home, where his wife observing his colour change, said, 'Are you not sick, my dear?' He replied, 'Bloody sick;' and incontinently fell a vomiting and straining in an uncommon and unnatural manner, the contents of his vomiting being as green as grass. His wife had been just reading a book of her husband's printing concerning Jane Wenham, the famous witch of Hertford, and her mind misgave her, that he was bewitched; but he soon let her know, that he suspected *poison*, and recounted to her, between the intervals of his yawnings and reachings, every circumstance of his interview with Mr. Pope.

Mr. Lintot in the mean time coming in, was extremely affrighted at the sudden alteration he observed in him: 'Brother Curll,' says he, 'I fear you have got the vomiting distemper; which (I have heard) kills in half an hour. This comes from your not following my advice, to drink old hock as I do, and abstain from sack.' Mr. Curll replied in a moving tone, 'Your author's sack, I fear, has done my business.' 'Z—ds,' says Mr. Lintot, 'My author!—Why did not you drink old hock?' Notwithstanding which rough remonstrance, he did in the most friendly manner press him to take warm water; but Mr. Curll did with great obstinacy refute it; which made Mr. Lintot infer, that he chose to die, as thinking to recover greater damages.

All this time the symptoms increased violently, with acute pains in the lower belly. 'Brother Lintot,' says he, 'I perceive my last hour approaching, do me the friendly office to call my partner, Mr. Pemberton, that we may settle our worldly affairs.' Mr. Lintot, like a kind neighbour, was hastening out of the room, while Mr. Curll raved aloud in this manner: 'If I survive this, I will be revenged on Tonson, it was he first detected me as the printer of these poems, and I will reprint these very poems in his name.' His wife admonished him not to think of revenge, but to take care of his stock and his soul: and in the same instant, Mr. Lintot (whose goodness can never be enough applauded) returned with Mr. Pemberton. After some tears jointly shed by these humane booksellers, Mr. Curll, being (as he said) in his perfect senses though in great bodily pain, immediately proceeded to make a verbal will (Mrs. Curll having first put on his nightcap) in the following manner.

'Gentlemen, in the first place, I do sincerely pray forgiveness for those indirect methods I have pursued in inventing new titles to old books, putting authors' names to things they never saw, publishing private quarrels for public entertainment; all which, I hope will be pardoned, as being done to get an honest livelihood.

I do also heartily beg pardon of all persons of honour, lords spiritual and temporal, gentry, burgesses, and commonalty, to whose abuse I have any, or every way, contributed by my publications. Particularly, I hope it will be considered, that if I have vilified his grace the duke of Marlborough, I have likewise aspersed the late duke of Ormond; if I have abused the honourable Mr. Walpole, I have also libelled the lord Bolingbroke; so that I have preserved that equality and impartiality which becomes an honest man in times of faction and division.

I call my conscience to witness, that many of these things, which may seem malicious, were done out of charity; I having made it wholly my business to print for poor disconsolate authors, whom all other booksellers refuse. Only God bless sir Richard Blackmore! you know he takes no copy-money.

The book of the *Conduct of the Earl of Nottingham*, is yet unpublished; as you are to have the profit of it, Mr. Pemberton, you are to run the risk of the resentments of all that noble family. Indeed I caused the author to assert several things in it as facts, which are only idle stories of the town; because I thought it would make the book sell. Do you pay the author for copy money, and the printer and publisher. I heartily beg God's, and my Lord Nottingham's pardon; but all trades must live.

The second collection of poems, which I groundlessly called Mr. Prior's, will sell for nothing, and has not yet paid the charge of the advertisements, which I was obliged to publish against him. Therefore you may as well suppress the edition, and beg that that gentleman's pardon in the name of a dying Christian.

The French *Cato*, with the criticisms showing how superior it is to Mr. Addison's, (which I wickedly ascribed to madam Dacier) may be suppressed at a reasonable rate, being damnably translated.

I protest I have no animosity to Mr. Rowe, having printed part of *Callipaedia*, and an incorrect edition of his poems without his leave, in quarto. Mr. Gildon's *Rehearsal*; or *Bays the Younger*, did more harm to me than to Mr. Rowe; though upon the faith of an honest man, I paid him double for abusing both him and Mr. Pope.

Heaven pardon me for publishing the *Trials of Sodomy* in an Elzevir letter; but I humbly hope, my printing sir Richard Blackmore's *Essays* will atone for them. I beg that you will take what remains of these last, which is near the whole impression, (presents excepted) and let my poor widow have in exchange the sole property of the copy of madam Mascranny.

Here Mr. Pemberton interrupted, and would by no means consent to this article, about which some dispute might have arisen, unbecoming a dying person, if Mr. Lintot had not interposed, and Mr. Curll vomited.

What this poor unfortunate man spoke afterward, was so indistinct, and in such broken accents (being perpetually interrupted by vomitings) that the reader is entreated to excuse the confusion and imperfection of this account.

Dear Mr. Pemberton, I beg you to beware of the indictment at Hick's Hall for publishing Rochester's bawdy poems; that copy will otherwise be my best legacy to my dear wife, and helpless child.

The Case of Impotence was my best support all the last long vacation.

In this last paragraph Mr. Curll's voice grew more free, for his vomitings abated upon his dejections, and he spoke what follows from his close-stool.

For the copies of noblemen's and bishops *Last Wills and Testaments*, I solemnly declare, I printed them not with any purpose of defamation; but merely as I thought those copies lawfully purchased from Doctors' Commons, at one shilling apiece. Our trade in wills turning to small account, we may divide them blindfold.

For Mr. Manwaring's *Life*, I ask Mrs. Oldfield's pardon. Neither *His* nor my Lord Halifax's Lives, though they were of service to their country, were of any to me: but I was resolved, since I could not print their works while they lived, to print their lives after they were dead.'

While he was speaking these words Mr. Oldmixon entered. 'Ah! Mr. Oldmixon' (said poor Mr. Curll) 'to what a condition have your works reduced me! I die a martyr to that unlucky preface. However, in these my last moments, I will be just to all men; you shall have your third share of the *Court Poems*, as was stipulated. When I am dead, where will you find another bookseller? Your *Protestant Packet* might have supported you, had you writ a little less scurrilously, There is a mean in all things.'

Then turning to Mr. Pemberton, he told him, he had several *taking title-pages*, that only wanted treatises to be wrote to them, and earnestly entreated, that when they were writ, his heirs might have some share of the profit of them.

After he had said this, he fell into horrible gripings, upon which Mr. Lintot advised him to repeat the Lord's Prayer. He desired his wife to step into the shop for a Common Prayer-Book, and read it by the help of a candle, without hesitation. He closed the book, fetched a groan, and recommended to Mrs. Curll to give forty shillings to the poor of the parish of St. Dunstan's, and a week's wages advance to each of his gentlemen authors, with some small gratuity in particular to Mrs. Centlivre.

The poor man continued for some hours with all his disconsolate family about him in tears, expecting his final dissolution; when of a sudden he was surprisingly relieved by a plentiful fetid stool, which obliged them all to retire out of the room. Notwithstanding, it is judged by sir Richard Blackmore, that the poison is still latent in his body, and will infallibly destroy him by slow degrees in less than a month. It is to be hoped the other enemies of this wretched stationer, will not farther pursue their revenge, or shorten this short period of his miserable life.

A FURTHER ACCOUNT
OF THE MOST DEPLORABLE CONDITION
OF MR. EDMUND CURLL, BOOKSELLER.
SINCE HIS BEING POISONED ON THE 28TH OF MARCH

The public is already acquainted with the manner of Mr. Curll's impoisonment, by a faithful, though unpolite historian of Grub-street. I am but the continuer of his history; yet I hope a due distinction will be made, between an undignified scribbler of a sheet and half, and the author of a three-penny stitched book, like myself.

'Wit,' (saith Sir Richard Blackmore)* 'proceeds from a concurrence of regular and exalted ferments, and an affluence of animal spirits rectified and refined to a degree of purity.' On the contrary, when the igneous particles rise with the vital liquor, they produce an abstraction of the rational part of the soul, which we commonly call madness. The verity of this hypothesis is justified by the symptoms with which the unfortunate Mr. Edmund Curll, bookseller, hath been afflicted, ever since his swallowing the poison at, the Swan tavern in Fleet-street. For though the neck of his retort, which carries up the animal spirits to the head, is of an extraordinary length; yet the said animal spirits rise muddy, being contaminated with the inflammable particles of this uncommon poison.

The symptoms of his departure from his usual temper of mind, were at first only *speaking civilly to his customers*, taking a fancy to *say his prayers, singeing a pig with a new purchased libel*, and *refusing two and nine-pence for Sir Richard Blackmore's Essays.*

As the poor man's frenzy increased, he began to *void his excrements in his bed, read Rochester's bawdy poems to his wife*, gave *Oldmixon a slap on the chops, and would have kissed Mr. Pembertons a— by violence.*

But at last he came to such a pass, that he would *dine upon nothing but copperplates, took a clyster for a whipped syllabub, and ate a suppository* for a *radish with bread and butter.*

We leave it to every tender wife to imagine, how sorely all this afflicted poor Mrs. Curll. At first she privately put a bill into several churches, desiring the prayers of the congregation for a *wretched stationer* distempered in mind. But when she was sadly convinced that his misfortune was public to all the world, writ the following letter to her good neighbour Mr. Lintot:

A true copy of Mrs. Curll's letter to Mr. Lintot.

Worthy Mr. Lintot,
You and all the neighbours know too well, the frenzy with which my poor man is visited. I never perceived he was out of himself, till that melancholy day that he thought he was poisoned in a glass of sack; upon this he ran a-vomiting all over the house, and in the new

washed dining-room. Alas! this is the greatest adversity that ever befell my poor man since he lost *one testicle* at school by the bite of a black boar. Good Lord! if he should die, where should I dispose of the stock? unless Mr. Pemberton or you would help a distressed widow; for God knows, he never published any books that lasted above a week, so that if he wanted *daily books*, we wanted *daily bread*. I can write no more, for I hear the rap of Mr. Curll's ivory-headed cane upon the counter.—Pray recommend me to your pastry-cook, who furnishes you yearly with tarts in exchange for your papers, for Mr. Curll has disobliged ours, since his fits came upon him;—before that we generally lived upon baked meats.—He is coming in, and I have but just time to put his son out of the way for fear of mischief: so wishing you a merry Easter, I remain your

most humble servant,
C. Curll.

P. S. As to the report of my poor husband's stealing a *calf*, it is really groundless, for he always binds in *sheep*.

But return we to Mr. Curll, who all Wednesday continued outrageously mad. On Thursday he had a *lucid interval*, that enabled him to send a general summons to all his authors. There was but one porter who could perform this office, to whom he gave the following bill of directions, where to find 'em. This bill, together with Mrs. Curll's original letter, lie at Mr. Lintot's shop to be perused by the curious.

Instructions to a Porter how to find Mr. Curll's Authors.

'At a tallow-chandler's in Petty France, halfway under the blind arch, ask for the *historian*.

'At the Bedstead and Bolster, a music-house in Moorfields, two translators in a bed together.

'At the Hercules and Still in Vinegar-Yard, a schoolmaster with carbuncles on his nose.

'At a blacksmith's shop in the Friars, a Pindaric writer in red stockings.

'In the Calendar-mill-room at Exeter-change, a composer of meditations.

'At the Three Tobacco-pipes in Dog and Bitch yard, one that has been a parson, he wears a blue camblet coat, trimmed with black: my best writer against *revealed religion*.

'At Mr. Summers, a thiefcatcher's, in Lewkners Lane, the man that wrote against the impiety of Mr. Rowe's plays.

'At the Farthing Pie House in Tooting Fields, the young man who is writing my new *Pastorals*.

'At the laundresses, at the Hole in the Wall in Cursitor's Alley, up three pair of stairs, the author of my *Church-History*— if his flux be over—you may also speak to the gentleman who lies by him in the flock bed, my *index-maker*.

'The cook's wife* in Buckingham Court; bid her bring along with her the *similes* that were lent her for her next new play.

'Call at Budge Row for the gentleman you use to go to in the cockloft; I have taken away the ladder, but his landlady has it in keeping.

'I don't much care if you ask at the Mint for the old beetle-browed critic, and the purblind poet at the Alley over against St. Andrew's Holborn. But this as you have time.'

All these gentlemen appeared at the hour appointed in Mr. Curll's dining-room, two excepted; one of whom was the gentleman in the cockloft, his landlady being out of the way, and the *Gradus ad Parnassum* taken down; the other happened to be too closely watched by the bailiffs.

They no sooner entered the room, but all of them showed in their behaviour some suspicion of each other; some turning away their heads with an air of contempt; others squinting with a leer, that showed at once fear and indignation, each with a haggard abstracted mien, the lively picture of *scorn, solitude*, and *short-commons*. So when a keeper feeds his hungry charge of vultures, panthers, and of Lybian leopards, each eyes his fellow with a fiery glare: high hung, the bloody liver tempts their maw. Or as a housewife stands before her pales, surrounded by her geese; they fight, they hiss, they gaggle, beat their wings, and down is scattered as the winter's snow, for a poor grain of oat, or tare, or barley. Such looks shot through the room transverse, oblique, direct; such was the stir and din, till Curll thus spoke, (but without rising from his close-stool.)

'*Whores* and *authors* must be paid beforehand to put them in good humour; therefore here is half a crown a-piece for you to drink your own healths, and confusion to Mr. Addison, and all other successful writers.

'Ah gentlemen! What have I not done, what have I not suffered, rather than the world should be deprived of your lucubrations? I have taken involuntary purges, I have been vomited, three times have I been caned, once was I hunted, twice was my head broke by a grenadier, twice was I tossed in a blanket; I have had boxes on the ear, slaps on the chops; I have been frighted, pumped, kicked, slandered, and beshitten.—I hope, Gentlemen, you are all convinced, that this author of Mr. Lintot's could mean nothing else but starving you, by poisoning me. It remains for us to consult the best and speediest methods of revenge.'

He had scarce done speaking, but the historian proposed a history of his life. The Exeter Exchange gentleman was for penning articles of his faith. Some pretty smart Pindaric (says the red-stocking gentleman) would effectually do his business. But the index-maker said, there was nothing like an index to his *Homer*.

After several debates, they came to the following resolutions.

'*Resolved*, That every member of this society, according to his several abilities, shall contribute some way or other to the defamation of Mr. Pope.

'*Resolved*, That towards the libelling of the said Pope there be a sum employed not exceeding six pounds sixteen shillings and ninepence (not including advertisements).

'*Resolved*, That Mr. Dennis make an affidavit before Mr. Justice Tully, that in Mr. Pope's *Homer*, there are several passages contrary to the established rules of OUR Sublime.

'*Resolved*, That he has on purpose, in several passages perverted the true ancient Heathen sense of *Homer*, for the more effectual propagation of the Popish religion.

'*Resolved*, That the printing of *Homer's* battles at this juncture, has been the occasion of all the disturbances of this kingdom.

'*Ordered*, That Mr. Barnivelt be invited to be a member of this society, in order to make further discoveries.

'*Resolved*, That a number of effective Erratas be raised out of Pope's *Homer* (not exceeding 1746) and that every gentleman, who shall send in one error, for his encouragement shall have the whole works of this society *gratis*.

'*Resolved*, That a sum not exceeding ten shillings and sixpence be distributed among the members of this society for *coffee* and *tobacco*, in order to enable them the more effectually to defame him in *coffee-houses*.

'*Resolved*, That towards the further lessening the character of the said Mr. Pope, some persons be deputed to abuse him at ladies' *tea tables*, and that in consideration our authors are not *well dressed* enough, Mr. C— y be deputed for that service.

'*Resolved*, That a *ballad* be made against Mr. Pope, and that Mr. Oldmixon, Mr. Gildon, and Mrs. Centlivre, do prepare and bring in the same.

'*Resolved*, That, above all, some effectual ways and means be found to increase the joint stock of the reputation of this society, which at present is exceeding low, and to give their works the greater currency; whether by raising the denomination of the said works by counterfeit title-pages, or mixing a greater quantity of the fine metal of other authors, with the alloy of this society.

'*Resolved*, That no member of this society for the future mix *stout* in his *ale* in a morning, and that Mr. *B* remove from the Hercules and Still.

'*Resolved*, That all our members (except the cook's wife) be provided with a sufficient quantity of the *vivifying drops*, or *Byfield's Sal Volatile*.

'*Resolved*, That Sir Richard Blackmore be appointed to endue this society with a large quantity of *regular and exalted ferments*, in order to *enliven their cold sentiments* (being his true receipt to make wits.)

These resolutions being taken, the assembly was ready to break up, but they took so near a part in Mr. Curll's afflictions, that none of them could leave him without giving him some advice to reinstate him in his health.

Mr. Gildon was of opinion, that in order to drive a Pope out of his belly, he should get the mummy of some deceased Moderator of the General Assembly in Scotland, to be taken inwardly, as an effectual antidote against Antichrist; but Mr. Oldmixon did conceive, that the *liver* of the person who administered the poison, boiled in broth, would be a more certain cure.

While the company were expecting the thanks of Mr. Curll, for these demonstrations of their zeal, a whole pile of *Essays* on a sudden fell on his head; the shock of which in an instant brought back his delirium. He immediately rose up, over-turned the close-stool, and beshit the *Essays* (which may probably occasion a second edition), then without putting up his breeches, in a most furious tone, he thus broke out to his books, which his distempered imagination represented to him as alive, coming down from their shelves, fluttering their leaves, and flapping their covers at him.

Now G—*d damn* all *folios, quartos, octavos,* and *duodecimos*! ungrateful varlets that you are, who have so long taken up my house without paying for your lodging?—Are you not the beggarly brood of fumbling *journeymen*; born in *garrets* among *lice* and *cobwebs*, nursed up on *grey peas, bullock's liver,* and *porter's ale*?—Was not the first light you saw, the farthing candle I paid for? Did you not come before your time into *dirty sheets* of brown paper? And have not I clothed you in double *Royal*, lodged you handsomely on *decent shelves*, laced your *backs* with *gold*, equipped you with splendid *titles*, and sent you into the world with the names of *persons of quality*? Must I be *always* plagued with you? Why flutter ye your leaves and flap your covers at me? Damn ye all, ye *wolves in sheep's clothing; rags ye were, and to rags ye shall return.* Why hold you forth your *texts* to me, ye paltry *sermons*? Why cry ye,—at every word to me, ye *bawdy poems*?—To my shop at Tunbridge ye shall go, by G—, and thence be drawn like the rest of your predecessors, bit by bit, to the *passage-house*: for in this present emotion of my bowels, how do I compassionate those who have great need, and nothing to wipe their breech with?'

Having said this, and at the same time recollecting that his own was yet unwiped, he abated of his fury, and with great gravity, applied to that function the unfinished sheets of the *Conduct of the Earl of Nottingham.*

POPE TO THE EARL OF BURLINGTON
NOVEMBER 1716.

My Lord,—If your mare could speak, she would give you an account of the extraordinary company she had on the road; which since she cannot, I will.

It was the enterprising Mr. Lintot, the redoubtable rival of Mr. Tonson, who mounted on a stone-horse, (no disagreeable companion to your Lordship's mare) overtook me in Windsor Forest. He said, he heard I designed for Oxford, the seat of the muses, and would, as my bookseller, by all means, accompany me thither.

I asked him where he got his horse? He answered, he got it of his publisher: 'For that rogue, my printer', said he, 'disappointed me: I hoped to put him in a good humour by a treat at the tavern, of a brown fricassee of rabbits which cost two shillings, with two quarts of wine, besides my conversation. I thought myself cocksure of his horse, which he readily promised me, but said that Mr. Tonson had just such another design of going to

Cambridge, expecting there the copy of a *Comment upon the Revelations*; and if Mr. Tonson went, he was preingaged to attend him, being to have the printing of the said copy.'

'So in short, I borrowed this stone-horse of my publisher, which he had of Mr. Oldmixon for a debt; he lent me too the pretty boy you see after me; he was a smutty dog yesterday, and cost me near two hours to wash the ink off his face: but the devil is a fair-conditioned devil, and very forward in his catechise: if you have any more bags, he shall carry them.'

I thought Mr. Lintot's civility not to be neglected, so gave the boy a small bag, containing three shirts and an Elzevir Virgil; and mounting in an instant proceeded on the road, with my man before, my courteous stationer beside, and the aforesaid devil behind.

Mr. Lintot began in this manner: 'Now damn them! what if they should put it into the newspaper, how you and I went together to Oxford? Why, what would I care? If I should go down into Sussex, they would say I was gone to the Speaker. But what of that? If my son were but big enough to go on with the business, by G—d I would keep as good company as old Jacob.'

Hereupon I inquired of his son. 'The lad,' says he, 'has fine parts, but is somewhat sickly, *much as you are*—I spare for nothing in his education at Westminster. Pray, don't you think Westminster to be the best school in England? Most of the late *ministry* came out of it; so did many of *this ministry*; I hope the boy will make his fortune.'

Don't you design to let him pass a year at Oxford? 'To what purpose?' said he, 'the universities do but make pedants, and I intend to breed him a man of business.'

As Mr. Lintot was talking, I observed he sat uneasy on his saddle, for which I expressed some solicitude. 'Nothing,' says he, 'I can bear it well enough; but since we have the day before us, methinks it would be very pleasant for you to rest awhile under the woods.' When we were alighted, 'See here, what a mighty pretty *Horace* I have in my pocket? what if you amused yourself in turning an ode, till we mount again? Lord! if you pleased, what a clever *Miscellany* might you make at leisure hours.' Perhaps I may, said I, if we ride on; the motion is an aid to my fancy; a round trot very much awakens my spirits. Then jog on apace, and I'll think as hard as I can.

Silence ensued for a full hour; after which Mr. Lintot lugged the reins, stopped short, and broke out, 'Well, sir, how far have you gone?' I answered seven miles. 'Z—ds, sir,' said Lintot, 'I thought you had done seven stanzas. Oldisworth in a ramble round Wimbledon Hill, would translate a whole ode in half this time. I'll say that for Oldisworth (though I lost by his *Timothy*'s) he translates an ode of Horace the *quickest* of any man in England. I remember Dr. King would write verses in a tavern three hours after he couldn't speak: and there's Sir Richard in that rumbling old chariot of his, between Fleet Ditch and St. Giles's pound shall make you half a *Job*.'

'Pray Mr. Lintot,' said I, 'now you talk of translators, what is your method of managing them?' 'Sir,' replied he, 'those are the saddest pack of rogues in the world. In a hungry fit, they'll swear they understand all the languages in the universe: I have known one of them take down a Greek book upon my counter and cry, Ay, this is Hebrew, I must read it from the latter end. By G—d, I can never be sure in these fellows, for I neither understand Greek, Latin, French, nor Italian myself. But this is my way: I agree with them for ten shillings per sheet, with a proviso, that I will have their doings corrected by whom I please; so by one or other they are led at last to the true sense of an author; my judgment giving the negative to all my translators.' But how are you secure that those correctors may not impose upon you? 'Why, I get any civil gentleman (especially any Scotchman) that comes into my shop to read the original to me in English; by this I know whether my first translator be deficient, and whether my corrector merits his money or no.

'I'll tell you what happened to me last month: I bargained with Sewell for a new version of *Lucretius* to publish against Tonson's; agreeing to pay the author so many shillings at his producing so many lines. He made a great progress in a very short time, and I gave it to the corrector to compare with the Latin; but he went directly to Creech's translation, and found it the same word for word, all but the first page. Now, what d'ye think I did? I arrested the *translator* for a cheat; nay, and I stopped the *corrector's pay* too, upon this proof that he had made use of Creech instead of the original.'

Pray tell me next how you deal with the critics? 'Sir,' said he, 'nothing more easy. I can silence the most formidable of them; the rich ones for a sheet apiece of the blotted manuscript, which costs me nothing. They'll go about with it to their acquaintance, and pretend they had it from the author, who submitted to their correction: this has given some of them such an air that in time they come to be consulted with, and dedicated to, as the top critics of the town. —As for the poor critics, I'll give you one instance of my management, by which you may guess the rest. A lean man that looked like a very good scholar came to me t'other day; he turned over *Homer*, shook his head, shrugged up his shoulders, and pished at every line of it; *'One would wonder,'* says he, *'at the strange presumption of men; Homer is no such easy task, that every stripling, every versifier'*—he was going on when my wife called to dinner: 'Sir,' said I, 'will you please to eat a *piece of beef* with me?' '*Mr. Lintot,*' said he, '*I am sorry you should be at the expense of this great book, I am really concerned on your account*' —'Sir, I am obliged to you: if you can dine upon a piece of beef, together with a slice of pudding' —'*Mr. Lintot, I do not say but Mr. Pope, if he would condescend to advise with men of learning*' —'Sir, the *pudding* is upon the table, if you please to go in.'—My critic complies, he comes to a taste of your poetry, and tells me in the same breath, that the *book* is commendable, and the *pudding* is excellent.'

'Now, sir,' concluded Mr. Lintot, 'in return to the frankness I have shown, pray tell me, Is it the opinion of your friends at court that my Lord Landsdown will be brought to the bar or not?' I told him I heard *not*, and I hoped it, my Lord being one I had particular obligations to. 'That may be,' replied Mr. Lintot, 'but by G—d if he is not, I shall lose the printing of a very good trial.'

These, my Lord, are a few traits by which you may discern the genius of my friend Mr. Lintot, which I have chosen for the subject of a letter. I dropped him as soon as I got to Oxford, and paid a visit to my Lord Carlton at Middleton.

The conversations I enjoy here are not to be prejudiced by my pen, and the pleasures from them only to be equaled when I meet your Lordship. I hope in a few days to cast myself from your horse at your feet.

I am, etc.

ELOISA TO ABELARD

ARGUMENT

Abelard and Eloisa flourished in the twelfth century; they were two of the most distinguished persons of their age in learning and beauty, but for nothing more famous than for their unfortunate passion. After a long course of calamities, they retired each to a several convent, and consecrated the remainder of their days to religion. It was many years after this separation that a letter of Abelard's to a friend, which contained the history of his misfortune, fell into the hands of Eloisa. This, awakening all her tenderness, occasioned those celebrated letters (out of which the following is partly extracted) which give so lively a picture of the struggles of grace and nature, virtue and passion.

> In these deep solitudes and awful cells,
> Where heavenly-pensive contemplation dwells,
> And ever-musing melancholy reigns;
> What means this tumult in a vestal's veins?
> Why rove my thoughts beyond this last retreat?
> Why feels my heart its long-forgotten heat?
> Yet, yet I love!—From Abelard it came,
> And Eloïsa yet must kiss the name.
> Dear fatal name! rest ever unrevealed,
> Nor pass these lips, in holy silence sealed:
> Hide it, my heart, within that close disguise,
> Where, mixed with God's, his loved idea lies:
> O write it not, my hand—the name appears
> Already written—wash it out, my tears!
> In vain lost Eloïsa weeps and prays,
> Her heart still dictates, and her hand obeys.
> Relentless walls! whose darksome round contains
> Repentant sighs, and voluntary pains:
> Ye rugged rocks! which holy knees have worn;
> Ye grots and caverns shagged with horrid thorn!
> Shrines! where their vigils pale-eyed virgins keep,
> And pitying saints, whose statues learn to weep!
> Though cold like you, unmoved and silent grown,
> I have not yet forgot myself to stone.
> All is not heaven's while Abelard has part,
> Still rebel nature holds out half my heart;
> Nor prayers nor fasts its stubborn pulse restrain,
> Nor tears, for ages taught to flow in vain.
> Soon as thy letters trembling I unclose,
> That well-known name awakens all my woes.
> Oh name for ever sad! for ever dear!
> Still breathed in sighs, still ushered with a tear.
> I tremble too where'er my own I find,
> Some dire misfortune follows close behind.

Line after line my gushing eyes o'erflow,
Led through a safe variety of woe:
Now warm in love, now withering in my bloom,
Lost in a convent's solitary gloom!
There stern religion quenched th' unwilling flame,
There died the best of passions, love and fame.
    Yet write, oh write me all, that I may join
Griefs to thy griefs, and echo sighs to thine.
Nor foes nor fortune take this power away;
And is my Abelard less kind than they?
Tears still are mine, and those I need not spare,
Love but demands what else were shed in prayer;
No happier task these faded eyes pursue;
To read and weep is all they now can do.
    Then share thy pain, allow that sad relief;
Ah, more than share it! give me all thy grief.
Heaven first taught letters for some wretch's aid,
Some banished lover, or some captive maid;
They live, they speak, they breathe what love inspires,
Warm from the soul, and faithful to its fires;
The virgin's wish without her fears impart,
Excuse the blush, and pour out all the heart,
Speed the soft intercourse from soul to soul,
And waft a sigh from Indus to the Pole.
    Thou knowst how guiltless first I met thy flame,
When love approached me under friendship's name;
My fancy formed thee of angelic kind,
Some emanation of th' all-beauteous mind.
Those smiling eyes, approached every ray,
Shone sweetly lambent with celestial day:
Guiltless I gazed; heaven listened while you sung;
And truths divine came mended from that tongue.
From lips like those what precept failed to move?
Too soon they taught me 'twas no sin to love:
Back through the paths of pleasing sense I ran,
Nor wished an angel whom I loved a man.
Dim and remote the joys of saints I see,
Nor envy them that Heaven I lose for thee.
    How oft, when pressed to marriage, have I said,
Curse on all laws but those which love has made?
Love, free as air, at sight of human ties,
Spreads his light wings, and in a moment flies.
Let wealth, let honour, wait the wedded dame,
August her deed, and sacred be her fame;
Before true passion all those views remove,
Fame, wealth, and honour! what are you to love?
The jealous God, when we profane his fires,
Those restless passions in revenge inspires,

And bids them make mistaken mortals groan,
Who seek in love for aught but love alone.
Should at my feet the world's great master fall,
Himself, his throne, his world, I'd scorn 'em all:
Not Caesar's empress would I deign to prove;
No, make me mistress to the man I love;
If there be yet another name more free,
More fond than mistress, make me that to thee!
Oh happy state! when souls each other draw,
When love is liberty, and nature law:
All then is full, possessing, and possessed,
No craving void left aching in the breast:
Even thought meets thought, ere from the lips it part,
And each warm wish springs mutual from the heart.
This sure is bliss (if bliss on earth there be),
And once the lot of Abelard and me.
    Alas how changed! what sudden horrors rise!
A naked lover bound and bleeding lies!
Where, where was Eloïse? her voice, her hand,
Her poniard, had opposed the dire command.
Barbarian, stay! that bloody stroke restrain;
The crime was common, common be the pain.
I can no more; by shame, by rage suppressed,
Let tears, and burning blushes speak the rest.
    Canst thou forget that sad, that solemn day,
When victims at you altar's foot we lay?
Canst thou forget what tears that moment fell,
When, warm in youth, I bade the world farewell?
As with cold lips I kissed the sacred veil,
The shrines all trembled, and the lamps grew pale:
Heaven scarce believed the conquest it surveyed,
And saints with wonder heard the vows I made.
Yet then, to those dread altars as I drew,
Not on the cross my eyes were fixed, but you:
Not grace, or zeal, love only was my call,
And if I lose thy love, I lose my all.
Come! with thy looks, thy words, relieve my woe;
Those still at least are left thee to bestow.
Still on that breast enamoured let me lie,
Still drink delicious poison from thy eye,
Pant on thy lip, and to thy heart be pressed;
Give all thou canst—and let me dream the rest.
Ah, no! instruct me other joys to prize,
With other beauties charm my partial eyes,
Full in my view set all the bright abode,
And make my soul quit Abelard for God.
    Ah, think at least thy flock deserves thy care,
Plants of thy hand, and children of thy prayer.

From the false world in early youth they fled,
By thee to mountains, wilds, and deserts led.
You raised these hallowed walls; the desert smiled,
And paradise was opened in the wild.
No weeping orphan saw his father's stores
Our shrines irradiate or emblaze the floors;
No silver saints, by dying misers given,
Here bribed the rage of ill-requited heaven;
But such plain roofs as piety could raise,
And only vocal with the Maker's praise.
In these lone walls (their day's eternal bound)
These moss-grown domes with spiry turrets crowned,
Where awful arches make a noon-day night,
And the dim windows shed a solemn light;
Thy eyes diffused a reconciling ray,
And gleams of glory brightened all the day.
But now no face divine contentment wears,
'Tis all blank sadness, or continual tears.
See how the force of others' prayers I try,
(O pious fraud of amorous charity!)
But why should I on others prayers depend?
Come thou, my father, brother, husband, friend!
Ah let thy handmaid, sister, daughter, move,
And all those tender names in one, thy love!
The darksome pines, that o'er yon rocks reclined,
Wave high, and murmur to the hollow wind,
The wandering streams that shine between the hills,
The grots that echo to the tinkling rills,
The dying gales that pant upon the trees,
The lakes that quiver to the curling breeze;
No more these scenes my meditation aid,
Or lull to rest the visionary maid.
But o'er the twilight groves and dusky caves,
Long-sounding aisles and intermingled graves,
Black Melancholy sits, and round her throws
A death-like silence, and a dread repose:
Her gloomy presence saddens all the scene,
Shades every flower, and darkens every green,
Deepens the murmur of the falling floods,
And breathes a browner horror on the woods.

    Yet here for ever, ever must I stay;
Sad proof how well a lover can obey!
Death, only Death can break the lasting chain;
And here, even then shall my cold dust remain,
Here all its frailties, all its flames resign,
And wait, till 'tis no sin to mix with thine.
    Ah wretch! believed the spouse of God in vain.
Confessed within the slave of love and man.

Assist me, heaven! but whence arose that prayer?
Sprung it from piety, or from despair?
Even here, where frozen chastity retires,
Love finds an altar for forbidden fires.
I ought to grieve, but cannot what I ought;
I mourn the lover, not lament the fault;
I view my crime, but kindle at the view,
Repent old pleasures, and solicit new;
Now turned to Heaven, I weep my past offence,
Now think of thee, and curse my innocence.
Of all affliction taught a lover yet,
'Tis sure the hardest science to forget!
How shall I lose the sin, yet keep the sense,
And love th' offender, yet detest th' offence?
How the dear object from the crime remove,
Or how distinguish penitence from love?
Unequal task! a passion to resign,
For hearts so touched, so pierced, so lost as mine.
Ere such a soul regains its peaceful state,
How often must it love, how often hate!
How often hope, despair, resent, regret,
Conceal, disdain—do all things but forget.
But let heaven seize it, all at once 'tis fired;
Not touched, but rapt; not wakened, but inspired!
Oh come! oh teach me nature to subdue,
Renounce my love, my life, myself—and you.
Fill my fond heart with God alone, for he
Alone can rival, can succeed to thee.
    How happy is the blameless vestal's lot?
The world forgetting, by the world forgot:
Eternal sunshine of the spotless mind!
Each prayer accepted, and each wish resigned;
Labour and rest, that equal periods keep;
'Obedient slumbers that can wake and weep;'
Desires composed, affections ever even;
Tears that delight, and sighs that waft to heaven.
Grace shines around her with serenest beams,
And whispering angels prompt her golden dreams.
For her th' unfading rose of Eden blooms,
And wings of seraphs shed divine perfumes,
For her the spouse prepares the bridal ring.
For her white virgins hymeneals sing;
To sounds of heavenly harps she dies away,
And melts in visions of eternal day.
    Far other dreams my erring soul employ,
Far other raptures of unholy joy:
When at the close of each sad, sorrowing day,
Fancy restores what vengeance snatched away,

Then conscience sleeps, and leaving nature free,
All my loose soul unbounded springs to thee.
Oh curst, dear horrors of all-conscious night!
How glowing guilt exalts the keen delight!
Provoking daemons all restraint remove,
And stir within me every source of love.
I hear thee, view thee, gaze o'er all thy charms,
And round thy phantom glue my clasping arms.
I wake—no more I hear, no more I view,
The phantom flies me, as unkind as you.
I call aloud; it hears not what I say:
I stretch my empty arms; it glides away.
To dream once more I close my willing eyes;
Ye soft illusions, dear deceits, arise!
Alas, no more! methinks we wandering go
Through dreary wastes, and weep each other's woe,
Where round some mouldering tower pale ivy creeps,
And low-browed rocks hang nodding o'er the deeps.
Sudden you mount! you beckon from the skies;
Clouds interpose, waves roar, and winds arise.
I shriek, start up, the same sad prospect find,
And wake to all the griefs I left behind.
  For thee the fates, severely kind, ordain
A cool suspense from pleasure and from pain;
Thy life a long dead calm of fixed repose;
No pulse that riots, and no blood that glows.
Still as the sea, ere winds were taught to blow,
Or moving spirit bade the waters flow;
Soft as the slumbers of a saint forgiven,
And mild as opening gleams of promised heaven.
  Come, Abelard! for what hast thou to dread?
The torch of Venus burns not for the dead.
Nature stands checked; Religion disapproves;
Even thou art cold—yet Eloïsa loves.
Ah hopeless, lasting flames! like those that burn
To light the dead, and warm th' unfruitful urn.
  What scenes appear where'er I turn my view?
The dear ideas, where I fly, pursue,
Rise in the grove, before the altar rise,
Stain all my soul, and wanton in my eyes.
I waste the matin lamp in sighs for thee,
Thy image steals between my God and me,
Thy voice I seem in every hymn to hear,
With every bead I drop too soft a tear.
When from the censer clouds of fragrance roll,
And swelling organs lift the rising soul,
One thought of thee puts all the pomp to flight,
Priests, tapers, temples, swim before my sight:

In seas of flame my plunging soul is drowned,
While altars blaze, and angels tremble round.
   While prostrate here in humble grief I lie,
Kind virtuous drops just gathering in my eye,
While praying, trembling, in the dust I roll,
And dawning grace is opening on my soul:
Come, if thou darest, all charming as thou art!
Oppose thyself to heaven; dispute my heart;
Come, with one glance of those deluding eyes
Blot out each bright idea of the skies;
Take back that grace, those sorrows, and those tears,
Take back my fruitless penitence and prayers,
Snatch me, just mounting, from the blest abode:
Assist the fiends, and tear me from my God!
   No, fly me, fly me, far as pole from pole;
Rise Alps between us! and whole oceans roll!
Ah, come not, write not, think not once of me,
Nor share one pang of all I felt for thee.
Thy oaths I quit, thy memory resign;
Forget, renounce me, hate whate'er was mine.
Fair eyes, and tempting looks (which yet I view),
Long loved, adored ideas, all adieu!
O grace serene! O virtue heavenly fair!
Divine Oblivion of low-thoughted care!
Fresh blooming Hope, gay daughter of the sky!
And faith, our early immortality!
Enter, each mild, each amicable guest;
Receive, and wrap me in eternal rest!
   See in her cell sad Eloïsa spread,
Propped on some tomb, a neighbour of the dead.
In each low wind methinks a spirit calls,
And more than echoes talk along the walls.
Here, as I watched the dying lamps around,
From yonder shrine I heard a hollow sound.
'Come, sister, come! (it said, or seemed to say)
'Thy place is here, sad sister, come away!
Once like thyself, I trembled, wept, and prayed,
Love's victim then, though now a sainted maid:
But all is calm in this eternal sleep;
Here grief forgets to groan, and love to weep,
Even superstition loses every fear:
For God, not man, absolves our frailties here.'
   I come, I come! prepare your roseate bowers,
Celestial palms, and ever-blooming flowers.
Thither, where sinners may have rest, I go,
Where flames refined in breasts seraphic glow;
Thou, Abelard! the last sad office pay,
And smooth my passage to the realms of day;

See my lips tremble, and my eye-balls roll,
Suck my last breath, and catch my flying soul!
Ah no—in sacred vestments mayst thou stand,
The hallowed taper trembling in thy hand,
Present the cross before my lifted eye,
Teach me at once, and learn of me, to die.
Ah then, thy once loved Eloïsa see!
It will be then no crime to gaze on me.
See from my cheek the transient roses fly!
See the last sparkle languish in my eye!
Till every motion, pulse, and breath be o'er,
And even my Abelard beloved no more.
O Death, all-eloquent! you only prove
What dust we dote on, when 'tis man we love.
    Then too, when Fate shall thy fair frame destroy,
(That cause of all my guilt, and all my joy)
In trance ecstatic may thy pangs be drowned,
Bright clouds descend, and angels watch thee round,
From opening skies may streaming glories shine,
And saints embrace thee with a love like mine.
    May one kind grave unite each hapless name,
And graft my love immortal on thy fame!
Then, ages hence, when all my woes are o'er,
When this rebellious heart shall beat no more;
If ever chance two wandering lovers brings
To Paraclete's white walls and silver springs,
O'er the pale marble shall they join their heads,
And drink the falling tears each other sheds;
Then sadly say, with mutual pity moved,
'Oh may we never love as these have loved!'
From the full choir, when loud hosannas rise,
And swell the pomp of dreadful sacrifice,
Amid that scene if some relenting eye
Glance on the stone where our cold relics lie,
Devotion's self shall steal a thought from heaven,
One human tear shall drop, and be forgiven.
And sure if fate some future bard shall join
In sad similitude of griefs to mine,
Condemned whole years in absence to deplore,
And image charms he must behold no more;
Such if there be, who loves so long, so well;
Let him our sad, our tender story tell;
The well-sung woes will soothe my pensive ghost;
He best can paint them who shall feel them most.

ELEGY
TO THE MEMORY OF AN
UNFORTUNATE LADY

What beckoning ghost along the moonlight shade
Invites my steps, and points to yonder glade?
'Tis she!—but why that bleeding bosom gored?
Why dimly gleams the visionary sword?
Oh ever beauteous, ever friendly! tell,
Is it, in heaven, a crime to love too well?
To bear too tender, or too firm a heart,
To act a lover's or a Roman's part?
Is there no bright reversion in the sky,
For those who greatly think, or bravely die?
Why bade ye else, ye Powers! her soul aspire
Above the vulgar flight of low desire?
Ambition first sprung from your blessed abodes;
The glorious fault of angels and of gods:
Thence to their images on earth it flows,
And in the breasts of kings and heroes glows.
Most souls, 'tis true, but peep out once an age,
Dull sullen prisoners in the body's cage;
Dim lights of life, that burn a length of years
Useless, unseen, as lamps in sepulchres;
Like eastern kings a lazy state they keep,
And, close confined to their own palace sleep.
From these, perhaps (ere Nature bade her die)
Fate snatched her early to the pitying sky.
As into air the purer spirits flow,
And separate from their kindred dregs below;
So flew the soul to its congenial place,
Nor left one virtue to redeem her race.
But thou, false guardian of a charge too good,
Thou, mean deserter of thy brother's blood!
See on these ruby lips the trembling breath,
These cheeks, now fading at the blast of death;
Cold is that breast which warmed the world before,
And those love-darting eyes must roll no more.
Thus, if eternal justice rules the ball,
Thus shall your wives, and thus your children fall:
On all the line a sudden vengeance waits,
And frequent hearses shall besiege your gates.
There passengers shall stand, and pointing say,
(While the long funerals blacken all the way)
Lo these were they whose souls the furies steeled,
And cursed with hearts unknowing how to yield.
Thus unlamented pass the proud away,

The gaze of fools, and pageant of a day!
So perish all, whose breast ne'er learned to glow
For others' good, or melt at others woe.
    What can atone (ever injured shade!)
Thy fate unpitied, and thy rites unpaid?
No friend's complaint, no kind domestic tear
Pleased thy pale ghost, or graced thy mournful bier;
By foreign hands thy dying eyes were closed,
By foreign hands thy decent limbs composed,
By foreign hands thy humble grave adorned,
By strangers honoured, and by strangers mourned.
What though no friends in sable weeds appear,
Grieve for an hour, perhaps, then mourn a year,
And bear about the mockery of woe
To midnight dances, and the public show?
What though no weeping loves thy ashes grace,
Nor polished marble emulate thy face?
What though no sacred earth allow thee room,
Nor hallowed dirge be muttered o'er thy tomb?
Yet shall thy grave with rising flowers be dressed,
And the green turf lie lightly on thy breast:
There shall the morn her earliest tears bestow,
There the first roses of the year shall blow;
While angels with their silver wings o'ershade
The ground, now sacred by thy relics made.
    So peaceful rests, without a stone, a name,
What once had beauty, titles, wealth and fame.
How loved, how honoured once, avails thee not,
To whom related, or by whom begot;
A heap of dust alone remains of thee;
'Tis all thou art, and all the proud shall be!
    Poets themselves must fall like those they sung;
Deaf the praised ear, and mute the tuneful tongue.
Even he whose soul now melts in mournful lays,
Shall shortly want the generous tear he pays;
Then from his closing eyes thy form shall part,
And the last pang shall tear thee from his heart,
Life's idle business at one gasp be o'er,
The Muse forgot, and thou beloved no more!

POPE TO TERESA AND MARTHA BLOUNT
September 1717

Ladies,—I came from Stonor (its master not being at home) to Oxford the same night. Nothing could have more of that melancholy which once used to please me, than my last day's journey: for after having passed through my favourite woods in the forest, with a thousand reveries of past pleasures; I rid over hanging hills, whose tops were edged with groves, and whose feet watered with winding rivers, listening to the falls of cataracts below, and the murmuring of the winds above. The gloomy verdure of Stonor succeeded to these, and then the shades of the evening overtook me, the moon rose in the clearest sky I ever saw, by whose solemn light I paced on slowly, without company, or any interruption to the range of my thoughts. About a mile before I reached Oxford, all the night bells tolled in different notes; the clocks of every college answered one another; and told me, some in a deeper, some in a softer voice, that it was eleven o'clock.

All this was no ill preparation to the life I have led since; among those old walls, venerable galleries, stone porticos, studious walks, and solitary scenes of the University. I wanted nothing but a black gown and a salary, to be as mere a bookworm as any there. I conformed myself to the college hours, was rolled up in books, wrapped in meditations, lay in one of the most ancient, dusky parts of the University, and was as dead to the world as any hermit of the desert. If anything was awake or alive in me it was a little vanity, such as even those good men used to entertain, when the monks of their own order extolled their piety and abstractedness. For I found myself received with a sort of respect, which this idle part of mankind, the learned, pay to their own species; who are as considerable here as the busy, the gay, and the ambitious are in your world. Indeed, I was so treated that I could not but ask myself in my mind, what college I was founder of, or what library I had built? Methinks I do very ill, to return to the world again, to leave the only place where I make a good figure, and from seeing myself seated with dignity on the most conspicuous shelves of a library, go to contemplate this wretched person in the abject condition of lying at a lady's feet in Bolton street.

I will not deny, but that like Alexander, in the midst of my glory, I am wounded, and find myself a mere man. To tell you from whence the dart comes, is to no purpose, since neither of you will take the tender care to draw it out of my heart, and suck the poison with your lips; or are in any disposition to take in a part of the venom yourselves, to ease me. Here, at my Lord Harcourt' s, I see a creature nearer an angel than a woman, (though a woman be very near as good as an angel). I think you have formerly heard me mention Mrs. Jennings as a credit to the maker of angels. She is a relation of his lordship's, and he gravely proposed her to me for a wife, being tender of her interests, and knowing (what is a shame to Providence) that she is less indebted to fortune than I. I told him, his Lordship could never have thought of, if it had not been his misfortune of being blind, and that I never could till I was so: but that, as matters now were, I did not care to force so fine a woman to give the finishing stroke to all my deformities, by the last mark of a beast, horns.

Now I am talking of beauty, I shall see my Lady Jane Hyde tomorrow at Cornbury. I shall pass a day and night at Blenheim Park, and will then hasten home, (taking Reading in my way). I have everywhere made inquiry if it be possible to get any annuities on sound security: it would really be an inexpressible joy to me if I could serve you, and I will always do my utmost to give myself pleasure.

I beg you both to think as well of me, that is to think me as much yours, as any one else. What degree of friendship and tenderness I feel for you, I must be content with being sure of myself; but I shall be glad if you believe it in any degree. Allow me as much as you can: and think as well as you are able of one whose imperfections are so manifest, and who thinks so little of himself, as to think ten times more of either of you.

POPE TO LADY MARY WORTLEY MONTAGU
1718

Dear Madam,—'Tis not possible to express the least part of the joy your return gives me. Time only, and experience, will convince you how very sincere it is—I excessively long to meet you; to say so much, so very much to you, that I believe I shall say nothing—I have given orders to be sent for the first minute of your arrival, (which I beg you will let them know at Mr. Jervas's.) I am fourscore miles from London, a short journey compared to that I so often thought at least of undertaking, rather than die without seeing you again. Though the place I am in is such as I would not quit for the town, if I did not value you more than any, nay everybody else there. And you'll be convinced how little the town has engaged my affections in your absence from it, when you know what a place this is which I prefer to it. I shall therefore describe it to you at large, as the true picture of a genuine ancient country seat.

You must expect nothing regular in my description of a house that seems to be built before rules were in fashion. The whole is so disjointed, and the parts so detached from each other, and yet so joining again, one cannot tell how; that in a poetical fit you would imagine it had been a village in Amphion's time, where twenty cottages had taken a dance together, were all out, and stood still in amazement ever since. A stranger would be grievously disappointed who should ever think to get into this house the right way. One would expect, after entering through the porch, to be let into the hall: alas nothing less— you find yourself in a brewhouse. From the parlor you think to step into the drawing-room, but upon opening the iron-nailed door, you are convinced by a flight of birds about your ears and a cloud of dust in your eyes, that 'tis the pigeon-house. On each side our porch are two chimneys, that wear their greens on the outside, which would do as well within, for whenever we make a fire, we let the smoke out of the windows. Over the parlor window hangs a sloping balcony, which time has turned to a very convenient penthouse. The top is crowned with a very venerable tower, so like that of the church just by, that the jackdaws build in it as if it were the true steeple.

The great hall is high and spacious, flanked with long tables (images of ancient hospitality) ornamented with monstrous horns, about twenty broken pikes, and a matchlock musket or two, which they say were used in the Civil Wars. Here is one vast arched window, beautifully darkened with divers scutcheons of painted glass. There seems to be great propriety in this old manner of blazoning upon glass, ancient families being like ancient windows, in the course of generations seldom free from cracks. One shining pane bears date 1286. There the face of Dame Elinor owes more to this single piece than to all the glasses she ever consulted in her life. Who can say after this that glass is frail, when it is not half so perishable as human beauty or glory? For in another pane you see the memory of a knight preserved, whose marble nose is moldered from his monument in the church adjoining. And yet, must not one sigh to reflect, that the most authentic record of so ancient a family should lie at the mercy of every boy that throws a stone? In this hall, in former days have dined gartered knights and courtly dames, with ushers, sewers, and seneschals; and yet it was but t'other night that an owl flew in hither, and mistook it for a barn.

This hall lets you up, (and down) over a very high threshold, into the parlor. It is furnished with historical tapestry, whose marginal fringes do confess the moisture of the air. The other contents of this room are a broken-bellied virginal, a couple of crippled velvet chairs, with two or three mildewed pictures of moldy ancestors, who look as dismally as if they came fresh from hell with all their brimstone about 'em. These are carefully set at the further corner; for the windows being everywhere broken, make it so convenient a place to dry poppies and mustard-seed in, that the room is appropriated to that use.

Next this parlor lies (as I said before) the pigeon-house: by the side of which runs an entry that leads, on one hand and t'other, into a bedchamber, a buttery, and a small hole called the chaplain's study. Then follow a brewhouse, a little green-and-gilt parlor, and the great stairs, under which is the dairy. A little further on the right, the servants' hall; and by the side of it, up six steps, the old lady's closet, which has a lattice into the said hall, that, while she said her prayers, she might cast an eye on the men and maids. There are upon this ground floor in all twenty-four apartments, hard to be distinguished by particular names; among which I must not forget a chamber that has in it a large antiquity of timber, which seems to have been either a bedstead or a cider-press.

Our best room above is very long and low; of the exact proportion of a bandbox. It has hangings of the finest work in the world, those I mean, which Arachne spins out of her own bowels. Indeed the roof is so decayed, that after a favorable shower of rain, we may (with God's blessing) expect a crop of mushrooms between the chinks of the floors.

All this upper story has for many years had no other inhabitants than certain rats, whose very age renders them worthy of this venerable mansion, for the very rats of this ancient seat are gray. Since these have not quitted it, we hope at least this house may stand during the small remainder of days these poor animals have to live, who are now too infirm to remove to another: they have still a small subsistence left them in the few remaining books of the library.

I had never seen half what I have described, but for an old starched gray-headed steward, who is as much an antiquity as any in the place, and looks like an old family picture walked out of its frame. He failed not, as we passed from room to room, to relate several memoirs of the family; but his observations were particularly curious in the cellar. He showed where stood the triple rows of butts of sack, and where were ranged the bottles of tent for toasts in the morning; he pointed to the stands that supported the iron-hooped hogsheads of strong beer; then stepping to a corner, he lugged out the tattered fragment of an unframed picture—'This,' says he, with tears in his eyes, 'was poor Sir Thomas! once master of all the drink I told you of: he had two sons (poor young masters!) that never arrived to the age of his beer! they both fell ill in this very cellar, and never went out upon their own legs.' He could not pass by a broken bottle without taking it up to show us the arms of the family on it. He then led me up the tower, by dark winding stone steps, which landed us into several little rooms, one above the other; one of these was nailed up, and my guide whispered to me the occasion of it. It seems the course of this noble blood was a little interrupted about two centuries ago by a freak of the Lady Frances, who was here taken with a neighboring prior: ever since which the room has been nailed up, and branded with the name of the adultery-chamber. The ghost of Lady Frances is supposed to walk here; some prying maids of the family formerly reported that they saw a lady in a farthingale through the keyhole; but this matter was hushed up, and the servants forbid to talk of it.

I must needs have tired you with this long letter: but what engaged me in the description was a generous principle to preserve the memory of a thing that must itself soon fall to ruin, nay perhaps, some part of it before this reaches your hands. Indeed I owe this old house the same sort of gratitude that we do to an old friend, that harbors us in his declining condition, nay even in his last extremities. I have found this an excellent place for retirement and study, where no one who passes by can dream there is an inhabitant, and even anybody that would visit me dares not venture under my roof. You will not wonder I have translated a great deal of Homer in this retreat; any one that sees it will own I could not have chosen a fitter or more likely place to converse with the dead. As soon as I return to the living, it shall be to converse with the best of them. I hope, therefore, very speedily to tell you in person how sincerely and unalterably I am

Madam

Your most faithful, obliged

& obedient servant,

A. Pope.

I beg Mr. Wortley to believe me his most humble Servant.

THE EIGHTEENTH BOOK
OF THE
ILIAD

THE ARGUMENT
The Gried of Achilles, and new Armour
Made him by Vulcan

The news of the death of Patroclus is brought to Achilles by Antilochus. Thetis, hearing his lamentations comes with all her sea-nymphs to comfort him. The speeches of the mother and son on this occasion. Iris appears to Achilles by the command of Juno, and orders him to show himself at the head of the entrenchments. The sight of him turns the fortunes of the day, and the body of Patroclus is carried off by the Greeks. The Trojans call a council, where Hector and Polydamas disagree in their opinions; but the advice of the former prevails, to remain encamped in the field. The grief of Achilles over the body of Patroclus.

Thetis goes to the palace of Vulcan to obtain new arms for her son. The description of the wonderful works of Vulcan, and, lastly, that noble one of the shield of Achilles.

The latter part of the nine-and-twentieth day, and the night ensuing, take up this book; the scene is at Achilles's tent on the sea-shore, from whence it changes to the palace of Vulcan.

Thus like the rage of fire the combat burns,
And now it rises, now it sinks by turns.
Meanwhile, where Hellespont's broad waters flow,
Stood Nestor's son, the messenger of woe:
There sat Achilles, shaded by his sails,
On hoisted yards extended to the gales;
Pensive he sate; for all that fate designed,
Rose in sad prospect to his boding mind.
Thus to his soul he said: 'Ah! what constrains
The Greeks, late victors, now to quit the plains?
Is this the day, which heaven so long ago
Ordained, to sink me with the weight of woe?
(So Thetis warned) when by a Trojan hand,

The bravest of the Myrmidonian band
Should lose the light! Fulfilled is that decree;
Fallen is the warrior, and Patroclus he!
In vain I charged him soon to quit the plain,
And warned to shun Hectorean force in vain!'
    Thus while he thinks, Antilochus appears,
And tells the melancholy tale with tears.
'Sad tidings, son of Peleus! thou must hear;
And wretched I, th' unwilling messenger!
Dead is Patroclus! For his corpse they fight;
His naked corpse: his arms are Hector's right.'
    A sudden horror shot through all the chief,
And wrapped his senses in the cloud of grief;
Cast on the ground, with furious hands he spread
The scorching ashes o'er his graceful head;
His purple garments, and his golden hairs,
Those he deforms with dust, and these he tears:
On the hard soil his groaning breast he threw,
And rolled and grovelled, as to earth he grew.
The virgin captives, with disordered charms,
(Won by his own, or by Patroclus' arms)
Rushed from their tents with cries; and gathering round
Beat their white breasts, and fainted on the ground:
While Nestor's son sustains a manlier part,
And mourns the warrior with a warrior's heart;
Hangs on his arms, amidst his frantic woe,
And oft prevents the meditated blow.
    Far in the deep abysses of the main,
With hoary Nereus, and the watery train,
The mother goddess from her crystal throne
Heard his loud cries, and answered groan for groan.
The circling Nereids with their mistress weep,
And all the sea-green sisters of the deep.
Thalia, Glauce, (every watery name)
Nesaea mild, and silver Spio came.
Cymothoe and Cymodoce were nigh,
And the blue languish of soft Alia's eye.
Their locks Actaea and Limnoria rear,
Then Proto, Doris, Panope appear,
Thoa, Pherusa, Doto, Melita;
Agave gentle, and Amphithoe gay:
Next Callianira, Callianassa show
Their sister looks; Dexamene the slow,
And swift Dynamene, now cut the tides:
Iaera now the verdant wave divides;
Nemertes with Apseudes lifts the head:
Bright Galatea quits her pearly bed;
These Orythia, Clymene, attend,

Maera, Amphinome, the train extend;
And black Janira, and Janassa fair.
And Amatheia with her amber hair.
All these, and all that deep in ocean held
Their sacred seats, the glimmering grotto filled;
Each beat her ivory breast with silent woe,
Till Thetis' sorrows thus began to flow.
    'Hear me, and judge, ye sisters of the main!
How just a cause has Thetis to complain!
How wretched, were I mortal, were my fate!
How more than wretched in the immortal state!
Sprung from my bed a godlike hero came,
The bravest far that ever bore the name;
Like some fair olive, by my careful hand
He grew, he flourished and adorned the land:
To Troy I sent him: but the fates ordain
He never, never must return again.
So short a space the light of heaven to view,
So short alas! and filled with anguish too.
Hear how his sorrows echo through the shore!
I cannot ease them, but I must deplore;
I go at least to bear a tender part,
And mourn my loved-one with a mother's heart.'
    She said, and left the caverns of the main.
All bathed in tears; the melancholy train
Attend her way. Wide-opening part the tides,
While the long pomp the silver waves divides.
Approaching now, they touched the Trojan land;
Then, two by two, ascended up the strand.
Th' immortal mother, standing close beside
Her mournful offspring, to his sighs replied;
Along the coast their mingled clamors ran.
And thus the silver-footed dame began.
    'Why mourns my son? thy late preferred request
The god has granted, and the Greeks distressed:
Why mourns my son? thy anguish let me share,
Reveal the cause, and trust a parent's care.'
    He, deeply groaning— 'To this cureless grief
Not even the Thunderer's favor brings relief.
Patroclus—Ah!—Say, Goddess, can I boast
A pleasure now? revenge itself is lost;
Patroclus, loved of all my martial train,
Beyond mankind, beyond myself, is slain!
Lost are those arms the gods themselves bestowed
On Peleus; Hector bears the glorious load.
Cursed be that day, when all the powers above
Thy charms submitted to a mortal love:
O hadst thou still, a sister of the main,

Pursued the pleasures of the watery reign;
And happier Peleus, less ambitious, led
A mortal beauty to his equal bed!
Ere the sad fruit of thy unhappy womb
Had caused such sorrows past, and woes to come.
For soon, alas! that wretched offspring slain,
New woes, new sorrows, shall create again:
'Tis not in fate the alternate now to give;
Patroclus dead, Achilles hates to live.
Let me revenge it on proud Hector's heart,
Let his last spirit smoke upon my dart;
On these conditions will I breathe: till then,
I blush to walk among the race of men.'
   A flood of tears, at this, the Goddess shed;
'Ah then, I see thee dying, see thee dead!
When Hector falls, thou diest.'—'Let Hector die,
And let me fall!', Achilles made reply,
'Far lies Patroclus from his native plain!
He fell, and falling wished my aid in vain.
Ah then, since from this miserable day
I cast all hope of my return away,
Since, unrevenged, a hundred ghosts demand
The fate of Hector from Achilles' hand;
Since here, for brutal courage far renowned,
I live an idle burden to the ground,
(Others in council famed for nobler skill,
More useful to preserve, than I to kill).
Let me—But oh! ye gracious powers above!
Wrath and revenge from men and gods remove:
Far, far too dear to every mortal breast,
Sweet to the soul, as honey to the taste;
Gathering like vapors of a noxious kind
From fiery blood, and darkening all the mind.
Me Agamemnon urged to deadly hate;
'Tis past—I quell it; I resign to fate.
Yes—I will meet the murderer of my friend,
Or (if the gods ordain it) meet my end.
The stroke of fate the strongest cannot shun:
The great Alcides, Jove's unequalled son,
To Juno's hate, at length resigned his breath,
And sunk the victim of all-conquering death.
So shall Achilles fall! stretched pale and dead,
No more the Grecian hope, or Trojan dread!
Let me, this instant, rush into the fields,
And reap what glory life's short harvest yields.
Shall I not force some widowed dame to tear
With frantic hands her long disheveled hair?
Shall I not force her breast to heave with sighs,

And the soft tears to trickle from her eyes?
Yes, I shall give the fair those mournful charms—
In vain you hold me—Hence! my arms, my arms!
Soon shall the sanguine torrent spread so wide,
That all shall know Achilles swells the tide.'
   'My son', Caerulean Thetis made reply,
To fate submitting with a secret sigh,
'The host to succor, and thy friends to save,
Is worthy thee; the duty of the brave.
But canst thou, naked, issue to the plains?
Thy radiant arms the Trojan foe detains,
Insulting Hector bears the spoils on high,
But vainly glories, for his fate is nigh.
Yet, yet awhile, thy generous ardor stay;
Assured, I meet thee at the dawn of day,
Charged with refulgent arms (a glorious load)
Vulcanian arms, the labor of a god.'
   Then turning to the daughters of the main.
The goddess thus dismissed her azure train.
   'Ye sister Nereids! to your deeps descend,
Haste, and our father's sacred seat attend,
I go to find the architect divine,
Where vast Olympus' starry summits shine:
So tell our hoary sire'—This charge she gave:
The sea-green sisters plunge beneath the wave:
Thetis once more ascends the blessed abodes,
And treads the brazen threshold of the Gods.
   And now the Greeks from furious Hector's force,
Urge to broad Hellespont their headlong course:
Nor yet their chiefs Patroclus' body bore
Safe through the tempest to the tented shore.
The horse, the foot, with equal fury joined,
Poured on the rear, and thundered close behind;
And like a flame through fields of ripened corn,
The rage of Hector o'er the ranks was borne:
Thrice the slain hero by the foot he drew;
Thrice to the skies the Trojan clamors flew.
As oft the Ajaces his assault sustain;
But checked, he turns; repulsed, attacks again.
With fiercer shouts his lingering troops he fires,
Nor yields a step, nor from his post retires:
So watchful shepherds strive to force, in vain,
The hungry lion from a carcass slain.
Even yet Patroclus had he borne away,
And all the dories of the extended day;
Had not high Juno from the realms of air,
Secret, dispatched her trusty messenger.
The various goddess of the showery bow,

Shot in a whirlwind to the shore below;
To great Achilles at his ships she came,
And thus began the many-coloured dame.
    'Rise, son of Peleus! rise, divinely brave!
Assist the combat, and Patroclus save:
For him the slaughter to the fleet they spread,
And fall by mutual wounds around the dead.
To drag him back to Troy the foe contends;
Nor with his death the rage of Hector ends:
A prey to dogs he dooms the corse to lie.
And marks the place to fix his head on high.
Rise, and prevent (if yet you think of fame)
Thy friend's disgrace, thy own eternal shame!'
    'Who sends thee, Goddess! from th' ethereal skies?'
Achilles thus. And Iris thus replies,
'I come, Pelides! from the Queen of Jove,
Th' immortal empress of the realms above;
Unknown to him who sits remote on high,
Unknown to all the synod of the sky.'
'Thou comest in vain' he cries (with fury warmed)
'Arms I have none, and can I fight unarmed?
Unwilling as I am, of force I stay,
Till Thetis bring me at the dawn of day
Vulcanian arms: what other should I wield?
Except the mighty Telamonian shield?
That, in my friend's defence, has Ajax spread,
While his strong lance around him heaps the dead:
The gallant chief defends Menoetius' son,
And does, what his Achilles should have done.'
    'Thy want of arms' said Iris, 'well we know,
But though unarmed, yet clad in terrors, go!
Let but Achilles o'er yon trench appear,
Proud Troy shall tremble, and consent to fear;
Greece from one glance of that tremendous eye
Shall take new courage, and disdain to fly.'
    She spoke, and passed in air. The hero rose;
Her Aegis, Pallas o'er his shoulder throws;
Around his brows a golden cloud she spread;
A stream of glory flamed above his head.
As when from some beleaguered town arise
The smokes high-curling to the shaded skies;
(Seen from some island, o'er the main afar,
When men distressed hang out the sign of war)
Soon as the sun in ocean hides his rays,
Thick on the hills the flaming beacons blaze;
With long-projected beams the seas are bright,
And heaven's high arch reflects the ruddy light;
So from Achilles' head the splendors rise,

Reflecting blaze on blaze, against the skies.
Forth marched the chief, and distant from the crowd,
High on the rampart raised his voice aloud;
With her own shout Minerva swells the sound;
Troy starts astonished, and the shores rebound.
As the loud trumpet's brazen mouth from far
With shrilling clangor sounds the alarm of war;
Struck from the walls, the echoes float on high,
And the round bulwarks, and thick towers reply:
So high his brazen voice the hero reared:
Hosts dropped their arms, and trembled as they heard;
And back the chariots roll, and coursers bound,
And steeds and men lie mingled on the ground.
Aghast they see the living lightnings play,
And turn their eye-balls from the flashing ray.
Thrice from the trench his dreadful voice he raised;
And thrice they fled, confounded and amazed.
Twelve in the tumult wedged, untimely rushed
On their own spears, by their own chariots crushed:
While shielded from the darts, the Greeks obtain
The long-contended carcass of the slain.

   A lofty bier the breathless warrior bears;
Around, his sad companions melt in tears:
But chief Achilles, bending down his head,
Pours unavailing sorrows o'er the dead.
Whom late, triumphant with his steeds and car,
He sent refulgent to the field of war;
(Unhappy change!) now senseless, pale, he found,
Stretched forth, and gashed with many a gaping wound.

   Meantime, unwearied with his heavenly way,
In ocean's waves th' unwilling light of day
Quenched his red orb, at Juno's high command,
And from their labors eased th' Achaean band.
The frighted Trojans (panting from the war,
Their steeds unharnessed from the weary car)
A sudden council called: each chief appeared
In haste, and standing; for to sit they feared.
'Twas now no season for prolonged debate;
They saw Achilles, and in him their fate.
Silent they stood: Polydamas at last,
Skilled to discern the future by the past,
The son of Panthus, thus expressed his fears;
(The friend of Hector, and of equal years:
The self-same night to both a being gave,
One wise in council, one in action brave.)

   'In free debate, my friends, your sentence speak
For me, I move, before the morning break
To raise our camp: too dangerous here our post,

Far from Troy walls, and on a naked coast.
I deemed not Greece so dreadful, while engaged
In mutual feuds, her king and hero raged;
Then, while we hoped our armies might prevail,
We boldly camped beside a thousand sail.
I dread Pelides now: his rage of mind
Not long continues to the shores confined,
Nor to the fields, where long in equal fray
Contending nations won and lost the day;
For Troy, for Troy, shall henceforth be the strife;
And the hard contest not for fame, but life.
Haste then to Ilion, while the favoring night
Detains these terrors, keeps that arm from fight;
If but the morrow's sun behold us here,
That arm, those terrors, we shall feel, not fear;
And hearts that now disdain, shall leap with joy,
If heaven permit them then to enter Troy.
Let not my fatal prophecy be true.
Nor what I tremble but to think, ensue.
Whatever be our fate, yet let us try
What force of thought and reason can supply;
Let us on counsel for our guard depend;
The town her gates and bulwarks shall defend:
When morning dawns, our well-appointed powers
Arrayed in arms, shall line the lofty towers.
Let the fierce hero then, when fury calls,
Vent his mad vengeance on our rocky walls,
Or fetch a thousand circles round the plain,
Till his spent coursers seek the fleet again:
So may his rage be tired, and labored down;
And dogs shall tear him, ere he sack the town.'
    'Return?', said Hector, fired with stern disdain,
'What! coop whole armies in our walls again?
Was't not enough, ye valiant warriors say,
Nine years imprisoned in those towers ye lay?
Wide o'er the world was Ilion famed of old
For brass exhaustless, and for mines of gold:
But while inglorious in her walls we stayed,
Sunk were her treasures, and her stores decayed;
The Phrygians now her scattered spoils enjoy.
And proud Maeonia wastes the fruits of Troy.
Great Jove at length my arms to conquest calls,
And shuts the Grecians in their wooden walls:
Darest thou dispirit whom the gods incite?
Flies any Trojan? I shall stop his flight.
To better counsel then attention lend,
Take due refreshment, and the watch attend.
If there be one whose riches cost him care,

Forth let him bring them for the troops to share;
'Tis better generously bestowed on those,
Than left the plunder of our country's foes.
Soon as the morn the purple orient warms
Fierce on yon navy will we pour our arms.
If great Achilles rise in all his might,
His be the danger: I shall stand the fight.
Honor, ye gods! or let me gain or give;
And live he glorious, whosoe'er shall live!
Mars is our common lord, alike to all;
And oft the victor triumphs, but to fall.'
 The shouting host in loud applauses joined;
So Pallas robbed the many of their mind;
To their own sense condemned! and left to choose
The worst advice, the better to refuse.
 While the long night extends her sable reign,
Around Patroclus mourned the Grecian train.
Stern in superior grief Pelides stood;
Those slaughtering arms, so used to bathe in blood.
Now clasp his clay-cold limbs: then gushing start
The tears, and sighs burst from his swelling heart.
The lion thus, with dreadful anguish stung,
Roars through the desert, and demands his young;
When the grim savage to his rifled den
Too late returning, snuffs the track of men,
And o'er the vales and o'er the forest bounds;
His clamorous grief the bellowing wood resounds.
So grieves Achilles; and impetuous, vents
To all his Myrmidons, his loud laments.
 'In what vain promise, gods! did I engage?
When to console Menaetius' feeble age,
I vowed his much-loved offspring to restore.
Charged with rich spoils, to fair Opuntia's shore!
But mighty Jove cuts short, with just disdain,
The long, long views of poor designing man!
One fate the warrior and the friend shall strike,
And Troy's black sands must drink our blood alike:
Me too, a wretched mother shall deplore,
An aged father never see me more!
Yet, my Patroclus! yet a space I stay,
Then swift pursue thee on the darksome way.
Ere thy dear relics in the grave are laid.
Shall Hector's head be offered to thy shade;
That, with his arms, shall hang before thy shrine,
And twelve, the noblest of the Trojan line,
Sacred to vengeance, by this hand expire;
Their lives effused around thy flaming pyre.
Thus let me lie till then! thus, closely pressed,

Bathe thy cold face, and sob upon thy breast!
While Trojan captives here thy mourners stay,
Weep all the night, and murmur all the day:
Spoils of my arms, and thine; when, wasting wide,
Our swords kept time, and conquered side by side.'
   He spoke, and bade the sad attendants round
Cleanse the pale corse, and wash each honoured wound.
A massy caldron of stupendous frame
They brought, and placed it o'er the rising flame:
Then heap the lighted wood; the flame divides
Beneath the vase, and climbs around the sides:
In its wide womb they pour the rushing stream;
The boiling water bubbles to the brim:
The body then they bathe with pious toil,
Embalm the wounds, anoint the limbs with oil;
High on a bed of state extended laid,
And decent covered with a linen shade;
Last, o'er the dead the milk-white veil they threw;
That done, their sorrows and their sighs renew.
   Meanwhile to Juno, in the realms above.
(His wife and sister), spoke almighty Jove.
'At last thy will prevails: great Peleus' son
Rises in arms: such grace thy Greeks have won.
Say (for I know not) is their race divine,
And thou the mother of that martial line?'
   'What words are these,' th' imperial dame replies,
While anger flashed from her majestic eyes,
'Succor like this a mortal arm might lend,
And such success mere human wit attend:
And shall not I, the second power above,
Heaven's queen, and consort of the thundering Jove,
Say, shall not I one nation's fate command,
Not wreak my vengeance on one guilty land?'
   So they. Meanwhile the silver-footed dame
Reached the Vulcanian dome, eternal frame!
High eminent amid the works divine,
Where heaven's far-beaming brazen mansions shine.
There the lame architect the goddess found,
Obscure in smoke, his forges flaming round,
While bathed in sweat from fire to fire he flew,
And puffing loud, the roaring billows blew.
That day no common task his labor claimed;
Full twenty tripods for his hall he framed,
That placed on living wheels of massy gold,
(Wondrous to tell) instinct with spirit rolled
From place to place, around the blessed abodes,
Self-moved, obedient to the beck of gods:
For their fair handles now, overwrought with flowers,

In moulds prepared, the glowing ore he pours.
Just as responsive to his thought, the frame
Stood prompt to move, the azure goddess came:
Charis, his spouse, a grace divinely fair,
(With purple fillets round her braided hair)
Observed her entering; her soft hand she pressed,
And smiling, thus the watery queen addressed.
　'What, goddess! this unusual favor draws?
All hail, and welcome! whatsoe'er the cause:
Till now a stranger, in a happy hour
Approach, and taste the dainties of the bower.'
　High on a throne, with stars of silver graced
And various artifice, the queen she placed;
A footstool at her feet: then calling, said,
'Vulcan draw near, 'tis Thetis asks your aid.'
　'Thetis,' replied the god, 'our powers may claim,
An ever-dear, an ever-honoured name!
When my proud mother hurled me from the sky,
(My awkward form, it seems, displeased her eye)
She, and Eurynome, my griefs redressed,
And soft received me on their silver breast.
Even then, these arts employed my infant thought;
Chains, bracelets, pendants, all their toys, I wrought.
Nine years kept secret in the dark abode,
Secure I lay, concealed from man and god:
Deep in a caverned rock my days were led;
The rushing ocean murmured o'er my head.
Now, since her presence glads our mansion, say,
For such desert what service can I pay?
Vouchsafe, O Thetis! at our board to share
The genial rites, and hospitable fare;
While I my labours of the forge forego,
And bid the roaring bellows cease to blow.'
　Then from his anvil the lame artist rose;
Wide with distorted legs oblique he goes,
And stills the bellows, and (in order laid)
Locks in their chests his instruments of trade.
Then with a sponge the sooty workman dressed
His brawny arms imbrowned, and hairy breast.
With his huge sceptre graced, and red attire,
Came halting forth the sovereign of the fire:
The monarch's steps two female forms uphold,
That moved, and breathed in, animated gold;
To whom was voice, and sense, and science given
Of works divine (such wonders are in heaven!)
On these supported, with unequal gait,
He reached the throne where pensive Thetis sate;
There placed beside her on the shining frame,

He thus addressed the silver-footed dame.
 'Thee, welcome goddess! what occasion calls,
(So long a stranger) to these honoured walls?
'Tis thine, fair Thetis, the command to lay,
And Vulcan's joy and duty to obey.'
 To whom the mournful mother thus replies,
(The crystal drops stood trembling in her eyes)
'O Vulcan! say, was ever breast divine
So pierced with sorrows, so o'erwhelmed as mine?
Of all the goddesses, did Jove prepare
For Thetis only such a weight of care?
I, only I, of all the watery race.
By force subjected to a man's embrace,
Who, sinking now with age, and sorrow, pays
The mighty fine imposed on length of days.
Sprung from my bed, a godlike hero came,
The bravest sure that ever bore the name;
Like some fair plant beneath my careful hand
He grew, he flourished, and he graced the land:
To Troy I sent him! but his native shore
Never, ah never, shall receive him more;
(Even while he lives, he wastes with secret woe)
Nor I, a goddess, can retard the blow!
Robbed of the prize the Grecian suffrage gave,
The king of nations forced his royal slave:
For this he grieved; and, till the Greeks oppressed
Required his arm, he sorrowed unredressed.
Large gifts they promise, and their elders send;
In vain—he arms not, but permits' his friend
His arms, his steeds, his forces to employ;
He marches, combats, almost conquers Troy:
Then slain by Phoebus (Hector had the name)
At once resigns his armor, life, and fame.
But thou, in pity, by my prayer be won;
Grace with immortal arms this short-lived son,
And to the field in martial pomp restore,
To shine with glory, till he shines no more!'
 To her the artist-god: 'Thy griefs resign,
Secure, what Vulcan can, is ever thine.
O could I hide him from the fates as well,
Or with these hands the cruel stroke repel,
As I shall forge most envied arms, the gaze
Of wondering ages, and the world's amaze!'
 Thus having said, the father of the fires
To the black labors of his forge retires.
Soon as he bade them blow, the bellows turned
Their iron mouths; and where the furnace burned,
Resounding breathed: at once the blast expires,

And twenty forges catch at once the fires;
Just as the god directs, now loud, now low,
They raise a tempest, or they gently blow.
In hissing flames huge silver bars are rolled,
And stubborn brass, and tin, and solid gold:
Before, deep fixed, th' eternal anvils stand;
The ponderous hammer loads his better hand,
His left with tongs turns the vexed metal round;
And thick, strong strokes, the doubling vaults rebound.
     Then first he formed the immense and solid shield;
Rich various artifice emblazed the field;
Its utmost verge a threefold circle bound;
A silver chain suspends the massy round,
Five ample plates the broad expanse compose,
And godlike labors on the surface rose.
There shone the image of the master-mind:
There earth, there heaven, there ocean he designed;
The unwearied sun, the moon completely round;
The starry lights that heaven's high convex crowned;
The Pleiads, Hyades, with the northern team;
And great Orion's more refulgent beam;
To which, around the axle of the sky,
The bear revolving, points his golden eye,
Still shines exalted on th' ethereal plain.
Nor bathes his blazing forehead in the main.
     Two cities radiant on the shield appear,
The image one of peace, and one of war.
Here sacred pomp, and genial feast delight,
And solemn dance, and Hymeneal rite;
Along the street the new-made brides are led,
With torches flaming, to the nuptial bed;
The youthful dancers in a circle bound
To the soft flute, and cittern's silver sound:
Through the fair streets the matrons in a row,
Stand in their porches, and enjoy the show.
     There in the forum swarm a numerous train;
The subject of debate, a townsman slain:
One pleads the fine discharged, which one denied,
And bade the public and the laws decide:
The witness is produced on either hand;
For this, or that, the partial people stand:
Th' appointed heralds still the noisy bands,
And form a ring, with sceptres in their hands;
On seats of stone, within the sacred place,
The reverend elders nodded o'er the case;
Alternate, each the attesting sceptre took,
And rising solemn, each his sentence spoke.
Two golden talents lay amidst, in sight,

The prize of him who best adjudged the right.
   Another part (a prospect differing far)
Glowed with refulgent arms, and horrid war.
Two mighty hosts a leaguered town embrace,
And one would pillage, one would burn the place.
Meantime the townsmen, armed with silent care,
A secret ambush on the foe prepare:
Their wives, their children, and the watchful band,
Of trembling parents, on the turrets stand.
They march; by Pallas and by Mars made bold;
Gold were the gods, their radiant garments gold,
And gold their armor: these the squadron led,
August, divine, superior by the head!
A place for ambush fit, they found, and stood
Covered with shields, beside a silver flood.
Two spies at distance lurk, and watchful seem
If sheep or oxen seek the winding stream.
Soon the white flocks proceeded o'er the plains,
And steers slow-moving, and two shepherd swains;
Behind them, piping on their reeds, they go,
Nor fear an ambush, nor suspect a foe.
In arms the glittering squadron rising round
Rush sudden; hills of slaughter heap the ground,
Whole flocks and herds lie bleeding on the plains,
And, all amidst them, dead, the shepherd swains!
The bellowing oxen the besiegers hear;
They rise, take horse, approach, and meet the war;
They fight, they fall, beside the silver flood;
The waving silver seemed to blush with blood.
There tumult, there contention stood confessed;
One reared a dagger at a captive's breast,
One held a living foe, that freshly bled
With new-made wounds; another dragged a dead;
Now here, now there, the carcasses they tore:
Fate stalked amidst them, grim with human gore.
And the whole war came out, and met the eye;
And each bold figure seemed to live or die.
   A field deep-furrowed, next the god designed,
The third time laboured by the sweating hind;
The shining shares full many ploughmen guide,
And turn their crooked yokes on every side.
Still as at either end they wheel around,
The master meets 'em with his goblet crowned;
The hearty draught rewards, renews their toil;
Then back the turning plough-shares cleave the soil:
Behind, the rising earth in ridges rolled;
And sable looked, though formed of molten gold.
   Another field rose high with waving grain;

With bended sickles stand the reaper-train:
Here stretched in ranks the levelled swarths are found,
Sheaves heaped on sheaves here thicken up the ground.
With sweeping stroke the mowers strow the lands;
The gatherers follow, and collect in bands;
And last the children, in whose arms are borne
(Too short to gripe them) the brown sheaves of com.
The rustic monarch of the field descries
With silent glee, the heaps around him rise.
A ready banquet on the turf is laid,
Beneath an ample oak's expanded shade.
The victim-ox the sturdy youth prepare;
The reaper's due repast, the woman's care.

Next, ripe in yellow gold, a vineyard shines,
Bent with the ponderous harvest of its vines;
A deeper dye the dangling clusters show,
And curled on silver props, in order glow:
A darker metal mixed entrenched the place,
And pales of glittering tin the enclosure grace.
To this, one pathway gently winding leads,
Where march a train with baskets on their heads,
(Fair maids and blooming youths) that smiling bear
The purple product of th' autumnal year.
To these a youth awakes the warbling strings,
Whose tender lay the fate of Linus sings;
In measured dance behind him move the train,
Tune soft the voice, and answer to the strain.

Here herds of oxen march, erect and bold,
Rear high their horns, and seem to low in gold,
And speed to meadows on whose sounding shores
A rapid torrent through the rushes roars:
Four golden herdsmen as their guardians stand,
And nine sour dogs complete the rustic band.
Two lions rushing from the wood appeared;
And seized a bull, the master of the herd:
He roared: in vain the dogs, the men withstood,
They tore his flesh, and drank his sable blood.
The dogs (oft cheered in vain) desert the prey,
Dread the grim terrors, and at distance bay.

Next this, the eye the art of Vulcan leads
Deep through fair forests, and a length of meads;
And stalls, and folds, and scattered cots between;
And fleecy flocks, that whiten all the scene.

A figured dance succeeds: such once was seen
In lofty Gnossus for the Cretan queen,
Formed by Daedalean art. A comely band
Of youths and maidens, bounding hand in hand:
The maids in soft cymars of linen dressed;

The youths all graceful in the glossy vest;
Of those the locks with flowery wreath enrolled,
Of these the sides adorned with swords of gold,
That glittering gay, from silver belts depend.
Now all at once they rise, at once descend,
With well-taught feet: now shape, in oblique ways,
Confusedly regular, the moving maze:
Now forth at once, too swift for sight, they spring,
And undistinguished blend the flying ring:
So whirls a wheel, in giddy circle tossed,
And rapid as it runs, the single spokes are lost.
The gazing multitudes admire around;
Two active tumblers in the centre bound;
Now high, now low, their pliant limbs they bend,
And general songs the sprightly revel end.

   Thus the broad shield complete the artist crowned
With his last hand, and poured the ocean round:
In living silver seemed the waves to roll,
And beat the buckler's verge, and bound the whole.

   This done, whate'er a warrior's use requires
He forged; the cuirass that outshone the fires;
The greaves of ductile tin, the helm impressed
With various sculpture, and the golden crest.
At Thetis' feet the finished labor lay;
She, as a falcon cuts the aerial way,
Swift from Olympus' snowy summit flies,
And bears the blazing present through the skies.

TO MR. GAY
Congratulating Pope on finishing his house and gardens

Ah, friend! 'tis true—this truth you lovers know—
In vain my structures rise, my gardens grow,
In vain fair Thames reflects the double scenes
Of hanging mountains, and of sloping greens:
Joy lives not here, to happier seats it flies,
And only dwells where WORTLEY casts her eyes.
What are the gay parterre, the chequered shade,
The morning bower, the evening colonnade,
But soft recesses of uneasy minds,
To sigh unheard in, to the passing winds?
So the struck deer in some sequestered part
Lies down to die, the arrow at his heart,
There, stretched unseen in coverts hid from day,
Bleeds drop by drop, and pants his life away.

TO MR. ADDISON
OCCASIONED BY HIS DIALOGUES ON MEDALS [3]

See the wild waste of all-devouring years!
How Rome her own sad sepulchre appears,
With nodding arches, broken temples spread!
The very tombs now vanished like their dead!
Imperial wonders raised on nations spoiled,
Where mixed with slaves the groaning martyr toiled:
Huge theatres, that now unpeopled woods,
Now drained a distant country of her floods:
Fanes, which admiring Gods with pride survey,
Statues of men, scarce less alive than they!
Some felt the silent stroke of mouldering age,
Some hostile fury, some religious rage.
Barbarian blindness, Christian zeal conspire,
And Papal piety, and Gothic fire.
Perhaps, by its own ruins saved from flame,
Some buried marble half preserves a name;
That name the learned with fierce disputes pursue,
And give to Titus old Vespasian's due.
   Ambition sighed: she found it vain to trust
The faithless column and the crumbling bust:
Huge moles, whose shadow stretched from shore to shore,
Their ruins perished, and their place no more!
Convinced, she now contracts her vast design,
And all her triumphs shrink into a coin:
A narrow orb each crowded conquest keeps,
Beneath her palm here sad Judea weeps,
Here scantier limits the proud arch confine,
And scarce are seen the prostrate Nile or Rhine;
A small Euphrates through the piece is rolled,
And little eagles wave their wings in gold.
   The medal, faithful to its charge of fame,
Through climes and ages bears each form and name:
In one short view subjected to our eye
Gods, emperors, heroes, sages, beauties, lie.
With sharpened sight pale antiquaries pore,
Th' inscription value, but the rust adore;
This the blue varnish, that the green endears,
The sacred rust of twice ten hundred years!
To gain Pescennius one employs his schemes,
One grasps a Cecrops in ecstatic dreams,
Poor Vadius, long with learned spleen devoured,
Can taste no pleasure since his shield was scoured;
And Curio, restless by the fair one's side,
Sighs for an Otho, and neglects his bride.

Theirs is the vanity, the learning thine:
Touched by thy hand, again Rome's glories shine;
Her gods and godlike Heroes rise to view,
And all her faded garlands bloom anew.
Nor blush, these studies thy regard engage;
These pleased the fathers of poetic rage;
The verse and sculpture bore an equal part,
And art reflected images to art.
    Oh, when shall Britain, conscious of her claim,
Stand emulous of Greek and Roman fame?
In living medals see her wars enrolled,
And vanquished realms supply recording gold?
Here, rising bold, the patriot's honest face;
There warriors frowning in historic brass:
Then future ages with delight shall see
How Plato's, Bacon's, Newton's looks agree;
Or in fair series laurelled bards be shown,
A Virgil there, and here an Addison.
Then shall thy CRAGGS (and let me call him mine)
On the cast ore another Pollio, shine;
With aspect open shall erect his head,
And round the orb in lasting notes be read,
'Statesman, yet friend to truth! of soul sincere,
In action faithful, and in honour clear;
Who broke no promise, served no private end,
Who gained no title, and who lost no friend;
Ennobled by himself, by all approved,
And praised, unenvied by the Muse he loved.'

[3] This was originally written in the year 1715, when Mr. Addison intended to publish his book of medals; it was some time before he was secretary of state; but not published till Mr. Tickell's edition of his works; at which time the verses on Mr. Craggs, which conclude the poem, were added, viz., in 1720.

EPISTLE
To
ROBERT EARL OF OXFORD
AND EARL MORTIMER

Such were the notes thy once-loved poet sung,
Till Death untimely stopped his tuneful tongue.
Oh, just beheld, and lost! admired and mourned!
With softest manners, gentlest arts adorned!
Blessed in each science, blessed in every strain!
Dear to the Muse! to HARLEY dear—in vain!
    For him thou oft hast bid the world attend,
Fond to forget the statesman in the friend;
For SWIFT and him despised the farce of state,

The sober follies of the wise and great;
Dexterous, the craving, fawning crowd to quit,
And pleased to 'scape from Flattery to Wit.
  Absent or dead, still let a friend be dear,
(A sigh the absent claims, the dead a tear)
Recall those nights that closed thy toilsome days,
Still hear thy Parnell in his living lays,
Who, careless now of interest, fame, or fate,
Perhaps forgets that OXFORD e'er was great;
Or deeming meanest what we greatest call,
Beholds thee glorious only in thy fall.
  And sure, if aught below the seats divine
Can touch immortals, 'tis a soul like thine:
A soul supreme, in each hard instance tried,
Above all pain, all passion, and all pride,
The rage of power, the blast of public breath,
The lust of lucre, and the dread of death.
  In vain to deserts thy retreat is made;
The Muse attends thee to thy silent shade:
'Tis hers the brave man's latest steps to trace,
Rejudge his acts, and dignify disgrace.
When interest calls off all her sneaking train,
And all th' obliged desert, and all the vain;
She waits, or to the scaffold or the cell,
When the last lingering friend has bid farewell.
Even now she shades thy evening walk with bays,
(No hireling she, no prostitute to praise)
Even now, observant of the parting ray,
Eyes the calm sunset of thy various day,
Through fortune's cloud one truly great can see,
Nor fears to tell that MORTIMER is he.

POPE TO SWIFT
August 1723

I Find a rebuke in a late Letter of yours, that both stings and pleases me extremely. Your saying that I ought to have writ a postscript to my friend Gay's, makes me not content to write less than a whole letter, and your seeming to take his kindly gives me hopes you will look upon this as a sincere effect of friendship. Indeed as I cannot but own, the laziness with which you tax me, and with which I may equally charge you (for both of us have had and one of us hath both had and given a surfeit of writing) so I really thought you would know yourself to be so certainly entitled to my friendship, that t'was a possession, you could not imagine stood in need of any further deeds or writings to assure you of it. It is an honest Truth, there's no one living or dead of whom I think oftener, or better than yourself. I look upon you to be, (as to me) in a state between both: you have from me all the passions, and good wishes, that can attend the living; and all that respect and tender sense of loss, that we feel for the dead. Whatever you seem to think of your withdrawn and separate state at this distance, and in this absence, Dr Swift lives still in

England, in every place and company where he would choose to live; and I find him in all the conversations I keep, and in all the hearts in which I would have any share. We have never met these many years without mention of you. Besides my old acquaintances I have found that all my friends of a later date, were such as were yours before. Lord Oxford, Lord Harcourt, and Lord Harley, may look upon me as one immediately entailed upon them by you. Lord Bolingbroke is now returned, as I hope, to take me with all his other hereditary rights; and indeed, he seems grown so much a philosopher as to set his heart upon some of them as little as upon the poet you gave him. It is sure my particular ill fate, that all those I have most loved, and with whom I have most lived, must be banished. After both of you left England, my constant host was the Bishop of Rochester. Sure this is a nation that is cursedly afraid of being overrun with too much politeness, and cannot regain one great genius, but at the expense of another. I tremble for my Lord Peterborough (whom I now lodge with) he has too much wit as well as courage, to make a solid General, and if he escapes being banished by others, I fear he will banish himself. This leads me to give you some account of the manner of my life and conversation which has been infinitely more various and dissipated than when you knew me, among all sexes, parties, and professions. A glut of study and retirement in the first part of my life cast me into this, and this, I begin to see, will throw me again into study and retirement. The civilities I have met with from opposite sets of people, have hindered me from being violent or sour to any party: but at the same time the observations and experiences I cannot but have collected, have made me less fond of, and less surprised at any. I am therefore the more afflicted and the more angry, at the violences and hardships I see practised by either. The merry vein you knew me in, is sunk into a turn of reflexion, that has made the world pretty indifferent to me, and yet I have acquired a quietness of mind, which by fits improves into a certain degree of cheerfulness, enough to make me just so good-humoured as to wish that world well. My friendships are increased by new ones, yet no part of the warmth I felt for the old is diminished. Aversions I have none but to knaves, (for fools I have learned to bear with) and those I cannot be commonly civil to: for I think those are next to knaves who converse with them. The greatest man in power of this sort shall hardly make me bow to him, unless I had a personal obligation to him and that I will take care not to have. The top-pleasure of my life is one I learned from you, both how to gain and how to use the freedoms' of friendship with men much my superiors. To have pleased great men, according to Horace, is a praise; but not to have flattered them, and yet not have displeased them, is a greater. I have carefully avoided all intercourse with poets and scribblers, unless where by great chance I find a modest one. By these means I have had no quarrels with any personally, and none have been enemies, but who were also strangers to me. And as there is no great need of eclaircissements with such, whatever they writ or said I never retaliated; not only never seeming to know, but often really never knowing anything of the matter. There are very few things that give me the anxiety of a wish: the strongest I have would be to pass my days with you, and a few such as you. But Fate has dispersed them all about the world. And I find to wish it is as vain as to wish to live to see the millennium, and the Kingdom of the Just upon earth.

If I have sinned in my long silence, consider there is one, to whom you yourself have been as great a sinner. As soon as you see his hand, you will learn to do me justice, and feel in your own heart how long a man may be silent to those he truly loves and respects.

I am, dear sir,

Your ever faithful servant

A. Pope

POPE TO MARTHA BLOUNT
22 June 1724

June 22nd

Madam,—I promised you an account of Sherborne, before I had seen it, or knew what I undertook. I imagined it to be one of those fine old seats of which there are numbers scattered over England. But this is so peculiar and its situation of so uncommon a kind, that it merits a more particular description.

The house is in the form of an H. The body of it, which was built by Sir Walter Ralegh, consists of four stories, with four six-angled towers at the ends. These have been since joined to four wings, with regular stone balustrade at the top, and four towers more that finish the building. The windows and gates are of a yellow stone throughout, and one of the flat sides towards the garden has the wings of a newer architecture with beautiful Italian window-frames done by the first Earl of Bristol, which, if they were joined in the middle by a portico covering the whole building, would be a noble front. The design of such an one I have been amusing myself with drawing, but 'tis a question whether my Lord Digby will not be better amused than to execute it. The finest room is a saloon fifty feet long, and a parlour hung with a very excellent tapestry of Rubens, which was a present from the king of Spain to the Earl of Bristol in his embassy there.

This stands in a park, finely crowned with very high woods, on all the tops of the hills, which form a great amphitheatre sloping down to the house. On the garden sides the woods approach close, so that it appears there with a thick line and depth of groves on each hand, and so it shows from most parts of the park. The gardens are so irregular, that 'tis very hard to give an exact idea of 'em but by a plan. Their beauty arises from this irregularity, for not only the several parts of the garden itself make the better contrast by these sudden rises, falls, and turns of ground; but the views about it are let in, and hang over the walls in very different figures and aspects. You come first out of the house into a green walk of standard limes, with a hedge behind them that makes a colonnade, thence into a little triangular wilderness, from whose centre von see the town of Sherborne in a valley, interspersed with trees. From the corner of this you issue at once upon a high preen terrace the whole breadth of the garden, which has five more green terraces hanging under each other, without hedges, only a few pyramid yews and large round honeysuckles between them. The honeysuckles hereabouts are the largest and finest I ever saw. You'll be pleased when I tell you the quartets of the above mentioned little wilderness are filled with these, and with cherry trees of the best kinds, all within reach of the hand. At the ends of these terraces run two long walks under the side walls of the garden which communicate with the other terrace that front these opposite. Between the valley is laid level, and divided into two irregular groves of horse chestnuts, and a bowling-green in the middle of about one hundred and eighty feet. This is bounded behind with a canal, that runs quite across the groves, and also along one side is the form of a T. Behind this is a semicircular berceau, and a thicket of mixed trees, that completes the crown of the amphitheatre which is of equal extent with the bowling-green. Beyond that runs a natural river through green banks of turf, over which rises another row of terraces, the first supported by a slope wall planted with vines (so is also the wall that bounds the channel of the river.) A second and third appeared above this, but they are to be turned into a line of wilderness with wild winding walks for the convenience of passing from one side to the other in shade, the heads of whole trees will lie below the uppermost terrace of all, which completes the garden, and overlooks both that and the country. Even above the wall of this the natural ground rises, and is crowned with several venerable ruins of an old castle, with arches and broken views, of which I must say more hereafter.

When you are at the left corner of the canal, and the chestnut-groves in the bottom, you turn of a sudden under very old trees, into the deepest shade. One walk winds you up a hill of venerable wood over-arched by nature, and of a vast height, into a circular grove, on one side of which is a close high arbour, on the other a sudden open sear, that overlooks the meadows and river with a distant large prospect. Another walk under this hill winds by the river side, quite covered with high trees on both banks, overhung with ivy, where falls a natural cascade, which never-ceasing murmurs. On the opposite hanging of the bank (which is a steep of fifty feet) is placed, with a very fine fancy, a rustic seat of stone, flagged and rough, with two urns in the same rude taste upon pedestals, on each side: from whence you lose your eyes upon the glimmering of the waters under the wood, and your ears in the constant dashing of the waves. In view of this, is a bridge that crosses this stream, built in the same ruinous taste: the wall of the garden hanging over it is humoured so as to appear the ruin of another arch or two above the bridge. Hence you mount the hill over the hermit's seat (as they call it) described before, and so lo the highest terrace, again.

On the left, full behind these old trees, which makes this whole part inexpressibly awful and solemn, runs a little, old, low wall, beside a trench, covered with elder-trees and ivies; which being crossed by another bridge, brings yon to the ruins, to complete the solemnity of the scene. You first see an old tower penetrated by a large arch, and others above it, through which the whole country appears in prospect, even when you are at the top of the other ruins; for they stand very high, and the ground slopes down in all sides. These venerable broken walls, some arches almost entire of thirty or forty feet deep, some open like porticoes, with fragments of pillars, some circular or enclosed on three sides, but exposed at top, with steps which time has made of disjointed stones to climb to the highest points of the ruin. These, I say, might have a prodigious beauty, mixed with greens and parterres from part to part; and the whole heap standing as it does on a round hill, kept smooth in green turf, which makes a bold basement to show it. The open courts from building to building might be thrown into circles or octagons of grass or flowers, and even in the gaming rooms you have fine trees grown, that might be made a natural tapestry to the walls, and arch you over-head, where time has uncovered them to the sky. Little paths of earth, or sand, might be made, up the half-tumbled walls; to guide from one view to another on the higher parts; and seats placed here and there, to enjoy these views, which are more romantic than imagination can form them. I could very much wish this were done, as well as a little temple built on a neighbouring round hill that is seen from all points of the garden and is extremely pretty. It would finish some walks, and particularly be a fine termination lo the river, and be seen from the entrance into that deep scene I have described by the cascade, where it would appear as in the clouds, between the tops of some very lofty trees that form an arch before it, with, a great slope downward to the end of the said river.

What should induce my Lord D. the rather to cultivate these ruins, and do honour to them, is that they do no small honour to his family; that castle, which was very ancient, being demolished in the civil wars, after it was nobly defended by one of his ancestors in the cause of the King. I would let up at the entrance of 'em an obelisk, with an inscription of the fact: which would be a monument erected to the very ruins; as the adoring and

142

beautifying them in the manner I have been imagining, would not be unlike the Egyptian finery of bestowing ornaments and curiosity on dead bodies. The present master of this place (and I verily believe I cast engage the same for the next successors) needs not to sear the record, or shun the remembrance of the actions of his forefathers. He will not disgrace them, as most modern progeny do, by an unworthy degeneracy of principle or of practice. When I have been describing his agreeable seat, I cannot make the reflection I have often done upon contemplating the beautiful villas of other noblemen, raised upon the spoils of plundered nations, or aggrandized by the wealth of the public. I cannot ask myself the question, 'What else has this man to be liked? What else has he cultivated or improved? What good or what desirable thing appears of him, without these walls?' I dare say his goodness and benevolence extend as far as his territories; that his peasants live almost as happy and contented as himself, and that not one of his children wishes to fee this seat his own. I have not looked much about since I was here. All I can tell you of my own knowledge is, that, going to see the cathedral in the town hard by, I took notice as the finest things, of a noble monuments, and a beautiful altar-piece of architecture; but, if I had not enquired in particular, he nor his, had never told me, that both the one and the other was erected by himself. The next pretty thing that catched any eye was a neat chapel for the use of the townspeople, (who are too numerous for the cathedral). My Lord modestly told me, he was glad I liked it, because it was of his own architecture.

I hope this long letter will be some entertainment to you, I was pleased not a little in writing it; but don't let any lady from hence imagine that my head is so full of any gardens as to forget hers. The greatest proof I could give her to the contrary is, that I have spent many hours here in studying for hers, and in drawing new plans for her. I shall soon come home, and have nothing to say when we meet, having here told you all that has pleased me. But Wilton is in my way, and I depend upon that for new matter. Believe me ever yours, with a sincerity as old-fashioned, and as different from modern sincerity, as this house, this family, and these ruins, are from the court, and all its neighbourhood.

Dear Madam, Adieu.

PREFACE TO
THE WORKS OF SHAKESPEARE

It is not my design to enter into a criticism upon this author; though to do it effectually and not superficially would be the best occasion that any just writer could take to form the judgment and taste of our nation. For of all English poets Shakespeare must be confessed to be the fairest and fullest subject for criticism, and to afford the most numerous, as well as most conspicuous instances both of beauties and faults of all sorts. But this far exceeds the bounds of a preface, the business of which is only to give an account of the fate of his works, and the disadvantages under which they have been transmitted to us. We shall hereby extenuate many faults which are his, and clear him from the imputation of many which are not: a design, which though it can be no guide to future critics to do him justice in one way, will at least be sufficient to prevent their doing him an injustice in the other.

I cannot however but mention some of his principal and characteristic excellencies, for which (notwithstanding his defects) he is justly and universally elevated above all other dramatic writers. Not that this is the proper place of praising him, but because I would not omit any occasion of doing it.

If ever any author deserved the name of an *original*, it was Shakespeare. Homer himself drew not his art so immediately from the fountains of nature, it proceeded through Egyptian strainers and channels, and came to him not without some tincture of the learning or some cast of the models, of those before him. The poetry of Shakespeare was inspiration indeed: he is not so much an imitator, as an instrument, of nature; and 'tis not so just to say that he speaks from her as that she speaks through him.

His *characters* are so much nature herself, that 'tis a sort of injury to call them by so distant a name as copies of her. Those of other poets have a constant resemblance, which shows that they received them from one another, and were but multipliers of the same image: each picture like a mock-rainbow is but the reflection of a reflection. But every single character in Shakespeare is as much an individual, as those in life itself; it is as impossible to find any two alike; and such as from their relation or affinity in any respect appear most to be twins will upon comparison be found remarkably distinct. To this life and variety of character, we must add the wonderful preservation of it; which is such throughout his plays, that had all the speeches been printed without the very names of the persons, I believe one might have applied them with certainty to every speaker.

The *power* over our *passions* was never possessed in a more eminent degree, or displayed in so different instances. Yet all along, there is seen no labour, no pains to raise them; no preparation to guide our guess to the effect or be perceived to lead toward it: but the heart swells, and the tears burst out, just at the proper places. We are surprised, the moment we weep; and yet upon reflection find the passion so just, that we should be surprised if we had not wept, and wept at that very moment.

How astonishing is it again, that the passions directly opposite to these, laughter and spleen, are no less at his command! that he is not more a master of the *great* than of the *ridiculous* in human nature; of our noblest tenderness, than of our vainest foibles; of our strongest emotions, than of our idlest sensations!

Nor does he only excel in the passions: in the coolness of Reflection and Reasoning he is full as admirable. His *sentiments* are not only in general the most pertinent and judicious upon every subject; but by a talent very peculiar, something between penetration and felicity, he hits upon that particular point on which the bent of each argument turns, or the force of each motive depends. This is perfectly amazing, from a man of no education or experience in those great and public scenes of life which are usually the subject of his thoughts: so that he seems to have known the word by intuition, to have looked through human nature at one glance, and to be the only author that gives ground for a very new opinion, that the philosopher and even the man of the world may be *born*, as well as the poet.

It must be owned that with all these great excellencies, he has almost as great defects; and that as he has certainly written better, so he has perhaps written worse than any other. But I think I can in some measure account for these defects from several causes and accidents, without which it is hard to imagine that so large and so enlightened a mind could ever have been susceptible to them. That all these contingencies should unite to his disadvantage seems to me almost as singularly unlucky, as that so many various (nay contrary) talents should meet in one man, was happy and extraordinary.

It must be allowed that stage-poetry of all other is more particularly leveled to please the *populace*, and its success more immediately depending upon the *common suffrage*. One cannot therefore wonder if Shakespeare, having at his first appearance no other aim in his writings than to procure a subsistence, directed his endeavours solely to hit the taste and humour that then prevailed. The audience was generally composed of the meaner sort

144

of people; and therefore the images of life were to be drawn from those of their own rank. Accordingly we find that not our author's only but almost all the old comedies have their scene among *tradesmen* and *mechanics*: and even their historical plays strictly follow the common *old stories* or *vulgar traditions* of that kind of people. In tragedy nothing was so sure to *surprise* and cause *admiration*, as the most strange, unexpected, and consequently most unnatural, events and incidents; the most exaggerated thoughts; the most verbose and bombast expression; the most pompous rhymes, and thundering versification. In comedy nothing was so sure to *please*, as mean buffoonery, vile ribaldry, and unmannerly jests of fools and clowns. Yet even in these our author's wit buoys up, and is borne above his subject. His genius in those low parts is like some prince of a romance in the disguise of a shepherd or peasant; a certain greatness and spirit now and then break out which manifest his higher extraction and qualities.

It may be added that not only the common audience had no notion of the rules of writing, but few even of the better sort piqued themselves upon any great degree of knowledge or nicety that way; till Ben Jonson, getting possession of the stage, brought critical learning into vogue. And that this was done without difficulty may appear from those frequent lessons (and indeed almost declamations) which he was forced to prefix to his first plays, and put into the mouth of his actors, the *Grex, Chorus*, etc. to remove the prejudices, and inform the judgment of his hearers. Till then our authors had no thoughts of writing on the model of the ancients: their tragedies were only histories in dialogue; and their comedies followed the thread of any novel as they found it, no less implicitly than if it had been true history.

To judge therefore of Shakespeare by Aristotle's rules, is like trying a man by the laws of one country, who acted under those of another. He writ to the *people*; and writ at first without patronage from the better sort, and therefore without aims of pleasing them; without assistance or advice from the learned, as without the advantage of education or acquaintance among them; without that knowledge of the best models, the ancients, to inspire him with an emulation of them; in a word, without any views of reputation, and of what poets are pleased to call immortality: some or all of which have encouraged the vanity or animated the ambition, of other writers.

Yet it must be observed that when his performances had merited the protection of his Prince, and when the encouragement of the court had succeeded to that of the town; the works of his riper years are manifestly raised above those of his former. The dates of his plays sufficiently evidence that his productions improved, in proportion to the respect he had for his auditors. And I make no doubt this observation would be found true in every instance, were but editions extant from which we might learn the exact time when every piece was composed, and whether writ for the town, or the court.

Another cause (and no less strong than the former) may be deduced from our Author's being a *player*, and forming himself first upon the judgments of that body of men whereof he was a member. They have ever had a standard to themselves, upon other principles than those of Aristotle. As they live by the majority, they know no rule but that of pleasing the present humour, and complying with the wit in fashion; a consideration which brings all their judgment to a short point. Players are just such judges of what is *right* as tailors are of what is *graceful*. And in this view it will be but fair to allow, that most of our author's faults are less to be ascribed to his wrong judgment as a poet, than to his right judgment as a player.

By these men it was thought a praise to Shakespeare, that he scarce ever *blotted a line*. This they industriously propagated, as appears from what we are told by Ben Jonson in his *Discoveries*, and from the preface of Hemings and Condell to their first folio edition. But in reality (however it has prevailed) there never was a more groundless report, or to the contrary of which there are more undeniable evidences. As, the comedy of the *Merry Wives of Windsor*, which he entirely new writ; the *History of Henry VI*, which was first published under the title of the *Contention of York and Lancaster*; and that of *Henry V*, extremely improved; that of *Hamlet* enlarged to almost as much again as at first, and many others. I believe the common opinion of his want of learning proceeded from no better ground. This too might be thought a praise by some, and to this his errors have as injudiciously been ascribed by others. For 'tis certain, were it true, it could concern but a small part of them; the most are such as are not properly defects, but superfetations: and arise not from the want of learning or reading but from want of thinking or judging: or rather (to be more just to our author) from a compliance to those wants in others. As to a wrong choice of the subject, a wrong conduct of the incidents, false thoughts, forced expressions, etc. if these are not to be ascribed to the foresaid accidental reasons, they must be charged upon the poet himself, and there is no help for it. But I think the two disadvantages which I have mentioned (to be obliged to please the lowest of people, and to keep the worst of company) if the consideration be extended as far as it reasonably may, will appear sufficient to mislead and depress the greatest genius upon earth. Nay the more modesty with which such a one is endued the more he is in danger of submitting and conforming to others against his own better judgment.

But as to his *want of learning*, it may be necessary to say something more: there is certainly a vast difference between *learning* and *languages*. How far he was ignorant of the latter I cannot determine; but 'tis plain he had much reading at least, if they will not call it learning. Nor is it any great matter, if a man has knowledge, whether he has it from one language or from another. Nothing is more evident than that he had a taste of natural philosophy, mechanics, ancient and modern history, poetical learning and mythology. We find him very knowing in the customs, rites, and manners of antiquity. In *Coriolanus* and *Julius Caesar*, not only the spirit, but manners of the Romans are exactly drawn; and still a nicer distinction is shown, between the manners, of the Romans in the time of the former and of the latter. His reading in the ancient historians is no less conspicuous, in many references to particular passages: and the speeches copied from Plutarch in *Coriolanus* may, I think, as well be made an instance of his learning, as those copied from Cicero in *Catilene* of Ben Jonson's. The manners of other nations in general, the Egyptians, Venetians, French, etc. are drawn with equal propriety. Whatever object of nature, or branch of science, he either speaks of or describes; it is always with competent, if not extensive knowledge: his descriptions are still exact; all his metaphors appropriated, and remarkably drawn from the true nature and inherent qualities of each subject. When he treats of ethic or politic we may constantly observe a wonderful justness of distinction as well as extent of comprehension. No one is more a master of the poetical story, or has more frequent allusions to the various parts of it: Mr. Waller (who has been celebrated for this last particular) has not shown more learning this way than Shakespeare. We have Translations from Ovid published in his name among those poems which pass for his and for some of which we have undoubted authority (being published by himself, and dedicated to his noble Patron the Earl of Southampton): He appears also to have been conversant in Plautus, from whom he has taken the plot of one of his plays: he follows the Greek authors, and particularly Dares Phrygius, in another (although I will not pretend to say in what language he read them). The modern Italian writers of novels he was manifestly acquainted with; and we may conclude him to be no less conversant with the ancients of his own country, from the use he has made of Chaucer in *Troilus and Cressida*, and in the *Two Noble Kinsmen*, if that play be his, as there goes a tradition it was (and indeed it has little resemblance of Fletcher, and more of our Author than some of those which have been received as genuine).

I am inclined to think, this opinion proceeded originally from the zeal of the partisans of our author and Ben Jonson; as they endeavoured to exalt one at the expense of the other. It is ever the nature of parties to be in extremes; and nothing is so probable, as that because Ben Jonson had much the most learning, it was said on the one hand that Shakespeare had none at all; and because Shakespeare had much the most wit and fancy, it was retorted on the other, that Jonson wanted both. Because Shakespeare borrowed nothing, it was said that Ben Jonson borrowed everything. Because Jonson did not write extempore, he was reproached with being a year about every piece; and because Shakespeare wrote with ease and rapidity, they cried, he never once made a blot. Nay the spirit of opposition ran so high, that whatever those of the one side objected to the other, was taken at the rebound, and turned into praises; as injudiciously as their antagonists before had made them objections.

Poets are always afraid of envy; but sure they have as much reason to be afraid of admiration. They are the Scylla and Charybdis of authors; those who escape one often fall by the other. *Pessimum genus inimicorum Laudantes*, says Tacitus: and Virgil desires to wear a charm against those who praise a poet without rule or reason.

> ——*Si ultra placitum laudarit, baccare frontem*
> *Cingito, ne Vati noceat*——

But however this contention might be carried on by the partisans on either side, I cannot help thinking those two great poets were good friends, and lived on amicable terms and in offices of society with each other. It is an acknowledged fact, that Ben Jonson was introduced upon the stage, and his first works encouraged, by Shakespeare. And after his death, that author writes *To the memory of his beloved Mr. William Shakespeare*, which shows as if the friendship had continued through life. I cannot for my own part find anything *invidious* or *sparing* in those verses, but wonder Mr. Dryden was of that opinion. He exalts him not only above his contemporaries, but above Chaucer and Spenser, whom he will not allow to be great enough to be ranked with him; and challenges the names of Sophocles, Euripides, and Aeschylus, nay all Greece and Rome at once, to equal him. And (which is very particular) expressly vindicates him from the imputation of wanting *art*, not enduring that all his excellencies should be attributed to *nature*. It is remarkable too, that the praise he gives him in his *Discoveries* seems to proceed from a *personal kindness*; he tells us that he loved the man as well as honoured his memory; celebrates the honesty, openness, and frankness of his temper; and only distinguishes, as he reasonably ought, between the real merit of the author, and the silly and derogatory applauses of the players. Ben Jonson might indeed be sparing in his commendations (though certainly he is not so in this instance) partly from his own nature and partly from judgment. For men of judgment think they do any man more service in praising him justly than lavishly. I say, I would fain believe they were friends, though the violence and ill-breeding of their followers and flatterers were enough to give rise to the contrary report. I would hope that it may be with *parties*, both in wit and state, as with those monsters described by the poets; and that their *heads* at least may have something humane though their *bodies* and *tails* are wild beasts and serpents.

As I believe that what I have mentioned gave rise to the opinions of Shakespeare's want of learning; so what has continued it down to us may have been the blunders and illiteracies of the first publishers of his works. In these editions their ignorance shines almost in every page; nothing is more common than *Actus tertia. Exit Omnes. Enter three Witches solus.* Their French is as bad as their Latin, both in construction and spelling; their very Welsh is false. Nothing is more likely than that those palpable blunders of Hector's quoting Aristotle, with others of that gross kind, sprung from the same root. It not being at all credible that these could be the errors of any man who had the least tincture of a school, or the least conversation with such as had. Ben Jonson (whom they will not think partial to him) allows him at least to have had *some Latin*, which is utterly inconsistent with mistakes like these. Nay the constant blunders in proper names of persons and places are such as must have proceeded from a man who had not so much as read any history in any language: so could not be Shakespeare's.

I shall now lay before the reader some of those almost innumerable errors, which have risen from one source, the ignorance of the players, both as his actors and as his editors. When the nature and kinds of these are enumerated and considered I dare to say that not Shakespeare only but Aristotle or Cicero, had their works undergone the same fate, might have appeared to want sense as well as learning.

It is not certain that any one of his plays was published by himself. During the time of his employment in the theatre, several of his pieces were printed separately in quarto. What makes me think that most of these were not published by him, is the excessive carelessness of the press: every page is so scandalously false spelled, and almost all the learned or unusual words so intolerably mangled, that it's plain there either was no corrector to the press at all or one totally illiterate. If any were supervised by himself I should fancy the two parts of *Henry IV*, and *Midsummer-Night's Dream* might have been so: because I find no other printed with any exactness; and (contrary to rest) there is very little variation in all the subsequent editions of them. There are extant two Prefaces, to the first quarto edition of *Troilus and Cressida* in 1609, and to that of *Othello*; by which it appears that the first was published without his knowledge or consent and even before it was acted, so late as seven or eight years before he died; and that the latter was not printed till after his death. The whole number of genuine plays which we have been able to find printed in his life-time amounts but to eleven. And of some of these we meet with two or more editions by different printers each of which has whole heaps of trash different from the other: which I should fancy was occasioned by their being taken from different copies belonging to different playhouses.

The folio edition (in which all the plays we now receive as his were first collected) was published by two players, Hemings and Condell, in 1623, seven years after his decease. They declare that all the other editions were stolen and surreptitious, and affirm theirs to be purged from the errors of the former. This is true as to the literal errors and no other, for in all respects else it is far worse than the quartos.

First, because the additions of trifling and bombast passages are in this edition far more numerous. For whatever had been added since those quartos by the actors, or had stolen from their mouths into the written parts, were from thence conveyed into the printed text and all stand charged upon the author. He himself complained of this usage in *Hamlet*, where he wishes that *Those who play the clowns would speak no more than is set down for them* (Act. 3. Sc. 4.) But as proof that he could not escape it, in the old editions of *Romeo and Juliet* there is no hint of a great number of the mean conceits and ribaldries now to be found there. In others the low scenes of mobs, plebeians and clowns are vastly shorter than at present. And I have seen one in particular (which seems to have belonged to the playhouse, by having the parts divided with lines and the Actors' names in the margin) where several of those very passages were added in a written hand, which are since to be found in the folio.

In the next place, a number of beautiful passages which are extant in the first single editions, are omitted in this: as it seems, without any other reason than their willingness to shorten some scenes: these men (as it was said of Procrustes) either lopping, or stretching an author, to make him just fit for their stage.

This edition is said to be printed from the *original copies*; I believe they meant those which had lain ever since the author's days in the playhouse, and had from time to time been cut, or added to, arbitrarily. It appears that this edition, as well as the quartos, was printed (at least partly) from no better copies than the *prompter's book*, or *piecemeal parts* written out for the use of the actors: for in some places their very names are through carelessness set down instead of the *Personae Dramatis*: and in others the notes of direction to the *property-men* for their *moveables*, and to the *players* for their *entries*, are inserted into the Text Through the ignorance of the transcribers.

The plays not having been before so much as distinguished by *acts* and *scenes*, they are in this edition divided according as they played them; often where there is no pause in the action, or where they thought fit to make a breach in it, for the sake of music, masques, or monsters.

Sometimes the scenes are transposed and shuffled backward and forward, a thing which could no otherwise happen, but by their being taken from separate and piecemeal-written parts.

Many verses are omitted entirely and others transposed, from whence invincible obscurities have arisen, past the guess of any Commentator to clear up, but just where the accidental glimpse of an old edition enlightens us.

Some Characters were confounded and mixed, or two put into one, for want of a competent number of actors. Thus in the quarto edition of *Midsummer-Night's Dream*, Act. 5, Shakespeare introduces a kind of Master of Revels called Philostratus, all whose part is given to another character (that of Aegeus) in the subsequent editions; so also in *Hamlet* and *King Lear*. This too makes it probable that the Prompter's Books were what they called the Original Copies.

From liberties of this kind, many speeches also were put into the mouths of wrong persons, where the author now seems chargeable with making them speak out of character; or sometimes perhaps for no better reason, than that a governing player, to have the mouthing of some favourite speech himself, would snatch it from the unworthy lips of an underling.

Prose from verse they did not know, and they accordingly printed one for the other throughout the volume.

Having been forced to say so much of the players, I think I ought in justice to remark that the judgment, as well as condition, of that class of people was then far inferior to what it is in our days. As then the best Playhouses were inns and taverns (the *Globe*, the *Hope*, the *Red Bull*, the *Fortune*, etc.) so the top of the profession were then mere players, not gentlemen of the stage. They were led into the buttery by the steward, not placed at the lord's table or lady's toilette: and consequently were entirely deprived of those advantages they now enjoy, in the familiar conversation of our nobility, and an intimacy (not to say dearness) with people of the first condition.

From what has been said, there can be no question but had Shakespeare published his works himself (especially in his latter time, and after his retreat from the stage) we should not only be certain which are genuine; but should find in those that are, the errors lessened by some thousands. If I may judge from all the distinguishing marks of his style, and his manner of thinking and writing, I make no doubt to declare that those wretched plays, *Pericles, Locrine, Sir John Oldcastle, Yorkshire Tragedy, Lord Cromwell, The Puritan,* and *London Prodigal* cannot be admitted as his. And I should conjecture of some of the others (particularly *Love's Labour Lost, The Winter's Tale,* and *Titus Andronicus*) that only some characters, single scenes, or perhaps a few particular passages were of his hand. It is very probable what occasioned some plays to be supposed Shakespeare's was only this; that they were pieces produced by unknown authors, or fitted up for the theatre while it was under his administration; and no owner claiming them they were adjudged to him, as they give strays to the lord of the manor. A mistake which (one may also observe) it was not for the interest of the house to remove. Yet the players themselves, Hemings and Condell, afterwards did Shakespeare the justice to reject those eight plays in their edition; though they were then printed in his name, in everybody's hands, and acted with some applause (as we learn from what Ben Jonson says of *Pericles* in his Ode on the *New Inn.*) That *Titus Andronicus* is one of this class I am the rather induced to believe by finding the same author openly express his contempt of it in the Induction to *Bartholomew Fair,* in the year 1614, when Shakespeare was yet living. And there is no better authority for these latter sort than for the former, which were equally published in his lifetime.

If we give in to this opinion, how many low and vicious parts and passages might no longer reflect upon this great genius, but appear unworthily charged upon him? And even in those which are really his how many faults may have been unjustly laid to his account from arbitrary additions, expunctions, transposition of scenes and lines, confusion of characters and persons, wrong application of speeches, corruptions of innumerable passages by the ignorance, and wrong corrections of 'em again by the impertinence, of his first editors? From one or other of these considerations, I am verily persuaded, that the greatest and the grossest part of what are thought his errors would vanish, and leave his character in a light very different from that disadvantageous one in which it now appears to us.

This is the state in which Shakespeare's writings lie at present; for since the above-mentioned folio edition, all the rest have implicitly followed it, without having recourse to any of the former, or ever making the comparison between them. It is impossible to repair the injuries already done him; too much time has elapsed, and the materials are too few. In what I have done I have rather given a proof of my willingness and desire, than of my ability to do him justice. I have discharged the dull duty of an editor, to my best judgment, with more labour than I expect thanks, with a religious abhorrence of all innovation, and without any indulgence to my private sense or conjecture. The method taken in this edition will show itself. The various readings are fairly put in the margin so that everyone may compare 'em; and those I have preferred into the Text are constantly *ex fide Codicum,* upon authority. The alterations or additions which Shakespeare himself made are taken notice of as they occur. Some suspected passages which are excessively bad (and which seem interpolations by being so inserted that one can entirely omit them without any chasm or deficience in the context), are degraded to the bottom of the page; with an asterisk referring to the places of their insertion. The scenes are marked so distinctly that every removal of place is specified; which is more necessary in this author

150

than any other since he shifts them more frequently: and sometimes without attending to this particular, the reader would have met with obscurities. The more obsolete or unusual words are explained. Some of the most shining passages are distinguished by comma's in the margin; and where the beauty lay not in particulars but in the whole, a star is prefixed to the scene. This seems to me a shorter and less ostentatious method of performing the better half of criticism (namely the pointing out an author's excellencies) than to fill a whole paper with citations of fine passages, with *general applauses*, or *empty exclamations* at the tail of them. There is also subjoined a catalogue of those first editions by which the greater part of the various readings and of the corrected passages are authorised (most of which are such as carry their own evidence along with them). These editions now hold the place of originals, and are the only materials left to repair the deficiencies or restore the corrupted sense of the author: I can only wish that the greater number of them (if a greater were ever published) may yet be found, by a search more successful than mine, for the better accomplishment of this end.

I will conclude by saying of Shakespeare that, with all his faults, and with all the irregularity of his *drama*, one may look upon his works, in comparison of those that are more finished and regular, as upon an ancient majestic piece of Gothic architecture compared with a neat modern building: the latter is more elegant and glaring, but the former is more strong and solemn. It must be allowed, that in one of these there are materials enough to make many of the other. It has much the greater variety, and much the nobler apartments; though we are often conducted to them by dark, odd, and uncouth passages. Nor does the whole fail to strike us with greater reverence, though many of the parts are childish, ill-placed, and unequal to its grandeur.

ΠΕΡΙ ΒΑΘΟΥΣ:
OR,
MARTINUS SCRIBLERUS
HIS
TREATISE
OF THE
ART OF SINKING
IN
POETRY

CONTENTS
TO THE
BATHOS

That the Bathos, *or* Profound, *is the natural Taste of Man, and in particular of the present Age.*
The Necessity of the Bathos, *physically considered.*
That there is an Art of the Bathos, *or* Profound.
Of the true Genius for the Profound, *and by what it is constituted.*
Of the several Kinds of Geniuses in the Profound, *and the Marks and Characters of each.*
Of the Profound, *when it consists in the Thought.*
Of the Profound, *consisting in the Circumstances, and of Amplification and Paraphrase in general.*
Of Imitation, and the manner of imitating.

CHAP. I.

It hath been long (my dear countrymen) the subject of my concern and surprise, that whereas numberless poets, critics, and orators, have compiled and digested the art of *ancient poesy*, there hath not risen among us one person so public-spirited, as to perform the like for the *modern*. Although it is universally known that our every way industrious moderns, both in the weight of their *writings*, and in the velocity of their *judgments*, do so infinitely excel the said ancients.

NEVERTHELESS, too true it is, that while a plain and direct road is paved to their ὕφος, or *sublime*; no track has been yet chalked out to arrive at our βάθος, or *profound*. The Latins, as they came between the Greeks and us, make use of the word *Altitudo*, which implies equally *height* and *depth*. Wherefore considering with no small grief, how many promising geniuses of this age are wandering (as I may say) in the dark without a guide, I have undertaken this arduous but necessary task, to lead them as it were by the hand, and step by step, the gentle down-hill way to the *Bathos*; the bottom, the end, the central point, the *non plus ultra*, of true modern poesy!

When I consider (my dear countrymen) the extent, fertility, and populousness of our *lowlands* of *Parnassus*, the flourishing state of our trade, and the plenty of our manufacture; there are two reflections, which administer great occasion of surprise; the one, that all dignities and honours should be bestowed upon the exceeding few meagre inhabitants of the top of the mountain; the other, that our own nation should have arrived to that pitch of greatness it now possesses, without any regular *system of laws*. As to the first, it is with great pleasure I have observed of late the gradual decay of delicacy and refinement among mankind, who are become too reasonable to require, that we should labour with infinite pains to come up to the taste of these mountaineers, when they without any may condescend to ours. But as we have now an *unquestionable majority* on our side, I doubt not but we shall shortly be able to level the Highlanders, and procure a farther vent for our own product, which is already so much relished, encouraged, and rewarded by the nobility and gentry of Great Britain.

THEREFORE, to supply our former defect, I purpose to collect the scattered rules of our art into regular institutes, from the example and practice of the deep geniuses of our nation; imitating herein my predecessors, the Master of Alexander, and the secretary of the renowned Zenobia. And in this my undertaking I am the more animated, as I expect more success than has attended even those great critics; since their laws (though they might be good) have ever been slackly executed, and their precepts (however strict) obeyed only by fits, and by a very small number.

AT the same time I intend to do justice upon our neighbours, inhabitants of the *upper Parnassus*; who taking advantage of the rising ground, are perpetually throwing down rubbish, dirt, and stones upon us, never suffering us to live in peace. These men, while they enjoy the crystal stream of Helicon, envy us our common water, which, (thank our stars) though it is somewhat muddy, flows in much greater abundance. Nor is this the greatest injustice, that we have to complain of; for, though it is evident that we never made the least *attempt* or *inroad* into *their* territories, but lived contented in our native fens; they have often not only committed *petty larcenies* upon our borders, but driven the country, and carried off at once *whole cartloads* of our *manufacture*; to reclaim some of which stolen goods is part of the design of this treatise.

FOR we shall see, in the course of this work, that our greatest adversaries have sometimes descended toward us; and doubtless might now and then have arrived at the *Bathos* itself, had it not been for that mistaken opinion they all entertained, that the *rules* of the *ancients* were *equally necessary* to the *moderns*, than which there cannot be a more grievous error, as will be amply proved in the following discourse.

AND indeed when any of these have gone so far, as by the light of their own genius to attempt *new models*, it is wonderful to observe, how nearly they have approached us in those particular pieces; though in their others they differed *toto coelo* from us.

CHAP. II.

That the Bathos, *or* Profound, *is the natural Taste of Man, and in particular of the present Age.*

The taste of the *Bathos* is implanted by Nature itself in the soul of man; till, perverted by custom or example he is taught, or rather compelled, to relish the *Sublime*. Accordingly, we see the unprejudiced minds of children delight only in such productions, and if such images, as our true modern writers set before them. I have observed how fast the general taste is returning to this first simplicity and innocence; and if the intent of all poetry be to divert and instruct, certainly that kind, which diverts and instructs the greatest number, is to be preferred. Let us look round among the admirers of poetry, we shall find those, who have a taste of the *Sublime*, to be very few: but the *Profound* strikes universally, and is adapted to every capacity. It is a fruitless undertaking to write for men of a nice and foppish *gusto*, whom, after all, it is almost impossible to please; and it is still more chimerical to write for *posterity*, of whose taste we cannot make any judgment, and whose applause we can never enjoy. It must be confessed, our wise authors have a present end,

Et prodesse volunt, & delectare Poetae.

Their true design is *profit* or *gain*; in order to acquire which, it is necessary to procure applause by administering *pleasure* to the reader. From whence it follows demonstrably, that their productions must be suited to the *present state*; and I cannot but congratulate our age on this peculiar felicity, that though we have made indeed great progress in all other branches of luxury, we are not yet debauched with any *high relish* in poetry, but are in this one taste, less *nice* than our ancestors. If an art is to be estimated by its success, I appeal to experience, whether there have not been, in proportion to their number, as many starving good poets as bad ones?

NEVERTHELESS, in making *gain* the principal end of our art, far be it from me to exclude any great *geniuses* of *rank* or *fortune* from diverting themselves this way. They ought to be praised no less than those princes who pass their vacant hours in some ingenious mechanical or manual art. And to such as these it would be ingratitude not to own, that our art has been often infinitely indebted.

CHAP. III.

The Necessity of the Bathos, Physically considered.

Farthermore, it were great cruelty and injustice, if all such authors as cannot write in the other way, were prohibited from writing at all. Against this I draw an argument from what seems to me an undoubted physical maxim, that poetry is a *natural* or *morbid secretion from the brain.* As I would not suddenly stop a cold in the head, or dry up my neighbour's issue, I would as little hinder him from necessary writing. It may be affirmed with great truth, that there is hardly any human creature past childhood, but at one time or other has had some poetical evacuation, and no question was much the better for it in his health; so true is the saying, *Nascimur poetae*: therefore is the desire o writing properly termed *Pruritus*, the *titillation of the generative faculty of the brain*; and the person is said to *conceive*; now, such as conceive, must *bring forth*. I have known a man thoughtful, melancholy, and raving for divers days, but forthwith grow wonderfully easy, lightsome and cheerful, upon a discharge of the peccant humour in exceeding purulent metre. Nor can I question, but abundance of untimely deaths are occasioned for want of this laudable vent of unruly passions: yea, perhaps, in poor wretches (which is very lamentable) for mere want of pen, ink, and paper! From hence it follows, that a suppression of the very worst poetry is of dangerous consequence to the state: we find by experience, that the same humours which vent themselves in summer in *ballads* and *sonnets* are condensed by the winter's cold into *pamphlets* and *speeches* for and against the *ministry*: nay, I know not, but many times a piece of poetry may be the most innocent composition of a *minister himself.*

It is therefore manifest, that *mediocrity* ought to be allowed, yea, indulge, to the good subjects of England. Nor can I conceive how the world has swallowed the contrary as a maxim, upon the single authority of Horace? Why should the *golden mean*, and quintessence of all virtues, be deemed so offensive in this art? Or *coolness* or *mediocrity* be so amiable a quality in a man, and so detestable in a poet?

HOWEVER, far be it from me to compare these writers with those *great spirits*, who are born with a *vivacité de pesanteur*, or (as an English author calls it) an *alacrity of sinking*; and who by *strength of nature* alone can excel. All I mean, is, to evince the *necessity* of rules to these lesser geniuses, as well as the *usefulness* of them to the greater.

CHAP. IV.

That there is an Art of the Bathos, or Profound

We come Dow to prove; that there is an *Art of Sinking* in poetry. Is there not an architecture of vaults and cellars, as well as of lofty domes and pyramids? Is there not as much skill and labour in making *dykes*, as in raising *mounts*? Is there not an art of *diving* as well as of *flying*? And will any sober practitioner affirm, that a diving engine is not of singular use in making him long-winded, assisting his descent, and furnishing him with more ingenious means of keeping under water?

If we search the authors of antiquity, we shall find as few to have been distinguished in the *true Profound*, as in the *true Sublime*. And the very same thing (as it appears from Longinus) had been imagined of that, as now of this; namely, that it was entirely the gift of nature. I grant, that to excel in the *Bathos* a genius is requisite; yet the rules of art must be allowed so far useful, as to add weight, or, as I may say, hang on lead, to facilitate and enforce our descent, to guide us to the most advantageous declivities, and habituate our imagination to a depth of thinking. Many there are that can full, but few can arrive at the felicity of falling gracefully; much more for a man, who is among the lowest of the creation, at the very bottom of the atmosphere; to descend *beneath himself*, is not so easy a task, unless he calls in art to his assistance. It is with the *Bathos* as with small beer, which is indeed vapid and insipid, if left at large and let abroad; but being by our rules confined, and well stopped, nothing grows so frothy, pert, and bouncing.

THE *Sublime* of nature is the sky, the sun, moon, stars, etc. The *Profound* of nature is gold, pearls, precious stones, and the treasures of the deep, which are inestimable as unknown. But all that lies between these, as corn, flowers, fruits, animals, and things for the mere use of man, are of mean price, and so common as not to be greatly esteemed by the curious: it being certain, that anything, of which we know the true use, cannot be invaluable: which affords a solution, why *common sense* hath either been totally despised, or held in small repute, by the greatest modern critics and authors.

CHAP. V.

Of the true Genius for the Profound, *and by what it is constituted*

And I will venture to lay it down, as the first maxim, and cornerstone of this our art, that whoever would excel therein must studiously avoid, detest, and turn his head from all the ideas, ways, and workings of that pestilent foe to wit, and destroyer of fine figures, which is known by the name of *common sense*. His business must be to contract the true *goût de travers*; and to acquire a most *happy, uncommon, unaccountable way of thinking.*

HE is to consider himself as a *grotesque* painter, whose works would be spoiled by an imitation of nature, or uniformity of design. He is to mingle bits of the most various, or discordant kinds, landscape, history, portraits, animals; and connect them with a great deal, of *flourishing*, by *heads* or *tails*, as it shall please his imagination, and contribute to his principal end; which is, to glare by strong oppositions of colours, and surprise by contrariety of images.

Serpentes avibus geminentur, tigribus agni.   *Horace.*

His design ought to be like a labyrinth, out of which nobody can get clear but himself. And since the great art of all poetry is to mix truth with fiction, in order to join the credible with the surprising, our author shall produce the *credible*, by painting nature in her *lowest simplicity*; and the *surprising*, by contradicting *common opinion*. In the very same *manner* he will affect the marvellous; he will draw Achilles with the patience of Job; a prince talking like a jack-pudding; a maid of honour selling bargains; a footman speaking like a philosopher; and a fine gentleman like a scholar. Whoever is conversant in *modern plays*, may make a most noble collection of this kind, and at the same time form a complete body of *modern ethics and morality.*

NOTHING seemed more plain to our great authors, than that the world had long been weary of natural things. How much the contrary are formed to please, is evident from the universal applause daily given to the admirable entertainments of harlequins and magicians on our stage. When an audience behold a coach turned into a wheelbarrow, a conjurer into an old woman, or a man's head where his heels should be, how are they struck with transport and delight? Which can only be imputed to this cause, that each object is changed into that which hath been suggested to them by their own low ideas before.

HE ought therefore to render himself master of this happy and anti-natural way of thinking, to such a degree, as to be able, on the appearance of any object, to furnish his imagination with ideas infinitely below it. And his eyes should be like unto the wrong end of a perspective glass, by which all the objects of nature are lessened.

FOR example, when a true genius looks upon the *sky*, he immediately catches the idea of a piece of *blue lutestring*, or a *child's mantle*.

> *The skies, whose spreading volumes scarce have room,*
> *Spun thin, and wove in nature's finest loom,*
> *The* new-born *world in their* soft lap *embraced,*
> *And all around their* starry mantle *cast.*
>
> *Pr. Arthur*, p. 41, 42.

IF he looks upon a *tempest*, he shall have an image of a tumbled bed, and describe a succeeding calm in this manner,

> *The ocean, joyed to see the tempest fled,*
> New lays *his waves, and* smooths his ruffled bed.
>
> p. 14.

The *triumphs* and *acclamations* of the *angels* at the creation of the universe present to his imagination the *rejoicings on the Lord Mayor's day*; and he beholds those glorious beings celebrating the creator, by huzzaing, making illuminations, and flinging squibs, crackers, and sky-rockets.

> *Glorious* illuminations, *made on high*
> *By all the stars and planets of the sky,*
> *In* just degrees, *and* shining order *placed,*
> *Spectators charmed, and the* blessed dwellings *graced.*
> *Through all th' enlightened air swift* fireworks *flew,*
> *Which with repeated* shouts *glad cherubs* threw,
> *Comets* ascended with their sweeping train,
> *Then fell in* starry showers *and* glittering rain.
> *In air ten thousand meteors* blazing hung,
> *Which from th' eternal* battlements *were* flung.
>
> page 50.

IF a man, who is violently fond of *wit*, will sacrifice to that passion his Trend or his God, would it no; be a shame, if he who is smit with the love of the *Bathos*, should not sacrifice to it all other transitory regards? You shall hear a zealous protestant deacon

156

invoke a saint, and modestly beseech her to do more for us than providence and destiny, for the sake of three or four weighty lines.

> *Look down, blessed saint, with pity then look down,*
> *Shed on this land thy kinder influence,*
> *And guide us through the mists of Providence,*
> *In which we stray.—*
>
> A. Philips. On the Death of Queen Mary.

Neither will he, if a goodly simile come in his way, scruple affirm himself an eye-witness of things never yet beheld by man, or never in existence; as thus,

> *Thus have I* seen, *in* Araby *the blessed,*
> *A* Phoenix *couched upon her funeral nest.*
>
> Anon.

BUT to convince you that nothing is so great which a marvellous genius, prompted by this laudable zeal, is not able to lessen; hear how the most sublime of all being is represented in the following images.

First he is a PAINTER.

> *Sometimes the Lord of Nature, in the air,*
> Spreads forth *his clouds, his* sable canvas, *where*
> *His* pencil, dipped *in heavenly* colour *bright,*
> Paints *his fair rainbow, charming to the sight.*
>
> Blackmore, Job, opt. edit. duod. 1716, p. 172.

Now he is a CHEMIST.

> *Th'* Almighty Chemist *does his work prepare,*
> *Pours down his* waters *on the thirsty plain,*
> Digests *his lightning, and* distils *his rain.*
>
> Blackmore, Ps. 104, p. 263.

Now he is a WRESTLER.

> *Me in his* griping arms *th' Eternal took,*
> *And with such* mighty force *my* body shook,
> *That the* strong grasp *my members* sorely bruised,
> Broke *all my* bones, *and all my* sinews loosed.
>
> Pg. 75.

Now a RECRUITING OFFICER.

> *For clouds the sunbeams* levy fresh supplies,
> *And raise* recruits *of vapours, which arise*
> Drawn *from the seas, to* muster *in the skies.*

Pg. 170.

Now a peaceable GUARANTEE.

In leagues *of* peace *the* neighbours *did agree,*
And to maintain them God was guarantee.

p. 70.

Then he is an ATTORNEY.

Job, *as a vile offender,* God indicts,
And terrible decrees against me writes.—
God *will not be my* advocate,
My cause *to* manage *or* debate.

p. 61.

In the following lines he is a GOLDBEATER.

Who the rich metal beats, *and then, with care,*
Unfolds *the* golden leaves, *to* gild *the fields of air.*

p. 181.

Then a FULLER.

—th' exhaling reeks that secret rise,
Borne on rebounding sunbeams through the skies;
Are thickened, wrought, *and* whitened, *till they grow*
A heavenly fleece.—

p. 180.

A MERCER or PACKER.

Didst thou one end *of air's wide* curtain *hold,*
And help the bales *of* ether *to* unfold;
Say, which cerulean pile *was by thy hand* unrolled?

p. 174.

A BUTLER.

He measures all the drops *with* wondrous skill,
Which the black clouds, his floating bottles, fill.

p. 131.

And a BAKER.

God in the wilderness his table spread,
And in his airy ovens baked their bread.

Blackmore, Song of *Moses,* p. 218.

158

CHAP. VI.

Of the several Kinds of Geniuses in the Profound, *and the Marks and Characters of each*

I DOUBT not but the reader, by this *cloud* of examples, begins to be convinced of the truth of our assertion, that the *Bathos* is an *art*, and that the genius of no mortal whatever, following the mere ideas of nature, and unassisted with an habitual, nay laborious peculiarity of thinking, could arrive at images so wonderfully low and unaccountable. The great author, from whose treasury we have drawn all these instances (the father of the *Bathos*, and indeed the Homer of it) has like that immortal Greek, confined his labours to the greater poetry, and thereby left room for others to acquire a due share of praise in inferior kinds. Many painters, who could never hit a nose or an eye, have with felicity copied a smallpox, .or been admirable at a toad or a red herring: and seldom are we without *geniuses* for *still-life*, which they can work up and stiffen with incredible accuracy.

AN universal genius rises not in an age; but when he rises, armies rise in him! he pours forth five or six epic poems with greater facility than five or six pages can be produced by an elaborate and servile copier after nature or the ancients. It is affirmed by Quintilian, that the same genius which made Germanicus so great a general, would with equal application have made him an excellent heroic poet. In like manner, reasoning from the affinity there appears between arts and sciences, I doubt not, but an active catcher of butterflies, a careful and fanciful pattern-drawer, an industrious collector of shells, a laborious and tuneful bagpiper, or a diligent breeder of tame rabbits, might severally excel in their respective parts of the *Bathos*.

I SHALL range these confined and less copious geniuses under proper classes, and (the better to give their pictures to the reader) under the names of animals of some sort or other; whereby he will be enabled, at the first sight of such as shall daily come forth, to know to what *kind* to refer, and with what *authors* to compare them.

1. THE *Flying Fishes*; these are writers who now and then *rise* upon their *fins*, and fly out of the *profound*; but their wings are soon *dry*, and they drop down to the *bottom*. G.S. A.H. C.G.

2. THE *Swallows* are authors, that are eternally *skimming* and *fluttering* up and down, but all their agility is employed to *catch flies*. L.T. W.P. Lord *R*.

3. THE *Ostriches* are such, whose heaviness rarely permits them to raise themselves from the ground; their wings are of no use to lift them up, and their motion is between *flying* and *walking*; but then they *run* very fast. D.F. L.E. The Hon. *E.H.*

4. THE *Parrots* are they that repeat *another's words* in such a *hoarse, odd* voice, as makes them seem *their own. W.B. W.H. C.C.* The Reverend *D.D.*

5. THE *Didappers* are authors, that keep themselves long *out of sight*, under water, and *come up* now and then, where you *least expected* them. *L.W.—D.* Esq; The Hon. Sir *W.Y.*

6. THE *Porpoises* are unwieldy and big; they put all their numbers into a great *turmoil* and *tempest*, but whenever they appear in *plain light* (which is seldom) they are only *shapeless* and *ugly monsters. J.D. C.G. J.O.*

7. THE *Frogs* are such, as can neither *walk* nor *fly*, but can *leap* and *bound* to admiration; they live generally in the *bottom of a ditch*, and make a *great noise*, whenever they thrust their *heads above water*. E.W. J.M. Esq. T.D. Gent.

8. THE *Eels* are obscure authors, that wrap themselves up in their *own mud*, but are mighty *nimble* and *pert*. L.W. L.T. P.M. General C.

9. THE *Tortoises* are *slow* and *chill*, and like *pastoral writers*, delight much in *gardens*: they have for the most part a *fine embroidered shell*, and underneath it *a heavy lump*. A.P. W.B. L.E. The Rt. Hon. E. of S.

THESE are the chief characteristics of the *Bathos*, and in each of these kinds we have the comfort to be blessed with sundry and manifold choice spirits in this our island.

CHAP. VII.

Of the Profound, *when it consists in the Thought.*

We have already laid down the principles, upon which our author is to proceed, and the manner of forming his thought by familiarizing his mind to the lowest objects; to which it may be added, that *vulgar* conversation will greatly contribute. There is no question, but the *garret* or the *printer's boy* may often be discerned in the compositions made in such scenes and company; and much of Mr. Curll himself has been insensibly infused into the works of his learned writers.

The physician, by the study and inspection of urine and ordure, approves himself in the science; and in like sort, should our author accustom and exercise his imagination upon the dregs of nature.

This will render his thoughts truly and fundamentally low, and carry him many fathoms beyond mediocrity. For, certain it is (though some lukewarm heads imagine they may be safe by temporizing between the extremes) that where there is not a triticalness or mediocrity in the *thought*, it can never be sunk into the genuine and perfect *Bathos* by the most elaborate low *expression*. It can, at most, be only carefully obscured, or metaphorically debased. But, it is the *thought* alone that strikes, and gives the whole that spirit, which we admire and stare at. For instance, in that ingenious piece on a lady's drinking the Bath waters.

> *She drinks! She drinks! Behold the matchless dame!*
> *To her 'tis water, but to us 'tis flame:*
> *Thus fire is water, water fire, by turns,*
> *And the same stream at once both cools and burns.*

Anon.

What can be more easy and unaffected, than the *diction* of these verses? It is the turn of *thought* alone, and the variety of imagination, that charm and surprise us. And when the same lady goes into the bath, the thought (as in justice it ought) goes still deeper.

> Venus *beheld her, 'midst her crowd of slaves,*
> *And thought* herself *just risen from the waves.*

Idem.

HOW much out of the way of common sense is this reflection of Venus, not knowing herself from the lady?

OF the same nature is that noble mistake of a frighted stag in a full chase, of which the poet,

> *Hears his own feet, and thinks they sound like more;*
> *And fears the hind-feet will o'ertake the fore.*

SO astonishing as these are, they yield to the following, which is *profundity* itself.

> *None but* himself *can be his* parallel.

Theobald, Double Distress

unless it may seem borrowed from the thought of that *master of a show* in Smithfield, who writ in large letters, over the picture of his elephant,

This is the greatest elephant in the world, except himself.

HOWEVER, our next instance is certainly an original: speaking of a beautiful infant,

> *So fair thou art, that if great* Cupid *be*
> *A child, as poets say, sure* thou *art* he.
> *Fair* Venus *would mistake thee for her own,*
> *Did not thy eyes proclaim thee* not *her son.*
> *There all the lightnings of thy* mother*'s shine,*
> *And with a fatal brightness* kill *in* thine.

FIRST he is Cupid, then he is not Cupid; first Venus would mistake him, then she would not mistake him; next his eyes are his mother's; and lastly they are not his mother's, but his own.

ANOTHER author, describing a poet that shines forth amid a circle of critics,

> *Thus* Phoebus *through the zodiac takes hit wa7,*
> *And amid* monsters *rises into day.*

WHAT a peculiarity is here of invention? The author's pencil, like the wand of Circe, turns all into *monsters* at a stroke. A great genius takes things in the lump, without stopping at minute considerations. In vain might the Ram, the Bull, the Goat, the Lion, the Crab, the Scorpion, the Fishes, all stand in its way, as mere natural animals: much more might it be pleaded, that a pair of Scales, an old man, and two innocent children, were no monsters: there were only the Centaur and the Maid, that could be esteemed out of nature. But what of that? with a boldness peculiar to these daring geniuses, what he found not monsters, he made so.

CHAP. VIII.

Of the Profound, *consisting in the Circumstances, and of Amplification and Paraphrase in general.*

What in a great measure distinguishes other writers from ours, is their choosing and separating such circumstances in a description, as illustrate or elevate the subject.

THE circumstances which are most natural, are obvious, therefore not astonishing or peculiar. But those that are far-fetched or unexpected, or hardly compatible, will surprise prodigiously. These therefore we must principally hunt out; but above all, preserve a laudable *prolixity*: presenting the whole and every side at once of the image to view. For, choice and distinction are not only a curb to the spirit, and limit the descriptive faculty, but also lessen the book, which is frequently the worst consequence of all to our author.

WHEN Job says in short, *He washed his feet in butter,* (a circumstance some poets would have softened, or passed over) hear how this butter is spread out by the great genius.

> *With teats distended with their milky store,*
> *Such numerous lowing herds, before my door,*
> *Their painful burden to unload did meet,*
> *That we with butter might have washed our feet.*
>
> *Blackmore, Job, p.133.*

HOW cautious and particular! He had, (says our author) so many herds, which herds thrived so well, and thriving so well, gave so much milk, and that milk produced so much butter, that if he *did not*, he *might* have washed his feet in it.

THE ensuing description of Hell is no less remarkable in the circumstances.

> *In flaming heaps the raging ocean rolls,*
> *Whose livid waves involve despairing souls;*
> *The liquid burnings dreadful colours show,*
> *Some deeply red and others faintly blue.*
>
> *Pr. Arth., p.89.*

COULD the most minute Dutch painter have been more exact? How inimitably circumstantial is this also of a war-horse!

> *His eyeballs burn, he wounds the smoking plain,*
> And knots of scarlet ribbon *deck* his *mane.*
>
> Anon.

Of certain cudgel-players:

> *They brandish high in air their threatening staves,*
> *Their* hands *a woven guard of osier* saves,
> *In which they fix their* hazel *weapon's* end.
>
> *Pr. Arth.*, p. 197

162

WHO would not think the poet had past his whole life at wakes in such laudable diversions? He even teaches us how to hold, and to make a cudgel!

Periphrase is another great aid to *prolixity*; being a diffused circumlocutory manner of expressing a known idea, which should be so mysteriously couched, as to give the reader the pleasure of guessing what it is that the author can possibly mean; and a strange surprise when he finds it.

THE poet I last mentioned is incomparable in this figure.

> *A waving sea of heads was round me spread,*
> *And still fresh streams the gazing deluge fed.*

Job, p. 78

HERE is a waving sea of heads, which by a fresh stream of heads grows to be a gazing deluge of heads. You come at last to find it means a *great crowd*.

How pretty and how genteel is the following.

> *Nature's confectioner—*
> *Whose suckets are moist alchemy:*
> *The still of his refining mould,*
> *Minting the garden into gold.*

Cleveland

What is this, but a *bee* gathering honey?

> *Little siren of the stage*
> *Empty warbler, breathing lyre,*
> *Wanton gale of fond desire,*
> *Tuneful mischief, vocal spell—*

Ph. to C—.

Who would think, this was only a poor gentlewoman, that sung finely?

WE may define *amplification* to be making the most of a *thought*; it is the spinning-wheel of the *Bathos*, which draws out and spreads it into the finest thread. There are amplifiers, who can extend half a dozen thin thoughts over a whole folio; but for which, the tale of many a vast romance, and the substance of many a fair volume, might be reduced to the size of a *primer*.

IN the book of *Job* are these words, '*Hast thou commanded the morning, and caused the day spring to know his place?*' How is this extended by the most celebrated amplifier of our age?

> *Canst thou set forth th' ethereal* mines on high,
> *Which the refulgent* ore *of light supply?*
> *Is the celestial* furnace *to thee known,*
> *In which I* melt *the golden* metal *down?*
> *Treasures, from whence I* deal *out light as fast,*
> *As all my stars and* lavish *suns can* waste.

Job, p. 180.

THE same author has amplified a passage in the 104th psalm; *'He looks on the earth, and it trembles. He touches the hills, and they smoke.'*

> *The hills* forget they're fixed, *and in their fright,*
> Cast off their weight, *and* ease *themselves for flight:*
> *The woods, with terror* winged, outfly *the wind,*
> *And leave the* heavy, panting *hills behind.*

YOU here see the hills not trembling, but shaking off woods from their backs, to run the faster. After this you are presented with a foot-race of mountains and woods, where the woods distance the mountains, that like corpulent pursy fellows, come puffing and panting a vast way behind them.

CHAP. IX.

Of Imitation, and the manner of Imitating.

That the true authors of the *Profound* are to imitate diligently the examples in their own way, is not to be questioned, and that divers have by this means attained to a depth whereunto their own weight could not have carried them, is evident by sundry instances. Who sees not that Defoe was the poetical son of Withers, T[a]te of Ogilby, E. Ward of John Taylor, and Eusden of Blackmore? Therefore when we sit down to write, let us bring some great author to our mind, and ask ourselves this question; how would Sir Richard have said this? Do I express myself as simply as A. Philips? or flow my numbers with the quiet thoughtlessness of Mr. Welsted?

BUT it may seem somewhat strange to assert, that our proficient should also read the works of those famous poets, who have excelled in the sublime: yet is not this a paradox? As Virgil is said to have read Ennius, out of his dunghill to draw gold; so may our author read Shakespeare, Milton, and Dryden, for the contrary end, to bury their gold in his own dunghill. A true genius, when he finds anything lofty or shining in them, will have the skill to bring it down, take off the gloss, or quite discharge the colour, by some ingenious circumstance, or periphrase, some addition or diminution, or by some of those figures, the use of which we shall show in our next chapter.

THE Book of *Job* is acknowledged to be infinitely sublime, and yet has not the father of the *Bathos* reduced it in every page? Is there a passage in all Virgil more painted up and laboured than the description of Etna in the third Aeneid.

> *—Horrificis juxta tonat Aetna ruinis,*
> *Interdumque atram prorumpit ad aethera nubem,*
> *Turbine fumantem piceo, & candente favilla,*
> *Attollitque globos flammarum, & sidera lambit*
> *Interdum scopulos avulsaque viscera montis*
> *Erigit eructans, liquefactaque saxa sub auras*
> *Cum gemitu glomerat, fundoque exaestuat imo.*

(I beg pardon of the gentle English reader, and such of our writers as understand not Latin) But lo! how this is taken down by our British poet, by the single happy thought of throwing the mountain into a fit of the *cholic.*

> Etna, *and all the burning mountains, find*
> *Their kindled stores with* inbred *storms of* wind
> Blown up *to rage; and* roaring out, *complain,*
> *As* torn *with* inward gripes, *and* torturing pain:
> *Labouring, they cast their dreadful* vomit *round,*
> *And with their* melted bowels, spread *the ground.*

Pr. Arth., Pag. 75.

HORACE, in search of the *Sublime,* struck his head against the stars; but Empedocles, to fathom the *Profound,* threw himself into Etna: And who but would imagine our excellent Modern had also been there, from this description?

IMITATION is of two sorts; the first is, when we force to our own purposes the thoughts of others; the second, consists in copying the imperfections, or blemishes of celebrated authors. I have seen a play professedly writ in the style of Shakespeare, wherein the resemblance lay in one single line,

And so good morrow t'ye, good Master Lieutenant.

And sundry poems in imitation of Milton, where with the utmost exactness, and not so much as one exception, nevertheless was constantly *nathless,* embroidered was *broidered,* hermits were *eremites,* disdained *'sdeigned,* shady *umbrageous,* enterprise *emprize,* pagan *paynim,* pinions *pennons,* sweet *dulcet,* orchards *orchats,* bridgework *pontifical;* nay, her was *hir,* and their was *thir* through the whole poem. And in very deed, there is no other way by which the true modern poet could read to any purpose the works of such men, as Milton and Shakespeare.

IT may be expected, that, like other critics, I should next speak of the PASSIONS: but as the main end and principal effect of the *Bathos* is to produce *tranquillity of mind* (and sure it is a better design to promote sleep than madness) we have little to say on this subject. Nor will the short bounds of this discourse allow us to treat at large of the *emollients* and *opiates* of *poesy;* of the *cool,* and the manner of producing it; or of the *methods* used by our authors in *managing* the *passions.* I shall but transiently remark, that nothing contributes so much to the *cool,* as the use of *wit* in expressing passion. The true genius rarely fails of *points, conceits,* and proper *similes* on such occasions: this we may term the *pathetic epigrammatical,* in which even puns are made use of with good success. Hereby our best authors have avoided throwing themselves or their readers into any indecent transports.

BUT, forasmuch as it la sometimes needful to excite the passions of our antagonist in the polemic way, the true students in the *law* have constantly taken their methods from *low*-life, where they observed, that to move *anger,* use is made of *scolding* and *railing;* to move *love,* of *bawdry;* to beget *favour* and friendship, of gross *flattery;* and to produce *fear,* of calumniating an adversary with *crimes* obnoxious to the *state.* As for *shame,* it is a silly passion, of which as our authors are incapable themselves, so they would not produce it in others.

CHAP. X.

Of Tropes *and* Figures: *and first of the variegating,*
confusing, and reversing Figures.

But we proceed to the *figures*. We cannot too earnestly recommend to our authors the study of the *abuse of speech*. They ought to lay down as a principle, to say nothing in the usual way, but (if possible) in the direct contrary. Therefore the figures must be so turned, as to manifest that intricate and wonderful *cast* of *head*, which distinguishes all writers of this genius; or (as I may say) to refer exactly the *mould* in which they were formed, in all its *inequalities*, *cavities*, *obliquities*, odd *crannies*, and *distortions*.

It would be endless, nay impossible, to enumerate all *such figures*, but we shall content ourselves to range the principal which most powerfully contribute to the *Bathos*, under three classes.

I. THE Variegating, Confusing, or Reversing *tropes* and *figures.*

II. THE Magnifying, and

III. THE Diminishing.

WE cannot avoid giving to these the Greek or He-man names; but in tenderness to our countrymen and fellow writers, many of whom, however exquisite, are wholly ignorant of those languages, we have also explained them in our mother tongue.

OF the first sort, nothing so much conduces to the *abuse* of *speech*, as the

CATACHRESIS.

A master of this will say,
    Mow the beard,
    Shave the grass,
    Pin the plank,
    Nail my sleeve.

From whence results the same kind of pleasure to the mind, as doth to the eye when we behold Harlequin trimming himself with a hatchet, hewing down a tree with a razor, making his tea in a cauldron, and brewing his ale in a tea-pot, to the incredible satisfaction of the British spectator. Another source of the *Bathos* is

The METONYMI,

the inversion of causes for effects, of inventors for inventions, etc.

> *Laced in her* *Cosins *new appeared the bride,*
> *A* *bubble-boy *and* *Tompion *at her side,*
> *And with an air divine her* *Colmar *plied.*
> *And 'oh!' she cries, 'what slaves I round me see?*
> *Here a bright* redcoat, *there a smart* *toupee'

166

The Synecdoche.

Which consists, in the use of a *part* for the *whole;* You may call a young woman sometimes pretty-*face* and pig's-*eyes*, and sometimes snotty-*nose* and draggle-*tail*. Or of *accidents* for *persons*; as a lawyer, is called *Split-cause* a tailor, *Prick-louse*, etc. Or of things belonging to a man, for the man himself; as a *Sword*-man, a *Gown*-man, a *Tom-Turd-man*; a *White staff*, a *Turnkey*, etc.

The Aposiopesis.

An excellent figure for the ignorant, as, *'What shall I say?'* when one has nothing to say; or, *'I can no more,'* when one really can no more: expressions which the gentle reader is so good, as never to take in earnest.

The Metaphor.

The first rule is to draw it from the lowest things, which is a certain way to sink the highest; as when you speak of the thunder of Heaven, say,

> *The* lords above *are* angry, *and* talk big.   *Lee, Alex.*

If you would describe a rich man refunding his treasures, express it thus,

> *Though he (as said) may riches* gorge, *the spoil*
> *Painful in* massy vomit *shall* recoil.
> *Soon shall he perish with a swift decay,*
> *Like his own* ordure, *cast with scorn away.*
>
> *Blackmore,* Job, p.91, 93.

The second, that whenever you *start* a metaphor, you must be sure to *run it down*, and pursue it as far as it can go. If you get the scent of a state negotiation, follow it in this manner.

> *The stones, and all the elements with thee*
> *Shall* ratify *a* strict confederacy;
> *Wild beasts their savage temper shall forget,*
> *And for a* firm alliance *with thee* treat;
> *The finny tyrant of the spacious seas*
> *Shall send a scaly* embassy *for* peace;
> *His* plighted faith *the* crocodile *shall keep,*
> *And seeing thee, for joy sincerely weep.*
>
> *Job,* p.22.

Or if you represent the Creator denouncing war against the wicked, be sure not to omit one circumstance' usual in proclaiming and levying war.

Envoys *and* agents, *who by my command*
Reside *in* Palestina*'s land,*
To whom commissions *I have given,*
To manage *there the* interests *of Heaven.*
Ye holy heralds, *who proclaim*
Or war *or* peace, *in mine* your master's *name.*
Ye pioneers *of Heaven, prepare a* road,
Make it plain, direct, and broad;—
For I in person will my people head;
—For the divine deliverer
Will on his march *in majesty appear,*
And needs the aid *of no* confederate power.

Blackmore, Isaiah, chap. 40.

UNDER the article of the *confusing,* we rank

THE MIXTURE OF FIGURES,

which raises so many images, as to give you no image at all. But its principal beauty is, when it gives an idea just opposite to what it seemed meant to describe. Thus an ingenious artist painting the *spring,* talks of a *snow* of blossoms, and thereby raises an unexpected picture of *winter.* Of this sort is the following:

The gaping clouds pour lakes of sulphur down,
Whose livid flashes sickening sunbeams drown.

Pr. Arthur, p. 73.

WHAT a noble confusion? Clouds, lakes, brimstone, flames, sun-beams, gaping, pouring, sickening, drowning! all in two lines.

The JARGON,

Thy head shall rise though buried in the dust,
And 'midst the stars his glittering turrets thrust

Job, p. 107

Quaere, what are the glittering turrets of a man's head?

Upon the shore; as frequent *as the* sand,
To meet the prince, the glad Dimetians *stand.*

Pr. Arthur, p. 157

Quaere, where these Dimetians stood? and of what size they were?

Destruction*'s empire shall no longer* last,
And desolation *lie for ever* waste.

Job, p. 89.

BUT for variegation and confusion of objects, nothing is more useful than

The ANTITHESIS, or SEE-SAW,

Whereby contraries and oppositions are balanced in such a way, as to cause a reader to remain suspended between them, to his exceeding delight and recreation. Such are these, on a lady who made herself appear out of size, by hiding a young princess under her clothes.

> *While the kind nymph, changing her faultless shape,*
> *Becomes* unhandsome, handsomely *to 'scape*

On the maids of honour in mourning:

> *Sadly they charm, and dismally they please.*

St-. on *Q. Mary.*

> —*His eyes so bright*
> *Let in the object and let out the light.*

Quarles.

> *The Gods look* pale *to see us look so* red.

Lee, Alex.

> —*The fairies and their queen,*
> *In mantles* blue *came tripping o'er the* green.

Phil. Past.

> *All nature felt a reverential shock,*
> *The sea* stood still *to see the mountains* rock.

Blackmore, Job, p.176.

CHAP. XI.

The Figures continued: Of the Magnifying and Diminishing Figures.

A genuine writer of the *Profound,* will take care never to *magnify* any object without *clouding* it at the same time; his thought will appear in a true *mist,* and very unlike what it is in nature. It must always be remembered that *darkness* is an essential quality of the *Profound,* or, if there chance to be a glimmering, it must be, as Milton expresses it,

> *No light, but rather darkness visible.*

The chief figure of this sort is,

The HYPERBOLE, or *Impossible,*
For instance, of a lion;

He roared so loud, and looked so wondrous grim,
His very shadow durst not follow him.

Vet. Aut.

Of a lady at dinner.

The silver whiteness that adorns thy neck,
Sullies the plate, and makes the napkin black.

Of the same.

—The obscureness of her birth
Cannot eclipse the lustre of her eyes,
Which make her all one light.

Theobald, *Double Distress*

Of a bull-baiting.

Up to the stars the sprawling mastiffs fly,
And add new monsters to the frighted sky.

Blackmore.

Of a scene of misery.

Behold a scene of misery and woe!
Here Argus *soon might weep himself quite blind,*
Even though he had Briareus' *hundred hands*
To wipe his hundred eyes—

Anon.

And that modest request of two absent lovers,

Ye gods! annihilate but space and time,
And make two lovers happy.—

The PERIPHRASIS, which the moderns call the *Circumbendibus,* whereof we have given examples in the ninth Chapter, and shall again in the twelfth.

TO the same class of the MAGNIFYING may be referred the following, which are so excellently modern, that we have yet no name for them. In describing a country prospect

I'd call them mountains, but can't call them so,
For fear to wrong them with a name too low;
While the fair vales beneath so humbly lie,
That even humble seems a term too high.

Anon.

    III. The third class remains; of the *Diminishing* figures: And first, The ANTICLIMAX, where the second line drops quite short of the first, than which nothing creates greater surprise.

On the extent of the British arms.

Under the tropics is our language spoke,
And part of Flanders hath received our yoke.

Waller.

On a warrior.

And thou, *Dalhousy,* the great god of war,
Lieutenant Colonel to the Earl of Mar.

Anon.

On the valour of the English.

Nor death, nor hell itself can keep them out,
—*Nor* fortified redoubt.

Dennis *on* Namur.

    AT other times this figure operates in a larger extent; and when the gentle reader is in expectation of some great image, he either finds it surprisingly *imperfect*, or is presented with something *low*, or quite *ridiculous*. A surprise resembling that of a curious person in a cabinet of antique statues, who beholds on the pedestal the names of Homer, or Cato; but looking up, finds Homer without a head, and nothing to be seen of Cato but his privy member. Such are these lines of a leviathan at sea.

His motion works, and beats the oozy mud,
And with its slime incorporates the flood,
'Till all th' encumbered, thick, fermenting stream
Does one vast pot of boiling ointment seem.
Where'er he swims, he leaves along the lake
Such frothy furrows, such a foamy track,
That all the waters of the deep appear
Hoary—*with* age, *or* grey *with sudden fear.*

Blackmore, Job, p. 197

BUT perhaps even these are excelled by the ensuing.

Now the resisted flames and fiery store,
By winds assaulted, in wide forges roar,
And raging seas flow down of melted ore.
Sometimes they hear long iron bars removed,
And to *and* fro *huge* heaps of cinders shoved.

The Vulgar

Is also a species of the *Diminishing*: by this a spear flying in the air is compared to a boy whistling as he goes on an errand.

> *The mighty* Stuffa *threw a massy spear.*
> *Which, with its* errand pleased, sung *through the air.*

Pr. Arthur

A man raging with grief to a mastiff dog.

> *I cannot stifle this gigantic woe,*
> *Nor on my raging grief a* muzzle *throw.*

Job, p. 41

And clouds big with water to a woman in great necessity.

> Distended *with the* waters *in 'em pent,*
> *The clouds* hang deep *in air, but* hang unrent.

The INFANTILE.

THIS is, when a poet grows so very simple, as to think and talk like a child. I shall take my examples from the greatest master in this way. Hear how he fondles like a mere stammerer:

> Little charm *of placid mien,*
> Miniature *of Beauty's Queen,*
> *Hither* British *muse* of mine,
> *Hither, all ye* Graecian nine,
> *With the lovely Graces* three,
> *And your* pretty nurseling *see.*
> *When the meadows next are seen,*
> *Sweet enamel, white and green.*
> *When again the lambkins play,*
> Pretty sportlings *full of* May,
> *Then the neck so white and round,*
> *(Little neck with brilliants bound.)*
> *And thy* gentleness *of mind,*
> *(Gentle from a gentle kind,)* etc.
> Happy *thrice, and* thrice again,
> Happiest *he of* happy *men,* etc.

A. Philips on Miss C——.

With the rest of those excellent *lullabies* of his composition.
How prettily he asks the sheep to teach him to bleat?

172

> *Teach me to grieve with bleating moan, my sheep.*   *Philips*, Past.

Hear how a babe would reason on his nurse's death:

> *That ever she could die! Oh most unkind!*
> *To die, and leave poor Colinet behind?*
> *And yet, —Why blame I her?—*
>
>   *Philips*, Past.

His shepherd reasons as much like an innocent, in love:

> *I love in secret all a beauteous maid,*
> *And have my love in secret all repaid:*
> *This coming night she does reserve for me.*
>
>   *Ibid.*

THE love of this maiden to him appears by her allowing him the reserve of one night from her other lovers; which you see he takes extremely kindly.

WITH no less simplicity does he suppose, that shepherdesses tear their hair and beat their breasts at then own deaths:

> *Ye brighter maids, faint emblems of my fair,*
> *With looks cast down, and with disheveled hair,*
> *In bitter anguish heat your breasts, and moan*
> *Her death untimely,* as it were your own.
>
>   *Ibid.*

The INANITY, or NOTHINGNESS.

OF this the same author furnishes us with most beautiful instances.

> *Ah silly I, more silly than my sheep,*
> *(Which on he flowery plain I once did keep.)*
>
>   *Philips*, Past.

> *To the grave senate she could counsel give,*
> *(Which with astonishment they did receive.)*
>
>   *Philips* on *Q.Mary.*

> *He whom loud cannon could not terrify,*
> *Falls (from the grandeur of his majesty.)*
>
>   *Ibid.*

> *The noise returning with returning light.*

What did it?

—Dispersed the silence, *and dispelled the* night.

Anon.

The glories of proud London *to survey,*
The sun himself shall rise—by break of day.

Autor Vet.

The EXPLETIVE,

admirably exemplified in the epithets of many authors.

Th' umbrageous shadow, and the verdant green,
The running current, and odorous fragrance,
Cheer my lone solitude with joyous gladness.

The MACROLOGY and PLEONASM,

are as generally coupled, as a lean rabbit with a fat one; nor is it a wonder, the superfluity of words and vacuity of sense, being just the same thing. I am pleased to see one of our greatest adversaries employ this figure.

The growth of meadows, and the pride of fields,
The food of armies and support of wars,
Refuse of swords, and gleanings of a fight;
Lessen his numbers and contract his host.
Where'er his friends retire, or foes succeed.
Covered with tempests, and in oceans drowned,

Camp.

Of all which the perfection is

The TAUTOLOGY.

Break through the billows, and—divide the main.
In smoother numbers, and—in softer verse.
Tonson, Misc. *duod.,* vol. 4, p. 291, fourth edition.

Divide—*and* part—*the* severed *world*—in two.
Ibid., vol. 6, p.121

WITH ten thousand others equally musical, and plentifully flowing through most of our celebrated modern poems.

CHAP. XII.

Of Expression, *and the several Sorts of* Style *of the present Age.*

The *Expression* is adequate, when it is proportion ably low to the profundity of the thought. It must not be always *grammatical*, lest it appear pedantic and ungentlemanly; nor too *clear,* for fear it become vulgar; for obscurity bestows a cast of the wonderful, and throws an oracular dignity upon a piece which hath no meaning.

FOR example, sometimes use the wrong number; *The sword and pestilence at once* devours, instead of *devour*. Sometimes the wrong case; *And who more fit to soothe the god than* thee, instead of *thou*: And rather than say, *Thetis saw Achilles* weep, she *heard* him weep.

Tickell, Hom. Il. 1.

WE must be exceeding careful in two things; first, in the *choice* of *low words*; secondly, in the *sober* and *orderly* way of *ranging* them. Many of our poets are naturally blessed with this talent, insomuch that they are in the circumstance of that honest citizen, who had made *prose* all his life without knowing it. Let verses run in this manner, just to be a vehicle to the words. (I take them from my last cited author, who though otherwise by no means of our rank, seemed once in his life to have a mind to be simple.)

> *If not, a prize I will myself decree,*
> *From him, or him, or else perhaps from thee.*

Tickell, Hom. Il. 1, p.11.

> *—Full of days was he;*
> *Two ages past, he lived the third to see.*

Idem. p. 17.

> *The king of forty kings, and honoured more*
> *By mighty Jove, than e'er was king before.*

p. 19.

> *That I may know, if thou my prayer deny,*
> *The most despised of all the gods am I.*

p. 34.

> *Then let my mother once be ruled by me,*
> *Though much more wise than I pretend to be.*

p. 38.

Or these, of the same hand.

I leave the arts of poetry and verse
To them that practise them with more success:
Of greater truths I now prepare to tell,
And so at once, dear friend and muse, farewell.

Tonson, Misc. 12ves, vol. 4, p. 292, fourth edition.

Sometimes a single *word* will familiarize a poetical idea; as where a ship set on fire owes all the spirit of the *Bathos* to one choice word that ends the line.

And his scorched ribs the hot contagion fried.

Pr. Arthur, p.151.

And in that description of a world in ruins.

Should the whole frame of nature round him break,
He unconcerned would hear the mighty crack.

Tonson, Misc. vol. 6, 119.

So also in these:

Beasts tame and savage to the river's brink
Come from the fields and wild abodes—to drink.

Job, p. 263.

FREQUENTLY two or three words will do it effectually.

He from the clouds does the sweet liquor squeeze,
That cheers the forest and the garden *trees.*

Id. Job, p. 264.

It is also useful to employ *technical terms,* which estrange your style from the great and general ideas of nature. And the higher your subject is, the lower should you search into mechanics for your expression. If you describe the garment of an angel, say that his *linen* was *finely spun,* and *bleached on the happy plains.* Call an army of angels, *angelic cuirassiers,* and if you have occasion to mention a number of misfortunes, style them

Pr. Arth., p. 19.
Ibid., p. 139.

Fresh troops *of pains, and* regimented *woes.*

Job, p.86.

STYLE is divided by the rhetoricians into the proper and figured. Of the figured we have already treated, and the proper is what our authors have nothing to do with. Of styles we shall mention only the principal, which owe to the *moderns* either their *chief improvement,* or entire *invention.*

176

1. The FLORID,

Than which none is more proper to the Bathos, as flowers which are the *lowest* of vegetables are most *gaudy*, and do many times grow in great plenty at the bottom of *ponds* and *ditches*.

A fine writer of this kind presents you with the following posy:

> *The groves appear all dressed with wreaths of flowers,*
> *And from their leaves drop aromatic showers,*
> *Whose fragrant heads in mystic twines above,*
> *Exchanged their sweets, and mixed with thousand kisses,*
> *As if the willing branches strove*
> *To beautify and shade the grove.——*

Behn's Poems, p. 2.

(Which indeed most branches do). But this is still excelled by our laureate.

> *Branches in branches twined compose the grove,*
> *And shoot and spread, and blossom into love.*
> *The trembling palms their mutual vows repeat,*
> *And bending poplars bending poplars meet.*
> *The distant platanes seems to press more nigh,*
> *And to the sighing alders, alders sigh.*

Guardian, 12ves, 127.

Hear also our Homer.

> *His* robe of state *is formed of light refined,*
> *An endless* train *of lustre* spreads behind.
> *His* thrones *of bright* compacted glory *made,*
> *With* pearls *celestial, and with gems* inlaid:
> *Whence* floods *of joy, and* seas *of splendour flow,*
> *On all the angelic gazing throng below.*

Blackmore, Ps. 104

2. The PERT *Style*.

This does in as peculiar a manner become the low in wit, as a pert air does the low in stature. Mr. Thomas Brown, the author of the *London Spy*, and all the *Spies* and *Trips* in general, are herein to be diligently studied: in verse, Mr. Cibber's *Prologues*.

BUT the beauty and energy of it is never so conspicuous, as when it is employed in *modernizing* and *adapting* to the *taste of the times* the works of the ancients. This we rightly phrase *doing* them *into English*, and *making* them *English*; two expressions of great propriety, the one denoting our *neglect* of the *manner how*, the other the *force* and *compulsion* with which, it is brought about. It is by virtue of this style that Tacitus talks like a coffee-house politician, Josephus like the *British Gazetteer*, Tully is as short and smart as Seneca or Mr. Asgill, Marcus Aurelius is excellent at *snipsnap*, and honest Thomas a Kempis as *prim* and *polite* as any preacher at court.

3. The ALAMODE Style,

Which is fine by being *new*, and has this happiness attending it, that it is as durable and extensive as the poem itself. Take some examples of it, in the description of the sun in a mourning coach upon the death of Queen Mary.

> *See* Phoebus *now, as once for* Phaeton,
> *Has* masked *his face; and put* deep mourning *on;*
> *Dark clouds his* sable chariot *do surround,*
> *And the* dull steeds stalk o'er *the* melancholy round.
>
> *A. Philips.*

Of Prince Arthur's Soldiers drinking.

> *While rich* Burgundian *wine, and bright* champagne,
> *Chase from their minds the terror of the main.*
>
> *Pr. Ar.*, p.16.

(Whence we also learn, that *burgundy* and *champagne* make a man on shore despise a storm at sea.)

Of the Almighty encamping his Regiments.

> *—He sunk a vast capacious deep,*
> *Where he his* liquid regiments *does keep.*
> *Thither the waves* file off, *and make their way,*
> *To form the mighty* body *of the sea;*
> *Where they encamp, and in their station stand,*
> Entrenched *in* works *of rock, and* lines *of sand.*
>
> *Blackmore,* Ps. 104, p.261.

Of two Armies on the Point of engaging.

> *Yon armies are the* cards *which both must play;*
> *At least come off a* saver, *if you may:*
> Throw boldly *at the* sum *the gods have* set;
> *These on your side will all their fortunes* bet.
>
> Lee, *Sophon.*

All perfectly agreeable to the present customs and best fashions of our metropolis.

BUT the principal branch of the *Alamode* is the PRURIENT, a style greatly advanced and honoured of late by the practice of persons of the *first quality*, and by the encouragement of the *ladies* not unsuccessfully introduced even into the *drawing-room*. Indeed its *incredible progress* and *conquests* may be compared to those of the great Sesostris, and are everywhere known by the *same marks*, the images of the genital parts of men or women. It consists wholly of metaphors drawn from two most fruitful sources or springs, the very *Bathos* of the human body, that is to say *** and **************** *Hiatus Magnus lachrymabilis.* ******************************. And *selling of bargains,* and *double entendre,* and Κιββερισμος and Ολφιελδισμος and, all derived from the said sources.

4. THE FINICAL which consists of the most curious, affected, mincing metaphors, and partakes of the last mentioned.

As this, of a brook dried by the sun.

Won by the summer's importuning ray.
Th' eloping stream did from her channel stray.
And with enticing sunbeams stole away.

Blackmore, Job, p.26.

Of an easy Death.

When watchful death shall on his harvest look,
And see thee ripe with age, invite *the hook;*
He'll gently *cut thy* bending *stalk, and thee*
Lay kindly *in the* grave, *his* granary.

Ibid., p. 23.

Of Trees in a Storm.

Oaks with extended arms the winds defy,
The tempest sees *their strength,* and sighs, and passes by.

Dennis.

Of Water simmering over the Fire.

The sparkling flames raise water to a smile,
Yet the pleased *liquor* pines, *and lessens all the while.*

Anon. in *Tonson's* Misc., Part 6, p. 234.

5. LASTLY, I shall place the CUMBROUS, which moves heavily under a load of metaphors, and draws after it a long train of words.

AND the BUSKIN, or *stately,* frequently and with great felicity mixed with the former. For as the first is the proper engine to depress what is high, so is the second to raise what is base and low to a ridiculous visibility: when both these can be done at once, then is the *Bathos* in perfection; as when a man is set with his head downward, and his breech upright, his degradation is complete: one end of him is as high as ever, only that end is the wrong one. Will not every true lover of the *Profound* be delighted to behold the most vulgar and low actions of life exalted in this manner?

Who knocks at the Door?

For whom thus rudely pleads my loud-tongued gate,
That he may enter?—

See who is there?

Advance the fringed curtains of thy eyes,
And tell me who comes yonder.—

Shut the Door.

The wooden guardian of our privacy
Quick on its axle turn.—

Bring my Clothes.

Bring me what nature, tailor to the bear,
To man himself denied: she gave me cold,
But would not give me clothes.—

Light the Fire.

Bring forth some remnant of Promethean *theft,*
Quick to expand th' inclement air congealed
By Boreas's *rude breath.—*

Snuff the candle.

Yon luminary amputation needs,
Thus shall you save its half-extinguished life.

Open the letter.

Wax! render up thy trust.—

Theobald, Double Distress.

Uncork the Bottle, and chip the Bread.

Apply thine engine to the spongy door,
Set Bacchus from his glassy prison free,
And strip white Ceres of her nut-brown coat.

APPENDIX

CHAP. XIII

A Project for the Advancement of the Bathos.

Thus have I (my dear countrymen) with incredible pains and diligence, discovered the hidden sources of the *Bathos*, or, as I may say broke open the abysses of this *Great Deep*. And having now established good and wholesome *laws*, what remains but that all true moderns with their utmost might do proceed to put the same in execution? In order whereto, I think I shall in the second place highly deserve of my country, by proposing such a *scheme*, as may facilitate this great end.

As our number is confessedly far superior to that of the enemy, there seems nothing wanting but unanimity among ourselves. It is therefore humbly offered, that all and every individual of the *Bathos*, do enter into a firm *association*, and incorporate into *one regular body*, whereof every member, even the meanest, will some way contribute to the support of the whole; in like manner as the weakest reeds when joined in one bundle, become infrangible. To which end our art ought to be put upon the same foot with other arts of this age. The vast improvement of modern manufactures ariseth from their being divided into several branches, and parcelled out to several *trades*. For instance, in *clockmaking*, one artist makes the balance, another the spring, another the crown-wheels, a fourth the case, and the principal workman puts all together; to this economy we owe the perfection of our modern watches; and doubtless we also might that of our modern poetry and rhetoric, were the several parts branched out in the like manner.

NOTHING is more evident than that divers persons, no other way remarkable, have each a strong disposition to the formation of some particular trope or figure. Aristotle saith, that the *Hyperbole* is an ornament fit for *young men of quality*; accordingly we find in those gentlemen a wonderful propensity toward it, which is marvellously improved by *travelling*. Soldiers also and seamen, are very happy in the same figure. The *Periphrasis*, or *Circumlocution* is the peculiar talent of *country farmers*, the Proverb and Apologue, of *old men* at clubs: the *Ellipsis* or Speech by half-words of *ministers* and *politicians*, the *Aposiopesis* of *courtiers*, the *Litotes* or Diminution of *ladies, whisperers,* and *backbiters*; and the *Anadyplosis* of common *criers* and *hawkers*, who by redoubling the same words, persuade people to buy their oysters, green hastings, or new ballads. *Epithets* may be found in great plenty at Billingsgate, *Sarcasm* and *Irony* learned upon the *water*, and the *Epiphonema*, or *Exclamation* frequently from the Bear-Garden, and as frequently from the 'Hear him' of the House of Commons.

Now each man applying his whole time and genius upon his particular figure, would doubtless attain to perfection; and when each became incorporated and sworn into the society, (as hath been, proposed;) a poet or orator would have no more to do, but to send to the particular traders in each kind; to the Metaphorist, for his *Allegories*, to the Simile-maker for his *Comparisons*, to the Ironist, for his *Sarcasms*; to the Apothegmatist, for his *Sentences*, etc. whereby a dedication or speech would be composed in a moment, the superior artist having nothing to do but to put together all the materials.

I THEREFORE propose, that there be contrived, with all convenient despatch, at the public expense, a *Rhetorical Chest of Drawers*, consisting of three stories, the highest for the *Deliberative*, the middle for the *Demonstrative*, and the lowest for the *Judicial*. These shall be divided into *loci* or *places*, being repositories for matter and argument in the several kinds of oration or writing; and every drawer shall again be subdivided into cells, resembling those of cabinets for rarities. The apartment for *peace* or *war*, and that of the *liberty* of the *press*, may in a very few days be filled with several arguments *perfectly new*; and the *vituperative partition* will as easily be replenished with a most choice collection, entirely of the growth and manufacture of the present age. Every composer will soon be taught the use of this cabinet, and how to manage all the registers of it, which will be drawn out much in the manner of those in an organ.

THE keys of it must be kept in honest hands, by some *reverend prelate*, or *valiant officer*, of unquestioned loyalty and affection to every present establishment in Church and State; which will sufficiently guard against any mischief, that might otherwise be apprehended from it.

AND being lodged in such hands, it may be at discretion *let out* by the *day* to several great orators in both Houses; from whence it is to be hoped much *profit* or *gain* will also accrue to our society.

CHAP. XIV

How to make Dedications, Panegyrics, *or* Satires, *and of*
the Colours *of Honourable and Dishonourable*

Now of what necessity the foregoing project may prove, will appear from this single consideration, that nothing is of equal consequence to the success of our works, as *speed* and *dispatch*. Great pity it is, that solid brains are not, like other solid bodies, constantly endowed with a *velocity* in sinking, proportioned to their *heaviness*: for it is with the *flowers* of the *Bathos*, as with those of nature, which, if the careful gardener brings not hastily to market in the *morning*, must unprofitably perish and wither before *night*. And of all our productions none is so short-lived as the *dedication* and *panegyric*, which are often but the *praise of a day*, and become by the next, utterly useless, improper, indecent, and false. This is the more to be lamented, inasmuch as these two are the sorts, whereon in a manner depends that *gain* or *profit*, which must still be remembered to be the main end of *our writers* and *speakers*.

WE shall therefore employ this chapter in showing the *quickest* method of composing them; after which we will teach a *short way* to epic poetry. And these being confessedly the works of most importance and difficulty, it is presumed we may leave the rest to each author's own learning or practice.

FIRST, of *panegyric*: every man is *honourable*, who is so by *law*, *custom* or *title*; the public are better judges of what is honourable than private men. The virtues of great men, like those of plants, are *inherent* in them, whether they are *exerted* or not; and the more strongly inherent, the less they are exerted; as a man is the more rich, the less he spends.

ALL great ministers, without either private or economical virtue, are virtuous by their *posts*; liberal and generous upon the *public money*, provident upon *parliamentary supplies*, just by paying *public interest*, courageous and magnanimous by the *fleets* and *armies*, magnificent upon the *public expenses*, and prudent by *public success*. They have, by their *office*, a right to a share of the *public stock* of virtues; besides they are by *prescription immemorial* invested in all the celebrated virtues of their *predecessors* in the same *stations*, especially those of their own *ancestors*.

As to what are commonly called the *colours* of *honourable* and *dishonourable*, they are various in different countries: in this they are *blue, green*, and *red*. But forasmuch as the duty we owe to the public doth often require that we should put some things in a strong light, and throw a shade over others, I shall explain the method of turning a vicious man into a hero.

THE first and chief rule is *the Golden Rule* of *Transformation*, which consists in converting vices into their *bordering* virtues. A man who is a spendthrift and will not pay a just debt, may have his injustice *transformed* into liberality; cowardice may be metamorphosed into prudence; intemperance into good nature and good fellowship, corruption into patriotism, and lewdness into tenderness and facility.

THE second is the *Rule of Contraries*: it is certain the less a man is endued with any virtue, the more need he has to have it plentifully bestowed, especially those good qualities of which the world generally believes he hath none at all: for who will thank a man for giving him that which he *has*?

THE reverse of these precepts win serve for *satire*, wherein we are ever to remark, that whoso loses his place, or becomes out of favour with the government, hath forfeited his share in *public praise* and *honour*. Therefore the truly public-spirited writer ought in duty to strip him whom the government hath stripped: which is the real *poetical justice* of this age. For a full collection of topics and epithets to be used in the praise and dispraise of ministerial and unministerial persons, I refer to our *rhetorical cabinet*; concluding with an earnest exhortation to all my brethren, to observe the precepts here laid down; the neglect of which hath cost some of them their *ears* in the *pillory*.

CHAP. XV

A Receipt to make an Epic Poem.

An epic poem, the critics agree, is the greatest work human nature is capable of. They have already laid down many mechanical rules for compositions of this sort, but at the same time they cut off almost all undertakers from the possibility of ever performing them; for the first qualification they unanimously require in a poet, is a *genius*. I shall here endeavour (for the benefit of my countrymen) to make it manifest, that epic poems may be made *without a genius*, nay without learning or much reading. This must necessarily be of great use to all those who confess they never *read*, and of whom the world is convinced they never *learn*. Molière observes of making a dinner, that any man can do it *with money*, and if a professed cook cannot do it *without* he has his art for nothing; the same may be said of making a poem, 'tis easily brought about by him that *has* a genius, but the skill lies in doing it without one. In pursuance of this end, I shall present the reader with a plain and certain *recipe*, by which any author in the *Bathos* may be qualified for this grand performance.

For the Fable.

TAKE out of any old poem, history-book, romance, or legend, (for instance, Geoffrey of Monmouth, or *Don Belianis of Greece*) those parts of the story which afford most scope for *long descriptions*. Put these pieces together, and throw all the adventures you fancy into *one tale*. Then take a hero, whom you may choose for the sound of his name, and put him into the midst of these adventures. There let him *work*, for twelve books; at the end of which you may take him out, ready prepared to *conquer* or to *marry*; it being necessary that the conclusion of an epic poem be *fortunate*.

To make an Episode.

TAKE any remaining adventure of your former collection, in which you could no way involve your hero; or any unfortunate accident, that was too good to be thrown away; and it will be of use, applied to any other person; who may be lost and *evaporate* in the course of the work, without the least damage to the composition.

For the Moral and Allegory.

THESE you may extract out of the fable afterwards, at your leisure: be sure you *strain* them sufficiently.

For the Manners.

For those of the *hero*, take all the best qualities you can find in the most celebrated heroes of antiquity; if they will not be reduced to a *consistency*, lay 'em *all on a heap* upon him. But be sure they are qualities, which your *patron* would be thought to have; and to prevent any mistake, which the world may be subject to, select from the alphabet those capital letters that compose his name, and set them at the head of a dedication before your poem. However, do not absolutely observe the exact quantity of these virtues, it not being determined whether or not it be necessary for the hero of a poem to be an *honest man*. For the *under-characters*, gather them from Homer and Virgil, and change the parries as occasion serves.

For the Machines.

TAKE of *deities*, male and female, as many as you can use. Separate them into two equal parts, and keep Jupiter in the middle. Let Juno put him in a ferment, and Venus mollify him. Remember on all occasions to make use of volatile Mercury. If you have need of devils, draw them out of Milton's Paradise, and extract your *spirits* from Tasso. The use of these machines is evident; for since no epic poem can possibly subsist without them, the wisest way is to reserve them for your greatest necessities. When you cannot extricate your hero by any human means, or yourself by your own wit, seek relief from heaven, and the Gods will do your business very readily. This is according to the direct prescription of Horace in his *Art of Poetry*.

Nec Deus intersit, nisi dignus vindice Nodus *Inciderit.—*

That is to say, '*A poet should never call upon the gods for their assistance, but when he is in great perplexity.*'

For the Descriptions.

FOR a *tempest*. Take Eurus, Zephyr, Auster and Boreas, and cast them together in one verse. Add to these of rain, lightning and thunder (the loudest you can) *quantum sufficit*. Mix your clouds and billows well together till they foam, and thicken your description here and there with a quicksand. Brew your tempest well in your head, before you set it a blowing.

FOR a *battle*. Pick a large quantity of images and descriptions from Homer's *Iliads*, with a spice or two of Virgil, and if there remain any overplus, you may lay them by for a *skirmish*. Season it well with *similes*, and it will make an *excellent battle*.

FOR a *burning town*. If such a description be necessary (because it is certain there is one in Virgil) old Troy is ready burnt to your hands. But if you fear that would be thought borrowed, a chapter or two of the *Conflagration*, well circumstanced, and done into verse, will be a good *succedaneum*.

As for *similes* and *metaphors*, they may be found all over the creation; the most ignorant may *gather* them, but the danger is in *applying* them. For this advise with your *bookseller*.

CHAP. XVI

A Project for the Advancement of the Stage.

It may be thought that we should not wholly omit the *drama*, which makes so great and so lucrative a part of poetry. But this province is so well taken care of by the present *managers* of the theatre, that it is perfectly needless to suggest to them any other methods than they have already practised for the advancement of the *Bathos*.

HERE therefore, in the name of all our brethren, let me return our sincere and humble thanks to the Most August Mr. Barton Booth, the Most Serene Mr. Robert Wilks, and the most undaunted Mr. Colley Cibber; of whom, let it be known *when the people of this age shall be ancestors*, and to all the *succession of our successors*, that to this present day they continue to outdo even their *own out-doings*. And when the inevitable hand of sweeping *Time* shall have brushed off all the works of *Today*, may this testimony of a *contemporary critic* to their fame be extended as far as *tomorrow*!

YET, if to so wise an administration it be possible anything can be added, it is that more ample and comprehensive scheme which Mr. Dennis and Mr. Gildon, (the two greatest critics and reformers then living) made public in the year 1720 in a project signed with their names, and dated the 2nd of February. I cannot better conclude than by presenting the reader with the substance of it.

1. IT is proposed, that the two *theatres* be incorporated into one company; that the Royal Academy of Music be added to them as an *orchestra*; and that Mr. Figg with his prize-fighters, and Violante with the rope-dancers, be admitted in partnership.

2. THAT a spacious building be erected at the public expense, capable of containing at least ten thousand spectators, which is become absolutely necessary by the great addition of children and nurses to the audience, since the new entertainments. That there be a stage as large as the Athenian, which was near ninety thousand geometrical paces square, and separate divisions for the two Houses of Parliament, my Lords the judges, the

honourable the Directors of the Academy, and the Court of Aldermen, who shall all have their places frank.

3. If Westminster-hall be not allotted to this service (which by reason of its proximity to the two chambers of parliament above mentioned, seems not altogether improper) it is left to the wisdom of the nation whether Somerset House may not be demolished, and a theatre built upon that site, which lies convenient to receive spectators from the County of Surrey, who may be wafted thither by water-carriage, esteemed by all projectors the cheapest whatsoever. To this may be added, that the River Thames may in the readiest manner convey those eminent personages from courts beyond the seas, who may be drawn either by curiosity to behold some of our most celebrated pieces, or by affection to see their countrymen the harlequins and eunuchs; of which convenient notice may be given for two or three months before, in the public prints.

4. THAT the theatre abovesaid be environed with a fair quadrangle of buildings, fitted for the accommodation of decayed critics and poets; out of whom six of the most aged (their age to be computed from the year wherein their first work was published) shall be elected to manage the affairs of the society, provided nevertheless that the Laureate for the time being, may be always one. The head or president over all, (to prevent disputes, but too frequent among the learned) shall be the *oldest poet* and *critic* to be found in the whole island.

5. The *male-players* are to be lodged in the garrets of the said quadrangle, and to attend the persons of the *poets*, dwelling under them, by brushing their apparel, drawing on their shoes, and the like. The *actresses* are to make their beds, and wash their linen.

6. A LARGE room shall be set apart for a *library*, to consist of all the modern dramatic poems, and all the criticisms extant. In the midst of this room shall be a round table for the Council of SIX to sit and deliberate on the merits of *plays*. The *majority* shall determine the dispute: and if it should happen, that *three* and *three* should be of each side, the president shall have a *casting voice*, unless where the contention may run so high as lo require a decision by *single combat*.

7. IT may be convenient to place the Council of SIX in some conspicuous situation in the theatre, where after the manner usually practised by composers in music, they may give *signs* (before settled and agreed upon) of dislike or approbation. In consequence of these signs the whole audience shall be required to *clap* or *hiss*, that the town may learn certainly, when and how far they ought to be pleased.

8. IT is submitted, whether it would not be proper to distinguish the Council of SIX by some particular habit or gown of an honourable shape and colour, to which may be added a square cap and a white wand.

9. THAT to prevent unmarried actresses making away with their infants, a competent provision be allowed for the nurture of them, who shall for that reason be deemed the *children of the society*; and that they may be educated according to the genius of their parents, the said actresses shall declare upon oath (as far as their memory will allow) the true names and qualities of their, several fathers. A private gentleman's son shall at the public expense be brought up a page to attend the Council of SIX. A more ample provision shall be made for the son of a *poet*, and a greater still for the son of a *critic*.

10. IF it be discovered, that any actress is got with child, during the interludes of any play, wherein she hath a part, it shall be reckoned a neglect of her business, and she shall *forfeit* accordingly. If any actor for the future shall commit *murder*, except upon the stage, he shall be left to the laws of the land; the like is to be understood of *robbery* and *theft*. In all other cases, particularly in those of *debt*, it is proposed that this, like the other

courts of Whitehall and St. James's, may be held a *place of privilege*. And whereas it has been found, that an obligation to satisfy *paltry creditors* has been a discouragement to *men of letters*, if any person of quality or others shall send for any *poet* or *critic* of this society to any remote quarter of the town, the said *poet* or *critic* shall freely pass and repass, without being liable to an *arrest*.

11. THE fore-mentioned scheme in its several regulations may be supported by profits arising from every third-night throughout the year. And as it would be hard to suppose, that so many persons could live without any food (though from the former course of their lives, a *very little* will be sufficient) the masters of calculation will, we believe, agree, that out of those profits, the said persons might be subsisted in a sober and decent manner. We will venture to affirm farther, that not only the proper magazines of thunder and lightning, but *paint, diet-drinks, spitting-pots*, and all other *necessaries* of *life*, may in like manner fairly be provided for.

12. IF some of the articles may at first view seem liable to objections, particularly those that give so vast a power to the Council of SIX (which is indeed larger than any entrusted to the great officers of state) this may be obviated by swearing those *six* persons of his majesty's Privy Council, and obliging them to pass everything of moment *previously* at that most honourable board.

Vale & Fruere.
MAR. SCRIB.

POPE TO JONATHAN SWIFT
28 November 1729

This letter (like all mine) will be a rhapsody; it is many years ago since I wrote as a wit. How many occurrences or informations must one omit, if one determined to say nothing that one could not say prettily? I lately received from the widow of one dead correspondent, and the father of another, several of my own letters of about fifteen and twenty years old; and it was not unentertaining to myself to observe, how and by what degrees I ceased to be a witty writer; as either my experience grew on the one hand, or my affection to my correspondents on the other. Now as I love you better than most I have ever met with in the world, and esteem you too the more the longer I have compared you with the rest of the world; so inevitably I write to you more negligently, that is, more openly, and what all but such as love one another will call writing worse. I smile to think how Curll would be bit, were our Epistles to fall into his hands, and how gloriously they would fall short of every ingenious reader's expectations?

You can't imagine what a vanity it is to me, to have something to rebuke you for in the way of economy? I love the man that builds a house *subito ingenio*, and makes a wall for a horse; then cries, 'We wife men must think of nothing but getting ready money.' I am glad you approve my annuity; all we have in this world is no more than an annuity, as to our own enjoyment. But I will increase your regard for my wisdom, and tell you, that this annuity includes also the life of another, whose concern ought to be as near me as my own, and with whom my whole prospects ought to finish. I throw my javelin of hope no farther, *Cur brevi fortes jaculamur aevo—etc.*

The second (as it is called, but indeed the eighth) edition of *The Dunciad*, with some additional notes and epigrams, shall be sent you if I know any opportunity ; if they reprint it with you, let them by all means follow that octavo edition.—The *Drapier's Letters* are again printed here, very laudably as to paper, print, etc. for you know I disapprove Irish politics (as my commentator tells you) being a strong and jealous subject of England. The lady you mention, you ought not to complain of for not acknowledging your present; she having just now received a much richer present from Mr. Knight of the South Sea; and you are sensible she cannot ever return it, to one in the condition of an outlaw: it's certain, as he can never expect any favour, his motive must be wholly disinterested. Will not this Reflection make you blush? Your continual deplorings of Ireland, make me wish, you were here long enough to forget those scenes that so afflict you. I am only in fear if you were, you would grow such a patriot here too, as not to be quite at ease, for your love of old England. It is very possible, your journey, in the time I compute, might exactly tally with my intended one to you; and if you must soon again go back, you would not be un-attended. For the poor woman decays perceptibly every week; and the winter may too probably put an end to a very long, and a very irreproachable, life. My constant attendance on her does indeed affect my mind very much, and lessen extremely my desires of long life; since I see the best that can come of it is a miserable benediction at most: so that I look upon myself to be many years older in two years since you saw me. The natural imbecility of my body, joined now to this acquired old age of the mind, makes me at least as old as you, and we are the fitter to crawl down the hill together; I only desire I may be able to keep pace with you. My first friendship at sixteen, was contracted with a man of seventy, and I found him not grave enough or consistent enough for me, though we lived well to his death. I speak of old Mr. Wycherley; some letters of whom (by the by) and of mine, the booksellers have got and printed not without the concurrence of a noble friend of mine and yours, I don't much approve of it; though there is nothing for me to be ashamed of, because I will not be ashamed of anything I do not do myself, or of anything that is not immoral but merely dull (as for instance, if they printed this letter I am now writing, which they easily may, if the underlings at the Post Office please to take a copy of it.) I admire on this consideration, your sending your last to me quite open, without a seal, wafer, or any closure whatever, manifesting the utter openness of the writer. I would do the same by this, but fear it would look like affectation to send two letters so together.—I will fully represent to our friend (and I doubt not it will touch his heart) what you so feelingly set forth as to the badness of your burgundy, etc. He is an extreme honest man, and indeed ought to be so, considering how very indiscreet and unreserved he is. But I do not approve this part of his character, and will never join with him in any of his idlenesses in the way of wit. You know my maxim to keep as clear of all offence, as I am clear of all interest in either party. I was once displeased before at you, for complaining to Mr. Dodington of my not having a pension, and am so again at your naming it to a certain Lord. I have given proof in the course of my whole life, (from the time when I was in the friendship of Lord Bolingbroke and Mr. Craggs even to this, when I am civilly treated by Sir R. Walpole) that I never thought myself so warm in any party's cause as to deserve their money; and therefore would never have accepted it: But give me leave to tell you, that of all mankind the two persons I would least have accepted any favour from, are those very two, to whom you have unluckily spoken of it. I desire you to take off any impressions which that dialogue may have left on his Lordship's mind, as if I ever had any thought of being beholden to him, or any other, in that way. And yet you know I am no enemy to the present constitution; I believe, as sincere a well-wisher to it, nay even to the church established, as any Minister in, or out of employment, whatever; or any bishop of England or Ireland. Yet am I of the religion of Erasmus, a Catholic; so I live; so I shall die; and hope one day to meet you, Bishop Atterbury, the younger Craggs, Dr. Garth, Dean Berkeley, and Mr. Hutchinson, in that place, To which God of his infinite mercy bring us, and everybody!

Lord B's answer to your letter I have just received, and join it to this packet. The work he speaks of with such abundant partiality, is a system of Ethics in the Horatian way.

EPITAPH
Intended for Sir ISAAC NEWTON
In Westminster-Abbey
ISAACUS NEWTONUS:

Quem Immortalem
Testantur *Tempus, Natura, Coelum*:
Mortalem
Hoc marmor fatetur.

Nature and Nature's Laws lay hid in Night.
GOD said, *Let Newton be!* and all was Light.

AN EPISTLE
TO
Richard Boyle, Earl Of *Burlington*

ARGUMENT
Of the Use of RICHES

The vanity of Expense in people of wealth and quality. The abuse of the word taste, v. 13. *That the first principle and foundation in this, as in every thing else, is* good sense, v. 40. *The chief proof of it is to* follow nature, *even in works of mere luxury and elegance. Instanced in* architecture *and* gardening, *where all must be adapted to the* genius *and* use *of the* place, *and the beauties not forced into it, but resulting from it,* v.50. *How men are disappointed in their most expensive undertakings for want of this true foundation, without which nothing can please* long, *if* at all; *and the best* examples *and* rules *will but be perverted into something* burdensome *or ridiculous,* v.65, *etc. to* 92. *A description of the* false taste *of* magnificence; *the first grand error of which is to imagine that* greatness *consists in the* size *and* dimension, *instead of the* proportion *and* harmony, *of the* whole, v. 97, *and the second, either in joining together* parts incoherent, *or too* minutely resembling, *or in the* repetition *of the* same *too frequently,* v. 105, *etc. A word or two of false taste in* books, *in* music, *in* painting, *even in* preaching *and* prayer, *and lastly in* entertainments, v. 133, *etc. Yet* PROVIDENCE *is justified in giving wealth to be squandered in this manner, since it is dispersed to the poor and laborious part of mankind,* v. 169. *[recurring to what is laid down in the first book, Ep.* ii. *and in the Epistle preceding this,* v. 159, *etc.] What are the* proper objects *of magnificence, and a proper field for the expense of* great men, v. 177, *etc. and finally, the great and public works which become a* prince, v. 191, *to the end.*

'Tis strange the miser should his cares employ
To gain those riches he can ne'er enjoy.
Is it less strange the prodigal should waste
His wealth, to purchase what he ne'er can taste?
Not for himself he sees, or hears, or eats;
Artists must choose his pictures, music, meats:
He buys for Topham, drawings and designs;
For Pembroke statues, dirty gods, and coins;
Rare monkish manuscripts for Hearne alone,
And books for Mead, and butterflies for Sloane.
Think we all these are for himself? no more
Than his fine wife, alas! or finer whore.

    For what has Virro painted, built, and planted?
Only to show, how many tastes he wanted.
What brought Sir Visto's ill got wealth to waste?
Some demon whispered, 'Visto! have a taste.'
Heaven visits with a taste the wealthy fool,
And needs no rod but Ripley with a rule.
See! sportive fate, to punish awkward pride,
Bids Bubo build, and sends him such a guide:
A standing sermon, at each year's expense,
That never coxcomb reached magnificence!

    You show us, Rome was glorious, not profuse,
And pompous buildings once were things of use.
Yet shall (my Lord) your just, your noble rules
Fill half the land with imitating fools;
Who random drawings from your sheets shall take,
And of one beauty many blunders make;
Load some vain church with old theatric state,
Turn arcs of triumph to a garden-gate;
Reverse your ornaments, and hang them all
On some patched dog-hole eked with ends of wall,
Then clap four slices of pilaster on't,
That, laced with bits of rustic, makes a front:
Or call the winds through long arcades to roar,
Proud to catch cold at a Venetian door;
Conscious they act a true Palladian part,
And if they starve, they starve by rules of art.

    Oft have you hinted to your brother peer,
A certain truth, which many buy too dear:
Something there is, more needful than expense,
And something previous even to taste—'tis sense:
Good sense, which only is the gift of heaven,
And though no science, fairly worth the seven:
A light, which in yourself you must perceive;
Jones and Le Nôtre have it not to give.

    To build, to plant, whatever you intend,

To rear the column, or the arch to bend,
To swell the terrace, or to sink the grot,
In all, let nature never be forgot.
But treat the goddess like a modest fair,
Nor over-dress, nor leave her wholly bare;
Let not each beauty everywhere be spied,
Where half the skill is decently to hide.
He gains all points, who pleasingly confounds,
Surprises, varies, and conceals the bounds.
   Consult the genius of the place in all;
That tells the waters or to rise, or fall,
Or helps th' ambitious hill the heavens to scale,
Or scoops in circling theatres the vale;
Calls in the country, catches opening glades,
Joins willing woods, and varies shades from shades;
Now breaks, or now directs, th' intending lines,
Paints as you plant, and as you work, designs.
   Still follow sense, of every art the soul,
Parts answering parts shall slide into a whole,
Spontaneous beauties all around advance,
Start even from difficulty, strike from chance;
Nature shall join you; time shall make it grow
A work to wonder at—perhaps a STOWE.
   Without it, proud Versailles! thy glory falls,
And Nero's terraces desert their walls:
The vast parterres a thousand hands shall make,
Lo! COBHAM comes, and floats them with a lake:
Or cut wide views through mountains to the plain,
You'll wish your hill or sheltered seat again.
Even in an ornament its place remark,
Nor in a hermitage set Dr. Clarke.
   Behold Villario's ten years' toil complete;
His arbours darkens, his espaliers meet;
The wood supports the plain, the parts unite,
And strength of shade contends with strength of light:
A waving glow the bloomy beds display,
Blushing in bright diversities of day,
With silver-quivering rills meandered o'er—
Enjoy them, you! Villario can no more;
Tired of the scene parterres and fountains yield,
He finds at last he better likes a field.
   Through his young woods how pleased Sabinus strayed
Or sat delighted in the thickening shade,
With annual joy the reddening shoots to greet,
Or see the stretching branches long to meet.
His son's fine taste an opener vista loves,
Foe to the dryads of his father's groves,
One boundless green, or flourished carpet views,

With all the mournful family of yews;
The thriving plants ignoble broomsticks made,
Now sweep those alleys they were born to shade.
    At Timon's villa let us pass a day,
Where all cry out, 'What sums are thrown away!'
So proud, so grand, of that stupendous air,
Soft and agreeable come never there.
Greatness, with Timon, dwells in such a draught
As brings all Brobdignag before your thought.
To compass this, his building is a town,
His pond an ocean, his parterre a down:
Who but must laugh, the master when he sees?
A puny insect, shivering at a breeze.
Lo! what huge heaps of littleness around!
The whole, a laboured quarry above ground.
Two cupids squirt before: a lake behind
Improves the keenness of the northern wind.
His gardens next your admiration call,
On every side you look, behold the wall!
No pleasing intricacies intervene,
No artful wildness to perplex the scene;
Grove nods at grove, each alley has a brother,
And half the platform just reflects the other.
The suffering eye inverted nature sees,
Trees cut to statues, statues thick as trees,
With here a fountain, never to be played,
And there a summer-house, that knows no shade.
Here Amphitrite sails through myrtle bowers;
There gladiators fight, or die, in flowers;
Un-watered see the drooping sea-horse mourn,
And swallows roost in Nilus' dusty urn.
    My Lord advances with majestic mien,
Smit with the mighty pleasure, to be seen:
But soft—by regular approach—not yet—
First through the length of yon hot terrace sweat,
And when up ten steep slopes you've dragged your thighs,
Just at his study door he'll bless your eyes.
    His study! with what authors is it stored?
In books, not authors, curious is my lord;
To all their dated backs he turns you round:
These Aldus printed, those Du Suëil has bound.
Lo some are vellum, and the rest as good
For all his Lordship knows, but they are wood.
For Locke or Milton 'tis in vain to look,
These shelves admit not any modern book.
    And now the chapel's silver bell you hear,
That summons you to all the pride of prayer:
Light quirks of music, broken and uneven,

Make the soul dance upon a jig to heaven.
On painted ceilings you devoutly stare,
Where sprawl the saints of Verrio or Laguerre,
On gilded clouds in fair expansion lie,
And bring all paradise before your eye.
To rest, the cushion and soft dean invite,
Who never mentions hell to ears polite.
   But hark! the chiming clocks to dinner call;
A hundred footsteps scrape the marble hall:
The rich buffet well-coloured serpents grace,
And gaping Tritons spew to wash your face.
Is this a dinner? this a genial room?
No, 'tis a temple, and a hecatomb,
A solemn sacrifice, performed in state,
You drink by measure, and to minutes eat.
So quick retires each flying course, you'd swear
Sancho's dread doctor and his wand were there.
Between each act the trembling salvers ring,
From soup to sweet-wine, and 'God bless the King'.
In plenty starving, tantalized in state,
And complaisantly helped to all I hate,
Treated, caressed, and tired, I take my leave,
Sick of his civil pride from morn to eve;
I curse such lavish cost, and little skill,
And swear no day was ever passed so ill.
   Yet hence the poor are clothed, the hungry fed;
Health to himself, and to his infants bread
The labourer bears: what his hard heart denies,
His charitable vanity supplies.
   Another age shall see the golden ear
Imbrown the slope, and nod on the parterre,
Deep harvests bury all his pride has planned,
And laughing Ceres reassume the land.
   Who then shall grace, or who improve the soil?
Who plants like BATHURST, or who builds like BOYLE.
'Tis use alone that sanctifies expense,
And splendour borrows all her rays from sense.
   His father's acres who enjoys in peace,
Or makes his neighbours glad, if he increase;
Whose cheerful tenants bless their yearly toil,
Yet to their Lord owe more than to the soil;
Whose ample lawns are not ashamed to feed
The milky heifer and deserving steed;
Whose rising forests, not for pride or show,
But future buildings, future navies, grow:
Let his plantations stretch from down to down,
First shade a country, and then raise a town.
   You too proceed! make falling arts your care,

Erect new wonders, and the old repair;
Jones and Palladio to themselves restore,
And be whate'er Vitruvius was before:
Till kings call forth th' ideas of your mind,
(Proud to accomplish what such hands designed,)
Bid harbours open, public ways extend,
Bid temples, worthier of the god, ascend,
Bid the broad arch the dangerous flood contain,
The mole projected break the roaring main;
Back to his bounds their subject sea command,
And roll obedient rivers through the land:
These honours, peace to happy Britain brings,
These are imperial works, and worthy kings.

AN EPISTLE
TO
Allen Lord *Bathurst*

ARGUMENT
Of the Use *of* RICHES

That it is known to few, most falling into one of the extremes, avarice *or* profusion, v. 1,
etc. *The point discussed, whether the invention of money has been more commodious or
pernicious to mankind, v. 21 to 77. That riches, either to the* avaricious *or the* prodigal,
*cannot afford happiness, scarcely necessaries, v. 85 to 106. That avarice is an absolute
frenzy, without an end or purpose, v. 107 etc. Conjectures about the motives of
avaricious men, v. 113 to 153. That the conduct of men, with respect to riches, can only
be accounted for by the* ORDER OF PROVIDENCE, *which works the general good out of
extremes, and brings all to its great end by perpetual revolutions, v. 161 to 178. How a
miser acts upon principles which appear to him reasonable, v. 179. How a prodigal does
the same, v. 199. The due medium and true use of riches v. 219. The* Man *of* Ross, v. 250.
*The fate of the profuse and the covetous, in two examples; both miserable in life and in
death, v. 300, etc. The story of Sir* Balaam, v. 339 to the end.*

Who shall decide, when doctors disagree,
And soundest casuists doubt, like you and me?
You hold the word from Jove to Momus given,
That man was made the standing jest of heaven;
And gold but sent to keep the fools in play,
For some to heap, and some to throw away.
  But I, who think more highly of our kind,
(And surely, heaven and I are of a mind)
Opine, that nature, as in duty bound,
Deep hid the shining mischief under ground:
But when by man's audacious labour won,
Flamed forth this rival to its sire the sun,
Then careful heaven supplied two sorts of men,

To squander these, and those to hide again.
   Like doctors thus, when much dispute has past,
We find our tenets just the same at last.
Both fairly owning, riches in effect,
No grace of heaven, or token of th' elect;
Given to the fool, the mad, the vain, the evil,
To Ward, to Waters, Chartres, and the devil.
What nature wants, commodious gold bestows,
'Tis thus we eat the bread another sows:
But how unequal it bestows, observe,
'Tis thus we riot, while who sow it, starve.
What nature wants (a phrase I much distrust)
Extends to luxury, extends to lust:
Useful, I grant, it serves what life requires,
But dreadful too, the dark assassin hires:
Trade it may help, Society extend;
But lures the pirate, and corrupts the friend:
It raises armies in a nation's aid,
But bribes a senate, and the land's betrayed.
In vain may heroes fight, and patriots rave;
If secret gold saps on from knave to knave.
Once, we confess, beneath the patriot's cloak,
From the cracked bag the dropping guinea spoke,
And gingling down the back-stairs, told the crew,
'Old Cato is as great a rogue as you.'
Blessed paper-credit! last and best supply!
That lends corruption lighter wings to fly!
Gold imped by thee, can compass hardest things,
Can pocket states, can fetch or carry kings;
A single leaf shall waft an army o'er,
Or ship off senates to some distant shore;
A leaf, like sibyl's, scatter to and fro
Our fates and fortunes, as the winds shall blow:
Pregnant with thousands flits the scrap unseen,
And silent sells a king, or buys a queen.
   Oh! that such bulky bribes as all might see,
Still, as of old, incumbered villainy!
Could France or Rome divert our brave designs,
With all their brandies or with all their wines?
What could they more than knights and squires confound,
Or water all the quorum ten miles round?
A statesman's slumbers how this speech would spoil!
'Sir, Spain has sent a thousand jars of oil;
Huge bales of British cloth blockade the door;
A hundred oxen at your levee roar.'
   Poor avarice one torment more would find;
Nor could Profusion squander all, in kind.
Astride his cheese Sir Morgan might we meet,

And Worldly crying coals from street to street,
Whom with a wig so wild, and mien so mazed,
Pity mistakes for some poor tradesman crazed.
Had Colepepper's whole wealth been hops and hogs,
Could he himself have sent it to the dogs?
His Grace will game: to White's a bull be led,
With spurning heels and with a butting head.
To White's be carried, as to ancient games,
Fair coursers, vases, and alluring dames.
Shall then Uxorio, if the stakes he sweep,
Bear home six whores, and make his lady weep?
Or soft Adonis, so perfumed and fine,
Drive to St. James's a whole herd of swine?
Oh filthy check on all industrious skill,
To spoil the nation's last great trade, quadrille!
Since then, my Lord, on such a world we fall,
What say you? 'Say? Why, take it, gold and all.'
   What riches give us let us then enquire:
Meat, fire, and clothes, what more? Meat, clothes, and fire.
Is this too little? would you more than live?
Alas! 'tis more than Turner finds they give.
Alas! 'tis more than (all his visions past)
Unhappy Wharton, waking, found at last!
What can they give? To dying Hopkins, heirs;
To Chartres, vigour; Japhet, nose and ears?
Can they, in gems bid pallid Hippia glow,
In Fulvia's buckle ease the throbs below;
Or heal, old Narses, thy obscener ail,
With all th' embroidery plastered at thy tail?
They might (were Harpax not too wise to spend)
Give Harpax' self the blessing of a friend;
Or find some doctor that would save the life
Of wretched Shylock, spite of Shylock's wife:
But thousands die, without or this or that,
Die, and endow a college, or a cat:
To some, indeed, heaven grants the happier fate,
T' enrich a bastard, or a son they hate.
   Perhaps you think the poor might have their part?
Bond damns the poor, and hates them from his heart:
The grave Sir Gilbert holds it for a rule,
That 'every man in want is knave or fool:'
'God cannot love' (says Blunt, with tearless eyes)
'The wretch he starves'—and piously denies:
But the good bishop, with a meeker air,
Admits, and leaves them, Providence's care.
   Yet, to be just to these poor men of pelf,
Each does but hate his neighbour as himself:
Damned to the mines, an equal fate betides

The slave that digs it, and the slave that hides.
Who suffer thus, mere charity should own,
Must act on motives powerful, though unknown:
Some war, some plague, or famine, they foresee,
Some revelation hid from you and me.
Why Shylock wants a meal, the cause is found,
He thinks a loaf will rise to fifty pound.
What made directors cheat in South Sea year?
To live on venison when it sold so dear.
Ask you why Phryne the whole auction buys?
Phryne foresees a general excise.
Why she and Sappho raise that monstrous sum?
Alas! they fear a man will cost a plum.
    Wise Peter sees the world's respect for gold,
And therefore hopes this nation may be sold:
Glorious ambition! Peter, swell thy store,
And be what Rome's great Didius was before.
    The crown of Poland, venal twice an age,
To just three millions stinted modest Gage.
But nobler scenes Maria's dreams unfold,
Hereditary realms, and worlds of gold.
Congenial souls! whose life one avarice joins,
And one fate buries in th' Asturian mines.
    Much-injured Blunt! why bears he Britain's hate?
A wizard told him in these words our fate:
'At length corruption, like a general flood
(So long by watchful ministers withstood)
Shall deluge all; and avarice, creeping on,
Spread like a low-born mist, and blot the sun;
Statesman and patriot ply alike the stocks,
Peeress and butler share alike the box,
And judges job, and bishops bite the town,
And mighty dukes pack cards for half a crown.
See Britain sunk in lucre's sordid charms,
And France revenged of ANNE'S and EDWARD'S arms!'
'Twas no court-badge, great scrivener! fired thy brain,
Nor lordly luxury, nor city gain:
No, 'twas thy righteous end, (ashamed to see
Senates degenerate, patriots disagree,
And nobly wishing party-rage to cease)
To buy both sides, and give thy country peace.
    'All this is madness,' cries a sober sage:
But who, my friend, has reason in his rage?
'The ruling passion, be it what it will,
The ruling passion conquers reason still.'
Less mad the wildest whimsy we can frame,
Than even that passion, if it has no aim;
For though such motives folly you may call,

The folly's greater to have none at all.
   Hear then the truth: "Tis heaven each passion sends,
And different men directs to different ends.
Extremes in nature equal good produce,
Extremes in man concur to general use.'
Ask me what makes one keep, and one bestow?
That POWER who bids the ocean ebb and flow;
Bids seed-time, harvest, equal course maintain,
Through reconciled extremes of drought and rain;
Builds life on death, on change duration founds,
And gives th' eternal wheels to know their rounds.
   Riches, like insects, when concealed they lie,
Wait but for wings, and in their season fly.
Who sees pale Mammon pine amidst his store,
Sees but a backward steward for the poor;
This year a reservoir, to keep and spare;
The next, a fountain, spouting through his heir,
In lavish streams to quench a country's thirst,
And men and dogs shall drink him till they burst.
   Old Cotta shamed his fortune and his birth,
Yet was not Cotta void of wit or worth:
What though (the use of barbarous spits forgot)
His kitchen vied in coolness with his grot?
His court with nettles, moats with cresses stored,
With soups unbought and salads blessed his board?
If Cotta lived on pulse, it was no more
Than Bramins, Saints, and Sages did before;
To cram the rich was prodigal expense,
And who would take the poor from Providence?
Like some lone Chartreux stands the good old hall,
Silence without, and fasts within the wall;
No raftered roofs with dance and tabor sound,
No noontide-bell invites the country round:
Tenants with sighs the smokeless towers survey,
And turn th' unwilling steeds another way:
Benighted wanderers, the forest o'er,
Curse the saved candle, and unopening door;
While the gaunt mastiff, growling at the gate,
Affrights the beggar whom he longs to eat.
   Not so his son, he marked this oversight,
And then mistook reverse of wrong for right.
(For what to shun will no great knowledge need,
But what to follow, is a task indeed.)
Yet sure, of qualities deserving praise,
More go to ruin fortunes, than to raise.
What slaughtered hecatombs, and floods of wine,
Fill the capacious squire and deep divine!
Yet no mean motive this profusion draws,

His oxen perish in his country's cause;
'tis GEORGE and LIBERTY that crowns the cup,
And zeal for that great house which eats him up.
The woods recede around the naked seat,
The sylvans groan—no matter—for the fleet:
Next goes his wool—to clothe our valiant bands,
Last, for his country's love, he sells his lands.
To town he comes, completes the nation's hope,
And heads the bold train-bands, and burns a Pope.
And shall not Britain now reward his toils,
Britain, that pays her patriots with her spoils?
In vain at court the bankrupt pleads his cause,
His thankless country leaves him to her laws.

    The sense to value riches, with the art
T' enjoy them, and the virtue to impart,
Not meanly, nor ambitiously pursued,
Not sunk by sloth, nor raised by servitude;
To balance fortune by a just expense,
Join with economy magnificence;
With splendour, charity; with plenty health;
O teach us, BATHURST! yet unspoiled by wealth!
That secret rare, between th' extremes to move
Of mad good-nature and of mean self-love.

    To worth or want well-weighed, be bounty given,
And ease, or emulate, the care of heaven;
(Whose measure full o'erflows on human race)
Mend fortune's fault, and justify her grace.
Wealth in the gross is death, but life diffused;
As poison heals, in just proportion used:
In heaps, like ambergris, a stink it lies,
But well-dispersed is incense to the skies.

    Who starves by nobles, or with nobles eats?
The wretch that trusts them, and the rogue that cheats.
Is there a lord, who knows a cheerful noon
Without a fiddler, flatterer, or buffoon?
Whose table, wit, or modest merit share,
Un-elbowed by a gamester, pimp, or player?
Who copies yours or OXFORD'S better part,
To ease th' oppressed, and raise the sinking heart?
Where'er he shines, oh fortune, gild the scene,
And angels guard him in the golden mean!
There, English bounty yet a while may stand,
And honour linger e'er it leaves the land.

    But all our praises why should lords engross?
Rise, honest Muse! and sing the MAN OF ROSS:
Pleased Vaga echoes through her winding bounds,
And rapid Severn hoarse applause resounds.
Who hung with woods yon mountain's sultry brow?

From the dry rock who bade the waters flow?
Not to the skies in useless columns tossed,
Or in proud falls magnificently lost,
But clear and artless, pouring through the plain
Health to the sick, and solace to the swain.
Whose causeway parts the vale with shady rows?
Whose seats the weary traveller repose?
Who taught that heaven-directed spire to rise?
'The MAN OF ROSS,' each lisping babe replies.
Behold the market-place with poor o'erspread!
The MAN OF ROSS divides the weekly bread:
He feeds yon alms-house, neat, but void of state,
Where age and want sit smiling at the gate:
Him portioned maids, apprenticed orphans blessed,
The young who labour, and the old who rest.
Is any sick? the MAN OF ROSS relieves,
Prescribes, attends, the medicine makes and gives.
Is there a variance? enter but his door,
Balked are the courts, and contest is no more.
Despairing quacks with curses fled the place,
And vile attorneys, now a useless race.
　　'Thrice happy man! enabled to pursue
What all so wish, but want the power to do!
Oh say, what sums that generous hand supply?
What mines, to swell that boundless charity?'
　　Of debts, and taxes, wife and children clear,
This man possessed—five hundred pounds a year.
Blush, grandeur, blush! proud courts, withdraw your blaze!
Ye little stars! hide your diminished rays.
　　'And what? no monument, inscription, stone?
His race, his form, his name almost unknown?'
　　Who builds a church to God, and not to fame,
Will never mark the marble with his name:
Go, search it there, where to be born and die,
Of rich and poor makes all the history;
Enough, that virtue filled the space between;
Proved, by the ends of being, to have been.
When Hopkins dies, a thousand lights attend
The wretch, who living saved a candle's end:
Shouldering God's altar a vile image stands,
Belies his features, nay extends his hands;
That livelong wig which Gorgon's self might own,
Eternal buckle takes in Parian stone.
Behold what blessings wealth to life can lend!
And see, what comfort it affords our end.
　　In the worst inn's worst room, with mat half-hung,
The floors of plaster, and the walls of dung,
On once a flock-bed, but repaired with straw,

With tape-tied curtains, never meant to draw,
The George and garter dangling from that bed
Where tawdry yellow strove with dirty red,
Great Villiers lies—alas! how changed from him,
That life or pleasure and that soul of whim!
Gallant and gay, in Cliveden's proud alcove,
The bower of wanton Shrewsbury and love;
Or just as gay, at council, in a ring
Of mimic statesmen, and their merry king.
No wit to flatter, left of all his store!
No fool to laugh at, which he valued more.
There, victor of his health, of fortune, friends,
And fame, this lord of useless thousands ends.

   His Grace's fate sage Cutler could foresee,
And well (he thought) advised him, 'Live like me.'
And well his Grace replied, 'Like you, Sir John?
That I can do, when all I have is gone.'
Resolve me, reason, which of these is worse,
Want with a full, or with an empty purse?
Thy life more wretched, Cutler, was confessed,
Arise, and tell me, was thy death more blessed?
Cutler saw tenants break, and houses fall,
For very want; he could not build a wall.
His only daughter in a stranger's power,
For very want; he could not pay a dower.
A few gray hairs his reverend temples crowned,
'Twas very want that sold them for two pound.
What even denied a cordial at his end,
Banished the doctor, and expelled the friend?
What but a want, which you perhaps think mad,
Yet numbers feel, the want of what he had!
Cutler and Brutus dying both exclaim,
'Virtue! and wealth! what are ye but a name!'

   Say, for such worth are other worlds prepared?
Or are they both, in this, their own reward?
A knotty point! to which we now proceed.
But you are tired—I'll tell a tale—'Agreed.'

   Where London's column, pointing at the skies,
Like a tall bully, lifts the head, and lies;
There dwelt a citizen of sober fame,
A plain good man, and Balaam was his name;
Religious, punctual, frugal, and so forth;
His word would pass for more than he was worth.
One solid dish his weekday meal affords,
An added pudding solemnized the Lord's:
Constant at church and Change; his gains were sure,
His givings rare, save farthings to the poor.

   The devil was piqued such saintship to behold,

And longed to tempt him like good Job of old:
But Satan now is wiser than of yore,
And tempts by making rich, not making poor.

    Roused by the prince of air, the whirlwinds sweep
The surge, and plunge his father in the deep;
Then full against his Cornish lands they roar,
And two rich shipwrecks bless the lucky shore.

    Sir Balaam now, he lives like other folks,
He takes his chirping pint, and cracks his jokes:
'Live like yourself,' was soon my Lady's word;
And lo! two puddings smoked upon the board.

    Asleep and naked as an Indian lay,
An honest factor stole a gem away:
He pledged it to the knight; the knight had wit,
So kept the diamond, and the rogue was bit.
Some scruple rose, but thus he eased his thought,
'I'll now give sixpence where I gave a groat;
Where once I went to church, I'll now go twice—
And am so clear too of all other vice.'

    The tempter saw his time; the work he plied;
Stocks and subscriptions pour on every side,
Till all the demon makes his full descent
In one abundant shower of cent per cent,
Sinks deep within him, and possesses whole,
Then dubs director, and secures his soul.

    Behold Sir Balaam, now a man of spirit,
Ascribes his gettings to his parts and merit;
What late he called a blessing now was wit,
And God's good Providence, a lucky hit.
Things change their titles as our manners turn:
His counting house employed the Sunday morn;
Seldom at church ('twas such a busy life)
But duly sent his family and wife.
There (so the devil ordained) one Christmas-tide
My good old lady catched a cold and died.

    A nymph of quality admires our knight;
He marries, bows at court, and grows polite:
Leaves the dull cits, and joins (to please the fair)
The well-bred cuckolds in St. James's air:
First, for his son a gay commission buys,
Who drinks, whores, fights, and in a duel dies:
His daughter flaunts a viscount's tawdry wife;
She bears a coronet and p—x for life.
In Britain's senate he a seat obtains,
And one more pensioner St. Stephen gains.
My Lady falls to play; so bad her chance,
He must repair it; takes a bribe from France;
The House impeach him; Coningsby harangues;

The court forsake him, and Sir Balaam hangs:
Wife, son, and daughter, Satan! are thy own,
His wealth, yet dearer, forfeit to the crown:
The devil and the king divide the prize,
And sad Sir Balaam curses God and dies.

THE
FIRST SATIRE
OF THE
SECOND BOOK
OF
HORACE IMITATED
To Mr. FORTESCUE

Advertisement

The occasion of publishing these *Imitations* was the clamour raised on some of my *Epistles*. An answer from *Horace* was both more full, and of more dignity, than any I could have made in my own person; and the example of much greater freedom in so eminent a divine as Dr. Donne, seemed a proof with what indignation and contempt a Christian may treat vice or folly, in ever so low, or ever so high, a station. Both these authors were acceptable to the princes and ministers under whom they lived. The Satires of Dr. Donne I versified, at the desire of the Earl of Oxford while he was Lord Treasurer, and of the Duke of Shrewsbury who had been Secretary of State; neither of whom looked upon a satire on vicious courts as any reflection on those they served in. And indeed there is not in the world a greater error, than that which fools are so apt to fall into, and knaves with good reason to encourage, the mistaking a *satirist* for a *libeller*; whereas to a *true satirist* nothing is so odious as a *libeller*, for the same reason as to a man *truly virtuous* nothing is so hateful as a *hypocrite*.

—Uni aequus Virtuti atque ejus Amicis.

P. There are (I scarce can think it, but am told)
There are, to whom my satire seems too bold:
Scarce to wise Peter complaisant enough,
And something said of Chartres much too rough.
The lines are weak, another's pleased to say,
Lord Fanny spins a thousand such a day.
Timorous by nature, of the rich in awe,
I come to counsel learned in the law:
You'll give me, like a friend both sage and free,
Advice; and (as you use) without a fee.
    F. I'd write no more.
          P. Not write? but then I think,
And for my soul I cannot sleep a wink.
I nod in company, I wake at night,
Fools rush into my head, and so I write.
    F. You could not do a worse thing for your life.

Why, if the nights seem tedious—take a wife:
Or rather truly, if your point be rest,
Lettuce and cowslip-wine: *probatum est.*
But talk with Celsus, Celsus will advise
Hartshorn, or something that shall close your eyes.
Or, if you needs must write, write CAESAR'S praise,
You'll gain at least a *knighthood,* or the *bays.*
    P. What? like Sir Richard, rumbling, rough, and fierce,
With ARMS, and GEORGE, and BRUNSWICK crowd the verse,
Rend with tremendous sound your ears asunder,
With gun, drum, trumpet, blunderbuss, and thunder?
Or nobly wild, with Budgell's fire and force,
Paint angels trembling round his falling horse?
    F. Then all your muse's softer art display,
Let CAROLINA smooth the tuneful lay,
Lull with AMELIA'S liquid name the nine,
And sweetly flow through all the royal line.
    P. Alas! few verses touch their nicer ear;
They scarce can bear their *Laureate* twice a year;
And justly CAESAR scorns the poet's lays,
It is to *history* he trusts for praise.
    F. Better be Cibber, I'll maintain it still,
Than ridicule all taste, blaspheme quadrille,
Abuse the city's best good men in metre,
And laugh at peers that put their trust in Peter.
Even those you touch not, hate you.
        P. What should ail them?
    F. A hundred smart in Timon and in Balaam:
The fewer still you name, you wound the more;
Bond is but one, but Harpax is a score.
    P. Each mortal has his pleasure: none deny
Scarsdale his bottle, Darty his ham-pie;
Ridotta sips and dances, till she see
The doubling lustres dance as fast as she;
Fox loves the senate, Hockley Hole his brother,
Like in all else, as one egg to another.
I love to pour out all myself, as plain
As downright SHIPPEN, or as old Montaigne:
In them, as certain to be loved as seen,
The soul stood forth, nor kept a thought within;
In me what spots (for spots I have) appear,
Will prove at least the medium must be clear.
In this impartial glass, my muse intends
Fair to expose myself, my foes, my friends;
Publish the present age; but where my text
Is vice too high, reserve it for the next:
My foes shall wish my life a longer date,
And every friend the less lament my fate.

My head and heart thus flowing through my quill,
Verse-man or prose-man, term me which you will,
Papist or Protestant, or both between,
Like good Erasmus in an honest mean,
In moderation placing all my glory,
While Tories call me Whig, and Whigs a Tory.
    Satire's my weapon, but I'm too discreet
To run amuck, and tilt at all I meet;
I only wear it in a land of Hectors,
Thieves, supercargoes, sharpers, and directors.
Save but our *army!* and let Jove encrust
Swords, pikes, and guns, with everlasting rust!
Peace is my dear delight—not FLEURY'S more:
But touch me, and no minister so sore.
Whoe'er offends, at some unlucky time
Slides into verse, and hitches in a rhyme,
Sacred to ridicule his whole life long,
And the sad burthen of some merry song.
    Slander or poison dread from Delia's rage,
Hard words or hanging, if your judge be Page.
From furious Sappho scarce a milder fate,
P-xed by her love, or libelled by her hate.
Its proper power to hurt, each creature feels;
Bulls aim their horns, and asses lift their heels;
'Tis a bear's talent not to kick, but hug;
And no man wonders he's not stung by Pug.
So drink with Walters, or with Chartres eat,
They'll never poison you, they'll only cheat.
    Then, learned Sir! (to cut the matter short)
Whate'er my fate, or well or ill at court,
Whether old age, with faint but cheerful ray,
Attends to gild the evening of my day,
Or death's black wing already be displayed,
To wrap me in the universal shade;
Whether the darkened room to muse invite,
Or whitened wall provoke the skewer to write:
In durance, exile, Bedlam or the Mint,
Like Lee or Budgell, I will rhyme and print.
    F. Alas young man! your days can ne'er be long,
In flower of age you perish for a song!
Plums and directors, Shylock and his wife,
Will club their testers, now, to take your life!
    P. What, armed for virtue when I point the pen,
Brand the bold front of shameless, guilty men;
Dash the proud gamester in his gilded car;
Bare the mean heart that lurks beneath a *star*;
Can there be wanting, to defend her cause,
Lights of the church, or guardians of the laws?

Could pensioned Boileau lash in honest strain
Flatterers and bigots even in Louis' reign?
Could Laureate Dryden pimp and friar engage,
Yet neither Charles nor James be in a rage?
And I not strip the gilding off a knave,
Unplaced, unpensioned, no man's heir, or slave?
I will, or perish in the generous cause:
Hear this, and tremble! you, who 'scape the Laws.
Yes, while I live, no rich or noble knave
Shall walk the world, in credit, to his grave.
To VIRTUE ONLY and HER FRIENDS, A FRIEND,
The world beside may murmur, or commend.
Know, all the distant din that world can keep,
Rolls o'er my grotto, and but soothes my sleep.
There, my retreat the best companions grace,
Chiefs out of war, and statesmen out of place.
There ST. JOHN mingles with my friendly bowl
The feast of reason and the flow of soul:
And HE, whose lightning pierced the Iberian lines,
Now forms my quincunx, and now ranks my vines,
Or tames the genius of the stubborn plain,
Almost as quickly as he conquered Spain.

Envy must own, I live among the great,
No pimp of pleasure, and no spy of state.
With eyes that pry not, tongue that ne'er repeats,
Fond to spread friendships, but to cover heats;
To help who want, to forward who excel;
This, all who know me, know; who love me, tell;
And who unknown defame me, let them be
Scribblers or peers, alike are *mob* to me.
This is my plea, on this I rest my cause—
What saith my counsel, learned in the laws?

F. Your plea is good; but still I say, beware!
Laws are explained by men—so have a care.
It stands on record, that in Richard's times
A man was hanged for very honest rhymes.
Consult the statute: *quart.* I think, it is,
Edwardi sext. or *prim. et quint. Eliz.*
See libels, satires—here you have it—read.

P. Libels and *Satires!* lawless things indeed!
But grave *Epistles*, bringing vice to light,
Such as a king might read, a bishop write,
Such as SIR ROBERT would approve—
                                        F. Indeed?
The case is altered—you may then proceed;
In such a cause the plaintiff would be hissed,
My lords the judges laugh, and you're dismissed.

AN
ESSAY ON MAN
IN
FOUR EPISTLES
TO
H. St. John Lord Bolingbroke

THE DESIGN

Having proposed to write some pieces of human life and manners, such as (to use my Lord Bacon's expression) 'come home to men's business and bosoms', I thought it more satisfactory to begin with considering *Man* in the abstract, his *Nature* and his *State*; since, to prove any moral duty, to enforce any moral precept, or to examine the perfection or imperfection of any creature whatsoever, it is necessary first to know what *condition* and *relation* it is placed in, and what is the proper *end* and *purpose* of its *being*.

The science of human nature is, like all other sciences, reduced to a *few clear points*: there are not *many certain truths* in this world. It is therefore in the anatomy of the mind as in that of the body; more good will accrue to mankind by attending to the large, open, and perceptible parts, than by studying too much such finer nerves and vessels, the conformations and uses of which will for ever escape our observation. The *disputes* are all upon these last, and, I will venture to say, they have less sharpened the *wits* than the *hearts* of men against each other, and have diminished the practice more than advanced the theory of morality. If I could flatter myself that this Essay has any merit, it is in steering betwixt the extremes of doctrines seemingly opposite, in passing over terms utterly unintelligible, and in forming a *temperate* yet not *inconsistent*, and a *short* yet not *imperfect* system of ethics.

This I might have done in prose; but I chose verse, and even rhyme, for two reasons. The one will appear obvious; that principles, maxims, or precepts so written, both strike the reader more strongly at first, and are more easily retained by him afterwards. The other may seem odd, but is true, I found I could express them more *shortly* this way than in prose itself; and nothing is more certain, than that much of the *force* as well as *grace* of arguments or instructions, depends on their conciseness. I was unable to treat this part of my subject more in *detail*, without becoming dry and tedious; or more *poetically*, without sacrificing perspicuity to ornament, without wandering from the precision, or breaking the chain of reasoning. If any man can unite all these without diminution of any of them, I freely confess he will compass a thing above my capacity.

What is now published is only to be considered as a *general map* of MAN, marking out no more than the *greater parts*, their *extent*, their *limits*, and their *connection*, but leaving the particular to be more fully delineated in the charts which are to follow. Consequently, these Epistles in their progress (if I have health and leisure to make any progress) will be less dry, and more susceptible of poetical ornament. I am here only opening the fountains, and clearing the passage. To deduce the rivers, to follow them in their course, and to observe their effects, may be a task more agreeable.

EPISTLE I.

ARGUMENT
Of the Nature and State of Man, with respect to the UNIVERSE

Of Man *in the abstract.*—I. *That we can judge only with regard to our* own system, *being ignorant of the* relations *of systems and things,* v.17, etc. II. *That Man is not to be deemed* imperfect, *but a being suited to his* place *and* rank *in the creation, agreeable to the* general order *of things, and conformable to* ends *and* relations *to him unknown,* v.35, etc. III. *That it is partly upon his* ignorance *of* future *events, and partly upon the* hope *of a* future *state, that all his happiness in the present depends,* v.77, etc. IV. *The* pride *of aiming at more knowledge, and pretending to more perfection, the cause of Man's error and misery. The* impiety *of putting himself in the place of* God, *and judging of the fitness or unfitness, perfection or imperfection, justice or injustice of His dispensations,* v.113, etc. V. *The* absurdity *of conceiting himself the* final cause *of the creation, or expecting that perfection in the* moral world, *which is not in the* natural, v.131, etc. VI. *The* unreasonableness *of his complaints against* Providence, *while on the one hand he demands the perfections of the angels, and on the other the bodily qualifications of the brutes; though to possess any of the* sensitive faculties *in a higher degree would render him miserable,* v.173, etc. VII. *That throughout the whole visible world, an universal* order *and* gradation *in the sensual and mental faculties is observed, which cause is a subordination of creature to creature, and of all creatures to Man. The gradations of* sense, instinct, thought, reflection, reason; *that reason alone countervails all the other faculties,* v.207. VIII. *How much further this* order *and* subordination *of living creatures may extend, above and below us; were any part of which broken, not that part only, but the whole connected creation, must be destroyed,* v.233. IX. *The* extravagance, madness, *and* pride *of such a desire,* v.259. X. *The consequence of all, the* absolute submission *due to Providence, both as to our* present *and* future state, v.281, etc., *to the end.*

Awake, my ST. JOHN! leave all meaner things
To low ambition, and the pride of kings.
Let us (since life can little more supply
Than just to look about us and to die)
Expatiate free o'er all this scene of Man;
A mighty maze! but not without a plan;
A wild, where weeds and flowers promiscuous shoot,
Or garden, tempting with forbidden fruit.
Together let us beat this ample field,
Try what the open, what the covert yield;
The latent tracts, the giddy heights explore
Of all who blindly creep, or sightless soar;
Eye nature's walks, shoot folly as it flies,
And catch the manners living as they rise;
Laugh where we must, be candid where we can;
But vindicate the ways of God to man.
    I. Say first, of God above, or Man below
What can we reason, but from what we know?
Of Man what see we, but his station here,

From which to reason, or to which refer?
Through worlds unnumbered though the God be known,
'Tis ours to trace him only in our own.
He, who through vast immensity can pierce,
See worlds on worlds compose one universe,
Observe how system into system runs,
What other planets circle other suns,
What varied being peoples every star,
May tell why Heaven has made us as we are.
But of this frame the bearings, and the ties,
The strong connections, nice dependencies,
Gradations just, has thy pervading soul
Looked through? or can a part contain the whole?
   Is the great chain, that draws all to agree,
And drawn supports, upheld by God, or thee?
   II. Presumptuous Man! the reason wouldst thou find,
Why formed so weak, so little, and so blind!
First, if thou canst, the harder reason guess,
Why formed no weaker, blinder, and no less!
Ask of thy mother earth, why oaks are made
Taller or stronger than the weeds they shade?
Or ask of yonder argent fields above,
Why JOVE'S satellites are less than JOVE?
   Of systems possible, if 'tis confessed
That wisdom infinite must form the best,
Where all must full or not coherent be,
And all that rises, rise in due degree;
Then in the scale of reasoning life, 'tis plain,
There must be, somewhere, such a rank as Man:
And all the question (wrangle e'er so long)
Is only this, if God has placed him wrong?
   Respecting Man, whatever wrong we call,
May, must be right, as relative to all.
In human works, though laboured on with pain,
A thousand movements scarce one purpose gain;
In God's one single can its end produce;
Yet serves to second too some other use.
So Man, who here seems principal alone,
Perhaps acts second to some sphere unknown,
Touches some wheel, or verges to some goal;
'Tis but a part we see, and not a whole.
   When the proud steed shall know why Man restrains
His fiery course, or drives him o'er the plains;
When the dull ox, why now he breaks the clod,
Is now a victim, and now Egypt's god:
Then shall man's pride and dulness comprehend
His actions', passions', being's, use and end;
Why doing, suffering, checked, impelled; and why

This hour a slave, the next a deity.

Then say not Man's imperfect, Heaven in fault;
Say rather, Man's as perfect as he ought:
His knowledge measured to his state and place,
His time a moment, and a point his space.
If to be perfect in a certain sphere,
What matter, soon or late, or here or there?
The blessed to-day is as completely so,
As who began a thousand years ago.

III. Heaven from all creatures hides the book of fate,
All but the page prescribed, their present state;
From brutes what men, from men what spirits know:
Or who could suffer being here below?
The lamb thy riot dooms to bleed today,
Had he thy reason, would he skip and play?
Pleased to the last, he crops the flowery food,
And licks the hand just raised to shed his blood.
Oh, blindness to the future! kindly given,
That each may fill the circle, marked by Heaven;
Who sees with equal eye, as God of all,
A hero perish, or a sparrow fall,
Atoms or systems into ruin hurled,
And now a bubble burst, and now a world.

Hope humbly then; with trembling pinions soar;
Wait the great teacher Death; and God adore!
What future bliss, He gives not thee to know,
But gives that hope to be thy blessing now.
Hope springs eternal in the human breast:
Man never is, but always to be blest:
The soul, uneasy and confined from home,
Rests and expatiates in a life to come.
Lo! the poor Indian, whose untutored mind
Sees God in clouds, or hears him in the wind;
His soul proud science never taught to stray
Far as the solar walk, or milky way;
Yet simple Nature to his hope has given,
Behind the cloud-topped hill, an humbler heaven;
Some safer world in depth of woods embraced,
Some happier island in the watery waste,
Where slaves once more their native land behold,
No fiends torment, no Christians thirst for gold!
To be, contents his natural desire,
He asks no angel's wing, no seraph's fire;
But thinks, admitted to that equal sky,
His faithful dog shall bear him company.

IV. Go, wiser thou! and, in thy scale of sense
Weigh thy opinion against providence;
Call imperfection what thou fanciest such,

Say, here he gives too little, there too much;
Destroy all creatures for thy sport or gust,
Yet cry, 'If Man's unhappy, God's unjust';
If Man alone engross not heaven's high care,
Alone made perfect here, immortal there:
Snatch from his hand the balance and the rod,
Re-judge his justice, be the GOD of GOD.
    In pride, in reasoning pride, our error lies;
All quit their sphere, and rush into the skies.
Pride still is aiming at the blessed abodes,
Men would be angels, angels would be gods.
Aspiring to be gods, if angels fell,
Aspiring to be angels, men rebel;
And who but wishes to invert the laws
OF ORDER, sins against the eternal cause.
    V. Ask for what end the heavenly bodies shine,
Earth for whose use? Pride answers, "Tis for mine:
For me kind Nature wakes her genial power,
Suckles each herb, and spreads out every flower;
Annual for me, the grape, the rose renew
The juice nectareous, and the balmy dew;
For me, the mine a thousand treasures brings;
For me, health gushes from a thousand springs;
Seas roll to waft me, suns to light me rise;
My footstool earth, my canopy the skies.'
    But errs not Nature from this gracious end,
From burning suns when livid deaths descend,
When earthquakes swallow, or when tempests sweep
Towns to one grave, whole nations to the deep?
'No' ('tis replied) 'the first almighty cause
Acts not by partial, but by general laws;
The exceptions few; some change since all began,
And what created perfect?'—Why then Man?
If the great end be human happiness,
Then nature deviates; and can Man do less?
As much that end a constant course requires
Of showers and sunshine, as of Man's desires;
As much eternal springs and cloudless skies,
As men for ever temperate, calm, and wise.
If plagues or earthquakes break not heaven's design,
Why then a Borgia, or a Catiline?
Who knows but he, whose hand the lightning forms,
Who heaves old ocean, and who wings the storms;
Pours fierce ambition in a Caesar's mind,
Or turns young Ammon loose to scourge mankind?
From pride, from pride, our very reasoning springs;
Account for moral, as for natural things:
Why charge we heaven in those, in these acquit?

In both, to reason right is to submit.
   Better for us, perhaps, it might appear,
Were there all harmony, all virtue here;
That never air or ocean felt the wind;
That never passion discomposed the mind:
But ALL subsists by elemental strife;
And passions are the elements of life.
The general ORDER, since the whole began,
Is kept in nature, and is kept in Man.
   VI. What would this Man? Now upward will he soar,
And little less than angel, would be more;
Now looking downwards, just as grieved appears
To want the strength of bulls, the fur of bears.
Made for his use all creatures if he call,
Say what their use, had he the powers of all?
Nature to these, without profusion kind,
The proper organs, proper powers assigned;
Each seeming want compensated of course,
Here with degrees of swiftness, there of force;
All in exact proportion to the state;
Nothing to add, and nothing to abate.
Each beast, each insect, happy in its own;
Is Heaven unkind to Man, and Man alone?
Shall he alone, whom rational we call,
Be pleased with nothing, if not blessed with all?
   The bliss of Man (could pride that blessing find)
Is not to act or think beyond mankind;
No powers of body or of soul to share,
But what his nature and his state can bear.
Why has not Man a microscopic eye?
For this plain reason, Man is not a fly.
Say what the use, were finer optics given,
To inspect a mite, not comprehend the heaven?
Or touch, if tremblingly alive all o'er,
To smart and agonize at every pore?
Or quick effluvia darting through the brain,
Die of a rose in aromatic pain?
If nature thundered in his opening ears,
And stunned him with the music of the spheres,
How would he wish that Heaven had left him still
The whispering zephyr, and the purling rill?
Who finds not Providence all good and wise,
Alike in what it gives, and what it denies?
   VII. Far as creation's ample range extends,
The scale of sensual, mental powers ascends:
Mark how it mounts, to man's imperial race,
From the green myriads in the peopled grass:
What modes of sight betwixt each wide extreme,

The mole's dim curtain, and the lynx's beam:
Of smell, the headlong lioness between,
And hound sagacious on the tainted green:
Of hearing, from the life that fills the flood,
To that which warbles through the vernal wood:
The spider's touch, how exquisitely fine!
Feels at each thread, and lives along the line:
In the nice bee, what sense so subtly true
From poisonous herbs extracts the healing dew:
How instinct varies in the grovelling swine,
Compared, half-reasoning elephant, with thine:
'Twixt that, and reason, what a nice barrier;
For ever separate, yet for ever near!
Remembrance and reflection how allied;
What thin partitions sense from thought divide:
And middle natures, how they long to join,
Yet never passed th' insuperable line!
Without this just gradation, could they be
Subjected these to those, or all to thee?
The powers of all subdued by thee alone,
Is not thy reason all these powers in one?
    VIII. See, through this air, this ocean, and this earth,
All matter quick, and bursting into birth.
Above, how high, progressive life may go!
Around, how wide! how deep extend below!
Vast chain of being, which from God began,
Natures ethereal, human, angel, man,
Beast, bird, fish, insect, what no eye can see,
No glass can reach! from infinite to thee,
From thee to nothing!—On superior powers
Were we to press, inferior might on ours:
Or in the full creation leave a void,
Where, one step broken, the great scale's destroyed:
From Nature's chain whatever link you strike,
Tenth or ten thousandth, breaks the chain alike.
    And, if each system in gradation roll,
Alike essential to the amazing whole,
The least confusion but in one, not all
That system only, but the whole must fall.
Let earth unbalanced from her orbit fly,
Planets and suns run lawless through the sky,
Let ruling angels from their spheres be hurled,
Being on being wrecked, and world on world,
Heaven's whole foundations to their centre nod,
And nature tremble to the throne of God:
All this dread ORDER break—for whom? for thee?
Vile worm!—Oh, madness, pride, impiety!
    IX. What if the foot, ordained the dust to tread,

Or hand to toil, aspired to be the head?
What if the head, the eye, or ear repined
To serve mere engines to the ruling mind?
Just as absurd for any part to claim
To be another, in this general frame:
Just as absurd, to mourn the tasks or pains
The great directing MIND OF ALL ordains.

All are but parts of one stupendous whole,
Whose body Nature is, and God the soul;
That, changed through all, and yet in all the same,
Great in the earth, as in the ethereal frame,
Warms in the sun, refreshes in the breeze,
Glows in the stars, and blossoms in the trees,
Lives through all life, extends through all extent,
Spreads undivided, operates unspent,
Breathes in our soul, informs our mortal part,
As full, as perfect, in a hair as heart;
As full, as perfect, in vile man that mourns,
As the rapt seraph that adores and burns;
To him no high, no low, no great, no small;
He fills, he bounds, connects, and equals all.

X. Cease, then, nor ORDER imperfection name:
Our proper bliss depends on what we blame.
Know thy own point: this kind, this due degree
Of blindness, weakness, Heaven bestows on thee.
Submit—in this, or any other sphere,
Secure to be as blest as thou canst bear:
Safe in the hand of one disposing power,
Or in the natal, or the mortal hour.
All nature is but art, unknown to thee;
All chance, direction, which thou canst not see;
All discord, harmony, not understood;
All partial evil, universal good:
And, spite of pride, in erring reason's spite,
One truth is clear, 'Whatever is, is RIGHT.'

EPISTLE II.

ARGUMENT
Of the Nature and State of Man *with respect to* Himself,
as an Individual.

I. *The business of Man not to pry into* God, *but to study* himself. *His* Middle Nature; *his powers and frailties*, v. 1 to 18. *The limits of his* capacity, v.19, etc. II. *The two principles of Man,* Self-love *and* Reason, *both necessary,* v.53, etc. Self-love *the stronger, and why,* v.67, *etc. Their end the same,* v.81, etc. III. *The* PASSIONS, *and their use,* v.93 to 130. *The* predominant passion, *and its force,* v.131 to 160. *Its necessity, in directing men to different purposes,* v.165, etc. *Its providential use, in fixing our principle, and* ascertaining our virtue, v.177. IV. Virtue *and* Vice *joined in our* mixed nature; *the limits near, yet the things* separate *and* evident: *What is the office of* reason, v.203 to 216. V. *How odious* vice *in itself, and how we deceive ourselves into it,* v.217. VI. *That, however, the* ends *of* Providence *and* general good *are answered in our passions and imperfections,* v.238, etc. *How usefully these are distributed to all* orders of Men, v.241. *How useful they are to* Society, v.249. *And to the* Individuals, v.261. *In every* state, *and every* age *of life,* v.271, etc.

> Know, then, thyself, presume not God to scan;
> The proper study of mankind is Man.
> Placed on this isthmus of a middle state,
> A being darkly wise, and rudely great:
> With too much knowledge for the sceptic side,
> With too much weakness for the stoic's pride,
> He hangs between; in doubt to act, or rest,
> In doubt to deem himself a god, or beast;
> In doubt his mind or body to prefer,
> Born but to die, and reasoning but to err;
> Alike in ignorance, his reason such,
> Whether he thinks too little, or too much:
> Chaos of thought and passion, all confused;
> Still by himself abused, or disabused;
> Created half to rise, and half to fall;
> Great lord of all things, yet a prey to all;
> Sole judge of truth, in endless error hurled:
> The glory, jest, and riddle of the world!
>   Go, wondrous creature! mount where science guides,
> Go, measure earth, weigh air, and state the tides;
> Instruct the planets in what orbs to run,
> Correct old time, and regulate the sun;
> Go, soar with Plato to th' empyreal sphere,
> To the first good, first perfect, and first fair;
> Or tread the mazy round his followers trod,
> And quitting sense call imitating God;
> As Eastern priests in giddy circles run,
> And turn their heads to imitate the sun.
> Go, teach Eternal Wisdom how to rule—
> Then drop into thyself, and be a fool!
>   Superior beings, when of late they saw
> A mortal man unfold all nature's law,
> Admired such wisdom in an earthly shape
> And showed a NEWTON as we show an ape.
>   Could he, whose rules the rapid comet bind,
> Describe or fix one movement of his mind?
> Who saw its fires here rise, and there descend,
> Explain his own beginning, or his end?
> Alas, what wonder! Man's superior part
> Unchecked may rise, and climb from art to art:

But when his own great work is but begun,
What reason weaves, by passion is undone.
  Trace science then, with modesty thy guide;
First strip off all her equipage of pride,
Deduct what is but vanity, or dress,
Or learning's luxury, or idleness;
Or tricks to show the stretch of human brain,
Mere curious pleasure, or ingenious pain:
Expunge the whole, or lop th' excrescent parts
Of all, our vices have created arts:
Then see how little the remaining sum,
Which served the past, and must the times to come!
  II. Two principles in human nature reign;
Self-love, to urge, and reason, to restrain;
Nor this a good, nor that a bad we call,
Each works its end, to move or govern all:
And to their proper operation still,
Ascribe all good; to their improper, ill.
  Self-love, the spring of motion, acts the soul;
Reason's comparing balance rules the whole.
Man, but for that, no action could attend,
And, but for this, were active to no end;
Fixed like a plant on his peculiar spot,
To draw nutrition, propagate, and rot;
Or, meteor-like, flame lawless through the void,
Destroying others, by himself destroyed.
  Most strength the moving principle requires;
Active its task, it prompts, impels, inspires.
Sedate and quiet the comparing lies,
Formed but to check, deliberate, and advise.
Self-love still stronger, as its objects nigh;
Reasons at distance, and in prospect lie:
That sees immediate good by present sense;
Reason, the future and the consequence.
Thicker than arguments, temptations throng,
At best more watchful this, but that more strong.
The action of the stronger to suspend
Reason still use, to reason still attend:
Attention, habit and experience gains,
Each strengthens reason, and self-love restrains.
  Let subtle schoolmen teach these friends to fight,
More studious to divide than to unite;
And grace and virtue, sense and reason split,
With all the rash dexterity of wit.
Wits, just like fools, at war about a name,
Have full as oft no meaning, or the same.
Self-love and reason to one end aspire,
Pain their aversion, pleasure their desire;

But greedy that, its object would devour,
This taste the honey, and not wound the flower:
Pleasure, or wrong or rightly understood,
Our greatest evil, or our greatest good.
   III. Modes of self-love the passions we may call:
'Tis real good, or seeming, moves them all:
But since not every good we can divide,
And reason bids us for our own provide;
Passions, though selfish, if their means be fair,
List under reason, and deserve her care;
Those, that imparted, court a nobler aim,
Exalt their kind, and take some virtue's name.
   In lazy apathy let Stoics boast
Their virtue fixed; 'tis fixed as in a frost,
Contracted all, retiring to the breast;
But strength of mind is exercise, not rest:
The rising tempest puts in act the soul,
Parts it may ravage, but preserves the whole.
On life's vast ocean diversely we sail,
Reason the card, but passion is the gale;
Nor God alone in the still calm we find,
He mounts the storm, and walks upon the wind.
   Passions, like elements, though born to fight,
Yet, mixed and softened, in his work unite:
These, 'tis enough to temper and employ;
But what composes Man, can Man destroy?
Suffice that reason keep to nature's road,
Subject, compound them, follow her and God.
Love, hope, and joy, fair pleasure's smiling train,
Hate, fear, and grief, the family of pain;
These mixed with art, and to due bounds confined,
Make and maintain the balance of the mind:
The lights and shades, whose well-accorded strife
Gives all the strength and colour of our life.
   Pleasures are ever in our hands or eyes,
And when in act they cease, in prospect rise;
Present to grasp, and future still to find,
The whole employ of body and of mind.
All spread their charms, but charm not all alike;
On different senses different objects strike;
Hence different passions more or less inflame,
As strong or weak, the organs of the frame;
And hence once master passion in the breast,
Like Aaron's serpent, swallows up the rest.
   As Man, perhaps, the moment of his breath,
Receives the lurking principle of death;
The young disease that must subdue at length,
Grows with his growth, and strengthens with his strength:

So, cast and mingled with his very frame,
The mind's disease, its ruling passion came;
Each vital humour which should feed the whole,
Soon flows to this, in body and in soul.
Whatever warms the heart, or fills the head,
As the mind opens, and its functions spread,
Imagination plies her dangerous art,
And pours it all upon the peccant part.

Nature its mother, habit is its nurse;
Wit, spirit, faculties, but make it worse;
Reason itself but gives it edge and power;
As Heaven's blessed beam turns vinegar more sour;
We, wretched subjects though to lawful sway,
In this weak queen, some favourite still obey.
Ah! if she lend not arms, as well as rules,
What can she more than tell us we are fools?
Teach us to mourn our nature, not to mend,
A sharp accuser, but a helpless friend!
Or from a judge turn pleader, to persuade
The choice we make, or justify it made;
Proud of an easy conquest all along,
She but removes weak passions for the strong:
So, when small humours gather to a gout
The doctor fancies he has driven them out.

Yes, Nature's road must ever be preferred;
Reason is here no guide, but still a guard:
'Tis hers to rectify, not overthrow,
And treat this passion more as friend than foe:
A mightier power the strong direction sends,
And several men impels to several ends.
Like varying winds, by other passions tossed,
This drives them constant to a certain coast.
Let power or knowledge, gold or glory, please,
Or (oft more strong than all) the love of ease;
Through life 'tis followed, even at life's expense;
The merchant's toil, the sage's indolence,
The monk's humility, the hero's pride,
All, all alike, find reason on their side.

The eternal art, educing good from ill,
Grafts on this passion our best principle:
'Tis thus the mercury of Man is fixed,
Strong grows the virtue with his nature mixed;
The dross cements what else were too refined,
And in one interest body acts with mind.

As fruits ungrateful to the planter's care
On savage stocks inserted, learn to bear;
The surest virtues thus from passions shoot,
Wild nature's vigour working at the root.

What crops of wit and honesty appear
From spleen, from obstinacy, hate, or fear!
See anger, zeal and fortitude supply;
Even avarice, prudence; sloth, philosophy;
Lust, through some certain strainers well refined,
Is gentle love, and charms all womankind:
Envy, to which th' ignoble mind's a slave,
Is emulation in the learned or brave:
Nor virtue, male or female, can we name,
But what will grow on pride, or grow on shame.
    Thus Nature gives us (let it check our pride)
The virtue nearest to our vice allied:
Reason the bias turns to good from ill,
And Nero reigns a Titus, if he will.
The fiery soul abhorred in Catiline,
In Decius charms, in Curtius is divine.
The same ambition can destroy or save,
And makes a patriot as it makes a knave.
    IV. This light and darkness in our chaos joined,
What shall divide? The God within the mind.
    Extremes in nature equal ends produce,
In Man they join to some mysterious use;
Though each by turns the other's bound invade,
As, in some well-wrought picture, light and shade,
And oft so mix, the difference is too nice
Where ends the virtue, or begins the vice.
    Fools! who from hence into the notion fall,
That vice or virtue there is none at all.
If white and black blend, soften, and unite
A thousand ways, is there no black or white?
Ask your own heart, and nothing is so plain;
'Tis to mistake them, costs the time and pain.
    V. Vice is a monster of so frightful mien,
As, to be hated, needs but to be seen;
Yet seen too oft, familiar with her face,
We first endure, then pity, then embrace.
But where th' extreme of vice, was ne'er agreed:
Ask where's the North? at York, 'tis on the Tweed;
In Scotland, at the Orcades; and there,
At Greenland, Zembla, or the Lord knows where:
No creature owns it in the first degree,
But thinks his neighbour farther gone than he.
Even those who dwell beneath its very zone,
Or never feel the rage, or never own;
What happier nations shrink at with affright,
The hard inhabitant contends is right.
    VI. Virtuous and vicious every man must be,
Few in th' extreme, but all in the degree;

The rogue and fool by fits is fair and wise,
And even the best, by fits, what they despise.
'Tis but by parts we follow good or ill,
For, vice or virtue, self directs it still;
Each individual seeks a several goal;
But HEAVEN'S great view is one, and that the whole:
That counter-works each folly and caprice;
That disappoints th' effect of every vice:
That happy frailties to all ranks applied,
Shame to the virgin, to the matron pride,
Fear to the statesman, rashness to the chief,
To kings presumption, and to crowds belief:
That, virtue's ends from vanity can raise,
Which seeks no interest, no reward but praise;
And build on wants, and on defects of mind,
The joy, the peace, the glory of mankind.
    Heaven forming each on other to depend,
A master, or a servant, or a friend,
Bids each on other for assistance call,
Till one man's weakness grows the strength of all.
Wants, frailties, passions, closer still ally
The common interest, or endear the tie:
To these we owe true friendship, love sincere,
Each home-felt joy that life inherits here:
Yet from the same we learn, in its decline,
Those joys, those loves, those interests to resign:
Taught half by reason, half by mere decay,
To welcome death, and calmly pass away.
    Whate'er the passion, knowledge, fame, or pelf,
Not one will change his neighbour with himself.
The learned is happy nature to explore,
The fool is happy that he knows no more;
The rich is happy in the plenty given,
The poor contents him with the care of Heaven.
See the blind beggar dance, the cripple sing,
The sot a hero, lunatic a king;
The starving chemist in his golden views
Supremely blessed, the poet in his muse.
    See some strange comfort every state attend,
And pride bestowed on all, a common friend;
See some fit passion every age supply,
Hope travels through, nor quits us when we die.
    Behold the child, by Nature's kindly law,
Pleased with a rattle, tickled with a straw:
Some livelier plaything gives his youth delight,
A little louder, but as empty quite:
Scarves, garters, gold, amuse his riper stage;
And beads and prayer-books are the toys of age:

Pleased with this bauble still, as that before;
Till tired he sleeps, and life's poor play is o'er!
  Meanwhile opinion gilds with varying rays
Those painted clouds that beautify our days;
Each want of happiness by hope supplied,
And each vacuity of sense by pride:
These build as fast as knowledge can destroy;
In folly's cup still laughs the bubble, joy;
One prospect lost, another still we gain;
And not a vanity is given in vain;
Even mean self-love becomes, by force divine,
The scale to measure others wants by thine.
See! and confess, one comfort still must rise,
'Tis this, though man's a fool, yet GOD IS WISE.

EPISTLE III.

ARGUMENT
Of the Nature and State of Man *with respect to* Society.

I. *The whole universe one system of society, v.* 7, *etc. Nothing made wholly for* itself, *nor yet wholly for* another, *v.*27. *The happiness of* animals *mutual, v.*49. II. Reason *or* instinct *operate alike to the good of each individual, v.*79. Reason *or* Instinct *operate also to Society, in all animals, v.*109. III. *How far* Society *carried by instinct, v.*115. *How much farther by reason, v.*131. IV. *Of that which is called the* State of Nature, *v.*147. *Reason instructed by instinct in the invention of* Arts, *v.*171, *and in the forms of* Society, *v.*179. V. *Origin of political societies, v.*199. *Origin of monarchy, v.*209. *Patriarchal government, v.*215. VI. *Origin of true religion and government, from the same principle, of love, v.*231, *etc. Origin of superstition and tyranny, from the same principle, of fear, v.*237, *etc. The influence of self-love operating to the* social *and* public *good, v.*269. *Restoration of true religion and government on their first principle, v.*283. *Mixed government, v.*294. *Various forms of each, and the true end of all, v.*300, *etc.*

Here, then, we rest: 'The universal cause
Acts to one end, but acts by various laws.'
In all the madness of superfluous health,
The trim of pride, the impudence of wealth,
Let this great truth be present night and day;
But most be present, if we preach or pray.
  Look round our world; behold the chain of love
Combining all below and all above.
See plastic nature working to this end,
The single atoms each to other tend,
Attract, attracted to, the next in place
Formed and impelled its neighbour to embrace.
See matter next, with various life endued,
Press to one centre still, the general good.
See dying vegetables life sustain,

See life dissolving vegetate again:
All forms that perish other forms supply,
(By turns we catch the vital breath, and die)
Like bubbles on the sea of matter borne,
They rise, they break, and to that sea return.
Nothing is foreign: parts relate to whole;
One all-extending, all-preserving soul
Connects each being, greatest with the least;
Made beast in aid of man, and man of beast;
All served, all serving! nothing stands alone;
The chain holds on, and where it ends, unknown.

    Has God, thou fool! worked solely for thy good,
Thy joy, thy pastime, thy attire, thy food?
Who for thy table feeds the wanton fawn,
For him as kindly spread the flowery lawn.
Is it for thee the lark ascends and sings?
Joy tunes his voice, joy elevates his wings:
Is it for thee the linnet pours his throat?
Loves of his own and raptures swell the note:
The bounding steed you pompously bestride,
Shares with his lord the pleasure and the pride:
Is thine alone the seed that strews the plain?
The birds of heaven shall vindicate their grain:
Thine the full harvest of the golden year?
Part pays, and justly, the deserving steer:
The hog, that ploughs not nor obeys thy call,
Lives on the labours of this lord of all.

    Know, Nature's children all divide her care;
The fur that warms a monarch, warmed a bear.
While Man exclaims, 'See all things for my use!'
'See man for mine!' replies a pampered goose;
And just as short of reason he must fall,
Who thinks all made for one, not one for all.

    Grant that the powerful still the weak control;
Be Man the wit and tyrant of the whole:
Nature that tyrant checks; he only knows,
And helps, another creature's wants and woes.
Say, will the falcon, stooping from above,
Smit with her varying plumage, spare the dove?
Admires the jay the insect's gilded wings?
Or hears the hawk when Philomela sings?
Man cares for all: to birds he gives his woods,
To beasts his pastures, and to fish his floods;
For some his interest prompts him to provide,
For more his pleasure, yet for more his pride:
All feed on one vain patron, and enjoy
The extensive blessing of his luxury.
That very life his learned hunger craves,

He saves from famine, from the savage saves;
Nay, feasts the animal he dooms his feast,
And, till he ends the being, makes it blest;
Which sees no more the stroke, or feels the pain,
Than favoured Man by touch ethereal slain.
The creature had his feast of life before;
Thou too must perish when thy feast is o'er.
  To each unthinking being, Heaven a friend,
Gives not the useless knowledge of its end:
To Man imparts it; but with such a view
As, while he dreads it, makes him hope it too:
The hour concealed, and so remote the fear,
Death still draws nearer, never seeming near.
Great standing miracle! that Heaven assigned
Its only thinking thing this turn of mind.
  II. Whether with reason, or with instinct blessed,
Know, all enjoy that power which suits them best;
To bliss alike by that direction tend,
And find the means proportioned to their end.
Say, where full instinct is th' unerring guide,
What Pope or Council can they need beside?
Reason, however able, cool at best,
Cares not for service, or but serves when pressed,
Stays till we call, and then not often near;
But honest instinct comes a volunteer;
Sure never to o'er-shoot, but just to hit;
While still too wide or short is human wit;
Sure by quick nature happiness to gain,
Which heavier reason labours at in vain,
This too serves always, reason never long;
One must go right, the other may go wrong.
See then the acting and comparing powers
One in their nature, which are two in ours,
And reason raise o'er instinct as you can,
In this 'tis God directs, in that 'tis Man.
  Who taught the nations of the field and wood
To shun their poison, and to choose their food?
Prescient, the tides or tempests to withstand,
Build on the wave, or arch beneath the sand?
Who made the spider parallels design,
Sure as Demoivre, without rule or line?
Who did the stork, Columbus-like, explore
Heavens not his own, and worlds unknown before?
Who calls the council, states the certain day,
Who forms the phalanx, and who points the way?
  III. God in the nature of each being founds
Its proper bliss, and sets its proper bounds:
But as he framed a whole, the whole to bless,

On mutual wants built mutual happiness:
So from the first, eternal ORDER ran,
And creature linked to creature, man to man.
Whate'er of life all-quickening ether keeps,
Or breathes through air, or shoots beneath the deeps,
Or pours profuse on earth; one nature feeds
The vital flame, and swells the genial seeds.
Not man alone, but all that roam the wood,
Or wing the sky, or roll along the flood,
Each loves itself, but not itself alone,
Each sex desires alike, till two are one.
Nor ends the pleasure with the fierce embrace;
They love themselves, a third time, in their race.
Thus beast and bird their common charge attend,
The mothers nurse it, and the sires defend;
The young dismissed to wander earth or air,
There stops the instinct, and there ends the care;
The link dissolves, each seeks a fresh embrace,
Another love succeeds, another race.
A longer care Man's helpless kind demands;
That longer care contracts more lasting bands:
Reflection, reason, still the ties improve,
At once extend the interest and the love;
With choice we fix, with sympathy we burn;
Each virtue in each passion takes its turn;
And still new needs, new helps, new habits rise,
That graft benevolence on charities.
Still as one brood, and as another rose,
These natural love maintained, habitual those:
The last, scarce ripened into perfect Man,
Saw helpless him from whom their life began:
Memory and forecast just returns engage,
That pointed back to youth, this on to age;
While pleasure, gratitude, and hope combined,
Still spread the interest, and preserved the kind.
    IV. Nor think, in NATURE'S STATE they blindly trod;
The state of nature was the reign of God:
Self-love and social at her birth began,
Union the bond of all things, and of Man.
Pride then was not; nor arts, that pride to aid;
Man walked with beast, joint tenant of the shade;
The same his table, and the same his bed;
No murder clothed him, and no murder fed.
In the same temple, the resounding wood,
All vocal beings hymned their equal God:
The shrine with gore unstained, with gold undressed,
Unbribed, unbloody, stood the blameless priest:
Heaven's attribute was universal care,

And man's prerogative to rule, but spare.
Ah! how unlike the man of times to come!
Of half that live the butcher and the tomb;
Who, foe to nature, hears the general groan,
Murders their species, and betrays his own.
But just disease to luxury succeeds,
And every death its own avenger breeds;
The fury-passions from that blood began,
And turned on Man a fiercer savage, Man.
　See him from Nature rising slow to art!
To copy instinct then was reason's part;
Thus then to Man the voice of Nature spake—
'Go, from the creatures thy instructions take:
Learn from the birds what food the thickets yield;
Learn from the beasts the physic of the field;
Thy arts of building from the bee receive;
Learn of the mole to plough, the worm to weave;
Learn of the little nautilus to sail,
Spread the thin oar, and catch the driving gale.
Here too all forms of social union find,
And hence let reason, late, instruct mankind:
Here subterranean works and cities see;
There towns aerial on the waving tree.
Learn each small people's genius, policies,
The ant's republic, and the realm of bees;
How those in common all their wealth bestow,
And anarchy without confusion know;
And these for ever, though a monarch reign,
Their separate cells and properties maintain.
Mark what unvaried laws preserve each state,
Laws wise as nature, and as fixed as fate.
In vain thy reason finer webs shall draw,
Entangle justice in her net of law,
And right, too rigid, harden into wrong;
Still for the strong too weak, the weak too strong.
Yet go! and thus o'er all the creatures sway,
Thus let the wiser make the rest obey,
And for those arts mere instinct could afford,
Be crowned as monarchs, or as gods adored.'
　V. Great Nature spoke; observant men obeyed;
Cities were built, societies were made:
Here rose one little state: another near
Grew by like means, and joined, through love or fear.
Did here the trees with ruddier burdens bend,
And there the streams in purer rills descend?
What war could ravish, commerce could bestow,
And he returned a friend, who came a foe.
Converse and love mankind might strongly draw,

When love was liberty, and nature law.
Thus states were formed; the name of king unknown,
Till common interest placed the sway in one.
'Twas VIRTUE ONLY (or in arts or arms,
Diffusing blessings, or averting harms)
The same which in a sire the sons obeyed,
A prince the father of a people made.
　VI. Till then, by Nature crowned, each patriarch sate,
King, priest, and parent of his growing state;
On him, their second providence, they hung,
Their law his eye, their oracle his tongue.
He from the wondering furrow called the food,
Taught to command the fire, control the flood,
Draw forth the monsters of the abyss profound,
Or fetch the aerial eagle to the ground.
Till drooping, sickening, dying they began
Whom they revered as God to mourn as Man:
Then, looking up, from sire to sire, explored
One great first father, and that first adored.
Or plain tradition that this all begun,
Conveyed unbroken faith from sire to son,
The worker from the work distinct was known,
And simple reason never sought but one:
Ere wit oblique had broke that steady light,
Man, like his Maker, saw that all was right,
To virtue, in the paths of pleasure, trod,
And owned a Father when he owned a God.
LOVE all the faith, and all the allegiance then;
For Nature knew no right divine in men,
No ill could fear in God; and understood
A sovereign being but a sovereign good.
True faith, true policy, united ran,
This was but love of God, and this of Man.
　Who first taught souls enslaved, and realms undone,
The enormous faith of many made for one;
That proud exception to all Nature's laws,
T' invert the world, and counter-work its cause?
Force first made conquest, and that conquest, law;
Till superstition taught the tyrant awe,
Then shared the tyranny, then lent it aid,
And gods of conquerors, slaves of subjects made:
She, 'midst the lightning's blaze, and thunder's sound,
When rocked the mountains, and when groaned the ground,
She taught the weak to bend, the proud to pray,
To power unseen, and mightier far than they:
She, from the rending earth and bursting skies,
Saw gods descend, and fiends infernal rise:
Here fixed the dreadful, there the blessed abodes;

Fear made her devils, and weak hope her gods;
Gods partial, changeful, passionate, unjust,
Whose attributes were rage, revenge, or lust;
Such as the souls of cowards might conceive,
And, formed like tyrants, tyrants would believe.
Zeal then, not charity, became the guide,
And hell was built on spite, and heaven on pride.
Then sacred seemed the ethereal vault no more;
Altars grew marble then, and reeked with gore:
Then first the flamen tasted living food;
Next his grim idol smeared with human blood;
With Heaven's own thunders shook the world below,
And played the god an engine on his foe.
    So drives self-love, through just and through unjust,
To one man's power, ambition, lucre, lust:
The same self-love, in all, becomes the cause
Of what restrains him, government and laws.
For, what one likes if others like as well,
What serves one will when many wills rebel?
How shall he keep, what, sleeping or awake,
A weaker may surprise, a stronger take?
His safety must his liberty restrain:
All join to guard what each desires to gain.
Forced into virtue thus by self-defence,
Even kings learned justice and benevolence:
Self-love forsook the path it first pursued,
And found the private in the public good.
    'Twas then, the studious head or generous mind,
Follower of God, or friend of humankind,
Poet or patriot, rose but to restore
The faith and moral, Nature gave before;
Relumed her ancient light, not kindled new;
If not God's image, yet His shadow drew:
Taught power's due use to people and to kings,
Taught nor to slack, nor strain its tender strings,
The less, or greater, set so justly true,
That touching one must strike the other too;
Till jarring interests, of themselves create
The according music of a well-mixed state.
Such is the world's great harmony, that springs
From order, union, full consent of things!
Where small and great, where weak and mighty, made
To serve, not suffer, strengthen, not invade,
More powerful each as needful to the rest,
And, in proportion as it blesses, blessed,
Draw to one point, and to one centre bring
Beast, man, or angel, servant, lord, or king.
    For forms of government let fools contest;

Whate'er is best administered is best:
For modes of faith let graceless zealots fight;
His can't be wrong whose life is in the right:
In faith and hope the world will disagree,
But all mankind's concern is charity:
All must be false that thwart this one great end,
And all of God, that bless mankind or mend.
    Man, like the generous vine, supported lives;
The strength he gains is from the embrace he gives.
On their own axis as the planets run,
Yet make at once their circle round the sun:
So two consistent motions act the soul;
And one regards itself, and one the whole.
    Thus God and Nature linked the general frame,
And bade self-love and social be the same.

EPISTLE IV.

ARGUMENT
Of the Nature and State of Man *with respect to* Happiness

    I. *False notions of happiness, philosophical and popular, answered from* v. 19 *to* 76. II. *It is the end of all men, and attainable by all,* v. 29. *God intends happiness to be* equal; *and to be so, it must be* social, *since all particular happiness depends on general, and since he governs by* general, *not* particular *laws,* v. 35. *As it is necessary for* order, *and the peace and welfare of society, that* external goods *should be* unequal, *happiness is not made to consist in these,* v. 49. *But, notwithstanding that inequality, the* balance *of happiness among mankind is kept even by Providence, by the two passions of* Hope *and* Fear, v. 67. III. *What the happiness of* Individuals *is, as far as is consistent with the constitution of this world; and that the* good Man *has here the advantage,* v. 77. *The error of imputing to* Virtue *what are only the calamities of* Nature, *or of* Fortune, v. 93. IV. *The folly of expecting that God should alter his general laws in favour of particulars,* v. 111. V. *That we are not judges who are good; but that, whoever they are, they must be happiest,* v. 131, *etc.* VI. *That* external goods *are not the proper rewards, but often inconsistent with, or destructive of virtue,* v. 167. *That even these can make no man happy without virtue: Instanced in* Riches, v. 185. Honours, v. 193. Nobility, v. 205. Greatness, v. 217. Fame, v. 237. Superior Talents, v. 259, *etc. With pictures of human infelicity in men possessed of them all,* v. 269, *etc.* VII. *That* Virtue *only constitutes a happiness, whose object is* universal, *and whose prospect* eternal, v. 309, *etc. That the* perfection *of* Virtue *and* Happiness *consists in a* conformity *to the* ORDER *of* PROVIDENCE *here, and a* Resignation *to it here and hereafter,* v. 327, *etc.*

    Oh, happiness! our being's end and aim!
Good, pleasure, ease, content! whate'er thy name:
That something still which prompts th' eternal sigh,
For which we bear to live, or dare to die,
Which still so near us, yet beyond us lies,
O'erlooked, seen double, by the fool, and wise.

Plant of celestial seed! if dropped below,
Say, in what mortal soil thou deignst to grow?
Fair opening to some court's propitious shine,
Or deep with diamonds in the flaming mine?
Twined with the wreaths Parnassian laurels yield,
Or reaped in iron harvests of the field?
Where grows?—where grows it not? If vain our toil,
We ought to blame the culture, not the soil:
Fixed to no spot is happiness sincere,
'Tis nowhere to be found, or everywhere;
'Tis never to be bought, but always free,
And fled from monarchs, ST. JOHN! dwells with thee.
    Ask of the learned the way? The learned are blind,
This bids to serve, and that to shun mankind;
Some place the bliss in action, some in ease,
Those call it pleasure, and contentment these;
Some, sunk to beasts, find pleasure end in pain;
Some, swelled to gods, confess even virtue vain;
Or indolent, to each extreme they fall,
To trust in everything, or doubt of all.
    Who thus define it, say they more or less
Than this, that happiness is happiness?
    II. Take Nature's path, and mad opinions leave;
All states can reach it, and all heads conceive;
Obvious her goods, in no extreme they dwell;
There needs but thinking right, and meaning well;
And mourn our various portions as we please,
Equal is common sense, and common ease.
    Remember, Man, 'the universal cause
Acts not by partial, but by general laws;'
And makes what happiness we justly call
Subsist not in the good of one, but all.
There's not a blessing individuals find,
But some way leans and hearkens to the kind.
No bandit fierce, no tyrant mad with pride,
No caverned hermit, rests self-satisfied;
Who most to shun or hate mankind pretend,
Seek an admirer, or would fix a friend.
Abstract what others feel, what others think,
All pleasures sicken, and all glories sink:
Each has his share; and who would more obtain,
Shall find, the pleasure pays not half the pain.
    ORDER is Heaven's first law; and this confessed,
Some are, and must be, greater than the rest,
More rich, more wise; but who infers from hence
That such are happier, shocks all common sense.
Heaven to mankind impartial we confess,
If all are equal in their happiness;

But mutual wants this happiness increase;
All Nature's difference keeps all Nature's peace.
Condition, circumstance is not the thing;
Bliss is the same in subject or in king,
In who obtain defence, or who defend,
In him who is, or him who finds a friend:
Heaven breathes through every member of the whole
One common blessing, as one common soul.
But fortune's gifts if each alike possessed,
And each were equal, must not all contest?
If then to all men happiness was meant,
God in externals could not place content.

Fortune her gifts may variously dispose,
And these be happy called, unhappy those;
But Heaven's just balance equal will appear,
While those are placed in hope, and these in fear:
Nor present good or ill, the joy or curse,
But future views of better, or of worse.

Oh, sons of earth! attempt ye still to rise,
By mountains piled on mountains, to the skies?
Heaven still with laughter the vain toil surveys,
And buries madmen in the heaps they raise.

III. Know, all the good that individuals find,
Or God and Nature meant to mere mankind,
Reason's whole pleasure, all the joys of sense,
Lie in three words, health, peace, and competence.
But health consists with temperance alone;
And peace, oh, virtue! peace is all thy own.
The good or bad the gifts of fortune gain;
But these less taste them, as they worse obtain.
Say, in pursuit of profit or delight,
Who risk the most, that take wrong means, or right?
Of vice or virtue, whether blest or cursed,
Which meets contempt, or which compassion first?
Count all th' advantage prosperous vice attains,
'Tis but what virtue flies from and disdains:
And grant the bad what happiness they would,
One they must want, which is, to pass for good.

Oh blind to truth, and God's whole scheme below,
Who fancy bliss to vice, to virtue woe!
Who sees and follows that great scheme the best,
Best knows the blessing, and will most be blessed.
But fools the good alone unhappy call,
For ills or accidents that chance to all.
See FALKLAND dies, the virtuous and the just!
See god-like TURENNE prostrate on the dust!
See SIDNEY bleeds amid the martial strife!
Was this their virtue, or contempt of life?

Say, was it virtue, more though Heaven ne'er gave,
Lamented DIGBY! sunk thee to the grave?
Tell me, if virtue made the son expire,
Why, full of days and honour, lives the sire?
Why drew Marseilles' good bishop purer breath,
When Nature sickened, and each gale was death?
Or why so long (in life if long can be)
Lent Heaven a parent to the poor and me?
    IV. What makes all physical or moral ill?
There deviates Nature, and here wanders will.
God sends not ill; if rightly understood,
Or partial ill is universal good,
Or change admits, or Nature lets it fall,
Short, and but rare, till Man improved it all.
We just as wisely might of Heaven complain
That righteous Abel was destroyed by Cain;
As that the virtuous son is ill at ease
When his lewd father gave the dire disease.
Think we, like some weak prince, th' eternal cause
Prone for his favourites to reverse his laws?
    Shall burning Etna, if a sage requires,
Forget to thunder, and recall her fires?
On air or sea new motions be impressed,
Oh, blameless Bethel! to relieve thy breast?
When the loose mountain trembles from on high,
Shall gravitation cease, if you go by?
Or some old temple, nodding to its fall,
For Chartres' head reserve the hanging wall?
    V. But still this world (so fitted for the knave)
Contents us not. A better shall we have?
A kingdom of the just then let it be:
But first consider how those just agree.
The good must merit God's peculiar care:
But who, but God, can tell us who they are?
One thinks on Calvin Heaven's own spirit fell,
Another deems him instrument of hell;
If Calvin feel Heaven's blessing, or its rod,
This cries there is, and that, there is no God.
What shocks one part will edify the rest,
Nor with one system can they all be blest.
The very best will variously incline,
And what rewards your virtue, punish mine.
'Whatever IS, is RIGHT'—This world, 'tis true,
Was made for Caesar—but for Titus too:
And which more blessed? who chained his country, say,
Or he whose virtue sighed to lose a day?
    'But sometimes virtue starves, while vice is fed.'
What then? Is the reward of virtue bread?

That, vice may merit, 'tis the price of toil;
The knave deserves it, when he tills the soil,
The knave deserves it, when he tempts the main,
Where folly fights for kings, or dives for gain.
The good man may be weak, be indolent;
Nor is his claim to plenty, but content.
But grant him riches, your demand is o'er?
'No—shall the good want health, the good want power?'
Add health, and power, and every earthly thing;
'Why bounded power? why private? why no king?'
Nay, why external for internal given?
Why is not Man a God, and earth a heaven?
Who ask and reason thus, will scarce conceive
God gives enough, while He has more to give:
Immense the power, immense were the demand;
Say, at what part of nature will they stand?
    VI. What nothing earthly gives, or can destroy,
The soul's calm sunshine, and the heartfelt joy,
Is virtue's prize: A better would you fix?
Then give humility a coach and six,
Justice a conqueror's sword, or truth a gown,
Or public spirit its great cure, a crown.
Weak, foolish man! will heaven reward us there
With the same trash mad mortals wish for here?
The boy and man an individual makes,
Yet sighest thou now for apples and for cakes?
Go, like the Indian, in another life
Expect thy dog, thy bottle, and thy wife:
As well as dream such trifles are assigned,
As toys and empires, for a god-like mind.
Rewards, that either would to virtue bring
No joy, or be destructive of the thing:
How oft by these at sixty are undone
The virtues of a saint at twenty-one!
To whom can riches give repute or trust,
Content, or pleasure, but the good and just?
Judges and senates have been bought for gold,
Esteem and love were never to be sold.
Oh, fool! to think God hates the worthy mind,
The lover and the love of humankind,
Whose life is healthful, and whose conscience clear;
Because he wants a thousand pounds a year.
    Honour and shame from no condition rise;
Act well your part, there all the honour lies.
Fortune in men has some small difference made,
One flaunts in rags, one flutters in brocade;
The cobbler aproned, and the parson gowned,
The friar hooded, and the monarch crowned,

'What differ more' (you cry) 'than crown and cowl?'
I'll tell you, friend! a wise man and a fool.
You'll find, if once the monarch acts the monk,
Or, cobbler-like, the parson will be drunk,
Worth makes the man, and want of it, the fellow;
The rest is all but leather or prunella.

    Stuck o'er with titles and hung round with strings,
That thou mayst be by kings, or whores of kings.
Boast the pure blood of an illustrious race,
In quiet flow from Lucrece to Lucrece:
But by your fathers' worth if yours you rate,
Count me those only who were good and great.
Go! if your ancient, but ignoble blood
Has crept through scoundrels ever since the flood,
Go! and pretend your family is young;
Nor own, your fathers have been fools so long.
What can ennoble sots, or slaves, or cowards?
Alas! not all the blood of all the HOWARDS.

    Look next on greatness; say where greatness lies?
'Where, but among the heroes and the wise?'
Heroes are much the same, the point's agreed,
From Macedonia's madman to the Swede;
The whole strange purpose of their lives, to find
Or make, an enemy of all mankind!
Not one looks backward, onward still he goes,
Yet ne'er looks forward farther than his nose.
No less alike the politic and wise;
All sly slow things, with circumspective eyes:
Men in their loose unguarded hours they take,
Not that themselves are wise, but others weak.
But grant that those can conquer, these can cheat;
'Tis phrase absurd to call a villain great:
Who wickedly is wise, or madly brave,
Is but the more a fool, the more a knave.
Who noble ends by noble means obtains,
Or failing, smiles in exile or in chains,
Like good Aurelius let him reign, or bleed
Like Socrates, that Man is great indeed.

    What's fame? a fancied life in others' breath,
A thing beyond us, even before our death.
Just what you hear, you have, and what's unknown
The same (my Lord) if Tully's, or your own.
All that we feel of it begins and ends
In the small circle of our foes or friends;
To all beside as much an empty shade,
An Eugene living, as a Caesar dead,
Alike or when, or where, they shone, or shine,
Or on the Rubicon, or on the Rhine.

A wit's a feather, and a chief a rod;
An honest man's the noblest work of God.
Fame but from death a villain's name can save,
As justice tears his body from the grave,
When what t' oblivion better were resigned,
Is hung on high, to poison half mankind.
All fame is foreign, but of true desert,
Plays round the head, but comes not to the heart:
One self-approving hour whole years outweighs
Of stupid starers, and of loud huzzas;
And more true joy Marcellus exiled feels,
Than Caesar with a senate at his heels.

   In parts superior what advantage lies?
Tell (for you can) what is it to be wise?
'Tis but to know how little can be known;
To see all others' faults, and feel our own:
Condemned in business or in arts to drudge,
Without a second or without a judge:
Truths would you teach or save a sinking land?
All fear, none aid you, and few understand.
Painful pre-eminence! yourself to view
Above life's weakness, and its comforts too.

   Bring, then, these blessings to a strict account,
Make fair deductions, see to what they mount.
How much of other each is sure to cost;
How each for other oft is wholly lost;
How inconsistent greater goods with these;
How sometimes life is risked, and always ease:
Think, and if still the things thy envy call,
Say, wouldst thou be the man to whom they fall?
To sigh for ribbons if thou art so silly,
Mark how they grace Lord Umbra, or Sir Billy:
Is yellow dirt the passion of thy life?
Look but on Gripus, or on Gripus' wife:
If parts allure thee, think how Bacon shined,
The wisest, brightest, meanest of mankind:
Or ravished with the whistling of a name,
See Cromwell, damned to everlasting fame!
If all, united, thy ambition call,
From ancient story learn to scorn them all.
There, in the rich, the honoured, famed, and great,
See the false scale of happiness complete!
In hearts of kings, or arms of queens who lay,
How happy! those to ruin, these betray.
Mark by what wretched steps their glory grows,
From dirt and seaweed as proud Venice rose;
In each how guilt and greatness equal ran,
And all that raised the hero, sunk the man:

Now Europe's laurels on their brows behold,
But stained with blood, or ill exchanged for gold:
Then see them broke with toils, or sunk with ease,
Or infamous for plundered provinces.
Oh, wealth ill-fated! which no act of fame
E'er taught to shine, or sanctified from shame!
What greater bliss attends their close of life?
Some greedy minion, or imperious wife,
The trophied arches, storied halls invade
And haunt their slumbers in the pompous shade.
Alas! not dazzled with their noontide ray,
Compute the morn and evening to the day;
The whole amount of that enormous fame,
A tale, that blends their glory with their shame!
   VII. Know, then, this truth (enough for Man to know)
'Virtue alone is happiness below.'
The only point where human bliss stands still,
And tastes the good without the fall to ill;
Where only merit constant pay receives,
Is blessed in what it takes, and what it gives;
The joy unequalled, if its end it gain,
And if it lose, attended with no pain:
Without satiety, though e'er so blessed,
And but more relished as the more distressed:
The broadest mirth unfeeling folly wears,
Less pleasing far than virtue's very tears.
Good, from each object, from each place acquired,
For ever exercised, yet never tired;
Never elated, while one man's oppressed;
Never dejected while another's blessed;
And where no wants, no wishes can remain,
Since but to wish more virtue, is to gain.
   See the sole bliss Heaven could on all bestow!
Which who but feels can taste, but thinks can know:
Yet poor with fortune, and with learning blind,
The bad must miss; the good, untaught, will find;
Slave to no sect, who takes no private road,
But looks through Nature up to Nature's God;
Pursues that chain which links the immense design,
Joins heaven and earth, and mortal and divine;
Sees, that no being any bliss can know,
But touches some above, and some below;
Learns, from this union of the rising whole,
The first, last purpose of the human soul;
And knows, where faith, law, morals, all began,
All end, in LOVE OF GOD, and LOVE OF MAN.
   For him alone, hope leads from goal to goal,
And opens still, and opens on his soul,

Till lengthened on to faith, and unconfined,
It pours the bliss that fills up all the mind.
He sees, why Nature plants in Man alone
Hope of known bliss, and faith in bliss unknown:
(Nature, whose dictates to no other kind
Are given in vain, but what they seek they find)
Wise is her present; she connects in this
His greatest virtue with his greatest bliss;
At once his own bright prospect to be blessed,
And strongest motive to assist the rest.

Self-love thus pushed to social, to divine,
Gives thee to make thy neighbour's blessing thine.
Is this too little for the boundless heart?
Extend it, let thy enemies have part:
Grasp the whole worlds of reason, life, and sense,
In one close system of benevolence:
Happier as kinder, in whate'er degree,
And height of bliss but height of charity.

God loves from whole to parts: but human soul
Must rise from individual to the whole.
Self-love but serves the virtuous mind to wake,
As the small pebble stirs the peaceful lake;
The centre moved, a circle straight succeeds,
Another still, and still another spreads;
Friend, parent, neighbour, first it will embrace,
His country next; and next all human race;
Wide and more wide, the o'erflowings of the mind
Take every creature in, of every kind;
Earth smiles around, with boundless bounty blest,
And Heaven beholds its image in his breast.

Come then, my friend, my genius, come along,
Oh master of the poet, and the song!
And while the muse now stoops, or now ascends,
To Man's low passions, or their glorious ends,
Teach me, like thee, in various nature wise,
To fall with dignity, with temper rise;
Formed by thy converse, happily to steer
From grave to gay, from lively to severe;
Correct with spirit, eloquent with ease,
Intent to reason, or polite to please.
Oh! while along the stream of time thy name
Expanded flies, and gathers all its fame,
Say, shall my little bark attendant sail,
Pursue the triumph, and partake the gale?
When statesmen, heroes, kings, in dust repose,
Whose sons shall blush their fathers were thy foes,
Shall then this verse to future age pretend
Thou wert my guide, philosopher, and friend?

That urged by thee, I turned the tuneful art
From sounds to things, from fancy to the heart;
From wit's false mirror held up Nature's light;
Showed erring pride, 'WHATEVER IS, IS RIGHT';
That REASON, PASSION, answer one great aim;
That true SELF-LOVE and SOCIAL are the same;
That VIRTUE only makes our bliss below;
And all our knowledge is, OURSELVES TO KNOW.

POPE TO JONATHAN SWIFT
20 April 1733

You say truly, that death is only terrible to us as it separates us from those we love, but I really think those have the worst of it who are left by us, if we are true friends. I have felt more (I fancy) in the loss of poor Mr. Gay, than I shall suffer in the thought of going away myself into a state that can feel none of this sort of losses. I wished vehemently to have seen him in a condition of living independent, and to have lived in perfect indolence the rest of our days together, the two most idle, most innocent, undesigning poets of our age. I now as vehemently wish, you and I might walk into the grave together, by as slow steps as you please, but contentedly and cheerfully: whether that ever can be, or in what country, I know no more than into what country we shall walk out of the grave. But it suffices me to know it will be exactly what region or state our Maker appoints, and that whatever *Is*, is *Right*. Our poor friend's papers are partly in my hands, and for as much as is so, I will take care to suppress things unworthy of him. As to the epitaph, I am sorry you gave a copy, for it will certainly by that means come into print, and I would correct it more, unless you will do it for me (and that I shall like as well). Upon the whole I earnestly wish your coming over hither, for this reason among many others, that your influence may be joined with mine to suppress whatever we may judge proper of his papers. To be plunged in my neighbours and my papers, will be your inevitable fate as soon as you come. That I am an author whose characters are thought of some weight, appears from the great noise and bustle that the court and town make about any I give: and I will not render them less important or less interesting, by sparing Vice or Folly, or by betraying the cause of Truth and Virtue. I will take care they shall be such as no man can be angry at, but the persons I would have angry. You are sensible with what decency and justice I paid homage to the royal family, at the same time that I satirized false courtiers and spies, etc. about 'em. I have not the courage, however, to be such a satirist as you, but I would be as much, or more, a philosopher. You call your satires libels; I would rather call my satires epistles. They will consist more of morality than of wit, and grow graver, which you will call duller. I shall leave it to my antagonists to be witty (if they can) and content myself to be useful and in the right. Tell me your opinion as to Lady Mary Wortley's or Lord Harvey's performance? they are certainly the top wits of the court, and you may judge by that single piece what can be done against me; for it was laboured, corrected, praecommended, and post-disapproved, so as to be dis-owned by themselves, after each had highly cried it up for the other's. I have met with some complaints, and heard at a distance of some threats occasioned by my satires: I sent fair messages to acquaint them where I was to be found in town, and to offer to call at their houses to satisfy them, and so it dropped. It is very poor in any one to rail and threaten at a distance, and have nothing to say to you when they see you.—I am glad you persist and abide by so good a thing as that poem, in which I am immortal for my morality: I never took any praise so kindly, and yet I think I deserve that praise better than I do any other.—When does your collection come out, and what will it consist of? I have but last week finished another of my *Epistles*, in the order of the system; and this week (*exercitandi gratia*) I have translated, or rather parodied, another of Horace's, in which I introduce you advising me about my expenses, house-keeping, etc. But these things shall lie by, till you come to carp at 'em, and alter rhymes, and grammar, and triplets, and cacophonies of all kinds. Our parliament will sit till midsummer, which I hope may be a motive to bring you rather in summer than so late as autumn: you used to love what I hate, a hurry of politics, etc. Courts I see not, courtiers I know not, kings I adore not, queens I compliment not; so I am never likely to be in fashion, nor in dependence. I heartily join with you in pitying our poor lady for her unhappiness, and should only pity her more, if she had more of what they at court call happiness. Come then, and perhaps we may go all together into France at the end of the season, and compare the liberties of both kingdoms. Adieu. Believe me dear Sir, (with a thousand warm wishes, mixed with short sighs) ever yours.

THE FOURTH SATIRE OF DR JOHN DONNE
VERSIFIED

Well, if it be my time to quit the stage,
Adieu to all the follies of the age!
I die in charity with fool and knave,
Secure of peace at least beyond the grave.
I've had my purgatory here betimes,
And paid for all my satires, all my rhymes:
The poet's hell, its tortures, fiends, and flames,
To this were trifles, toys and empty names.

    With foolish pride my heart was never fired,
Nor the vain itch t' admire, or be admired;
I hoped for no commission from his Grace;
I bought no benefice, I begged no place;
Had no new verses, nor new suit to show;
Yet went to court!—the devil would have it so.
But, as the fool that in reforming days
Would go to mass in jest (as story says)
Could not but think, to pay his fine was odd,
Since 'twas no formed design of serving God;
So was I punished, as if full as proud,
As prone to ill, as negligent of good.
As deep in debt, without a thought to pay,
As vain, as idle, and as false, as they
Who live at court, for going once that way!
Scarce was I entered, when, behold! there came
A thing which Adam had been posed to name;
Noah had refused it lodging in his ark,
Where all the race of reptiles might embark:
A verier monster, than on Afric's shore

The sun e'er got, or slimy Nilus bore,
Or Sloane or Woodward's wondrous shelves contain,
Nay, all that lying travellers can feign.
The watch would hardly let him pass at noon,
At night, would swear him dropped out of the moon.
One whom the mob, when next we find or make
A Popish plot, shall for a Jesuit take,
And the wise Justice starting from his chair
Cry: 'By your priesthood tell me what you are?'
    Such was the wight: the apparel on his back
Though coarse, was reverend, and though bare, was black:
The suit, if by the fashion one might guess,
Was velvet in the youth of good Queen *Bess*,
But mere tuftaffeta what now remained;
So time, that changes all things, had ordained!
Our sons shall see it leisurely decay,
First turn plain rash, then vanish quite away.
    This thing has travelled, speaks each language too,
And know what's fit for very state to do;
Of whose best phrase and courtly accent joined,
He forms one tongue, exotic and refined,
Talkers I've learned to bear; Motteux I knew,
Henley himself I've heard, and Budgell too.
The Doctor's wormwood style, the hash of tongues
A pedant makes, the storm of Gonson's lungs,
The whole artillery of the terms of war,
And (all those plagues in one) the bawling bar:
These I could bear; but not a rogue so civil,
Whose tongue will compliment you to the devil.
A tongue that can cheat widows, cancel scores,
Make Scots speak treason, cozen subtlest whores,
With royal favourites in flattery vie,
And Oldmixon and Burnet both outlie.
    He spies me out, I whisper: 'Gracious God!
What sin of mine could merit such a rod?
That all the shot of dulness now must be
From this thy blunderbuss discharged on me!'
'Permit,' he cries, 'no stranger to your fame
To crave your sentiment, if ——'s your name.
What *speech* esteem you most?' 'The *King's*,' said I.
'But the best *words*?'—'O, sir, the *Dictionary*.'
'You miss my aim; I mean the most acute
And perfect *Speaker*?'—'Onslow, past dispute.'
'But, Sir, of writers?' 'Swift, for closer style,
But Hoadly for a period of a mile.'
'Why, yes, 'tis granted, these indeed may pass
Good common linguists, and so Panurge was;
Nay troth, th' apostles (though perhaps too rough)

Had once a pretty gift of tongues enough:
Yet these were all poor gentlemen! I dare
Affirm, 'twas travel made them what they were.'
   Thus others' talents having nicely shown,
He came by sure transition to his own:
Till I cried out: 'You prove yourself so able,
Pity! you was not druggerman at Babel;
For had they found a linguist half so good
I make no question but the tower had stood.'
   'Obliging sir! for courts you sure were made:
Why then for ever buried in the shade?
Spirits like you should see and should be seen,
The King would smile on you—at least the Queen.'
'Ah, gentle sir! you courtiers so cajole us—
But Tully has it, *Nunquam minus solus:*
And as for courts, forgive me, if I say
No lessons now are taught the Spartan way:
Though in his pictures lust be full displayed,
Few are the converts Aretine has made;
And though the court show vice exceeding clear,
None should, by my advice, learn virtue there.'
   At this entranced, he lifts his hands and eyes,
Squeaks like a high-stretched lutestring, and replies:
'Oh, 'tis the sweetest of all earthly things
To gaze on princes, and to talk of kings!'
'Then, happy man who shows the tombs!' said I,
'He dwells amidst the royal family;
He every day, from king to king can walk,
Of all our Harries, all our Edwards talk,
And get by speaking truth of monarchs dead,
What few can of the living, ease and bread.'
'Lord, sir, a mere mechanic! strangely low,
And coarse of phrase,—your English all are so.
How elegant your Frenchmen?' 'Mine, d'ye mean?
I have but one, I hope the fellow's clean.'
'Oh! sir, politely so! nay, let me die,
Your only wearing is your paduasoy.'
'Not, Sir, my only, I have better still,
And this you see is but my dishabille'—
Wild to get loose, his patience I provoke,
Mistake, confound, object at all he spoke.
But as coarse iron, sharpened, mangles more,
And itch most hurts when angered to a sore;
So when you plague a fool, 'tis still the curse,
You only make the matter worse and worse.
   He past it o'er; affects an easy smile
At all my peevishness, and turns his style.
He asks, 'What news?' I tell him of new plays,

New eunuchs, harlequins, and operas.
He hears, and as a still with simples in it,
Between each drop it gives, stays half a minute,
Loth to enrich me with too quick replies,
By little, and by little, drops his lies.
Mere household trash! of birth-nights, balls, and shows,
More than ten Holinsheds, or Halls, or Stows.
When the Queen frowned, or smiled, he knows; and what
A subtle minister may make of that:
Who sins with whom: who got his pension rug.
Or quickened a reversion by a drug:
Whose place is quartered out, three parts in four,
And whether to a bishop, or a whore:
Who having lost his credit, pawned his rent,
Is therefore fit to have a government:
Who in the secret, deals in stocks secure,
And cheats the unknowing widow and the poor:
Who makes a trust or charity a job,
And gets an Act of Parliament to rob:
Why turnpikes rise, and now no cit nor clown
Can gratis see the country, or the town:
Shortly no lad shall chuck, or lady vole,
But some excising courtier will have toll.
He tells what strumpet places sells for life,
What squire his lands, what citizen his wife:
And last (which proves him wiser still than all)
What lady's face is not a whited wall.
　　As one of Woodward's patients, sick, and sore,
I puke, I nauseate—yet he thrusts in more:
Trims Europe's balance, tops the statesman's part,
And talks *Gazettes* and *Post-Boys* o'er by heart.
Like a big wife at sight of loathsome meat,
Ready to cast, I yawn, I sigh, and sweat.
Then as a licensed spy, whom nothing can
Silence or hurt, he libels the great man;
Swears every place entailed for years to come,
In sure succession to the day of doom:
He names the price for every office paid,
And says our wars thrive ill, because delayed:
Nay hints, 'tis by connivance of the court,
That Spain robs on, and Dunkirk's still a port.
Not more amazement seized on Circe's guests,
To see themselves fall endlong into beasts,
Than mine, to find a subject staid and wise
Already half turned traitor by surprise.
I felt the infection slide from him to me,
As in the pox, some give it to get free;
And quick to swallow me, methought I saw

One of our giant statutes ope its jaw.
   In that nice moment, as another lie
Stood just atilt, the minister came by.
To him he flies, and bows, and bows again,
Then, close as Umbra, joins the dirty train.
Not Fannius' self more impudently near,
When half his nose is in his prince's ear.
I quaked at heart; and still afraid to see
All the court filled with stranger things than he,
Ran out as fast as one that pays his bail
And dreads more actions, hurries from a jail.
   Bear me, some god, oh, quickly bear me hence
To wholesome solitude, the nurse of sense:
Where contemplation plumes her ruffled wings,
And the free soul looks down to pity kings!
There sober thought pursued the amusing theme,
Till fancy coloured it, and formed a dream.
A vision hermits can to hell transport,
And forced even me to see the damned at court.
Not Dante dreaming all the infernal state,
Beheld such scenes of envy, sin, and hate.
Base fear becomes the guilty, not the free;
Suits tyrants, plunderers, but suits not me:
Shall I, the terror of this sinful town,
Care, if a liveried lord or smile or frown?
Who cannot flatter, and detest who can,
Tremble before a noble serving-man?
O, my fair mistress, truth! shall I quit thee
For huffing, braggart, puffed nobility?
Thou, who since yesterday hast rolled o'er all
The busy, idle blockheads of the ball,
Hast thou, oh, sun! beheld an emptier fort,
Than such who swell this bladder of a court?
Now pox on those who show a *court in wax!*
It ought to bring all courtiers on their backs:
Such painted puppets! such a varnished race
Of hollow gewgaws, only dress and face!
Such waxen noses, stately staring things—
No wonder some folks bow, and think them kings.
   See! where the British youth, engaged no more
At Figg's, at White's, with felons, or a whore,
Pay their last duty to the court, and come
All fresh and fragrant, to the drawing-room;
In hues as gay, and odours as divine,
As the fair fields they sold to look so fine.
'That's velvet for a king!' the flatterer swears;
'Tis true, for ten days hence 'twill be King Lear's.
Our Court may justly to our stage give rules,

That helps it both to fool's coats and to fools.
And why not players strut in courtiers' clothes?
For these are actors too, as well as those:
Wants reach all states; they beg but better dressed,
And all is splendid poverty at best.
   Painted for sight, and essenced for the smell,
Like frigates fraught with spice and cochineal,
Sail in the ladies: how each pirate eyes
So weak a vessel, and so rich a prize!
Top-gallant he, and she in all her trim,
He boarding her, she striking sail to him:
'Dear Countess! you have charms all hearts to hit!'
And 'Sweet Sir Fopling! you have so much wit!'
Such wits and beauties are not praised for nought,
For both the beauty and the wit are bought.
'Twould burst even Heraclitus with the spleen
To see those antics, Fopling and Courtin:
The presence seems, with things so richly odd,
The mosque of Mahound, or some queer pagod.
See them survey their limbs by Dürer's rules,
Of all beau-kind the best proportioned fools!
Adjust their clothes, and to confession draw
Those venial sins, an atom, or a straw;
But oh! what terrors must distract the soul
Convicted of that mortal crime, a hole;
Or should one pound of powder less bespread
Those monkey tails that wag behind their head.
Thus finished, and corrected to a hair,
They march, to prate their hour before the fair.
So first to preach a white-gloved chaplain goes,
With band of lily, and with cheek of rose,
Sweeter than Sharon, in immaculate trim,
Neatness itself impertinent in him.
Let but the ladies smile, and they are blessed:
Prodigious! how the things *protest, protest:*
Peace, fools, or Gonson will for papists seize you,
If once he catch you at your *Jesu! Jesu!*
   Nature made every fop to plague his brother,
Just as one beauty mortifies another.
But here's the captain that will plague them both,
Whose air cries 'Arm!', whose very look's an oath:
The captain's honest, sirs, and that's enough,
Though his soul's bullet, and his body buff.
He spits fore-right; his haughty chest before,
Like battering rams, beats open every door:
And with a face as red, and as awry,
As Herod's hangdogs in old tapestry,
Scarecrow to boys, the breeding woman's curse,

Has yet a strange ambition to look worse;
Confounds the civil, keeps the rude in awe,
Jests like a licensed fool, commands like law.
 Frighted, I quit the room, but leave it so
As men from gaols to execution go;
For hung with deadly sins I see the wall,
And lined with giants deadlier than 'em all:
Each man an Askapart, of strength to toss
For quoits, both Temple Bar and Charing Cross.
Scared at the grizzly forms, I sweat, I fly,
And shake all o'er, like a discovered spy.
 Courts are too much for wits so weak as mine:
Charge them with Heaven's artillery, bold divine!
From such alone the great rebukes endure,
Whose satire's sacred, and whose rage secure:
'Tis mine to wash a few light stains, but theirs
To deluge sin, and drown a court in tears.
However, what's now Apocrypha, my wit,
In time to come, may pass for holy writ.

AN EPISTLE

TO

Sir *Richard Temple*, Lord *Cobham*

ARGUMENT

Of the Knowledge *and* Characters *of* MEN

That it is not sufficient for this knowledge to consider Man in the abstract: books *will not serve the purpose, nor yet our own* experience *singly,* v.1. *General maxims, unless they be formed upon* both, *will be but notional,* v.10. *Some peculiarity in every man, characteristic to himself, yet varying from himself,* v.15. *Difficulties arising from our own passions, fancies, faculties, etc.,* v.31. *The shortness of life, to observe in, and the uncertainty of the* principles of action *in men, to observe by,* v.37, *etc. Our* own *principle of action often hid from ourselves,* v.41. *Some few characters plain, but in general confounded, dissembled, or inconsistent,* v.51. *The same man utterly different in different places and seasons,* v.71. *Unimaginable weaknesses in the greatest,* v.70, *etc. Nothing constant and certain but* God *and* Nature, v.95. *No judging of the* motives *from the actions; the same actions proceeding from contrary motives, and the same motives influencing contrary actions* v.100. II. *Yet to form* characters, *we can only take the strongest actions of a man's life, and try to make them* agree. *The utter uncertainty of this, from* Nature *itself, and from* policy, v.120. Characters *given according to the* rank *of men of the world,* v.135. *And some reason for it,* v.140. Education *alters the* nature, *or at least* character *of many,* v.149. Actions, passions, opinions, manners, humours, *or* principles *all subject to change. No judging by* Nature, *from* v.158 *to* 178. III. *It only remains to find (if we can) his* RULING PASSION. *That will certainly influence all the rest, and can reconcile the seeming or real inconsistency of all his actions,* v.175. *Instanced in the extraordinary character of* Clodio, v.179. *A caution against mistaking* second qualities *for* first, *which will destroy all possibility of the knowledge of mankind,* v.210. *Examples of the strength of the* ruling passion, *and its continuation to the last breath,* v.222, etc.

Yes, you despise the man to books confined,
Who from his study rails at human kind;
Though what he learns, he speaks, and may advance
Some general maxims, or be right by chance.
The coxcomb bird, so talkative and grave,
That from his cage cries cuckold, whore, and knave,
Though many a passenger he rightly call,
You hold him no philosopher at all.
    And yet the fate of all extremes is such,
Men may be read as well as books, too much.
To observations which ourselves we make,
We grow more partial for the observer's sake;
To written wisdom, as another's, less:
Maxims are drawn from notions, those from guess.
There's some peculiar in each leaf and grain,
Some unmarked fibre, or some varying vein:
Shall only man be taken in the gross?
Grant but as many sorts of mind, as moss.
    That each from other differs, first confess;
Next, that he varies from himself no less:
Add nature's, custom's reason's passion's strife,
And all opinion's colours cast on life.
    Our depths who fathoms, or our shallows finds,
Quick whirls, and shifting eddies, of our minds?
On human actions reason though you can,
It may be reason, but it is not man:
His principle of action once explore,
That instant 'tis his principle no more.
Like following life through creatures you dissect,
You lose it in the moment you detect.
    Yet more; the difference is as great between
The optics seeing, as the object seen.
All manners take a tincture from our own;
Or come discoloured through our passions shown.
Or fancy's beam enlarges, multiplies,
Contracts, inverts, and gives ten thousand dyes.
    Nor will life's stream for observation stay,
It hurries all too fast to mark their way:
In vain sedate reflections we would make,
When half our knowledge we must snatch, not take.
Oft, in the passion's wild rotation tossed,
Our spring of action to ourselves is lost:
Tired, not determined, to the last we yield,
And what comes then is master of the field.
As the last image of that troubled heap,

When sense subsides, and fancy sports in sleep,
(Though past the recollection of the thought)
Becomes the stuff of which our dream is wrought;
Something as dim to our internal view,
Is thus perhaps the cause of most we do.
    True, some are open, and to all men known;
Others so very close, they're hid from none;
(So darkness strikes the sense no less than light)
Thus gracious CHANDOS is beloved at sight;
And every child hates Shylock, though his soul
Still sits at squat, and peeps not from its hole.
At half mankind when generous Manly raves,
All know 'tis virtue, for he thinks them knaves:
When universal homage Umbra pays,
All see 'tis vice, and itch of vulgar praise.
When flattery glares, all hate it in a queen,
While one there is who charms us with his spleen.
    But these plain characters we rarely find;
Though strong the bent, yet quick the turns of mind:
Or puzzling contraries confound the whole,
Or affectations quite reverse the soul.
The dull, flat falsehood serves for policy,
And in the cunning, truth itself's a lie:
Unthought-of frailties cheat us in the wise;
The fool lies hid in inconsistencies.
    See the same man, in vigour, in the gout;
Alone, in company; in place, or out;
Early at business, and at hazard late;
Mad at a fox-chase, wise at a debate;
Drunk at a borough, civil at a ball;
Friendly at Hackney, faithless at Whitehall.
    Catius is ever moral, ever grave,
Thinks who endures a knave is next a knave,
Save just at dinner—then prefers, no doubt,
A rogue with venison to a saint without.
    Who would not praise Patritio's high desert,
His hand unstained, his uncorrupted heart,
His comprehensive head? all interests weighed,
All Europe saved, yet Britain not betrayed.
He thanks you not, his pride is in piquet,
Newmarket-fame, and judgment at a bet.
    What made (say Montaigne, or more sage Charron!)
Otho a warrior, Cromwell a buffoon?
A perjured prince a leaden saint revere?
A godless regent tremble at a star?
The throne a bigot keep, a genius quit,
Faithless through piety, and duped through wit?
Europe a woman, child, or dotard rule,

And just her wisest monarch made a fool?
　　Know, GOD and NATURE only are the same:
In man, the judgment shoots at flying game,
A bird of passage! gone as soon as found,
Now in the moon, perhaps, now under ground.
　　In vain the sage, with retrospective eye,
Would from the apparent what conclude the why,
Infer the motive from the deed, and show
That what we chanced, was what we meant to do.
Behold! if fortune or a mistress frowns,
Some plunge in business, others shave their crowns:
To ease the soul of one oppressive weight,
This quits an empire, that embroils a state:
The same adust complexion has impelled
Charles to the convent, Philip to the field.
　　Not always actions show the man: we find
Who does a kindness, is not therefore kind;
Perhaps prosperity becalmed his breast,
Perhaps the wind just shifted from the east:
Not therefore humble he who seeks retreat,
Pride guides his steps, and bids him shun the great:
Who combats bravely is not therefore brave,
He dreads a death-bed like the meanest slave:
Who reasons wisely is not therefore wise,
His pride in reasoning, not in acting lies.
　　But grant that actions best discover man;
Take the most strong, and sort them as you can.
The few that glare each character must mark,
You balance not the many in the dark.
What will you do with such as disagree?
Suppress them, or miscall them policy?
Must then at once (the character to save)
The plain rough hero turn a crafty knave?
Alas! in truth the man but changed his mind,
Perhaps was sick, in love, or had not dined.
Ask why from Britain Caesar would retreat?
Caesar himself might whisper he was beat.
Why risk the world's great empire for a punk?
Caesar perhaps might answer he was drunk.
But, sage historians! 'tis your task to prove
One action, conduct; one, heroic love.
　　'Tis from high life high characters are drawn;
A saint in crape is twice a saint in lawn;
A judge is just, a chancellor juster still;
A gownman, learned; a bishop, what you will;
Wise, if a minister; but, if a king,
More wise, more learned, more just, more everything.
Court-virtues bear, like gems, the highest rate,

Born where Heaven's influence scarce can penetrate:
In life's low vale, the soil the virtues like,
They please as beauties, here as wonders strike.
Though the same sun with all-diffusive rays
Blush in the rose, and in the diamond blaze,
We prize the stronger effort of his power,
And justly set the gem above the flower.

   'Tis education forms the common mind,
Just as the twig is bent, the tree's inclined.
Boastful and rough, your first son is a squire;
The next a tradesman, meek, and much a liar;
Tom struts a soldier, open, bold, and brave;
Will sneaks a scrivener, an exceeding knave:
Is he a churchman? then he's fond of power:
A quaker? sly: a presbyterian? sour:
A smart freethinker? all things in an hour.

   Ask men's opinions: Scoto now shall tell
How trade increases, and the world goes well;
Strike off his pension, by the setting sun,
And Britain, if not Europe, is undone.

   That gay freethinker, a fine talker once,
What turns him now a stupid silent dunce?
Some god, or spirit he has lately found:
Or chanced to meet a minister that frowned.

   Judge we by Nature? Habit can efface,
Interest o'ercome, or policy take place:
By actions? those uncertainty divides:
By passions? these dissimulation hides:
Opinions? they still take a wider range:
Find, if you can, in what you cannot change.

   Manners with fortunes, humours turn with climes.
Tenets with books, and principles with times.

   Search then the RULING PASSION: there, alone,
The wild are constant, and the cunning known;
The fool consistent, and the false sincere;
Priests, princes, women, no dissemblers here.
This clue once found, unravels all the rest,
The prospect clears, and Wharton stands confessed.
Wharton, the scorn and wonder of our days,
Whose ruling passion was the lust of praise;
Born with whate'er could win it from the wise,
Women and fools must like him or he dies;
Though wondering senates hung on all he spoke,
The club must hail him master of the joke.
Shall parts so various aim at nothing new?
He'll shine a Tully and a Wilmot too.
Then turns repentant, and his God adores
With the same spirit that he drinks and whores;

Enough if all around him but admire,
And now the punk applaud, and now the friar.
Thus, with each gift of nature and of art,
And wanting nothing but an honest heart;
Grown all to all, from no one vice exempt,
And most contemptible, to shun contempt;
His passion still, to covet general praise,
His life, to forfeit it a thousand ways;
A constant bounty which no friend has made;
An angel tongue, which no man can persuade;
A fool, with more of wit than half mankind,
Too rash for thought, for action too refined;
A tyrant to the wife his heart approves;
A rebel to the very king he loves;
He dies, sad outcast of each church and state,
And, harder still! flagitious, yet not great.
Ask you why Wharton broke through every rule?
'Twas all for fear the knaves should call him fool.

 Nature well known, no prodigies remain,
Comets are regular and Wharton plain.

 Yet, in this search, the wisest may mistake,
If second qualities for first they take.
When Catiline by rapine swelled his store;
When Caesar made a noble dame a whore;
In this the lust, in that the avarice
Were means, not ends; ambition was the vice.
That very Caesar, born in Scipio's days,
Had aimed, like him, by chastity at praise.
Lucullus, when frugality could charm,
Had roasted turnips in the Sabine farm.
In vain the observer eyes the builder's toil,
But quite mistakes the scaffold for the pile.

 In this one passion man can strength enjoy,
As fits give vigour, just when they destroy.
Time, that on all things lays his lenient hand,
Yet tames not this; it sticks to our last sand.
Consistent in our follies and our sins,
Here honest Nature ends as she begins.

 Old politicians chew on wisdom past,
And totter on in business to the last;
As weak, as earnest; and as gravely out,
As sober Lanesborough dancing in the gout.

 Behold a reverend sire, whom want of grace
Has made the father of a nameless race,
Shoved from the wall perhaps, or rudely pressed
By his own son, that passes by unblessed:
Still to his wench he crawls on knocking knees,
And envies every sparrow that he sees.

A salmon's belly, Helluo, was thy fate;
The doctor called, declares all help too late:
'Mercy!' cries Helluo, 'mercy on my soul!
Is there no hope?—Alas!—then bring the jowl.'
    The frugal crone, whom praying priests attend,
Still tries to save the hallowed taper's end,
Collects her breath, as ebbing life retires,
For one puff more, and in that puff expires.
    'Odious! in woollen! 'twould a saint provoke'
(Were the last words that poor Narcissa spoke);
'No, let a charming chintz, and Brussels lace
Wrap my cold limbs, and shade my lifeless face:
One would not, sure, be frightful when one's dead—
And—Betty—give this cheek a little red.'
    The courtier smooth, who forty years had shined
An humble servant to all human kind,
Just brought out this, when scarce his tongue could stir,
'If—where I'm going—I could serve you, Sir?'
    'I give and I devise' (old Euclio said,
And sighed) 'my lands and tenements to Ned.'
'Your money, Sir; 'My money, Sir, what all?
Why—if I must'—(then wept) 'I give it Paul.'
'The manor, Sir?—'The manor! hold,' he cried,
'Not that—I cannot part with that'—and died.
    And you! brave COBHAM, to the latest breath
Shall feel your ruling passion strong in death:
Such in those moments as in all the past,
'Oh, save my country, Heaven!' shall be your last.

THE SECOND SATIRE
OF THE
SECOND BOOK
OF
HORACE IMITATED
To Mr. Bethel

What, and how great, the virtue and the art
To live on little with a cheerful heart
(A doctrine sage, but truly none of mine)
Let's talk, my friends, but talk before we dine:
Not when a gilt buffet's reflected pride
Turns you from sound philosophy aside,
Not when from plate to plate your eyeballs roll,
And the brain dances to the mantling bowl.
Hear BETHEL'S sermon, one not versed in schools,
But strong in sense, and wise without the rules.
    'Go work, hunt, exercise!' he thus began,
'Then scorn a homely dinner, if you can.

Your wine locked up, your butler strolled abroad,
Or fish denied (the river yet unthawed)
If then plain bread and milk will do the feat,
The pleasure lies in you, and not the meat.
    Preach as I please, I doubt our curious men
Will choose a pheasant still before a hen;
Yet hens of Guinea full as good I hold,
Except you eat the feathers green and gold.
Of carps and mullets why prefer the great,
(Though cut in pieces 'ere my lord can eat)
Yet for small turbots such esteem profess?
Because God made these large, the other less.
Oldfield with more than harpy throat endued,
Cries 'Send me, gods! a whole hog barbecued!'
Oh blast it, south-winds! till a stench exhale
Rank as the ripeness of a rabbit's tail.
By what criterion do ye eat, d'ye think,
If this is prized for sweetness, that for stink?
When the tired glutton labours through a treat,
He finds no relish in the sweetest meat;
He calls for something bitter, something sour,
And the rich feast concludes extremely poor:
Cheap eggs, and herbs, and olives still we see;
Thus much is left of old simplicity!
The robin-redbreast till of late had rest,
And children sacred held a martin's nest,
Till beccaficos sold so devilish dear
To one that was, or would have been a peer.
Let me extol a cat, on oysters fed,
I'll have a party at the Bedford Head;
Or even to crack live crawfish recommend;
I'd never doubt at Court to make a friend.
    'Tis yet in vain, I own, to keep a pother
About one vice, and fall into the other:
Between excess and famine lies a mean;
Plain, but not sordid; though not splendid, clean.
    Avidien, or his wife (no matter which,
For him you'll call a dog, and her a bitch)
Sell their presented partridges, and fruits,
And humbly live on rabbits and on roots:
One half-pint bottle serves them both to dine,
And is at once their vinegar and wine.
But on some lucky day (as when they found
A lost bank-bill, or heard their son was drowned)
At such a feast, old vinegar to spare,
Is what two souls so generous cannot bear:
Oil, though it stink, they drop by drop impart,
But souse the cabbage with a bounteous heart.

He knows to live, who keeps the middle state,
And neither leans on this side, nor on that:
Nor stops, for one bad cork, his butler's pay,
Swears, like Albutius, a good cook away;
Nor lets, like Naevius, every error pass,
The musty wine, foul cloth, or greasy glass.

'Now hear what blessings temperance can bring:'
(Thus said our friend, and what he said I sing)
'First health: The stomach (crammed from every dish,
A tomb of boiled and roast, and flesh and fish,
Where bile, and wind, and phlegm, and acid jar,
And all the man is one intestine war)
Remembers oft the schoolboy's simple fare,
The temperate sleeps, and spirits light as air.

How pale, each worshipful and reverend guest
Rise from a clergy, or a city feast!
What life in all that ample body, say?
What heavenly particle inspires the clay?
The soul subsides, and wickedly inclines
To seem but mortal, even in sound divines.

On morning wings how active springs the mind
That leaves the load of yesterday behind?
How easy every labour it pursues?
How coming to the poet every muse?
Not but we may exceed, some holy time,
Or tired in search of truth, or search of rhyme.
Ill health some just indulgence may engage,
And more the sickness of long life, old age;
For fainting age what cordial drop remains,
If our intemperate youth the vessel drains?

Our fathers praised rank venison. You suppose,
Perhaps, young men! our fathers had no nose?
Not so: a buck was then a week's repast,
And 'twas their point, I ween, to make it last;
More pleased to keep it till their friends could come,
Than eat the sweetest by themselves at home.
Why had not I in those good times my birth,
Ere coxcomb pies or coxcombs were on earth?

Unworthy he, the voice of fame to hear,
That sweetest music to an honest ear;
(For 'faith, Lord Fanny! you are in the wrong,
The world's good word is better than a song)
Who has not learned fresh sturgeon and ham-pie
Are no rewards for want, and infamy!
When luxury has licked up all thy pelf,
Cursed by thy neighbours, thy trustees, thyself,
To friends, to fortune, to mankind a shame,
Think how posterity will treat thy name;

And buy a rope, that future times may tell
Thou hast at least bestowed one penny well.
   'Right,' cries his lordship, 'for a rogue in need
To have a taste, is insolence indeed:
In me 'tis noble, suits my birth and state,
My wealth unwieldy, and my heap too great.'
Then, like the sun, let bounty spread her ray,
And shine that superfluity away.
Oh, impudence of wealth! with all thy store,
How darest thou let one worthy man be poor?
Shall half the new-built churches round thee fall?
Make quays, build bridges, or repair Whitehall:
Or to thy country let that heap be lent,
As Marlborough's was, but not at five per cent.
   Who thinks that fortune cannot change her mind,
Prepares a dreadful jest for all mankind.
And who stands safest? tell me, is it he
That spreads and swells in puffed posterity,
Or blessed with little, whose preventing care
In peace provides fit arms against a war?'
Thus BETHEL spoke, who always speaks his thought,
And always thinks the very thing he ought:
His equal mind I copy what I can,
And as I love, would imitate the man.
In South-Sea days not happier, when surmised
The lord of thousands, than if now *excised;*
In forest planted by a father's hand,
Than in five acres now of rented land.
Content with little, I can piddle here
On broccoli and mutton, round the year;
But ancient friends (though poor, or out of play)
That touch my bell, I cannot turn away.
'Tis true, no turbots dignify my boards,
But gudgeons, flounders, what my Thames affords:
To Hounslow Heath I point and Banstead Down,
Thence comes your mutton, and these chicks my own:
From yon old walnut-tree a shower shall fall;
And grapes, long lingering on my only wall,
And figs, from standard and espalier join;
The devil is in you if you cannot dine:
Then cheerful healths (your mistress shall have place)
And, what's more rare, a poet shall say grace.
   Fortune not much of humbling me can boast;
Though double taxed, how little have I lost?
My life's amusements have been just the same,
Before, and after, standing armies came.
My lands are sold, my father's house is gone;
I'll hire another's; is not that my own,

And yours, my friends? through whose free-opening gate
None comes too early, none departs too late;
(For I, who hold sage Homer's rule the best,
Welcome the coming, speed the going guest.)
'Pray heaven it last!' cries SWIFT, 'as you go on;
I wish to God this house had been your own:
Pity! to build, without a son or wife:
Why, you'll enjoy it only all your life.'
Well, if the use be mine, can it concern one,
Whether the name belong to Pope or Vernon?
What's *property?* dear Swift! you see it alter
From you to me, from me to Peter Walter;
Or, in a mortgage, prove a lawyer's share;
Or, in a jointure, vanish from the heir;
Or in pure equity (the case not clear)
The Chancery takes your rents for twenty year:
At best, it falls to some ungracious son,
Who cries, 'My father's damned, and all's my own.'
Shades, that to BACON could retreat afford,
Become the portion of a booby lord;
And Helmsley, once proud Buckingham's delight,
Slides to a scrivener or a city knight.
Let lands and houses have what lords they will,
Let us be fixed, and our own masters still.

THE
SECOND SATIRE
OF THE
FIRST BOOK
OF
HORACE

Imitated in the manner of Mr. POPE

The tribe of templars, players, apothecaries,
Pimps, poets, wits, Lord Fanny's, Lady Mary's,
And all the court in tears, and half the town,
Lament dear charming Oldfield, dead and gone!
Engaging Oldfield! who, with grace and ease,
Could join the arts, to ruin and to please.
    Not so, who of ten thousand gulled her knight,
Then asked ten thousand for a second night:
The gallant too, to whom she paid it down,
Lived to refuse that mistress half a crown.
    Con. Philips cries, 'A sneaking dog I hate,'
That's all three lovers have for their estate!
'Treat on, treat on,' is her eternal note,
And lands and tenements go down her throat.

Some damn the jade, and some the cullies blame,
But not Sir Herbert, for he does the same.
  With all a woman's virtues but the p—x,
Fufidia thrives in money, land, and stocks;
For interest, ten per cent, her constant rate is;
Her body? hopeful heirs may have it *gratis*.
She turns her very sister to a job,
And, in the happy minute, picks your fob:
Yet starves herself, so little her own friend,
And thirsts and hungers only at one end:
A self-tormentor, worse than (in the play)
The wretch, whose avarice drove his son away.
  But why all this? beloved, 'tis my theme:
'Women and fools are always in extreme.'
Rufa's at either end a common shore,
Sweet Moll and Jack are civet-cat and boar:
Nothing in nature is so lewd as Peg,
Yet for the world she would not show her leg!
While bashful Jenny, ev'n at morning prayer,
Spreads her fore-buttocks to the navel bare.
But different taste in different men prevails,
And one is fired by heads, and one by tails;
Some feel no flames but at the court or ball,
And others hunt white aprons in the Mall.
  My Lord of London, chancing to remark
A noted Dean much busied in the Park,
'Proceed', (he cried), 'proceed, my reverend brother,
'Tis *fornicatio simplex*, and no other:
Better than lust for boys, with Pope and Turk,
Or others' spouses, like my Lord of York'.
  'May no such praise', cries Jefferies, 'e'er be mine!'
Jefferies, who bows at Hillsborough's hoary shrine.
All you who think the city ne'er can thrive,
Till every cuckold-maker's flayed alive;
Attend, while I their miseries explain,
And pity men of pleasure still in pain!
Survey the pangs they bear, the risks they run,
Where the most lucky are but last undone.
See! wretched Monsieur flies to save his throat,
And quits his mistress, money, ring, and note!
See good Sir George of ragged livery stripped,
By worthier footmen pissed upon and whipped!
Plundered by thieves, (or lawyers, which is worse)
One bleeds in person, and one bleeds in purse;
This meets a blanket, and that meets a cudgel—
And all applaud the justice—all, but Budgell.
  How much more safe, dear countrymen! his state,
Who trades in frigates of the second rate?

And yet some care of Sallust should be had,
Nothing so mean for which he can't run mad;
His wit confirms him but a slave the more,
And makes a princess whom he found a whore:
The youth might save much trouble and expense,
Were he a dupe of only common sense.
But here's his point; 'A wench' (he cries) 'for me!
'I never touch a dame of quality.'

To Palmer's bed no actress comes amiss,
He courts the whole *personae dramatis:*
He too can say, 'With wives I never sin.'
But singing-girls and mimics draw him in.
Sure, worthy sir, the difference is not great,
With whom you lose your credit and estate?
This, or that person, what avails to shun?
What's wrong is wrong, wherever it be done;
The ease, support, and lustre of your life,
Destroyed alike with strumpet, maid, or wife.

What pushed poor Ellis on th' imperial whore?
'Twas but to be where CHARLES had been before.
The fatal steel unjustly was applied,
When not his lust offended, but his pride:
Too hard a penance for defeated sin,
Himself shut out, and Jacob Hall let in.

Suppose that honest part that rules us all,
Should rise, and say—'Sir Robert! or Sir Paul!
Did I demand, in my most vigorous hour,
A thing descended from the Conqueror?
Or when my pulse beat highest, ask for any
Such nicety as Lady or Lord Fanny?'——
What would you answer? could you have the face,
When the poor sufferer humbly mourned his case,
To cry, 'You weep the favours of her GRACE?'

Hath not indulgent nature spread a feast,
And given enough for man, enough for beast?
But man corrupt, perverse in all his ways,
In search of vanities from nature strays:
Yea, though the blessing's more than he can use,
Shuns the permitted, the forbid pursues!
Weigh well the cause from whence these evils spring,
'Tis in thyself, and not in God's good thing:
Then, lest repentance punish such a life,
Never, ah, never! kiss thy neighbour's wife.

First, silks and diamonds veil no finer shape,
Or plumper thigh, than lurk in humble crape:
And secondly, how innocent a belle
Is she who shows what ware she has to sell?
Not ladylike, displays a milk-white breast,

And hides in sacred sluttishness, the rest.
   Our ancient kings (and sure those kings were wise,
Who judged themselves, and saw with their own eyes)
A war-horse never for the service chose,
But eyed him round, and stripped off all the clothes;
For well they knew, proud trappings serve to hide
A heavy chest, thick neck, or heaving side.
But fools are ready chaps, agog to buy,
Let but a comely forehand strike the eye:
No eagle sharper, every charm to find,
To all defects, Tyrawley not so blind:
Goose-rumped, hawk-nosed, swan-footed is my dear?
They'll praise her elbow, heel, or tip o'th' ear.
   A lady's face is all you see undressed;
(For none but Lady Mary shows the rest)
But if to charms more latent you pretend,
What lines encompass, and what works defend!
Dangers on dangers! Obstacles by dozens!
Spies, guardians, guests, old women, aunts, and cousins!
Could you directly to her person go,
Stays will obstruct above, and hoops below,
And if the dame says yes, the dress says no.
Not thus at Needham's; your judicious eye
May measure there the breast, the hip, the thigh!
And will you run to perils, sword, and law,
All for a thing you ne'er so much as saw?
'The hare once seized, the hunter heeds no more
The little scut he so pursued before;
Love follows flying game (as Suckling sings)
And 'tis for that the wanton boy has wings.'
Why let him sing—but when you're in the wrong,
Think ye to cure the mischief with a song?
Has nature set no bounds to wild desire?
No sense to guide, no reason to enquire,
What solid happiness, what empty pride,
And what is best indulged, or best denied?
If neither gems adorn, nor silver tip
The flowing bowl, will you not wet your lip?
When sharp with hunger, scorn you to be fed
Except on peachicks, at the Bedford Head?
Or when a tight neat girl, will serve the turn,
In errant pride, continue stiff and burn?
I'm a plain man, whose maxim is professed,
'The thing at hand is of all things the best.'
But her who will, and then will not comply,
Whose word is 'If', 'Perhaps', and 'By-and-by',
Z—ds! let some eunuch or Platonic take—'
So Bathurst cries, philosopher and rake!

Who asks no more (right reasonable peer)
Than not to wait too long, nor pay too dear.
Give me a willing nymph! ('tis all I care,)
Extremely clean, and tolerably fair;
Her shape her own, whatever shape she have,
And just that white and red which Nature gave:
Her I transported touch, transported view,
And call her angel! goddess! Montague!
No furious husband thunders at the door;
No barking dog, no household in a roar;
From gleaming swords no shrieking women run;
No wretched wife cries out, 'Undone! Undone'
Seized in the fact, and in her cuckold's power,
She kneels, she weeps, and worse! resigns her dower.
Me, naked me, to posts, to pumps they draw,
To shame eternal, or eternal law.
Oh love, be deep tranquillity my luck,
No mistress Heysham near, no Lady Buck:
For, to be taken, is the devil in hell;
This truth let Liddel, Jefferies, Onslow tell.

EPISTLE TO DR ARBUTHNOT

Neque sermonibus *Vulgi* dederis te, nec in *Praemiis* humanis spem posueris rerum tuarum; suis te oportet illecebris *ipsa Virtus* trahat ad verum decus. Quid de te alii loquantur, ipsi videant, sed loquentur tamen.

TULLY [De Re Publica, vi. 23].

Advertisement

This paper is a sort of bill of complaint, begun many years since, and drawn up by snatches, as the several occasions offered. I had no thoughts of publishing it, till it pleased some persons of rank and fortune [the authors of Verses *to the Imitator of Horace*, and of an *Epistle to a Doctor of Divinity from a Nobleman at Hampton Court*] to attack in a very extraordinary manner, not only my writings (of which being public the public may judge) but my *person, morals,* and *family,* whereof to those who know me not, a truer Information may be requisite. Being divided between the necessity to say something of *myself,* and my own laziness to undertake so awkward a task, I thought it the shortest way to put the last hand to this epistle. If it have anything pleasing, it will be that by which i am most desirous to please, the *truth* and the *sentiment*; and if anything offensive, it will be only to those I am least sorry to offend, the *vicious* or the *ungenerous.*

Many will know their own pictures in it, there being not a circumstance but what is true; but I have, for the most part spared their *names,* and they may escape being laughed at, if they please.

I would have some of them know, it was owing to the Request of the learned and candid Friend to whom it is inscribed, that I make not as free use of theirs as they have done of mine. However I shall have this advantage, and honour, on my side, that whereas by their proceeding, any abuse may be directed at any man, no injury can possibly be done by mine, since a nameless character can never be found out, but by its *truth* and *likeness.*

'Shut, shut the door, good John!', fatigued I said,
'Tie up the knocker, say I'm sick, I'm dead.'
The dog-star rages! nay 'tis past a doubt,
All Bedlam, or Parnassus, is let out:
Fire in each eye, and papers in each hand,
They rave, recite, and madden round the land.
    What walls can guard me, or what shades can hide?
They pierce my thickets, through my grot they glide,
By land, by water, they renew the charge,
They stop the chariot, and they board the barge.
No place is sacred, not the church is free,
Even Sunday shines no sabbath day to me:
Then from the Mint walks forth the man of rhyme,
Happy! to catch me just at dinner time.
    Is there a parson, much bemused in beer,
A maudlin poetess, a rhyming peer,
A clerk, foredoomed his father's soul to cross,
Who pens a stanza, when he should *engross?*
Is there, who, locked from ink and paper, scrawls
With desperate charcoal round his darkened walls?
All fly to TWIT'NAM, and in humble strain
Apply to me, to keep them mad or vain.
Arthur, whose giddy son neglects the laws,
Imputes to me and my damned works the cause:
Poor Cornus sees his frantic wife elope,
And curses wit, and poetry, and Pope.
    Friend to my life! (which did not you prolong,
The world had wanted many an idle song)
What *drop* or *nostrum* can this plague remove?
Or which must end me, a fool's wrath or love?
A dire dilemma! either way I'm sped,
If foes, they write, if friends, they read me dead.
Seized and tied down to judge, how wretched I!
Who can't be silent, and who will not lie:
To laugh, were want of goodness and of grace,
And to be grave, exceeds all power of face.
I sit with sad civility, I read
With honest anguish, and an aching head;
And drop at last, but in unwilling ears,
This saving counsel, 'Keep your piece nine years.'
    'Nine years!' cries he, who high in Drury Lane
Lulled by soft zephyrs through the broken pane,
Rhymes ere he wakes, and prints before *term* ends,
Obliged by hunger, and request of friends:

'The piece, you think, is incorrect? why take it,
I'm all submission, what you'd have it, make it.'
   Three things another's modest wishes bound,
My friendship, and a prologue, and ten pound.
   Pitholeon sends to me: 'You know his Grace,
I want a patron; ask him for a place.'
Pitholeon libelled me—'but here's a letter
Informs you, sir, 'twas when he knew no better.
Dare you refuse him? Curll invites to dine,
He'll write a *Journal*, or he'll turn divine.'
   Bless me! a packet—"Tis a stranger sues,
A virgin tragedy, an orphan muse.'
If I dislike it, 'Furies, death and rage!'
If I approve, 'Commend it to the stage.'
There (thank my stars) my whole commission ends,
The players and I are, luckily, no friends.
Fired that the house reject him, "Sdeath I'll print it,
And shame the fools—your interest, sir, with Lintot.'
'Lintot, dull rogue! will think your price too much:
'Not, sir, if you revise it, and retouch.'
All my demurs but double his attacks;
At last he whispers, 'Do; and we go snacks.'
Glad of a quarrel, straight I clap the door,
Sir, let me see your works and you no more.
   'Tis sung, when Midas' ears began to spring,
(Midas, a sacred person and a king)
His very minister who spied them first,
(Some say his queen) was forced to speak, or burst.
And is not mine, my friend, a sorer case,
When every coxcomb perks them in my face?
   'Good friend, forbear! you deal in dangerous things.
I'd never name queens, ministers, or kings;
Keep close to ears, and those let asses prick,
'Tis nothing'—Nothing? if they bite and kick?
Out with it, *Dunciad*! let the secret pass,
That secret to each fool, that he's an ass:
The truth once told (and wherefore should we lie?)
The Queen of Midas slept, and so may I.
   You think this cruel? take it for a rule,
No creature smarts so little as a fool.
Let peals of laughter, Codrus! round thee break,
Thou unconcerned canst hear the mighty crack:
Pit, box, and gallery in convulsions hurled,
Thou standst unshook amidst a bursting world.
Who shames a scribbler? break one cobweb through,
He spins the slight, self-pleasing thread anew:
Destroy his fib or sophistry; in vain,
The creature's at his dirty work again,

Throned in the centre of his thin designs,
Proud of a vast extent of flimsy lines!
Whom have I hurt? has poet yet, or peer,
Lost the arched eyebrow, or Parnassian sneer?
And has not Colley still his lord, and whore?
His butchers Henley, his freemasons Moor?
Does not one table Bavius still admit?
Still to one bishop Philips seem a wit?
Still Sappho—'Hold! for God sake—you'll offend,
No names—be calm—learn prudence of a friend:
I too could write, and I am twice as tall;
But foes like these' One flatterer's worse than all;
Of all mad creatures, if the learned are right,
It is the slaver kills, and not the bite.
A fool quite angry is quite innocent:
Alas! 'tis ten times worse when they *repent*.

   One dedicates in high heroic prose,
And ridicules beyond a hundred foes:
One from all Grub Street will my fame defend,
And more abusive, calls himself my friend.
This prints my *Letters*, that expects a bribe,
And others roar aloud, 'Subscribe, subscribe.'

   There are, who to my person pay their court:
I cough like Horace, and, though lean, am short,
Ammon's great son one shoulder had too high,
Such Ovid's nose, and 'Sir! you have an eye—'
Go on, obliging creatures, make me see
All that disgraced my betters, met in me.
Say for my comfort, languishing in bed,
'Just so immortal Maro held his head:'
And when I die, be sure you let me know
Great Homer died three thousand years ago.

   Why did I write? what sin to me unknown
Dipped me in ink, my parents', or my own?
As yet a child, nor yet a fool to fame,
I lisped in numbers, for the numbers came.
I left no calling for this idle trade,
No duty broke, no father disobeyed.
The Muse but served to ease some friend, not wife,
To help me through this long disease, my life,
To second, ARBUTHNOT! thy art and care,
And teach the being you preserved, to bear.

   But why then publish? Granville the polite,
And knowing Walsh, would tell me I could write;
Well-natured Garth inflamed with early praise,
And Congreve loved, and Swift endured my lays;
The courtly Talbot, Somers, Sheffield read,
Even mitred Rochester would nod the head,

And St. John's self (great Dryden's friends before)
With open arms received one poet more.
Happy my studies, when by these approved!
Happier their author, when by these beloved!
From these the world will judge of men and books,
Not from the Burnets, Oldmixons, and Cookes.

   Soft were my numbers; who could take offence
While pure description held the place of sense?
Like gentle Fanny's was my flowery theme,
A painted mistress, or a purling stream.
Yet then did Gildon draw his venal quill;
I wished the man a dinner, and sate still.
Yet then did Dennis rave in furious fret;
I never answered, I was not in debt:
If want provoked, or madness made them print,
I waged no war with Bedlam or the Mint.

   Did some more sober critic come abroad?
If wrong, I smiled; if right, I kissed the rod.
Pains, reading, study, are their just pretence,
And all they want is spirit, taste, and sense.
Commas and points they set exactly right,
And 'twere a sin to rob them of their mite.
Yet ne'er one sprig of laurel graced these ribalds,
From slashing Bentley down to piddling Tibbalds:
Each wight who reads not, and but scans and spells,
Each word-catcher that lives on syllables,
Even such small critics some regard may claim,
Preserved in Milton's or in Shakespeare's name.
Pretty! in Amber to observe the forms
Of hairs, or straws, or dirt, or grubs, or worms!
The things, we know, are neither rich nor rare,
But wonder how the Devil they got there?

   Were others angry? I excused them too;
Well might they rage, I gave them but their due.
A man's true merit 'tis not hard to find,
But each man's secret standard in his mind,
That casting-weight pride adds to emptiness,
This, who can gratify? for who can *guess?*
The bard whom pilfered pastorals renown,
Who turns a Persian tale for half a crown,
Just writes to make his barrenness appear,
And strains, from hard-bound brains, eight lines a year;
He, who still wanting, though he lives on theft,
Steals much, spends little, yet has nothing left:
And he, who now to sense, now nonsense leaning,
Means not, but blunders round about a meaning:
And he, whose fustian's so sublimely bad,
It is not poetry, but prose run mad:

All these, my modest satire bad *translate,*
And owned, that nine such poets made a Tate.
How did they fume, and stamp, and roar, and chafe!
And swear, not ADDISON himself was safe.

    Peace to all such! but were there one whose fires
True genius kindles, and fair fame inspires,
Blessed with each talent and each art to please,
And born to write, converse, and live with ease:
Should such a man, too fond to rule alone,
Bear, like the Turk, no brother near the throne,
View him with scornful, yet with jealous eyes,
And hate for arts that caused himself to rise;
Damn with faint praise, assent with civil leer,
And without sneering, teach the rest to sneer;
Willing to wound, and yet afraid to strike,
Just hint a fault, and hesitate dislike;
Alike reserved to blame, or to commend,
A timorous foe, and a suspicious friend;
Dreading even fools, by flatterers besieged,
And so obliging, that he ne'er obliged;
Like Cato, give his little senate laws,
And sit attentive to his own applause;
While wits and templars every sentence raise,
And wonder with a foolish face of praise—
Who but must laugh, if such a man there be?
Who would not weep, if ATTICUS were he?

    What though my name stood rubric on the walls,
Or plastered posts, with claps, in capitals?
Or smoking forth, a hundred hawkers load,
On wings of winds came flying all abroad?
I sought no homage from the race that write;
I kept, like Asian monarchs, from their sight:
Poems I heeded (now berhymed so long)
No more than thou, great GEORGE! a birthday song.
I ne'er with wits or witlings passed my days,
To spread about the itch of verse and praise;
Nor like a puppy daggled through the town,
To fetch and carry sing-song up and down;
Nor at rehearsals sweat, and mouthed, and cried,
With handkerchief and orange at my side;
But sick of fops, and poetry, and prate,
To Bufo left the whole Castalian state.

    Proud as Apollo on his forked hill,
Sat full-blown Bufo, puffed by every quill;
Fed with soft dedication all day long,
Horace and he went hand in hand in song.
His library, (where busts of poets dead
And a true Pindar stood without a head)

Received of Wits an undistinguished race,
Who first his judgment asked, and then a place:
Much they extolled his pictures, much his seat,
And flattered every day, and some days eat:
Till grown more frugal in his riper days,
He paid some bards with port, and some with praise,
To some a dry rehearsal was assigned,
And others (harder still) he paid in kind.
Dryden alone (what wonder?) came not nigh,
Dryden alone escaped this judging eye:
But still the great have kindness in reserve,
He helped to bury whom he helped to starve.
    May some choice patron bless each grey goose quill!
May every Bavius have his Bufo still!
So when a statesman wants a day's defence,
Or envy holds a whole week's war with sense,
Or simple pride for flattery makes demands,
May dunce by dunce be whistled off my hands!
Blessed be the Great! for those they take away,
And those they left me; for they left me GAY,
Left me to see neglected genius bloom,
Neglected die! and tell it on his tomb:
Of all thy blameless life the sole return
My verse, and QUEENSBERRY weeping o'er thy urn!
    Oh let me live my own! and die so too!
(To live and die is all I have to do:)
Maintain a poet's dignity and ease,
And see what friends, and read what books I please:
Above a patron, though I condescend
Sometimes to call a minister my friend:
I was not born for courts or great affairs;
I pay my debts, believe, and say my prayers;
Can sleep without a poem in my head,
Nor know, if Dennis be alive or dead.
    Why am I asked what next shall see the light?
Heavens! was I born for nothing but to write?
Has life no joys for me? or (to be grave)
Have I no friend to serve, no soul to save?
'I found him close with Swift'—'Indeed? no doubt'
(Cries prating Balbus) 'something will come out.'
'Tis all in vain, deny it as I will.
'No, such a genius never can lie still;'
And then for mine obligingly mistakes
The first lampoon Sir Will. or Bubo makes.
Poor guiltless I! and can I choose but smile,
When every coxcomb knows me by my *style?*
    Curst be the verse, how well soe'er it flow,
That tends to make one worthy man my foe,

Give virtue scandal, innocence a fear,
Or from the soft-eyed virgin steal a tear!
But he who hurts a harmless neighbour's peace,
Insults fallen worth, or beauty in distress,
Who loves a lie, lame slander helps about,
Who writes a libel, or who copies out:
That fop, whose pride affects a patron's name,
Yet absent, wounds an Author's honest fame:
Who can *your* merit *selfishly* approve,
And show the *sense* of it without the *love*;
Who has the vanity to call you friend,
Yet wants the honour, injured, to defend;
Who tells whate'er you think, whate'er you say,
And, if he lie not, must at least betray:
Who to the Dean and *silver bell* can swear,
And sees at Cannons what was never there;
Who reads, but with a lust to misapply,
Make satire a lampoon, and fiction, lie.
A lash like mine no honest man shall dread,
But all such babbling blockheads in his stead.
　　Let Sporus tremble—'What? that thing of silk,
Sporus, that mere white curd of ass's milk?
Satire or sense, alas! can Sporus feel?
Who breaks a Butterfly upon a Wheel?'
　　Yet let me flap this bug with gilded wings,
This painted child of dirt that stinks and stings;
Whose buzz the witty and the fair annoys,
Yet wit ne'er tastes, and beauty ne'er enjoys:
So well-bred spaniels civilly delight
In mumbling of the Game they dare not bite.
Eternal smiles his emptiness betray,
As shallow streams run dimpling all the way.
Whether in florid Impotence he speaks,
And, as the prompter breathes, the puppet squeaks;
Or at the ear of Eve, familiar toad,
Half froth, half venom, spits himself abroad,
In puns, or politicks, or tales, or lies,
Or spite, or smut, or rhymes, or blasphemies.
His wit all see-saw between *that* and *this*,
Now high, now low, now master up, now miss,
And he himself one vile antithesis.
Amphibious thing! that acting either part,
The trifling head, or the corrupted heart!
Fop at the toilet, flatterer at the board,
Now trips a lady, and now struts a lord.
Eve's tempter thus the rabbins have expressed,
A cherub's face, a reptile all the rest;
Beauty that shocks you, parts that none will trust,

Wit that can creep, and pride that licks the dust.
   Not fortune's worshipper, nor fashion's fool,
Not lucre's madman, nor ambition's tool,
Not proud, nor servile; be one poet's praise,
That, if he pleased, he pleased by manly ways:
That flattery, even to kings, he held a shame,
And thought a lie in verse or prose the same:
That not in fancy's maze he wandered long,
But stooped to truth, and moralized his song:
That not for fame, but virtue's better end,
He stood the furious foe, the timid friend,
The damning critic, half-approving wit,
The coxcomb hit, or fearing to be hit;
Laughed at the loss of friends he never had,
The dull, the proud, the wicked, and the mad;
The distant threats of vengeance on his head,
The blow unfelt, the tear he never shed;
The tale revived, the lie so oft overthrown;
Th' imputed trash, and dulness not his own;
The morals blackened when the writings 'scape,
The libelled person, and the pictured shape;
Abuse on all he loved, or loved him, spread,
A friend in exile, or a father, dead;
The whisper, that to greatness still too near,
Perhaps, yet vibrates on his SOVEREIGN'S ear—
Welcome for thee, fair virtue! all the past:
For thee, fair virtue! welcome even the *last!*
   'But why insult the poor, affront the great?'
A knave's a knave, to me, in every state:
Alike my scorn, if he succeed or fail,
Sporus at court, or Japhet in a jail,
A hireling scribbler, or a hireling peer,
Knight of the post corrupt, or of the shire;
If on a pillory, or near a throne,
He gain his prince's ear, or lose his own.
   Yet soft by nature, more a dupe than wit,
Sappho can tell you how this man was bit:
This dreaded satirist Dennis will confess
Foe to his pride, but friend to his distress:
So humble, he has knocked at Tibbald's door,
Has drunk with Cibber, nay has rhymed for Moore.
Full ten years slandered, did he once reply?
Three thousand Suns went down on Welsted's lie.
To please a mistress, one aspersed his life;
He lashed him not, but let her be his wife:
Let Budgell charge low Grub Street on his quill,
And write whate'er he pleased, except his will;
Let the Two Curls of Town and Court, abuse

His father, mother, body, soul, and muse.
Yet why? that father held it for a rule,
It was a sin to call our neighbour fool:
That harmless mother thought no wife a whore:
Hear this! and spare his family, James Moore!
Unspotted names! and memorable long,
If there be force in virtue, or in song.
    Of gentle blood (part shed in honour's cause,
While yet in Britain honour had applause)
Each parent sprung — 'What fortune, pray?' — Their own,
And better got, than Bestia's from the throne.
Born to no pride, inheriting no strife,
Nor marrying discord in a noble wife,
Stranger to civil and religious rage,
The good man walked innoxious through his age.
No courts he saw, no suits would ever try,
Nor dared an oath, nor hazarded a lie:
Unlearned, he knew no schoolman's subtle art,
No language, but the language of the heart.
By nature honest, by experience wise,
Healthy by temperance and by exercise;
His life, though long, to sickness past unknown,
His death was instant, and without a groan.
O grant me, thus to live, and thus to die!
Who sprung from kings shall know less joy than I.
    O friend! may each domestic bliss be thine!
Be no unpleasing melancholy mine:
Me, let the tender office long engage
To rock the cradle of reposing age,
With lenient arts extend a mother's breath,
Make languor smile, and smooth the bed of death,
Explore the thought, explain the asking eye,
And keep a while one parent from the sky!
On cares like these if length of days attend,
May heaven, to bless those days, preserve my friend,
Preserve him social, cheerful, and serene,
And just as rich as when he served a QUEEN!
Whether that blessing be denied or given,
Thus far was right, the rest belongs to heaven.

AN EPISTLE
TO
A LADY
Of the Characters *of* WOMEN.

Nothing so true as what you once let fall,
'Most women have no characters at all.'
Matter too soft a lasting mark to bear,
And best distinguished by black, brown, or fair.
   How many pictures of one nymph we view,
All how unlike each other, all how true!
Arcadia's Countess, here, in ermined pride,
Is, there, Pastora by a fountain side.
Here Fannia, leering on her own good man,
And there, a naked Leda with a swan.
Let then the fair one beautifully cry,
In Magdalen's loose hair, and lifted eye,
Or dressed in smiles of sweet Cecilia shine,
With simpering angels, palms, and harps divine;
Whether the charmer sinner it, or saint it,
If folly grow romantic, I must paint it!
   Come then, the colours and the ground prepare!
Dip in the rainbow, trick her off in air;
Choose a firm cloud, before it fall, and in it
Catch, e'er she change, the Cynthia of this minute.
   Rufa, whose eye, quick-glancing o'er the park,
Attracts each light gay meteor of a spark,
Agrees as ill with Rufa studying Locke,
As Sappho's diamonds with her dirty smock;
Or Sappho at her toilet's greasy task,
With Sappho fragrant at an evening mask:
So morning insects that in muck begun,
Shine, buzz, and fly-blow in the setting-sun.
   How soft is Silia! fearful to offend,
The frail one's advocate, the weak one's friend:
To her, Calista proved her conduct nice,
And good Simplicius asks of her advice.
Sudden, she storms! she raves! You tip the wink,
But spare your censure; Silia does not drink.
All eyes may see from what the change arose,
All eyes may see—a pimple on her nose.
   Papillia, wedded to her amorous spark,
Sighs for the shades—'How charming is a park!'
A park is purchased, but the fair he sees
All bathed in tears—'Oh, odious, odious trees!'
   Ladies, like variegated tulips show;
'Tis to their changes half their charms we owe;

Their happy spots the nice admirer take,
Fine by defect, and delicately weak,
'Twas thus Calypso once each heart alarmed,
Awed without virtue, without beauty charmed;
Her tongue bewitched as oddly as her eyes,
Less wit than mimic, more a wit than wise;
Strange graces still, and stranger flights she had,
Was just not ugly, and was just not mad;
Yet ne'er so sure our passion to create,
As when she touched the brink of all we hate.
   Narcissa's nature, tolerably mild,
To make a wash, would hardly stew a child;
Has even been proved to grant a lover's prayer,
And paid a tradesman once to make him stare;
Gave alms at Easter, in a Christian trim,
And made a widow happy, for a whim.
Why then declare good-nature is her scorn,
When 'tis by that alone she can be borne?
Why pique all mortals, yet affect a name?
A fool to pleasure, yet a slave to fame:
Now deep in Taylor and the Book of Martyrs,
Now drinking citron with his Grace and Chartres:
Now conscience chills her, and now passion burns;
And atheism and religion take their turns;
A very heathen in the carnal part,
   See sin in state, majestically drunk;
Proud as peeress, prouder as a punk;
Chaste to her husband, frank to all beside,
A teeming mistress, but a barren bride.
What then? let blood and body bear the fault,
Her head's untouched, that noble seat of thought:
Such this day's doctrine—in another fit
She sins with poets through pure love of wit.
What has not fired her bosom or her brain?
Caesar and Tall-boy, Charles and Charlemagne.
As Helluo, late dictator of the feast,
The nose of hautgout, and the tip of taste,
Critiqued your wine, and analyzed your meat,
Yet on plain pudding deigned at home to eat;
So Philomedé, lecturing all mankind
On the soft passion, and the taste refined,
The address, the delicacy—stoops at once,
And makes her hearty meal upon a dunce.
   Flavia's a wit, has too much sense to pray;
To toast our wants and wishes, is her way;
Nor asks of God, but of her stars, to give
The mighty blessing, 'while we live, to live.'
Then all for death, that opiate of the soul!

Lucretia's dagger, Rosamonda's bowl.
Say, what can cause such impotence of mind?
A spark too fickle, or a spouse too kind.
Wise wretch! with pleasures too refined to please,
With too much spirit to be e'er at ease,
With too much quickness ever to be taught,
With too much thinking to have common thought:
You purchase pain with all that joy can give,
And die of nothing but a rage to live.
   Turn then from wits; and look on Simo's mate,
No ass so meek, no ass so obstinate:
Or her, that owns her faults, but never mends,
Because she's honest, and the best of friends:
Or her, whose life the Church and scandal share,
For ever in a passion, or a prayer:
Or her, who laughs at hell, but (like her Grace)
Cries, 'Ah! how charming, if there's no such place!'
Or who in sweet vicissitude appears
Of mirth and opium, ratafee and tears,
The daily anodyne, and nightly draught,
To kill those foes to fair ones, time and thought.
Woman and fool are two hard things to hit;
For true no-meaning puzzles more than wit.
   But what are these to great Atossa's mind?
Scarce once herself, by turns all womankind!
Who, with herself, or others, from her birth
Finds all her life one warfare upon earth:
Shines in exposing knaves, and painting fools,
Yet is, whate'er she hates and ridicules.
No thought advances, but her eddy brain
Whisks it about, and down it goes again.
Full sixty years the world has been her trade,
The wisest fool much time has ever made.
From loveless youth to unrespected age,
No passion gratified except her rage.
So much the fury still outran the wit,
The pleasure missed her, and the scandal hit.
Who breaks with her, provokes revenge from hell,
But he's a bolder man who dares be well.
Her every turn with violence pursued,
Nor more a storm her hate than gratitude:
To that each passion turns, or soon or late;
Love, if it makes her yield, must make her hate:
Superiors? death! and equals? what a curse!
But an inferior not dependent? worse.
Offend her, and she knows not to forgive;
Oblige her, and she'll hate you while you live:
But die, and she'll adore you—Then the bust

And temple rise—then fall again to dust.
Last night, her lord was all that's good and great;
A knave this morning, and his will a cheat.
Strange! by the means defeated of the ends,
By spirit robbed of power, by warmth of friends,
By wealth of followers! without one distress
Sick of herself through very selfishness!
Atossa, cursed with every granted prayer,
Childless with all her children, wants an heir.
To heirs unknown descends th' unguarded store
Or wanders, heaven-directed, to the poor.
    Pictures like these, dear Madam, to design,
Asks no firm hand, and no unerring line;
Some wandering touches, some reflected light,
Some flying stroke alone can hit 'em right:
For how should equal colours do the knack?
Chameleons who can paint in white and black?
    'Yet Cloe sure was formed without a spot'—
Nature in her then erred not, but forgot.
'With every pleasing, every prudent part,
Say, what can Cloe want?'—She wants a heart.
She speaks, behaves, and acts just as she ought;
But never, never, reached one generous thought.
Virtue she finds too painful an endeavour,
Content to dwell in decencies for ever.
So very reasonable, so unmoved,
As never yet to love, or to be loved.
She, while her lover pants upon her breast,
Can mark the figures on an Indian chest;
And when she sees her friend in deep despair,
Observes how much a chintz exceeds mohair.
Forbid it, Heaven, a favour or a debt
She e'er should cancel—but she may forget.
Safe is your secret still in Cloe's ear;
But none of Cloe's shall you ever hear.
Of all her dears she never slandered one,
But cares not if a thousand are undone.
Would Cloe know if you're alive or dead?
She bids her footman put it in her head.
Cloe is prudent—would you too be wise?
Then never break your heart when Cloe dies.
    One certain portrait may (I grant) be seen,
Which heaven has varnished out, and made a Queen.
THE SAME FOR EVER! and described by all
With truth and goodness, as with crown and ball.
Poets heap virtues, painters gems at will,
And show their zeal, and hide their want of skill.
'Tis well—but, artists! who can paint or write,

To draw the naked is your true delight.
That robe of quality so struts and swells,
None see what parts of nature it conceals:
The exactest traits of body or of mind,
We owe to models of an humble kind.
If QUEENSBURY to strip there's no compelling,
'Tis from a handmaid we must take a Helen,
From peer or bishop 'tis no easy thing
To draw the man who loves his God or king:
Alas! I copy (or my draught would fail)
From honest Mah'met, or plain Parson Hale.

But grant, in public men sometimes are shown,
A woman's seen in private life alone:
Our bolder talents in full light displayed;
Your virtues open fairest in the shade.
Bred to disguise, in public 'tis you hide;
There, none distinguish 'twixt your shame or pride,
Weakness or delicacy; all so nice,
That each may seem a virtue, or a vice.

In men, we various ruling passions find;
In women, two almost divide the kind;
Those, only fixed, they first or last obey,
The love of pleasure, and the love of sway.

That, nature gives; and where the lesson taught
Is but to please, can pleasure seem a fault?
Experience, this; by man's oppression cursed,
They seek the second not to lose the first.

Men, some to business, some to pleasure take;
But every woman is at heart a rake:
Men, some to quiet, some to public strife;
But every lady would be queen for life.

Yet mark the fate of a whole sex of queens!
Power all their end, but beauty all the means:
In youth they conquer, with so wild a rage,
As leaves them scarce a subject in their age:
For foreign glory, foreign joy, they roam;
No thought of peace or happiness at home.
But wisdom's triumph is well-timed retreat,
As hard a science to the fair as great!
Beauties, like tyrants, old and friendless grown,
Yet hate repose, and dread to be alone,
Worn out in public, weary every eye,
Nor leave one sigh behind them when they die.

Pleasures the sex, as children birds, pursue,
Still out of reach, yet never out of view;
Sure, if they catch, to spoil the toy at most,
To covet flying, and regret when lost:
At last, to follies youth could scarce defend,

It grows their age's prudence to pretend;
Ashamed to own they gave delight before,
Reduced to feign it, when they give no more:
As hags hold Sabbaths, less for joy than spite,
So these their merry, miserable night;
Still round and round the ghosts of beauty glide,
And haunt the places where their honour died.

See how the world its veterans rewards!
A youth of frolics, an old age of cards;
Fair to no purpose, artful to no end,
Young without lovers, old without a friend;
A fop their passion, but their prize a sot;
Alive, ridiculous, and dead, forgot!

Ah! friend! to dazzle let the vain design;
To raise the thought, and touch the heart be thine!
That charm shall grow, while what fatigues the ring
Flaunts and goes down, an unregarded thing:
So when the sun's broad beam has tired the sight,
All mild ascends the moon's more sober light,
Serene in virgin modesty she shines,
And unobserved the glaring orb declines.

Oh! blessed with temper whose unclouded ray
Can make to-morrow cheerful as today;
She, who can love a sister's charms, or hear
Sighs for a daughter with unwounded ear;
She, who ne'er answers till a husband cools,
Or, if she rules him, never shows she rules;
Charms by accepting, by submitting sways,
Yet has her humour most, when she obeys;
Let fops or fortune fly which way they will;
Disdains all loss of tickets, or codille;
Spleen, vapours, or small-pox, above them all,
And mistress of herself, though China fall.

And yet, believe me, good as well as ill,
Woman's at best a contradiction still.
Heaven, when it strives to polish all it can
Its last best work, but forms a softer man;
Picks from each sex, to make the favourite blest,
Your love of pleasure, our desire of rest:
Blends, in exception to all general rules,
Your taste of follies, with our scorn of fools,
Reserve with frankness, art with truth allied,
Courage with softness, modesty with pride,
Fixed principles, with fancy ever new;
Shakes all together, and produces—You.

Be this a woman's fame: with this unblessed,
Toasts live a scorn, and queens may die a jest.
This Phoebus promised (I forget the year)

When those blue eyes first opened on the sphere;
Ascendant Phoebus watched that hour with care,
Averted half your parents' simple prayer,
And gave you beauty, but denied the pelf
That buys your sex a tyrant o'er itself.
The generous God, who wit and gold refines,
And ripens spirits as he ripens mines,
Kept dross for duchesses, the world shall know it,
To you gave sense, good-humour, and a poet.

THE SECOND SATIRE OF DR. JOHN DONNE VERSIFIED

Yes; thank my stars! as early as I knew
This town, I had the sense to hate it too:
Yet here, as even in hell, there must be still
One giant-vice, so excellently ill,
That all beside, one pities, not abhors;
As who knows Sappho, smiles at other whores.
    I grant that poetry's a crying sin;
It brought (no doubt) the Excise and Army in:
Catched like the plague, or love, the Lord knows how,
But that the cure is starving, all allow.
Yet like the papist's, is the poet's state,
Poor and disarmed, and hardly worth your hate!
    Here a lean bard, whose wit could never give
Himself a dinner, makes an actor live:
The thief condemned, in law already dead,
So prompts, and saves a rogue who cannot read.
Thus, as the pipes of some carved organ move,
The gilded puppets dance and mount above.
Heaved by the breath the inspiring bellows blow:
The inspiring bellows lie and pant below.
    One sings the fair; but songs no longer move;
No rat is rhymed to death, nor maid to love:
In love's, in nature's spite, the siege they hold,
And scorn the flesh, the devil, and all but gold.
    These write to lords, some mean reward to get,
As needy beggars sing at doors for meat.
Those write because all write, and so have still
Excuse for writing, and for writing ill.
    Wretched, indeed! but far more wretched yet
Is he who makes his meal on others' wit:
'Tis changed, no doubt, from what it was before,
His rank digestion makes it wit no more:
Sense, passed through him, no longer is the same;
For food digested takes another name.
    I pass o'er all those confessors and martyrs,

Who live like Sutton, or who die like Chartres,
Outcant old Esdras, or out-drink his heir,
Out-usure Jews, or Irishmen out-swear;
Wicked as pages, who in early years
Act sins which Prisca's confessor scarce hears.
Even those I pardon, for whose sinful sake
Schoolmen new tenements in hell must make;
Of whose strange crimes no canonist can tell
In what commandment's large contents they dwell.
   One, one man only breeds my just offence;
Whom crimes gave wealth, and wealth gave impudence:
Time, that at last matures a clap to pox,
Whose gentle progress makes a calf an ox,
And brings all natural events to pass,
Hath made him an attorney of an ass.
No young divine, new-beneficed, can be
More pert, more proud, more positive than he.
What further could I wish the fop to do,
But turn a wit, and scribble verses too;
Pierce the soft labyrinth of a lady's ear
With rhymes of this *per cent.* and that *per year?*
Or court a wife, spread out his wily parts,
Like nets or lime-twigs, for rich widows' hearts?
Call himself barrister to every wench,
And woo in language of the Pleas and Bench?
Language, which Boreas might to Auster hold
More rough than forty Germans when they scold.
   Cursed be the wretch! so venal and so vain;
Paltry and proud, as drabs in Drury Lane.
'Tis such a bounty as was never known,
If PETER deigns to help you to your *own*:
What thanks, what praise, if Peter but supplies,
And what a solemn face if he denies!
Grave, as when prisoners shake the head and swear
'Twas only suretyship that brought 'em there.
His *office* keeps your parchment fates entire,
He starves with cold to save them from the fire;
For you he walks the streets through rain or dust,
For not in chariots Peter puts his trust;
For you he sweats and labours at the laws,
Takes God to witness he affects your cause,
And lies to every lord in everything,
Like a king's favourite—or like a king.
These are the talents that adorn them all,
From wicked waters even to godly * *
Not more of simony beneath black gowns,
Nor more of bastardy in heirs to crowns.
In shillings and in pence at first they deal;

And steal so little, few perceive they steal;
Till, like the sea, they compass all the land,
From Scots to Wight, from Mount to Dover strand:
And when rank widows purchase luscious nights,
Or when a duke to Jansen punts at White's,
Or city-heir in mortgage melts away;
Satan himself feels far less joy than they.
Piecemeal they win this acre first, then that,
Glean on, and gather up the whole estate.
Then strongly fencing ill-got wealth by law,
Indentures, covenants, articles thy draw,
Large as the fields themselves, and larger far
Than civil codes, with all their glosses, are;
So vast, our new divines, we must confess,
Are fathers of the Church for writing less.
But let them write for you, each rogue impairs
The deeds, and dexterously omits, *ses heires*:
No commentator can more slily pass
O'er a learned, unintelligible place;
Or, in quotation, shrewd divines leave out
Those words, that would against them clear the doubt.
    So Luther thought the Paternoster long,
When doomed to say his beads and evensong;
But having cast his cowl, and left those laws,
Adds to Christ's prayer, the 'power and glory' clause.
    The lands are bought; but where are to be found
Those ancient woods, that shaded all the ground?
We see no new-built palaces aspire,
No kitchens emulate the vestal fire.
Where are those troops of poor, that thronged of yore
The good old landlord's hospitable door?
Well, I could wish, that still in lordly domes
Some beasts were killed, though not whole hecatombs;
That both extremes were banished from their walls,
Carthusian fasts, and fulsome bacchanals;
And all mankind might that just mean observe,
In which none e'er could surfeit, none could starve.
These as good works, 'tis true, we all allow;
But oh! these works are not in fashion now:
Like rich old wardrobes, things extremely rare,
Extremely fine, but what no man will wear.
    Thus much I've said, I trust, without offence;
Let no court sycophant pervert my sense,
Nor sly informer watch these words to draw
Within the reach of treason, or the law.

POPE TO JONATHAN SWIFT
25 March 1736

If ever I write more epistles in verse, one of them shall be addressed to you. I have long concerted it, and begun it, but I would make what bears your name as finished as my last work ought to be, that is to say, more finished than any of the rest. The subject is large, and will divide into four epistles, which naturally follow the *Essay on Man*, *viz.* 1. Of the extent and limits of human reason and science, 2. A view of the useful and therefore attainable, and of the un-useful and therefore unattainable, arts. 3. Of the nature, ends, application, and use of different capacities. 4. Of the use of *learning*, of the *science* of the *world*, and of *wit*. It will conclude with a satire against the misapplication of all these, exemplified by pictures, characters, and examples.

But, alas! the task is great, and *non sum qualis eram*! My understanding, indeed, such as it is, is extended rather than diminished: I see things more in the whole, more consistent, and more clearly deduced from, and related to, each other. But what I gain on the side of philosophy, I lose on the side of poetry: the flowers are gone, when the fruits begin to ripen, and the fruits perhaps will never ripen perfectly. The climate (under our heaven of a court) is but cold and uncertain: the winds rise and the winter comes on. I find myself but little disposed to build a new house; I have nothing left but to gather up the relics of a wreck, and look about me to see what friends I have! Pray, whose esteem or admiration should I desire now to procure by my writings? whose friendship or conversation to obtain by 'em? I am a man of desperate fortunes, that is a man whose friends are dead: for I never aimed at any other fortune than in friends. As soon as I had sent my last letter, I received a most kind one from you, expressing great pain for my late illness at Mr. Cheselden's. I conclude you was eased of that friendly apprehension in a few days after you had dispatched yours, for mine must have reached you then. I wondered a little at your query, who Cheselden was? it shows that the truest merit does not travel so far any way as on the wings of poetry; he is the most noted, and most deserving man in the whole profession of chirurgery; and has saved the lives of thousands by his manner of cutting for the stone.—I am now well, or what I must call so.

I have lately seen some writings of Lord B's, since he went to France. Nothing can depress his genius: whatever befalls him, he will still be the greatest man in the world, either in his own time, or with posterity.

Every man you know or care for here, enquires of you, and pays you the only devoir he can, that of drinking your health. Here are a race sprung up of young patriots, who would animate you. I wish you had any motive to see this kingdom. I could keep you, for I am rich, that is, I have more than I want. I can afford room for yourself and two servants; I have indeed room enough; nothing but myself at home! the kind and hearty housewife is dead! the agreeable and instructive neighbour is gone! yet my house is enlarged, and the gardens extend and flourish, as knowing nothing of the guest they have lost. I have more fruit-trees and kitchen-garden than you have any thought of; nay I have good melons and pine-apples of my own growth. I am as much a better gardener as I am a worse poet than when you saw me: but gardening is near akin to philosophy, for Tully says, *Agricultura proxima sapientiae*. For God's sake, why should not you, (that are a step higher than a philosopher, a divine, yet have more grace and wit than to be a bishop) e'en give all you have to the poor of Ireland (for whom you have already done everything else) so quit the place, and live and die with me? And let *Tales Animae Concordes* be our motto and our epitaph.

THE
SECOND EPISTLE
OF THE
SECOND BOOK
OF
HORACE IMITATED

Ludentis speciem dabit et torquebitur.
Horace.

Dear Colonel, COBHAM'S and your country's friend!
You love a verse, take such as I can send.
A Frenchman comes, presents you with his boy,
Bows and begins—'This lad, sir, is of Blois:
Observe his shape how clean! his locks how curled!
My only son, I'd have him see the world:
His French is pure; his voice too—you shall hear—
Sir, he's your slave for twenty pound a year.
Mere wax as yet, you fashion him with ease,
Your barber, cook, upholsterer, what you please:
A perfect genius at an opera song—
To say too much might do my honour wrong.
Take him with all his virtues, on my word;
His whole ambition was to serve a lord;
But, sir, to you, with what would I not part?
Though faith, I fear 'twill break his mother's heart.
Once (and but once) I caught him in a lie,
And then, unwhipped, he had the grace to cry:
The fault he has I fairly shall reveal,
(Could you o'erlook but that) it is to steal.'
    If, after this, you took the graceless lad,
Could you complain, my friend, he proved so bad?
Faith, in such case, if you should prosecute,
I think Sir Godfrey should decide the suit;
Who sent the thief that stole the cash away,
And punished him that put it in his way.
    Consider then, and judge me in this light;
I told you when I went, I could not write;
You said the same; and are you discontent
With laws to which you gave your own assent?
Nay worse, to ask for verse at such a time!
D'ye think me good for nothing but to rhyme?
    In ANNA'S wars, a soldier poor and old
Had dearly earned a little purse of gold:
Tired with a tedious march, one luckless night,

He slept, poor dog! and lost it, to a doit.
This put the man in such a desperate mind,
Between revenge, and grief, and hunger joined
Against the foe, himself, and all mankind,
He leaped the trenches, scaled a castle-wall,
Tore down a standard, took the fort and all.
'Prodigious well,' his great commander cried,
Gave him much praise and some reward beside.
Next pleased his excellence a town to batter:
(Its name I know not, and it's no great matter)
'Go on, my friend,' he cried, 'see yonder walls!
Advance and conquer! go where glory calls!
More honours, more rewards, attend the brave.'
Don't you remember what reply he gave?
'D'ye think me, noble general, such a sot?
Let him take castles who has ne'er a groat.'
    Bred up at home, full early I begun
To read in Greek the wrath of Peleus' son.
Besides, my father taught me from a lad,
The better art to know the good from bad:
(And little sure imported to remove,
To hunt for truth in Maudlin's learned grove.)
But knottier points we knew not half so well,
Deprived us soon of our paternal cell;
And certain laws, by sufferers thought unjust,
Denied all posts of profit or of trust:
Hopes after hopes of pious papists failed,
While mighty WILLIAM'S thundering arm prevailed.
For right hereditary taxed and fined,
He stuck to poverty with peace of mind;
And me, the Muses helped to undergo it;
Convict a papist he, and I a poet.
But (thanks to Homer) since I live and thrive,
Indebted to no prince or peer alive,
Sure I should want the care of ten Munroes,
If I would scribble, rather than repose.
    Years following years, steal something every day,
At last they steal us from ourselves away;
In one our frolics, one amusements end,
In one a mistress drops, in one a friend:
This subtle thief of life, this paltry time,
What will it leave me, if it snatch my rhyme?
If every wheel of that unwearied mill
That turned ten thousand verses, now stands still.
    But after all, what would you have me do?
When out of twenty I can please not two;
When this heroics only deigns to praise,
Sharp satire that, and that Pindaric lays?

One likes the pheasant's wing, and one the leg;
The vulgar boil, the learned roast an egg;
Hard task! to hit the palate of such guests,
When Oldfield loves what Dartineuf detests.
    But grant I may relapse, for want of grace,
Again to rhyme; can London be the place?
Who there his muse, or self, or soul attends,
In crowds, and courts, law, business, feasts, and friends?
My counsel sends to execute a deed:
A poet begs me I will hear him read:
'In Palace Yard at nine you'll find me there—
At ten for certain, sir, in Bloomsbury Square—
Before the Lords at twelve my cause comes on—
There's a rehearsal, sir, exact at one.'—
'Oh, but a wit can study in the streets,
And raise his mind above the mob he meets.'
Not quite so well, however, as one ought;
A hackney coach may chance to spoil a thought;
And then a nodding beam or pig of lead,
God knows, may hurt the very ablest head.
Have you not seen, at Guildhall's narrow pass,
Two aldermen dispute it with an ass?
And peers give way, exalted as they are,
Even to their own s-r-v-nce in a car?
    Go, lofty poet! and in such a crowd,
Sing thy sonorous verse—but not aloud.
Alas! to grottoes and to groves we run,
To ease and silence, every muse's son:
Blackmore himself, for any grand effort,
Would drink and doze at Tooting or Earl's Court.
How shall I rhyme in this eternal roar?
How match the bards whom none e'er matched before?
The man, who, stretched in Isis' calm retreat,
To books and study gives seven years complete,
See! strowed with learned dust, his night-cap on,
He walks, an object new beneath the sun!
The boys flock round him, and the people stare:
So stiff, so mute! some statue you would swear,
Stepped from its pedestal to take the air!
And here, while town, and court, and city roars,
With mobs, and duns, and soldiers at their doors;
Shall I, in London, act this idle part?
Composing songs for fools to get by heart?
    The Temple late two brother sergeants saw,
Who deemed each other oracles of law;
With equal talents these congenial souls
One lulled th' Exchequer, and one stunned the Rolls;
Each had a gravity would make you split,

And shook his head at Murray as a wit.
'Twas, 'Sir, your law'—and 'Sir, your eloquence'
'Yours, Cowper's manner—and yours, Talbot's sense.'
   Thus we dispose of all poetic merit,
Yours Milton's genius, and mine Homer's spirit.
Call Tibbald Shakespeare, and he'll swear the nine,
(Dear Cibber!) never matched one ode of thine.
Lord! how we strut through Merlin's Cave, to see
No poets there, but Stephen, you, and me.
Walk with respect behind, while we at ease
Weave laurel crowns, and take what names we please.
'My dear Tibullus!' if that will not do,
'Let me be Horace, and be Ovid you:
Or, I'm content, allow me Dryden's strains,
And you shall rise up Otway for your pains.'
Much do I suffer, much, to keep in peace
This jealous, waspish, wrong-head, rhyming race;
And much must flatter, if the whim should bite
To court applause by printing what I write:
But let the fit pass o'er, I'm wise enough,
To stop my ears to their confounded stuff.
   In vain, bad rhymers all mankind reject,
They treat themselves with most profound respect;
'Tis to small purpose that you hold your tongue,
Each praised within, is happy all day long,
But how severely with themselves proceed
The men, who write such verse as we can read?
Their own strict judges, not a word they spare
That wants, or force, or light, or weight, or care,
Howe'er unwillingly it quits its place,
Nay though at court, perhaps, it may find grace:
Such they'll degrade; and sometimes, in its stead,
In downright charity revive the dead;
Mark where a bold expressive phrase appears,
Bright through the rubbish of some hundred years;
Command old words that long have slept, to wake,
Words, that wise Bacon, or brave Raleigh spake;
Or bid the new be English, ages hence,
(For use will farther what's begot by sense)
Pour the full tide of eloquence along,
Serenely pure, and yet divinely strong,
Rich with the treasures of each foreign tongue;
Prune the luxuriant, the uncouth refine
But show no mercy to an empty line:
Then polish all, with so much life and ease,
You think 'tis nature, and a knack to please:
'But ease in writing flows from art, not chance;
As those move easiest who have learned to dance.'

If such the plague and pains to write by rule,
Better (say I) be pleased and play the fool;
Call, if you will, bad rhyming a disease,
It gives men happiness, or leaves them ease.
There lived *in primo Georgii*, (they record)
A worthy member, no small fool, a lord;
Who, though the House was up, delighted sate,
Heard, noted, answered, as in full debate:
In all but this, a man of sober life,
Fond of his friend, and civil to his wife;
Not quite a madman, though a pasty fell,
And much too wise to walk into a well:
Him, the damned doctors and his friends immured,
They bled, they cupped, they purged; in short, they cured:
Whereat the gentleman began to stare—
'My friends!' he cried, 'p—x take you for your care!
That from a patriot of distinguished note,
Have bled and purged me to a simple vote.'

    Well, on the whole, plain prose must be my fate:
Wisdom (curse on it) will come soon or late.
There is a time when poets will grow dull:
I'll e'en leave verses to the boys at school:
To rules of poetry no more confined,
I learn to smooth and harmonize my mind,
Teach every thought within its bounds to roll,
And keep the equal measure of the soul.

    Soon as I enter at my country door,
My mind resumes the thread it dropped before;
Thoughts, which at Hyde Park Corner I forgot,
Meet and rejoin me, in the pensive grot.
There all alone, and compliments apart,
I ask these sober questions of my heart.

    If, when the more you drink, the more you crave,
You tell the doctor; when the more you have,
The more you want, why not with equal ease
Confess as well your folly, as disease?
The heart resolves this matter in a trice,
'Men only feel the smart but not the vice.'

    When golden angels cease to cure the evil,
You give all royal witchcraft to the devil:
When servile chaplains cry, that birth and place
Endue a peer with honour, truth, and grace,
Look in that breast, most dirty Duke! be fair,
Say, can you find out one such lodger there?
Yet still, not heeding what your heart can teach,
You go to church to hear these flatterers preach.

    Indeed, could wealth bestow or wit or merit,
A grain of courage, or a spark of spirit,

The wisest man might blush, I must agree,
If Devonshire loved sixpence, more than he.
   If there be truth in law, and use can give
A property, that's yours on which you life.
Delightful Abscourt, if its fields afford
Their fruits to you, confesses you its lord:
All Worldly's hens, nay partridge, sold to town,
His venison too, a guinea makes your own:
He bought at thousands, what with better wit
You purchase as you want, and bit by bit;
Now, or long since, what difference will be found?
You pay a penny, and he paid a pound.
   Heathcote himself, and such large-acred men,
Lords of fat Evesham, or of Lincoln fen,
Buy every stick of wood that lends them heat,
Buy every pullet they afford to eat.
Yet these are wights, who fondly call their own
Half that the Devil o'erlooks from Lincoln town.
The laws of God, as well as of the land,
Abhor, a perpetuity should stand:
Estates have wings and hang in fortune's power
Loose on the point of every wavering hour,
Ready, by force, or of your own accord,
By sale, at least by death, to change their lord.
Man? and *for ever?* wretch! what wouldst thou have?
Heir urges heir, like wave impelling wave.
All vast possessions (just the same the case
Whether you call them villa, park, or chase).
Alas, my BATHURST! what will they avail?
Join Cotswold hills to Sapperton's fair dale,
Let rising granaries and temples here,
There mingled farms and pyramids appear,
Link towns to towns with avenues of oak,
Enclose whole downs in walls, 'tis all a joke!
Inexorable Death shall level all,
And trees, and stones, and farms, and farmer fall.
   Gold, silver, ivory, vases sculptured high,
Paint, marble, gems, and robes of Persian dye,
There are who have not—and thank heaven there are,
Who, if they have not, think not worth their care,
   Talk what you will of taste, my friend, you'll find,
Two of a face, as soon as of a mind.
Why, of two brothers, rich and restless one
Ploughs, burns, manures, and toils from sun to sun;
The other slights, for women, sports, and wines,
All Townshend's turnips, and all Grosvenor's mines:
Why one like Bubb with pay and scorn content,
Bows and votes on, in court and parliament;

One, driven by strong benevolence of soul,
Shall fly, like Oglethorpe, from pole to pole:
Is known alone to that directing power,
Who forms the genius in the natal hour;
That God of Nature, who, within us still,
Inclines our action, not constrains our will;
Various of temper, as of face or frame,
Each individual: His great end the same.

    Yes, sir, how small soever be my heap,
A part I will enjoy, as well as keep.
My heir may sigh, and think it want of grace
A man so poor would live without a place:
But sure no statute in his favour says,
How free, or frugal, I shall pass my days:
I, who at some times spend, at others spare,
Divided between carelessness and care.
'Tis one thing madly to disperse my store:
Another, not to heed to treasure more;
Glad, like a boy, to snatch the first good day,
And pleased, if sordid want be far away.

    What is't to me (a passenger, God wot)
Whether my vessel be first-rate or not?
The ship itself may make a better figure,
But I that sail, am neither less nor bigger.
I neither strut with every favouring breath,
Nor strive with all the tempest in my teeth.
In power, wit, figure, virtue, fortune, placed
Behind the foremost and before the last.

    'But why all this of avarice? I have none.'
I wish you joy, sir, of a tyrant gone;
But does no other lord it at this hour,
As wild and mad: the avarice of power?
Does neither rage inflame, nor fear appal?
Not the black fear of death, that saddens all?
With terrors round, can reason hold her throne,
Despise the known, nor tremble at the unknown!
Survey both worlds, intrepid and entire,
In spite of witches, devils, dreams, and fire?
Pleased to look forward, pleased to look behind,
And count each birthday with a grateful mind?
Has life no sourness, drawn so near its end?
Canst thou endure a foe, forgive a friend?
Has age but melted the rough parts away,
As winter fruits grow mild e'er they decay?
Or will you think, my friend, your business done,
When, of a hundred thorns, you pull out one?

    Learn to live well, or fairly make your will;
You've played, and loved, and eat, and drunk your fill:

Walk sober off; before a sprightlier age
Comes tittering on, and shoves you from the stage:
Leave such to trifle with more grace and ease,
Where folly pleases, and whose follies please.

THE
FIRST EPISTLE
OF THE
SECOND BOOK
OF
HORACE IMITATED
TO AUGUSTUS

Advertisement

The reflections of *Horace*, and the judgments past in his *Epistle to Augustus*, seemed so seasonable to the present times, that i could not help applying them to the use of my own country. The author thought them considerable enough to address them to his prince; whom he paints with all the great and good qualities of a monarch, upon whom the Romans depended for the increase of an *absolute empire*. But to make the poem entirely English, I was willing to add one or two of those which contribute to the happiness of a *free people*, and are more consistent with the welfare of *our neighbours*.

This Epistle will show the learned world to have fallen into two mistakes: one, that *Augustus was a patron of poets in general*; whereas he not only prohibited all but the best writers to name him, but recommended that care even to the civil magistrate: *Admonebat praetores, ne paterentur nomen suum obsolefieri*, etc. The other, that this piece was only a *general discourse of poetry*; whereas it was an *apology for the poets*, in order to render *Augustus* more their patron. *Horace* here pleads the cause of his contemporaries, first against the taste of the *town*, whose humour it was to magnify the authors of the preceding age; secondly against the *court* and *nobility*, who encouraged only the writers for the theatre; and lastly against the Emperor himself, who had conceived them of little use to the government. He shows (by a view of the progress of learning, and the change of taste among the Romans) that the introduction of the polite arts of Greece had given the writers of his time great advantages over their predecessors; that their *morals* were much improved, and the license of those ancient poets restrained: that *satire* and *comedy* were become more just and useful; that, whatever extravagances were left on the stage, were owing to the *ill taste* of the *nobility*; that poets, under due regulations, were in many respects useful to the *state*, and concludes, that it was upon them the Emperor himself must depend for his fame with posterity.

We may farther learn from this Epistle, that Horace made his court to this great prince by writing with a decent freedom toward him, with a just contempt of his low flatterers, and with a manly regard to his own character.

While you, great patron of mankind! sustain
The balanced world, and open all the main;
Your country, chief, in arms abroad defend,
At home, with morals, arts, and laws amend;
How shall the muse, from such a monarch, steal

An hour, and not defraud the public weal?
  Edward and Henry, now the boast of fame,
And virtuous Alfred, a more sacred name,
After a life of generous toils endured,
The Gaul subdued, or property secured,
Ambition humbled, mighty cities stormed,
Our laws established, and the world reformed;
Closed their long glories with a sigh, to find
Th' unwilling gratitude of base mankind!
All human virtue, to its latest breath,
Finds envy never conquered, but by death.
The great Alcides, every labour past,
Had still this monster to subdue at last.
Sure fate of all, beneath whose rising ray
Each star of meaner merit fades away!
Oppressed we feel the beam directly beat,
Those suns of glory please not till they set.
  To thee, the world its present homage pays,
The harvest early, but mature the praise:
Great friend of LIBERTY! in *kings* a name
Above all Greek, above all Roman fame:
Whose word is truth, as sacred and revered,
As heaven's own oracles from altars heard.
Wonder of kings! like whom, to mortal eyes
None e'er has risen, and none e'er shall rise.
  Just in one instance be it yet confessed
Your people, sir, are partial in the rest:
Foes to all living worth except your own,
And advocates for folly dead and gone.
Authors, like coins, grow dear as they grow old;
It is the rust we value, not the gold.
Chaucer's worst ribaldry is learned by rote,
And beastly Skelton heads of houses quote:
One likes no language but the *Faery Queene*;
A Scot will fight for *Christ's Kirk o' the Green*;
And each true Briton is to Ben so civil,
He swears the muses met him at the devil.
  Though justly Greece her eldest sons admires,
Why should not we be wiser than our sires?
In every public virtue we excel;
We build, we paint, we sing, we dance as well,
And learned Athens to our art must stoop,
Could she behold us tumbling through a hoop.
  If time improve our wit as well as wine,
Say at what age a poet grows divine?
Shall we, or shall we not, account him so,
Who died, perhaps, an hundred years ago?
End all dispute; and fix the year precise

When British bards begin t' immortalize?
  'Who lasts a century can have no flaw,
I hold that wit a classic, good in law.'
  Suppose he wants a year, will you compound?
And shall we deem him ancient, right and sound,
Or damn to all eternity at once,
At ninety-nine, a modern and a dunce?
  'We shall not quarrel for a year or two;
By courtesy of England, he may do.'
  Then by the rule that made the horse-tail bare,
I pluck out year by year, as hair by hair,
And melt down ancients like a heap of snow:
While you to measure merits, look in Stow,
And estimating authors by the year,
Bestow a garland only on a bier.
  Shakespeare (whom you and every playhouse bill
Style the divine, the matchless, what you will)
For gain, not glory, winged his roving flight,
And grew immortal in his own despite.
Ben, old and poor, as little seemed to heed
The life to come, in every poet's creed.
Who now reads Cowley? if he pleases yet,
His moral pleases, not his pointed wit;
Forget his epic, nay Pindaric art,
But still I love the language of his heart.
  'Yet surely, surely, these were famous men!
What boy but hears the sayings of old Ben?
In all debates where Critics bears a part,
Not one but nods, and talks of Jonson's art,
Of Shakespeare's nature, and of Cowley's wit;
How Beaumont's judgment checked what Fletcher writ;
How Shadwell hasty, Wycherley was slow;
But for the passions, Southern sure and Rowe.
These, only these, support the crowded stage,
From eldest Heywood down to Cibber's age.'
  All this may be; the people's voice is odd,
It is, and it is not, the voice of God.
To *Gammer Gurton* if it give the bays,
And yet deny *The Careless Husband* praise.
Or say our fathers never broke a rule;
Why then, I say, the public is a fool.
But let them own, that greater faults than we
They had, and greater virtues, I'll agree.
Spenser himself affects the obsolete,
And Sidney's verse halts ill on Roman feet:
Milton's strong pinion now not heaven can bound,
Now serpent-like, in prose he sweeps the ground,
In quibbles, angel and archangel join,

And God the Father turns a school-divine.
Not that I'd lop the beauties from his book,
Like slashing Bentley with his desperate hook;
Or damn all Shakespeare, like the affected fool
At court, who hates whate'er he read at school.
    But for the wits of either Charles's days,
The mob of gentlemen who wrote with ease;
Sprat, Carew, Sedley, and a hundred more,
(Like twinkling stars the miscellanies o'er)
One simile, that solitary shines
In the dry desert of a thousand lines,
Or lengthened thought that gleams through many a page,
Has sanctified whole poems for an age.
I lose my patience, and I own it too,
When works are censured, not as bad, but new;
While if our elders break all reason's laws,
These fools demand not pardon, but applause.
    On Avon's bank, where flowers eternal blow,
If I but ask, if any weed can grow?
One tragic sentence if I dare deride
Which Betterton's grave action dignified,
Or well-mouthed Booth with emphasis proclaims,
(Though but, perhaps, a muster-roll of names)
How will our fathers rise up in a rage,
And swear, all shame is lost in George's age!
You'd think no fools disgraced the former reign,
Did not some grave examples yet remain,
Who scorn a lad should teach his father skill,
And, having once been wrong, will be so still.
He, who to seem more deep than you or I,
Extols old bards, or Merlin's prophecy,
Mistake him not; he envies, not admires,
And to debase the sons, exalts the sires.
Had ancient times conspired to disallow
What then was new, what had been ancient now?
Or what remained, so worthy to be read
By learned critics, of the mighty dead?
    In days of ease, when now the weary sword
Was sheathed, and *luxury* with Charles restored;
In every taste of foreign courts improved,
'All, by the King's example, lived and loved.'
Then peers grew proud in horsemanship t'excel,
Newmarket's glory rose, as Britain's fell;
The soldier breathed the gallantries of France,
And every flowery courtier writ romance.
Then marble, softened into life, grew warm:
And yielding metal flowed to human form:
Lely on animated canvas stole

The sleepy eye, that spoke the melting soul.
No wonder then, when all was love and sport,
The willing Muses were debauched at court:
On each enervate string they taught the note
To pant, or tremble through an eunuch's throat.
  But Britain, changeful as a child at play,
Now calls in princes, and now turns away.
Now Whig, now Tory, what we loved we hate;
Now all for pleasure, now for church and state;
Now for prerogative, and now for laws;
Effects unhappy! from a noble cause.
  Time was, a sober Englishman would knock
His servants up, and rise by five o'clock,
Instruct his family in every rule,
And send his wife to church, his son to school.
To worship like his fathers, was his care;
To teach their frugal virtues to his heir;
To prove, that luxury could never hold;
And place, on good security, his gold.
Now times are changed, and one poetic itch
Has seized the court and city, poor and rich:
Sons, sires, and grandsires, all will wear the bays,
Our wives read Milton, and our daughters plays,
To theatres, and to rehearsals throng,
And all our grace at table is a song.
I, who so oft renounce the muses, lie,
Not ——'s self e'er tells more *fibs* than I;
When sick of muse, our follies we deplore,
And promise our best friends to rhyme no more;
We wake next morning in a raging fit,
And call for pen and ink to show our wit.
  He served a 'prenticeship, who sets up shop;
Ward tried on puppies, and the poor, his drop;
Even Radcliff's doctors travel first to France,
Nor dare to practise till they've learned to dance.
Who builds a bridge that never drove a pile?
(Should Ripley venture, all the world would smile)
But those who cannot write, and those who can,
All rhyme, and scrawl, and scribble, to a man.
  Yet, sir, reflect, the mischief is not great;
These madmen never hurt the Church or State;
Sometimes the folly benefits mankind;
And rarely avarice taints the tuneful mind.
Allow him but his plaything of a pen,
He ne'er rebels, or plots, like other men:
Flight of cashiers, or mobs, he'll never mind;
And knows no losses while the muse is kind.
To cheat a friend, or Ward, he leaves to Peter;

The good man heaps up nothing but mere metre,
Enjoys his garden and his book in quiet;
And then—a perfect hermit in his diet.
　Of little use the man you may suppose,
Who says in verse what others say in prose;
Yet let me show, a poet's of some weight,
And (though no soldier) useful to the state.
What will a child learn sooner than a song?
What better teach a foreigner the tongue?
What's long or short, each accent where to place,
And speak in public with some sort of grace.
I scarce can think him such a worthless thing,
Unless he praise some monster of a king;
Or virtue, or religion turn to sport,
To please a lewd or unbelieving court.
Unhappy Dryden!—In all Charles's days,
Roscommon only boasts unspotted bays;
And in our own (excuse some courtly stains)
No whiter page than Addison remains.
He, from the taste obscene reclaims our youth,
And sets the passions on the side of truth,
Forms the soft bosom with the gentlest art,
And pours each human virtue in the heart.
Let Ireland tell, how wit upheld her cause,
Her trade supported, and supplied her laws;
And leave on SWIFT this grateful verse engraved,
The rights a court attacked, a poet saved.
Behold the hand that wrought a nation's cure,
Stretched to relieve the idiot and the poor,
Proud vice to brand, or injured worth adorn,
And stretch the ray to ages yet unborn.
Not but there are, who merit other palms:
Hopkins and Sternhold glad the heart with Psalms:
The boys and girls whom charity maintains,
Implore your help in these pathetic strains:
How could devotion touch the country pews,
Unless the gods bestowed a proper muse?
Verse cheers their leisure, verse assists their work,
Verse prays for peace, or sings down Pope and Turk.
The silenced preacher yields to potent strain,
And feels that grace his prayer besought in vain;
The blessing thrills through all the labouring throng,
And heaven is won by violence of song.
　Our rural ancestors, with little blessed,
Patient of labour when the end was rest,
Indulged the day that housed their annual grain,
With feasts, and offerings, and a thankful strain:
The joy their wives, their sons, and servants share,

Ease of their toil, and partners of their care:
The laugh, the jest, attendants on the bowl,
Smoothed every brow, and opened every soul:
With growing years the pleasing licence grew,
And taunts alternate innocently flew.
But times corrupt, and nature, ill-inclined,
Produced the point that left a sting behind;
Till friend with friend, and families at strife,
Triumphant malice raged through private life.
Who felt the wrong, or feared it, took th' alarm,
Appealed to law, and justice lent her arm.
At length, by wholesome dread of statutes bound,
The poets learned to please, and not to wound:
Most warped to flattery's side; but some more nice,
Preserved the freedom, and forebore the vice.
Hence satire rose, that just the medium hit.
And heals with morals what it hurts with wit.
    We conquered France, but felt our captive's charms;
Her arts victorious triumphed o'er our arms:
Britain to soft refinements less a foe,
Wit grew polite, and numbers learned to flow.
Waller was smooth; but Dryden taught to join
The varying verse, the full-resounding line,
The long majestic march, and energy divine.
Though still some traces of our rustic vein
And splay-foot verse, remained, and will remain.
Late, very late, correctness grew our care,
When the tired nation breathed from civil war.
Exact Racine, and Corneille's noble fire,
Showed us that France had something to admire.
Not but the tragic spirit was our own,
And full in Shakespeare, fair in Otway shone:
But Otway failed to polish or refine,
And fluent Shakespeare scarce effaced a line.
Ev'n copious Dryden wanted, or forgot,
The last and greatest art, the art to blot.
Some doubt, if equal pains, or equal fire
The humbler muse of comedy require?
But in known images of life, I guess
The labour greater, as th' indulgence less.
Observe how seldom ev'n the best succeed:
Tell me if Congreve's fools are fools indeed?
What pert, low dialogue has Farquhar writ!
How Van wants grace, who never wanted wit!
The stage how loosely does Astraea tread,
Who fairly puts all characters to bed!
And idle Cibber, how he breaks the laws,
To make poor Pinky eat with vast applause!

But fill their purse, our poet's work is done,
Alike to them, by pathos or by pun.
   O you! whom vanity's light bark conveys
On fame's mad voyage by the wind of praise,
With what a shifting gale your course you ply,
For ever sunk too low, or borne too high!
Who pants for glory finds but short repose,
A breath revives him, or a breath o'erthrows.
Farewell the stage! if just as thrives the play,
The silly bard grows fat, or falls away.
   There still remains, to mortify a wit,
The many-headed monster of the pit:
A senseless, worthless, and unhonoured crowd;
Who, to disturb their betters mighty proud,
Clattering their sticks before ten lines are spoke,
Call for the farce, the bear, or the 'Black-Joke'.
What dear delight to Britons farce affords!
Ever the taste of mobs, but now of lords;
(Taste, that eternal wanderer, which flies
From heads to ears, and now from ears to eyes.)
The play stands still; damn action and discourse,
Back fly the scenes, and enter foot and horse;
Pageants on pageants, in long order drawn,
Peers, heralds, bishops, ermine, gold, and lawn;
The Champion too! and, to complete the jest,
Old Edward's armour beams on Cibber's breast,
With laughter sure Democritus had died,
Had he beheld an audience gape so wide.
Let bear or elephant be e'er so white,
The people, sure, the people are the sight!
Ah luckless poet! stretch thy lungs and roar,
That bear or elephant shall heed thee more;
While all its throats the gallery extends,
And all the thunder of the pit ascends!
Loud as the wolves, on Orcas' stormy steep,
Howl to the roarings of the northern deep,
Such is the shout, the long-applauding note,
At Quin's high plume, or Oldfield's petticoat;
Or when from court a birthday suit bestowed,
Sinks the lost actor in the tawdry load.
Booth enters—hark! the universal peal!
'But has he spoken?' Not a syllable.
What shook the stage, and made the people stare?
Cato's long wig, flowered gown, and lacquered chair.
   Yet lest you think I rally more than teach,
Or praise malignly arts I cannot reach,
Let me for once presume t' instruct the times,
To know the poet from the man of rhymes:

'Tis he, who gives my breast a thousand pains,
Can make me feel each passion that he feigns;
Enrage, compose, with more than magic art,
With pity, and with terror, tear my heart;
And snatch me, o'er the earth, or through the air,
To Thebes, to Athens, when he will, and where.
   But not this part of the poetic state
Alone, deserves the favour of the great:
Think of those authors, sir, who would rely
More on a reader's sense, than gazer's eye.
Or who shall wander where the muses sing?
Who climb their mountain, or who taste their spring?
How shall we fill a library with wit,
When Merlin's Cave is half unfurnished yet?
My liege! why writers little claim your thought,
I guess; and, with their leave, will tell the fault:
We poets are (upon a poet's word)
Of all mankind, the creatures most absurd:
The season, when to come, and when to go,
To sing, or cease to sing, we never know;
And if we will recite nine hours in ten,
You lose your patience, just like other men.
Then too we hurt ourselves, when to defend
A single verse, we quarrel with a friend;
Repeat unasked; lament, the wit's too fine
For vulgar eyes, and point out every line.
But most, when straining with too weak a wing,
We needs will write epistles to the King;
And from the moment we oblige the town,
Expect a place, or pension from the crown;
Or dubbed historians by express command,
T' enroll your triumphs o'er the seas and land;
Be called to court to plan some work divine,
As once for LOUIS, Boileau and Racine.
   Yet think, great sir! (so many virtues shown)
Ah think, what poet best may make them known?
Or choose at least some minister of grace,
Fit to bestow the laureate's weighty place.
   Charles, to late times to be transmitted fair,
Assigned his figure to Bernini's care;
And great Nassau to Kneller's hand decreed
To fix him graceful on the bounding steed;
So well in paint and stone they judged of merit:
But kings in wit may want discerning spirit.
The hero William and the martyr Charles,
One knighted Blackmore, and one pensioned Quarles;
Which made old Ben, and surly Dennis swear,
'No Lord's anointed, but a Russian bear.'

Not with such majesty, such bold relief,
The forms august, of king, or conquering chief,
E'er swelled on marble; as in verse have shined
(In polished verse) the manners and the mind.
Oh! could I mount on the Maeonian wing,
Your arms, your actions, your repose to sing!
What seas you traversed, and what fields you fought!
Your country's peace, how oft, how dearly bought!
How barbarous rage subsided at your word,
And nations wondered while they dropped the sword!
How, when you nodded, o'er the land and deep,
Peace stole her wing, and wrapped the world in sleep;
Till earth's extremes your mediation own,
And Asia's tyrants tremble at your throne—
But verse, alas! your majesty disdains;
And I'm not used to panegyric strains:
The zeal of fools offends at any time,
But most of all, the zeal of fools in rhyme.
Besides, a fate attends on all I write,
That when I aim at praise, they say I bite.
A vile encomium doubly ridicules:
There's nothing blackens like the ink of fools.
If true, a woeful likeness; and if lies,
'Praise undeserved is scandal in disguise:'
Well may he blush, who gives it, or receives;
And when I flatter, let my dirty leaves
(Like journals, odes, and such forgotten things
As Eusden, Philips, Settle, writ of kings)
Clothe spice, line trunks, or, fluttering in a row,
Befringe the rails of Bedlam and Soho.

THE
SIXTH EPISTLE
OF THE
FIRST BOOK
OF
HORACE IMITATED
To Mr. Murray

'Not to admire, is all the art I know,
To make men happy, and to keep them so.'
(Plain truth, dear Murray, needs no flowers of speech,
So take it in the very words of Creech.)
    This vault of air, this congregated ball,
Self-centred sun, and stars that rise and fall,
There are, my friend! whose philosophic eyes
Look through, and trust the ruler with his skies,
To him commit the hour, the day, the year,

And view this dreadful all without a fear.
Admire we, then, what earth's low entrails hold,
Arabian shores, or Indian seas enfold?
All the mad trade of fools and slaves for gold?
Or popularity? or stars and strings?
The mob's applauses, or the gifts of kings?
Say with what eyes we ought at courts to gaze,
And pay the great our homage of amaze?
   If weak the pleasure that from these can spring,
The fear to want them is as weak a thing:
Whether we dread, or whether we desire,
In either case, believe me, we admire;
Whether we joy or grieve, the same the curse,
Surprised at better, or surprised at worse.
Thus good or bad, to one extreme betray
Th' unbalanced mind, and snatch the man away;
For virtue's self may too much zeal be had;
The worst of madmen is a saint run mad.
   Go then, and if you can, admire the state
Of beaming diamonds, and reflected plate;
Procure a TASTE to double the surprise,
And gaze on Parian charms with learnèd eyes:
Be struck with bright brocade, or Tyrian dye,
Our birthday nobles' splendid livery.
If not so pleased, at council-board rejoice,
To see their judgments hang upon thy voice;
From morn to night, at senate, Rolls, and Hall,
Plead much, read more, dine late, or not at all.
But wherefore all this labour, all this strife?
For fame, for riches, for a noble wife?
Shall one whom nature, learning, birth, conspired
To form not to admire but be admired,
Sigh, while his Cloe blind to wit and worth
Weds the rich dulness of some son of earth?
Yet time ennobles, or degrades each line;
It brightened CRAGGS'S, and may darken thine:
And what is fame? the meanest have their day,
The greatest can but blaze and pass away.
Graced as thou art, with all the power of words,
So known, so honoured, at the House of Lords:
Conspicuous scene! another yet is nigh,
(More silent far) where kings and poets lie;
Where MURRAY (long enough his country's pride)
Shall be no more than TULLY, or than HYDE!
   Racked with sciatics, martyred with the stone,
Will any mortal let himself alone?
See Ward by battered beaux invited over,
And desperate misery lays hold on Dover.

The case is easier in the mind's disease;
There all men may be cured, whene'er they please.
Would ye be blessed? despise low joys, low gains;
Disdain whatever CORNBURY disdains;
Be virtuous and be happy for your pains.
    But art thou one, whom new opinions sway,
One who believes as Tindal leads the way,
Who virtue and a church alike disowns,
Thinks that but words, and this but brick and stones?
Fly then on all the wings of wild desire,
Admire whate'er the maddest can admire.
Is wealth thy passion? Hence! from pole to pole,
Where winds can carry, or where waves can roll,
For Indian spices, for Peruvian gold,
Prevent the greedy, and outbid the bold:
Advance thy golden mountain to the skies;
On the broad base of fifty thousand rise,
Add one round hundred, and (if that's not fair)
Add fifty more, and bring it to a square.
For, mark th' advantage; just so many score
Will gain a wife with half as many more,
Procure her beauty, make that beauty chaste,
And then such friends—as cannot fail to last.
A man of wealth is dubbed a man of worth,
Venus shall give him form, and Anstis birth.
(Believe me, many a German prince is worse,
Who proud of pedigree, is poor of purse.)
His wealth brave Timon gloriously confounds;
Asked for a groat, he gives a hundred pounds;
Or if three ladies like a luckless play,
Takes the whole house upon the poet's day.
Now, in such exigencies not to need,
Upon my word, you must be rich indeed;
A noble superfluity it craves,
Not for yourself, but for your fools and knaves;
Something, which for your honour they may cheat,
And which it much becomes you to forget.
If wealth alone then make and keep us blessed,
Still, still be getting, never, never rest.
    But if to power and place your passion lie,
If in the pomp of life consist the joy;
Then hire a slave, or (if you will) a lord
To do the honours, and to give the word;
Tell at your levee, as the crowds approach,
To whom to nod, whom take into your coach,
Whom honour with your hand: to make remarks,
Who rules in Cornwall, or who rules in Berks:
'This may be troublesome, is near the chair:

That makes three members, this can choose a mayor.'
Instructed thus, you bow, embrace, protest,
Adopt him son, or cousin at the least,
Then turn about, and laugh at your own jest.
  Or if your life be one continued treat,
If to live well means nothing but to eat;
Up, up! cries gluttony, 'tis break of day,
Go drive the deer, and drag the finny prey;
With hounds and horns go hunt an appetite—
So Russel did, but could not eat at night,
Called happy dog! the beggar at his door,
And envied thirst and hunger to the poor.
  Or shall we every decency confound,
Through taverns, stews, and bagnios take our round,
Go dine with Chartres, in each vice outdo
Kinnoul's lewd cargo, or Tyrawley's crew,
From Latian sirens, French Circean feasts,
Return well travelled, and transformed to beasts,
Or for a titled pink, or foreign name?
Renounce our country, and degrade our name?
  If, after all, we must with Wilmot own,
The cordial drop of life is love alone,
And SWIFT cry wisely, 'Vive la bagatelle!'
The man that loves and laughs, must sure do well.
Adieu—if this advice appear the worst,
E'en take the counsel which I gave you first:
Or better precepts if you can impart,
Why do, I'll follow them with all my heart.

THE
FIRST EPISTLE
OF THE
FIRST BOOK
OF
HORACE IMITATED

To LORD BOLINGBROKE

St. John, whose love indulged my labours past,
Matures my present, and shall bound my last!
Why will you break the sabbath of my days?
Now sick alike of envy and of praise.
Public too long, ah let me hide my age!
See modest Cibber now has left the stage:
Our generals now, retired to their estates,
Hang their old trophies o'er the garden gates,
In life's cool evening satiate of applause,
Nor fond of bleeding, even in BRUNSWICK'S cause.

A voice there is, that whispers in my ear,
('Tis reason's voice, which sometimes one can hear)
'Friend Pope, be prudent, let your muse take breath,
And never gallop Pegasus to death;
Lest stiff, and stately, void of fire or force,
You limp, like Blackmore, on a Lord Mayor's horse.'
    Farewell then verse, and love, and every toy,
The rhymes and rattles of the man or boy;
What right, what true, what fit we justly call,
Let this be all my care—for this is all:
To lay this harvest up, and hoard with haste
What every day will want, and most, the last.
    But ask not, to what doctors I apply?
Sworn to no master, of no sect am I:
As drives the storm, at any door I knock:
And house with Montaigne now, or now with Locke.
Sometimes a patriot, active in debate,
Mix with the world, and battle for the state,
Free as young Lyttelton, her cause pursue,
Still true to virtue, and as warm as true:
Sometimes with Aristippus, or St. Paul,
Indulge my candour, and grow all to all;
Back to my native moderation slide,
And win my way by yielding to the tide.
    Long, as to him who works for debt, the day;
Long as the night to her whose love's away;
Long as the year's dull circle seems to run,
When the brisk minor pants for twenty-one:
So slow th' unprofitable moments roll,
That lock up all the functions of my soul;
That keep me from myself; and still delay
Life's instant business to a future day:
That task, which as we follow, or despise,
The eldest is a fool, the youngest wise;
Which done, the poorest can no wants endure,
And which not done, the richest must be poor.
    Late as it is, I put myself to school,
And feel some comfort, not to be a fool.
Weak though I am of limb, and short of sight,
Far from a lynx, and not a giant quite;
I'll do what Mead and Cheselden advise,
To keep these limbs, and to preserve these eyes.
Not to go back, is somewhat to advance,
And men must walk at least before they dance.
    Say, does thy blood rebel, thy bosom move
With wretched avarice, or as wretched love?
Know, there are words and spells, which can control
Between the fits this fever of the soul:

Know, there are rhymes, which fresh and fresh applied
Will cure the arrant'st puppy of his pride.
Be furious, envious, slothful, mad, or drunk,
Slave to a wife, or vassal to a punk,
A Switz, a High Dutch, or a Low Dutch bear;
All that we ask is but a patient ear.

'Tis the first virtue, vices to abhor;
And the first wisdom, to be fool no more.
But to the world no bugbear is so great,
As want of figure, and a small estate.
To either India see the merchant fly,
Scared at the spectre of pale poverty!
See him, with pains of body, pangs of soul,
Burn through the Tropic, freeze beneath the Pole!
Wilt thou do nothing for a nobler end,
Nothing, to make philosophy thy friend?
To stop thy foolish views, thy long desires,
And ease thy heart of all that it admires?

Here, wisdom calls: 'Seek virtue first, be bold!
As gold to silver, virtue is to gold.'
There, London's voice: 'Get money, money still!
And then let virtue follow, if she will.'
This, this the saving doctrine, preached to all,
From low St. James's up to high St. Paul;
From him whose quills stand quivered at his ear,
To him who notches sticks at Westminster.

Barnard in spirit, sense, and truth abounds;
'Pray then, what wants he?' Fourscore thousand pounds;
A pension, or such harness for a slave
As Bug now has, and Dorimant would have.
Barnard, thou art a cit, with all thy worth;
But Bug and D*l, their *honours*, and so forth.

Yet every child another song will sing,
'Virtue, brave boys! 'tis virtue makes a king.'
True, conscious honour is to feel no sin,
He's armed without that's innocent within;
Be this thy screen, and this thy wall of brass;
Compared to this, a minister's an ass.

And say, to which shall our applause belong,
This new court jargon, or the good old song?
The modern language of corrupted peers,
Or what was spoke at CRESSY and POITIERS?
Who counsels best? who whispers, 'Be but great,
With praise or infamy leave that to fate;
Get place and wealth, if possible, with grace;
If not, by any means get wealth and place.'
For what? to have a box where eunuchs sing,
And foremost in the circle eye a king.

Or he, who bids thee face with steady view
Proud fortune, and look shallow greatness through:
And, while he bids thee, sets th' example too?
If such a doctrine, in St. James's air,
Should chance to make the well-dressed rabble stare;
If honest Schutz take scandal at a spark,
That less admires the palace than the park;
Faith I shall give the answer Reynard gave:
'I cannot like, dread sir, your royal cave;
Because I see, by all the tracks about,
Full many a beast goes in, but none come out.'
Adieu to virtue, if you're once a slave:
Send her to Court, you send her to her grave.

　　Well, if a king's a lion, at the least
The people are a many-headed beast:
Can they direct what measures to pursue,
Who know themselves so little what to do?
Alike in nothing but one lust of gold,
Just half the land would buy, and half be sold:
Their country's wealth our mightier misers drain,
Or cross, to plunder provinces, the main;
The rest, some farm the poor-box, some the pews;
Some keep assemblies, and would keep the stews;
Some with fat bucks on childless dotards fawn;
Some win rich widows by their chine and brawn;
While with the silent growth of ten per cent.
In dirt and darkness, hundreds stink content.

　　Of all these ways, if each pursues his own,
Satire be kind, and let the wretch alone:
But show me one who has it in his power
To act consistent with himself an hour.
Sir Job sailed forth, the evening bright and still,
'No place on earth,' he cried, 'like Greenwich Hill!'
Up starts a palace; lo, th' obedient base
Slopes at its foot, the woods its sides embrace,
The silver Thames reflects its marble face.
Now let some whimsy, or that devil within
Which guides all those who know not what they mean,
But give the knight (or give his lady) spleen;
'Away, away! take all your scaffolds down,
For snug's the word. My dear! we'll live in town.'

　　At amorous Flavio is the stocking thrown?
That very night he longs to lie alone.

　　The fool, whose wife elopes some thrice a quarter,
For matrimonial solace dies a martyr.
Did ever Proteus, Merlin, any witch,
Transform themselves so strangely as the rich?
Well, but the poor—the poor have the same itch;

They change their weekly barber, weekly news,
Prefer a new japanner to their shoes,
Discharge their garrets, move their beds, and run
(They know not whither) in a chaise and one;
They hire their sculler, and when once aboard,
Grow sick, and damn the climate—like a lord.
   You laugh, half beau, half sloven if I stand,
My wig all powder, and all snuff my band;
You laugh, if coat and breeches strangely vary,
White gloves, and linen worthy Lady Mary!
But when no prelate's lawn with hair-shirt lined,
Is half so incoherent as my mind,
When (each opinion with the next at strife,
One ebb and flow of follies all my life)
I plant, root up; I build, and then confound;
Turn round to square, and square again to round;
You never change one muscle of your face,
You think this madness but a common case,
Nor once to Chancery, nor to Hale apply;
Yet hang your lip, to see a seam awry!
Careless how ill I with myself agree,
Kind to my dress, my figure, not to me.
Is this my guide, philosopher, and friend?
This, he who loves me, and who ought to mend?
Who ought to make me (what he can, or none,)
That man divine whom wisdom calls her own;
Great without title, without fortune blessed;
Rich even when plundered, honoured while oppressed;
Loved without youth, and followed without power;
At home, though exiled; free, though in the Tower;
In short, that reasoning, high, immortal thing,
Just less than Jove, and much above a king,
Nay, half in heaven—except (what's mighty odd)
A fit of vapours clouds this demigod.

EPILOGUE
TO THE
SATIRES
Written in MDCCXXXVIII
DIALOGUE I

Fr. Not twice a twelve-month you appear in print,
And when it comes, the Court see nothing in't.
You grow *correct*, that once with rapture writ,
And are, besides, too *moral* for a wit.
Decay of parts, alas! we all must feel—
Why now, this moment, don't I see you steal?
'Tis all from Horace; Horace long before ye

Said, 'Tories called him Whig, and Whigs a Tory;'
And taught his Romans, in much better metre,
'To laugh at fools who put their trust in Peter.'
   But Horace, sir, was delicate, was nice;
Bubo observes, he lashed no sort of *vice:*
Horace would say, Sir Billy *served the crown,*
Blunt could *do business,* Huggins *knew the town*;
In Sappho touch the *failings of the sex,*
In reverend bishops note some *small neglects,*
And own, the Spaniard did a *waggish thing,*
Who cropped our ears, and sent them to the King.
His sly, polite, insinuating style
Could please at Court, and make AUGUSTUS smile:
An artful manager, that crept between
His friend and shame, and was a kind of *screen.*
But 'faith, your friends will soon be sore;
Patriots there are, who wish you'd jest no more—
And where's the glory? 'twill be only thought
The Great Man never offered you a groat.
Go, see SIR ROBERT—
          P. See Sir Robert!—hum—
And never laugh—for all my life to come?
Seen him I have, but in his happier hour
Of social pleasure, ill-exchanged for power;
Seen him, unencumbered with the venal tribe,
Smile without art, and win without a bribe.
Would he oblige me? let me only find
He does not think me what he thinks mankind.
Come, come, at all I laugh he laughs, no doubt;
The only difference is, I dare laugh out.
   F. Why, yes: with *scripture* still you may be free;
A horse-laugh, if you please, at *honesty*;
A joke on *Jekyll,* or some odd *Old Whig*
Who never changed his principle, or wig:
A patriot is a fool in every age,
Whom all Lord Chamberlains allow the stage:
These nothing hurts; they keep their fashion still,
And wear their strange old virtue, as they will.
   If any ask you, 'Who's the man, so near
His prince, that writes in verse, and has his ear?'
Why, answer, LYTTELTON, and I'll engage
The worthy youth shall ne'er be in a rage:
But were his verses vile, his whisper base,
You'd quickly find him in Lord Fanny's case.
Sejanus, Wolsey, hurt not honest FLEURY,
But well may put some statesmen in a fury.
   Laugh then at any, but at fools or foes;
These you but anger, and you mend not those.

Laugh at your friends, and, if your friends are sore,
So much the better, you may laugh the more.
To vice and folly to confine the jest,
Sets half the world, God knows, against the rest;
Did not the sneer of more impartial men
At sense and virtue, balance all again.
Judicious wits spread wide the ridicule,
And charitably comfort knave and fool.
    P. Dear sir, forgive the prejudice of youth:
Adieu distinction, satire, warmth, and truth!
Come, harmless characters, that no one hit;
Come, Henley's oratory, Osborne's wit!
The honey dropping from Favonio's tongue,
The flowers of Bubo, and the flow of Young!
The gracious dew of pulpit eloquence,
And all the well-whipped cream of courtly sense,
That first was Hervey's, Fox's next, and then
The senate's, and then Hervey's once again.
O, come, that easy Ciceronian style,
So Latin, yet so English all the while,
As, though the pride of Middleton and Bland,
All boys may read, and girls may understand!
Then might I sing, without the least offence,
And all I sung should be the *nation's sense*;
Or teach the melancholy muse to mourn,
Hang the sad verse on CAROLINA'S urn,
And hail her passage to the realms of rest,
All parts performed, and *all* her children blessed!
So—satire is no more—I feel it die—
No *gazetteer* more innocent than I—
And let, a-God's name, every fool and knave
Be graced through life, and flattered in his grave.
    F. Why so? if satire knows its time and place,
You still may lash the greatest—in disgrace:
For merit will by turns forsake them all;
Would you know when? exactly when they fall.
But let all satire in all changes spare
Immortal Selkirk, and grave De la Ware.
Silent and soft, as saints remove to heaven,
All ties dissolved and every sin forgiven,
These may some gentle ministerial wing
Receive, and place for ever near a king!
There, where no passion, pride, or shame transport,
Lulled with the sweet nepenthe of a court;
There, where no father's, brother's, friend's disgrace
Once break their rest, or stir them from their place:
But past the sense of human miseries,
All tears are wiped for ever from all eyes;

No cheek is known to blush, no heart to throb,
Save when they lose a question, or a job.
  P. Good heaven forbid, that I should blast their glory,
Who know how like Whig ministers to Tory,
And, when three sovereigns died, could scarce be vexed,
Considering what a *gracious Prince* was next.
Have I, in silent wonder, seen such things
As pride in slaves, and avarice in kings;
And at a peer, or peeress, shall I fret,
Who starves a sister, or forswears a debt?
Virtue, I grant you, is an empty boast;
But shall the dignity of *Vice* be lost?
Ye gods! shall Cibber's son, without rebuke,
Swear like a lord, or Rich out-whore a duke?
A favourite's porter with his master vie,
Be bribed as often, and as often lie?
Shall Ward draw contracts with a statesman's skill?
Or Japhet pocket, like his Grace, a will?
Is it for Bond, or Peter (paltry things)
To pay their debts, or keep their faith, like kings?
If Blount dispatched himself, he played the man,
And so mayst thou, illustrious Passeran!
But shall a printer, weary of his life,
Learn, from their books, to hang himself and wife?
This, this, my friend, I cannot, must not bear;
Vice thus abused, demands a nation's care:
This calls the Church to deprecate our sin,
And hurls the thunder of the laws on *gin.*
  Let modest Foster, if he will, excel
Ten Metropolitans in preaching well;
A simple Quaker, or a Quaker's wife,
Outdo Llandaff in doctrine,—yea in life:
Let humble ALLEN, with an awkward shame,
Do good by stealth, and blush to find it fame.
Virtue may choose the high or low degree,
'Tis just alike to Virtue, and to me;
Dwell in a monk, or light upon a king,
She's still the same, beloved, contented thing.
Vice is undone, if she forgets her birth,
And stoops from angels to the dregs of earth:
But 'tis the *fall* degrades her to a whore;
Let *Greatness* own her, and she's mean no more;
Her birth, her beauty, crowds and courts confess;
Chaste matrons praise her, and grave bishops bless;
In golden chains the willing world she draws,
And hers the Gospel is, and hers the laws,
Mounts the tribunal, lifts her scarlet head,
And sees pale Virtue carted in her stead.

Lo! at the wheels of her triumphal car,
Old England's genius, rough with many a scar,
Dragged in the dust! his arms hang idly round,
His flag inverted trails along the ground!
Our youth, all liveried o'er with foreign gold,
Before her dance: behind her, crawl the old!
See thronging millions to the pagod run,
And offer country, parent, wife, or son!
Hear her black trumpet through the land proclaim,
That 'not to be corrupted is the shame.'
In soldier, churchman, patriot, man in power,
'Tis avarice all, ambition is no more!
See, all our nobles begging to be slaves!
See, all our fools aspiring to be knaves!
The wit of cheats, the courage of a whore,
Are what ten thousand envy and adore:
All, all look up, with reverential awe,
At crimes that 'scape, or triumph o'er the law:
While truth, worth, wisdom, daily they decry—
'Nothing is sacred now but villainy.'
    Yet may this verse (if such a verse remain)
Show there was one who held it in disdain.

EPILOGUE
TO THE
SATIRES
DIALOGUE II

Fr. 'Tis all a libel—Paxton, sir will say.
    P. Not yet, my friend! tomorrow 'faith it may;
And for that very cause I print today.
How should I fret, to mangle every line,
In reverence to the sins of thirty-nine!
Vice with such giant strides comes on amain,
Invention strives to be before in vain;
Feign what I will, and paint it e'er so strong,
Some rising genius sins up to my song.
    F. Yet none but you by name the guilty lash;
Even Guthrie saves half Newgate by a dash.
Spare, then, the person, and expose the vice.
    P. How, sir? not damn the sharper, but the dice?
Come on then, satire! general, unconfined,
Spread thy broad wing, and souze on all the kind.
Ye statesmen, priests, of one religion all!
Ye tradesmen vile, in army, court, or hall!
Ye reverend atheists. *F*. Scandal! name them, who?
    P. Why that's the thing you bid me not to do.
'Who starved a sister, who forswore a debt,'

I never named; the town's enquiring yet.
The poisoning dame—*F.* You mean—*P.* I don't. *F.* You do.
    P. See, now I keep the secret, and not you!
The bribing statesman—*F.* Hold, too high you go.
    P. The bribed elector—*F.* There you stoop too low.
    P. I fain would please you, if I knew with what;
Tell me, which knave is lawful game, which not?
Must great offenders, once escaped the crown,
Like royal harts, be never more run down?
Admit your law to spare the knight requires,
As beasts of nature may we hunt the squires?
Suppose I censure—you know what I mean—
To save a bishop, may I name a dean?
    F. A dean, sir? no: his fortune is not made,
You hurt a man that's rising in the trade.
    P. If not the tradesman who set up today,
Much less the 'prentice who tomorrow may.
Down, down, proud satire! though a realm be spoiled,
Arraign no mightier thief than wretched Wild;
Or, if a court or country's made a job,
Go drench a pickpocket, and join the mob.
    But, sir, I beg you (for the love of vice!)
The matter's weighty, pray consider twice:
Have you less pity for the needy cheat,
The poor and friendless villain, than the great?
Alas! the small discredit of a bribe
Scarce hurts the lawyer, but undoes the scribe.
Then better, sure, it charity becomes
To tax directors, who (thank God!) have plums;
Still better, ministers; or, if the thing
May pinch ev'n there—why lay it on a king.
    F. Stop! stop!
             P. Must satire, then, nor rise nor fall?
Speak out, and bid me blame no rogues at all.
    F. Yes, strike that Wild, I'll justify the blow.
        P. Strike? why the man was hanged ten year ago:
Who now that obsolete example fears?
Ev'n Peter trembles only for his ears.
    F. What always Peter? Peter thinks you mad,
You make men desperate if they once are bad:
Else might he take to virtue some years hence—
    P. As Selkirk, if he lives, will love the PRINCE.
    F. Strange spleen to Selkirk!
                 P. Do I wrong the man?
God knows, I praise a courtier where I can.
When I confess, there is who feels for fame,
And melts to goodness, need I SCARBOROUGH name?
Please let me own, in Esher's peaceful grove

(Where Kent and Nature vie for PELHAM'S love)
The scene, the master, opening to my view,
I sit and dream I see my CRAGGS anew!
    Ev'n in a bishop I can spy desert;
Secker is decent, Rundle has a heart,
Manners with candour are to Benson given,
To Berkeley, every virtue under heaven.
    But does the court a worthy man remove?
That instant, I declare, he has my love:
I shun his zenith, court his mild decline;
Thus SOMERS once, and HALIFAX, were mine.
Oft, in the clear, still mirror of retreat,
I studied SHREWSBURY, the wise and great:
CARLETON'S calm sense, and STANHOPE'S noble flame,
Compared, and knew their generous end the same:
How pleasing ATTERBURY'S softer hour!
How shined the soul, unconquered in the Tower!
How can I PULTENEY, CHESTERFIELD forget,
While Roman spirit charms, and Attic wit:
ARGYLL, the state's whole thunder born to wield,
And shake alike the senate and the field:
Or WYNDHAM, just to freedom and the throne,
The master of our passions, and his own.
Names, which I long have loved, nor loved in vain,
Ranked with their friends, not numbered with their train:
And if yet higher the proud list should end,
Still let me say: 'No follower, but a friend.'
    Yet think not, friendship only prompts my lays;
I follow *virtue*: where she shines, I praise:
Point she to priest or elder, Whig or Tory,
Or round a Quaker's beaver cast a glory.
I never (to my sorrow, I declare)
Dined with the MAN OF ROSS, or my LORD MAYOR.
Some in their choice of friends (nay, look not grave)
Have still a secret bias to a knave:
To find an honest man I beat about,
And love him, court him, praise him, in or out.
    F. Then why so few commended?
                             P. Not so fierce;
Find you the virtue, and I'll find the verse.
But random praise—the task can ne'er be done;
Each mother asks it for her booby son,
Each widow asks it for *the best of men*,
For him she weeps, and him she weds again.
Praise cannot stoop, like satire, to the ground;
The number may be hanged, but not be crowned.
Enough for half the greatest of these days,
To 'scape my censure, not expect my praise.

And they not rich? what more can they pretend?
Dare they to hope a poet for their friend?
What RICHELIEU wanted, LOUIS scarce could gain,
And what young AMMON wished, but wished in vain.
No power the muse's friendship can command;
No power when virtue claims it, can withstand:
To Cato, Virgil paid one honest line;
O let my country's friends illumine mine!
—What are you thinking? *F.* Faith, the thought's no sin,
I think your friends are out, and would be in.
　　P. If merely to come in, sir, they go out,
The way they take is strangely round about.
　　F. They too may be corrupted, you'll allow?
　　P. I only call those knaves who are so now.
　　Is that too little? Come then, I'll comply—
Spirit of *Arnall!* aid me while I lie.
COBHAM'S a coward, POLWARTH is a slave,
And LYTTELTON a dark, designing knave,
ST. JOHN has ever been a wealthy fool—
But let me add, SIR ROBERT'S mighty dull,
Has never made a friend in private life,
And was, besides, a tyrant to his wife.
　　But pray, when others praise him, do I blame?
Call Verres, Wolsey, any odious name?
Why rail they, then, if but a wreath of mine,
Oh, all-accomplished ST. JOHN! deck thy shrine?
　　What? shall each spur-galled hackney of the day,
When Paxton gives him double pots and pay,
Or each new-pensioned sycophant, pretend
To break my windows, if I treat a friend?
Then wisely plead, to me they meant no hurt,
But 'twas my guest at whom they threw the dirt?
Sure, if I spare the minister, no rules
Of honour bind me, not to maul his tools;
Sure, if they cannot cut, it may be said
His saws are toothless, and his hatchets lead.
　　If angered TURENNE, once upon a day,
To see a footman kicked that took his pay:
But when he heard the affront the fellow gave,
Knew one a man of honour, one a knave;
The prudent general turned it to a jest,
And begged, he'd take the pains to kick the rest:
Which not at present having time to do—
　　F. Hold sir! for God's sake where's the affront to you?
Against your worship when had Selkirk writ?
Or Page poured forth the torrent of his wit?
Or grant the bard whose distich all commend
'In power a servant, out of power a friend'

To Walpole guilty of some venial sin;
What's that to you who ne'er was out nor in?
 The priest whose flattery bedropped the crown,
How hurt he you? he only stained the gown.
And how did, pray, the florid youth offend,
Whose speech you took, and gave it to a friend?
 P. Faith, it imports not much from whom it came,
Whoever borrowed, could not be to blame,
Since the whole house did afterwards the same.
Let courtly wits to wits afford supply,
As hog to hog in huts of Westphaly;
If one, through nature's bounty, or his lord's,
Has what the frugal, dirty soil affords,
From him the next receives it, thick or thin,
As pure a mess almost as it came in;
The blessed benefit, not there confined,
Drops to the third, who nuzzles close behind;
From tail to mouth, they feed and they carouse:
The last full fairly gives it to the House.
 F. This filthy simile, this beastly line,
Quite turns my stomach—
      P. So does flattery mine;
And all your courtly civet-cats can vent,
Perfume to you, to me is excrement.
But hear me further—Japhet, 'tis agreed,
Writ not, and Chartres scarce could write or read,
In all the courts of Pindus guiltless quite;
But pens can forge, my friend, that cannot write;
And must no egg in Japhet's face be thrown
Because the deed he forged was not my own?
Must never patriot, then, declaim at gin,
Unless, good man! he has been fairly in?
No zealous pastor blame a failing spouse,
Without a staring reason on his brows?
And each blasphemer quite escape the rod
Because the insult's not on man, but God?
 Ask you what provocation I have had?
The strong antipathy of good to bad.
When truth or virtue an affront endures,
The affront is mine, my friend, and should be yours.
Mine, as a foe professed to false pretence,
Who think a coxcomb's honour like his sense;
Mine, as a friend to every worthy mind;
And mine as man, who feel for all mankind.
 F. You're strangely proud.
     P. So proud, I am no slave:
So impudent I own myself no knave:
So odd, my country's ruin makes me grave.

Yes, I am proud; I must be proud to see
Men not afraid of God, afraid of me:
Safe from the bar, the pulpit, and the throne,
Yet touched and shamed by ridicule alone.
    O sacred weapon! left for truth's defence,
Sole dread of folly, vice, and insolence!
To all but heaven-directed hands denied,
The muse may give thee, but the God must guide:
Reverent I touch thee! but with honest zeal;
To rouse the watchmen of the public weal,
To virtue's work provoke the tardy Hall,
And goad the prelate slumbering in his stall.
Ye tinsel insects whom a court maintains
That counts your beauties only by your stains,
Spin all your cobwebs o'er the eye of day!
The muse's wing shall brush you all away:
All his Grace preaches, all his Lordship sings,
All that makes saints of queens, and gods of kings.
All, all but truth, drops dead-born from the press,
Like the last Gazette or the last address.
    When black ambition stains a public cause,
A monarch's sword when mad vainglory draws,
Not Waller's wreath can hide the nation's scar,
Nor Boileau turn the feather to a star.
    Not so, when diademed with rays divine,
Touched with the flame that breaks from virtue's shrine,
Her priestess muse forbids the good to die,
And opes the temple of eternity.
There, other trophies deck the truly brave,
Than such as Anstis casts into the grave;
Far other stars than * and * * wear,
And may descend to Mordington from STAIR:
(Such as on HOUGH'S unsullied mitre shine,
Or beam, good DIGBY, from a heart like thine)
Let envy howl, while heaven's whole chorus sings,
And bark at honour not conferred by kings;
Let flattery sickening see the incense rise,
Sweet to the world, and grateful to the skies:
Truth guards the poet, sanctifies the line,
And makes immortal, verse as mean as mine.
    Yes, the last pen for freedom let me draw,
When truth stands trembling on the edge of law;
Here, last of Britons! let your names be read;
Are none, none living? let me praise the dead,
And for that cause which made your fathers shine,
Fall by the votes of their degenerate line.
    F. Alas! alas! pray end what you began,
And write next winter more *Essays on Man.*

310

EPIGRAM
*Engraved on the Collar of a Dog which
I gave to his Royal Highness*

I am his Highness' dog at Kew;
Pray tell me, sir, whose dog are you?

EPITAPH
For One who would not be buried in
Westminster Abbey

Heroes and kings, your distance keep:
In peace let one poor poet sleep,
Who never flattered folks like you:
Let Horace blush, and Virgil too.

POPE TO HUGH BETHEL
19 March 1744

I am very solicitous to know how you proceed in your health, and these inveterate north-easterly winds give me much apprehension for yours, as they vey greatly affect mine. Within these three weeks I have been excessive ill. The asthma in every symptom increased, with a swelling in my legs and a low fever. I have been so long and yet am confined to my chamber at Twitnam and the whole business of my two servants night and day to attend me. Dr Burton is very watchful over me, he changed the warm pills into a cooler regimen. I drink no wine, and take scarce any meat. Asses' milk twice a day. My only medicines are millepedes and garlic, and horehound tea. He is against crude quicksilver till he is sure there is no fever, but prescribes alkalized mercury in five pills a day: and proposes an issue, which I fear may drain and waste me too much, it can't be imagined how weak I am, and how unable to move, or walk, or use any exercise, but going in a coach, for which the weather is yet too cold. These are all discouraging things, to cure me of buying houses, so I've determined not to purchase this, which will cost me £1200 and instead of it to lay out three upon a cheap one in London, seated in an airy high place. If I live but five months I shall never be able to live about, as I used, in other peoples houses, but quite at ease, to keep my own hours, and with my own servants: and if I don't live there, it will do for a friend, which Twitnam would not suit at all. Give me leave therefore to pay in to your brother what I don't want of the sum I drew upon him by your kind order.—I told you in my last how very welcome was your kind present of your picture which he transmitted very safe. The last thing I did before I was confined, was to sit the first time to Mr. Kent, for you: it wants but one sitting more, and pray tell me, where, or with whom it shall be left for you?

Now I have said a great deal, all I could, of my own state, pray be as particular as to yours. I every morning and night see you in my bedchamber and think of you: nothing can be more resembling, but I wish your complexion be in reality as healthy. Dear Sir, if you are not worse, do not let me wait long for the comfort of knowing it, though you employ any hand, and spare your own eyes. Above all, what is your scheme, as to coming to London, and when? Me you cannot miss; and we may truly say of each other, that we shall be friends to the last breath. Pray remember me to Mr. Moyser.

Ever yours
A. Pope

Twitnam
March 19th
I must desire you to say nothing of what I tell you concerning my purchase of the house in town, which is done in another's name.

THE
DUNCIAD
IN
FOUR BOOKS
Printed according to the complete Copy
found in the Year 1742
WITH THE
PROLEGOMENA OF SCRIBLERUS
AND
NOTES VARIORUM

To which are added SEVERAL NOTES now published, the HYPERCRITICS of ARISTARCHUS, and his *Dissertation* on the HERO of the POEM

Tandem *Phoebus* adest, morsusque inferred parantem Congelat, et patulos, ut errant, indurate hiatus.

OVID.

By AUTHORITY

By virtue of the Authority in Us vested by the Act for subjecting Poets to the power of a Licenser, we have revised this Piece; where finding the style and appellation of KING to have been given to a certain Pretender, Pseudo-Poet, or Phantom, of the name of TIBBALD; and apprehending the same may be deemed in some sort a Reflection on Majesty, or at least an insult on that Legal Authority which has bestowed on another person the Crown of Poesy: we have ordered the said Pretender, Pseudo-Poet, or Phantom, utterly to vanish and evaporate out of this work: And do declare the said Throne of Poesy from henceforth to be abdicated and vacant, unless duly and lawfully supplied by the LAUREATE himself. And it is hereby enacted that no other person do presume to fill the same.

ƆC. Ch.

MARTINUS SCRIBLERUS
HIS
Prolegomena and Illustrations
To the
DUNCIAD
WITH THE
Hyper-critics of ARISTARCHUS

A
LETTER
TO THE
PUBLISHER

Occasioned by the first correct
EDITION of the DUNCIAD.

It is with pleasure I hear that you have procured a correct copy of the *Dunciad*, which the many surreptitious ones have rendered so necessary; and it is yet with more, that I am informed it will be attended with a COMMENTARY: a work so requisite, that I cannot think the author himself would have omitted it, had he approved of the first appearance of this poem.

Such notes as have occurred to me I herewith send you. You will oblige me by inserting them amongst those which are, or will be, transmitted to you by others; since not only the author's friends but even strangers appear engaged by humanity, to take some care of an orphan of so much genius and spirit, which its parent seems to have abandoned from the very beginning, and suffered to step into the world naked, unguarded, and unattended.

It was upon reading some of the abusive papers lately published, that my great regard to a person, whose friendship I esteem as one of the chief honours of my life, and a much greater respect to truth, than to him or any man living, engaged me in inquiries, of which the enclosed notes are the fruit.

I perceived, that most of these authors had been (doubtless very wisely) the first aggressors. They had tried, till they were weary, what was to be got by railing at each other: nobody was either concerned or surprised, if this or that scribbler was proved a dunce. But everyone was curious to read what could be said to prove Mr. POPE one, and was ready to pay something for such a discovery: a stratagem, which would they fairly own, it might not only reconcile them to me, but screen them from the resentment of their lawful superiors, whom they daily abuse, only (as I charitably hope) to get that *by* them, which they cannot get *from* them.

I found this was not all: ill success in that had transported them to personal abuse, either of himself, or (what I think he could less forgive) of his friends. They had called men of virtue and honour bad men, long before he had either leisure or inclination to call them bad writers: and some had been such old offenders, that he had quite forgotten their persons as well as their slanders, till they were pleased to revive them.

Now what had Mr. POPE done before to incense them? He had published those works which are in the hands of everybody, in which not the least mention is made of any of them. And what has he done since? He has laughed, and written the *Dunciad*. What has that said of them? A very serious truth, which the public had said before, that they were dull. And what it had no sooner said, but they themselves were at great pains to procure, or even purchase, room in the prints to testify under their hands to the truth of it.

I should still have been silent, if either I had seen any inclination in my friend to be serious with such accusers, or if they had only meddled with his writings; since whoever publishes, puts himself on his trial by his country. But when his moral character was attacked, and in a manner from which neither truth nor virtue can secure the most innocent; in a manner which, though it annihilates the credit of the accusation with the just and impartial, yet aggravates very much the guilt of the accusers; I mean by authors *without names*: then I thought, since the danger was common to all, the concern ought to be so; and that it was an act of justice to detect the authors, not only on this account, but as many of them are the same who, for several years past, have made free with the greatest names in church and state, exposed to the world the private misfortunes of families, abused all, even to women, and whose prostituted papers (for one or other party, in the unhappy divisions of their country) have insulted the fallen, the friendless, the exiled, and the dead.

Besides this, which I take to be a public concern, I have already confessed I had a private one. I am one of that number who have long loved and esteemed Mr. POPE; and had often declared it was not his capacity or writings (which we ever thought the least valuable part of his character) but the honest, open, and beneficent man, that we most esteemed, and loved in him. Now if what these people say were believed, I must appear to all my friends either a fool, or a knave; either imposed on myself, or imposing on them; so that I am as much interested in the confutation of these calumnies as he is himself.

I am no author, and consequently not to be suspected either of jealousy or resentment against any of the men, of whom scarce one is known to me by sight; and as for their writings, I have sought them (on this one occasion) in vain, in the closets and libraries of all my acquaintance. I had still been in the dark if a gentleman had not procured me (I suppose from some of themselves, for they are generally much more dangerous friends than enemies) the passages I send you. I solemnly protest I have added nothing to the malice or absurdity of them; which it behoves me to declare, since the vouchers themselves will be so soon and so irrecoverably lost. You may in some measure prevent it, by preserving at least their titles, and discovering (as far as you can depend on the truth of your information) the names of the concealed authors.

The first objection I have heard made to the poem is, that the persons are too *obscure* for satire. The persons themselves, rather than allow the objection, would forgive the satire; and if one could be tempted to afford it a serious answer, were not all assassinates, popular insurrections, the insolence of the rabble without doors, and of domestics within, most wrongfully chastised, if the meanness of offenders indemnified them from punishment? On the contrary, obscurity renders them more dangerous, as less thought of: law can pronounce judgment only on open facts; morality alone can pass censure on intentions of mischief; so that for secret calumny, or the arrow flying in the dark, there is no public punishment left, but what a good writer inflicts.

The next objection is, that these sort of authors are *poor*. That might be pleaded as an excuse at the Old Bailey for lesser crimes than defamation (for 'tis the case of almost all who are tried there), but sure it can be none: for who will pretend that the robbing another of his reputation supplies the want of it in himself? I question not but such authors are poor, and heartily wish the objection were removed by any honest livelihood. But poverty is here the accident, not the subject: he who describes malice and villany to be pale and meagre, expresses not the least anger against paleness or leanness, but against malice and villainy. The apothecary in *Romeo and Juliet* is poor; but is he therefore justified in vending poison? Not but poverty itself becomes a just subject of satire, when it is the consequence of vice, prodigality, or neglect of one's lawful calling; for then it increases the public burden, fills the streets and highways with robbers, and the garrets with clippers, coiners, and weekly journalists.

But admitting that two or three of these offend less in their morals than in their writings; must poverty make nonsense sacred? If so, the fame of bad authors would be much better consulted than that of all the good ones in the world; and not one of a hundred had ever been called by his right name.

They mistake the whole matter: it is not charity to encourage them in the way they follow, but to get them out of it; for men are not bunglers because they are poor, but they are poor because they are bunglers.

Is it not pleasant enough to hear our authors crying out on the one hand, as if their persons and characters were too sacred for satire; and the public objecting on the other, that they are too mean even for ridicule? But whether bread or fame be their end, it must be allowed, our author, by and in this poem, has mercifully given them a little of both.

There are two or three who, by their rank and fortune, have no benefit from the former objections, supposing them good; and these I was sorry to see in such company. But if, without any provocation, two or three gentlemen will fall upon one, in an affair wherein his interest and reputation are equally embarked, they cannot, certainly, after they have been content to print themselves his enemies, complain of being put into the number of them.

Others, I am told, pretend to have been once his friends. Surely they are their enemies who say so, since nothing can be more odious than to treat a friend as they have done. But of this I cannot persuade myself, when I consider the constant and eternal aversion of all bad writers to a good one.

Such as claim a merit from being his admirers, I would gladly ask, if it lays him under a personal obligation? At that rate, he would be the most obliged humble servant in the world. I dare swear for these in particular, he never desired them to be his admirers, nor promised in return to be theirs: that had truly been a sign he was of their acquaintance; but would not the malicious world have suspected such an approbation of some motive worse than ignorance in the author of the *Essay on Criticism*? Be it as it will, the reasons of their admiration and of his contempt are equally subsisting, for his works and theirs are the very same that they were.

One, therefore, of their assertions I believe may be true, 'That he has a contempt for their writings.' And there is another, which would probably be sooner allowed by himself than by any good judge beside, 'That his own have found too much success with the public.' But as it cannot consist with his modesty to claim this as justice, it lies not on him, but entirely on the public, to defend its own judgment.

There remains what in my opinion might seem a better plea for these people than any they have made use of. If obscurity or poverty were to exempt a man from satire, much more should folly or dulness, which are still more involuntary; nay, as much so as personal deformity. But even this will not help them: deformity becomes an object of ridicule when a man sets up for being handsome; and so must dulness when he sets up for a wit. They are not ridiculed because ridicule in itself is, or ought to be, a pleasure, but because it is just to undeceive and vindicate the honest and unpretending part of mankind from imposition, because particular interest ought to yield to general, and a great number who are not naturally fools ought never to be made so, in complaisance to a few who are. Accordingly we find that in all ages, all vain pretenders, were they ever so poor or ever so dull, have been constantly the topics of the most candid satirists, from the Codrus of JUVENAL to the Damon of BOILEAU.

Having mentioned BOILEAU, the greatest poet and most judicious critic of his age and country, admirable for his talents, and yet perhaps more admirable for his judgment in the proper application of them, I cannot help remarking the resemblance betwixt him and our author, in qualities, fame, and fortune, in the distinctions shown them by their superiors, in the general esteem of their equals, and in their extended reputation amongst foreigners; in the latter of which ours has met with the better fate, as he has had for his translators persons of the most eminent rank and abilities in their respective nations. But the resemblance holds in nothing more than in their being equally abused by the ignorant pretenders to poetry of their times, of which not the least memory will remain but in their own writings, and in the notes made upon them. What BOILEAU has done in almost all his poems, our author has only in this: I dare answer for him he will do it in no more; and on this principle, of attacking few but who had slandered him, he could not have done it at all, had he been confined from censuring obscure and worthless persons, for scarce any other were his enemies. However, as the parity is so remarkable, I hope it will continue to the last; and if ever he shall give us an edition of this poem himself, I may see some of them treated as gently, on their repentance or better merit, as Perrault and Quinault were at last by BOILEAU.

In one point I must be allowed to think the character of our English poet the more amiable. He has not been a follower of fortune or success; he has lived with the great without flattery—been a friend to men in power, without pensions, from whom, as he asked, so he received no favour but what was done him in his friends. As his satires were the more just for being delayed, so were his panegyrics; bestowed only on such persons as he had familiarly known, only for such virtues as he had long observed in them, and only at such times as others cease to praise, if not begin to calumniate them, I mean, when out of power or out of fashion. A satire, therefore, on writers so notorious for the contrary practice, became no man so well as himself; as none, it is plain, was so little in their friendships, or so much in that of those whom they had most abused, namely, the greatest and best of all parties. Let me add a further reason, that, though engaged in their friendships, he never espoused their animosities; and can almost singly challenge this honour, not to have written a line of any man, which, through guilt, through shame, or through fear, through variety of fortune, or change of interests, he was ever unwilling to own.

I shall conclude with remarking what a pleasure it must be to every reader of humanity, to see all along, that our author in his very laughter is not indulging his own ill-nature, but only punishing that of others. As to his poem, those alone are capable of doing it justice, who, to use the words of a great writer, know how hard it is (with regard both to his subject and his manner) VETUSTIS DARE NOVITATEM, OBSOLETIS NITOREM, OBSCURIS LUCEM, FASTIDITIS GRATIAM. I am

Your most humble servant,
WILLIAM CLELAND.

St. James's
Dec. 22, 1728.

MARTIN SCRIBLERUS
of the POEM

    This poem, as it celebrateth the most grave and ancient of things, Chaos, Night, and Dulness; so is it of the most grave and ancient kind. Homer (saith Aristotle) was the first who gave the *form*, and, saith Horace, who adapted the *measure*, to heroic poesy. But even before this, may be rationally presumed from what the ancients have left written, was a piece by Homer, composed of like nature and matter with this of our poet. For of epic sort it appeareth to have been, yet of matter surely not unpleasant, witness what is reported of it by the learned archbishop Eustathius, in *Odyss.* x. And accordingly Aristotle, in his *Poetics*, chap. iv, does further set forth, that as the *Iliad* and *Odyssey* gave example to tragedy, so did this poem to comedy its first idea.

    From these authors also it should seem that the hero or chief personage of it was no less *obscure*, and his understanding and sentiments no less quaint and strange (if indeed not more so), than any of the actors of our poem. MARGITES was the name of this personage, whom antiquity recordeth to have been *Dunce the first*; and surely, from what we hear of him, not unworthy to be the root of so spreading a tree and so numerous a posterity. The poem therefore celebrating him was properly and absolutely a *Dunciad*; which, though now unhappily lost, yet is its nature sufficiently known by the infallible tokens aforesaid. And thus it doth appear that the first *Dunciad* was the first epic poem, written by Homer himself, and anterior even to the *Iliad* or *Odyssey*.

    Now, forasmuch as our poet had translated those two famous works of Homer which are yet left, he did conceive it in some sort his duty to imitate that also which was lost: and was therefore induced to bestow on it the same form which Homer's is reported to have had, namely, that of epic poem; with a title also framed after the ancient Greek manner, to wit, that of *Dunciad*.

    Wonderful it is that so few of the moderns have been stimulated to attempt some *Dunciad*! since, in the opinion of the multitude, it might cost less pain and oil than an imitation of the greater epic. But possible it is also, that, on due reflection, the maker might find it easier to paint a Charlemagne, a Brute, or a Godfrey, with just pomp and dignity heroic, than a Margites, a Codrus, or a Flecknoe.

    We shall next declare the occasion and the cause which moved our poet to this particular work. He lived in those days, when (after Providence had permitted the invention of printing as a scourge for the sins of the learned) paper also became so cheap, and printers so numerous, that a deluge of authors covered the land: whereby not only the peace of the honest unwriting subject was daily molested, but unmerciful demands were made of his applause, yea of his money, by such as would neither earn the one nor deserve the other. At the same time, the licence of the press was such, that it grew dangerous to refuse them either: for they would forthwith publish slanders unpunished, the authors being anonymous, and skulking under the wings of publishers, a set of men who never scrupled to vend either calumny or blasphemy, as long as the town would call for it.

    Now our author, living in those times, did conceive it an endeavour well worthy an honest satirist to dissuade the dull and punish the wicked, *the only way that was left*. In that public-spirited view he laid the plan of this poem, as the greatest service he was capable (without much hurt, or being slain) to render his dear country. First, taking things from their original, he considereth the causes creative of such authors—namely, *dulness* and *poverty*; the one born with them, the other contracted by neglect of their proper talents, through self-conceit of greater abilities. This truth he wrapped in an *allegory* (as the construction of epic poesy requireth), and feigns that one of these goddesses had taken up her abode with the other, and that they jointly inspired all such writers and such works. He proceedeth to show the *qualities* they bestow on these authors, and the *effects* they produce; then the *materials*, or *stock*, with which they furnish them; and (above all) that *self-opinion* which causeth it to seem to themselves vastly greater than it is, and is the prime motive of their setting up in this sad and sorry merchandise. The great power of these goddesses acting in alliance (whereof as the one is the mother of industry, so is the other of plodding) was to be exemplified in some *one, great* and *remarkable action*. And none could be more so than that which our poet hath chosen, viz. the restoration of the reign of Chaos and Night, by the ministry of Dulness their daughter, in the removal of her imperial seat from the city to the polite world; as the action of the *Aeneid* is the restoration of the empire of Troy, by the removal of the race from thence to Latium. But as Homer singing only the *wrath* of Achilles, yet includes in his poem the whole history of the Trojan war; in like manner our author hath drawn into this single action the whole history of Dulness and her children.

A *person* must next be fixed upon to support this action. This *phantom* in the poet's mind must have a *name*. He finds it to be —; and he becomes of course the hero of the poem.

The *fable* being thus, according to the best example, one and entire, as contained in the proposition, the *machinery* is a continued chain of allegories, setting forth the whole power, ministry, and empire of Dulness, extended through her subordinate instruments, in all her various operations.

This is branched into *episodes*, each of which hath its moral apart, though all conducive to the main end. The crowd assembled in the second book demonstrates the design to be more extensive than to bad poets only, and that we may expect other episodes of the patrons, encouragers, or paymasters of such authors, as occasion shall bring them forth. And the third book, if well considered, seemeth to embrace the whole world. Each of the games relateth to some or other vile class of writers: the first concerneth the Plagiary, to whom he giveth the name of More; the second the libellous Novelist, whom he styleth Eliza; the third, the flattering Dedicator; the fourth, the bawling Critic, or noisy Poet; the fifth, the dark and dirty Party-writer; and so of the rest; assigning to each some *proper name* or other, such as he could find.

As for the *characters*, the public hath already acknowledged how justly they are drawn. The manners are so depicted, and the sentiments so peculiar to those to whom applied, that surely to transfer them to any other or wiser personages would be exceeding difficult: and certain it is, that every person concerned, being consulted apart, hath readily owned the resemblance of every portrait, his own excepted. So Mr. Cibber calls them 'a parcel of *poor wretches*, so many '*silly flies*': but adds, 'our author's wit is remarkably more bare and barren whenever it would fall foul on Cibber, than upon any other person whatever.'

The *descriptions* are singular, the *comparisons* very quaint, the *narration* various, yet of one colour. The purity and chastity of *diction* is so preserved, that in the places most suspicious, not the *words* but only the *images* have been censured, and yet are those images no other than have been sanctified by ancient and classical authority (though, as was the manner of those good times, not so curiously wrapped up), yea, and commented upon by the most grave doctors and approved critics.

318

As it beareth the name of *epic*, it is thereby subjected to such severe indispensable rules as are laid on all neoterics—a strict imitation of the ancients; insomuch that any deviation, accompanied with whatever poetic beauties, hath always been censured by the sound critic. How exact that imitation hath been in this piece, appeareth not only by its general structure, but by particular allusions infinite, many whereof have escaped both the commentator and poet himself; yea, divers by his exceeding diligence are so altered and interwoven with the rest, that several have already been, and more will be, by the ignorant abused, as altogether and originally his own.

In a word, the whole poem proveth itself to be the work of our author when his faculties were in full vigour and perfection; at that exact time when years have ripened the judgment without diminishing the imagination: which by good critics is held to be punctually at *forty*. For at that season it was that Virgil finished his *Georgics*; and Sir Richard Blackmore at the like age composing his *Arthurs*, declared the same to be the very *acme* and pitch of life for epic poesy—though since he hath altered it to *sixty*, the year in which he published his *Alfred*. True it is, that the talents for *criticism*—namely smartness, quick censure, vivacity of remark, certainty of asseveration, indeed all but acerbity—seem rather the gifts of youth than of riper age. But it is far otherwise in *poetry*; witness the works of Mr. Rymer and Mr. Dennis, who, beginning with criticism, became afterwards such poets as no age hath paralleled. With good reason, therefore, did our author choose to write his *Essay* on that subject at twenty, and reserve for his maturer years this great and wonderful work of the *Dunciad*.

RICARDUS ARISTARCHUS
OF THE
HERO OF THE POEM

Of the nature of *Dunciad* in general, whence derived, and on what authority founded, as well as of the art and conduct of this our poem in particular, the learned and laborious Scriblerus hath, according to his manner, and with tolerable share of judgment, dissertated. But when he cometh to speak of the *person* of the *hero* fitted for such poem, in truth he miserably halts and hallucinates. For, misled by one Monsieur Bossu, a Gallic critic, he prateth of I cannot tell what *phantom of a hero*, only raised up to support the fable. A putrid conceit! As if Homer and Virgil, like modern undertakers, who first build their house, and then seek out for a tenant, had contrived the story of a war and a wandering, before they once thought either of Achilles or Aeneas. We shall therefore set our good brother and the world also right in this particular, by giving our word, that, in the *greater epic*, the prime intention of the muse is to exalt heroic virtue, in order to propagate the love of it among the children of men; and, consequently, that the poet's first thought must needs be turned upon a real subject meet for laud and celebration; not one whom he is to make, but one whom he may find, truly illustrious. This is the *primum mobile* of his poetic world, whence everything is to receive life and motion. For this subject being found, he is immediately ordained, or rather acknowledged, a *hero*, and put upon such action as befitteth the dignity of his character.

But the muse ceases not here her eagle-flight. For sometimes, satiated with the contemplation of these *suns* of glory, she turneth downward on her wing, and darts like lightning on the *goose* and *serpent* kind. For we may apply to the muse in her various moods, what an ancient master of wisdom affirmeth of the gods in general: '*Si Dii non irascuntur impiis et injustis, nec pios utique justosque diligunt. In rebus enim diversis, aut in utramque partem moveri necesse est, aut in neutram. Itaque qui bonos diligit, & malos odit; & qui malos non odit, nec bonos diligit. Quia & diligere bonos ex odio malorum venit; & malos odisse ex bonorum caritate descendit.*' Which, in our vernacular idiom, may be thus interpreted: 'If the gods be not provoked at evil men, neither are they delighted with the good and just. For contrary objects must either excite contrary affections, or no affections at all. So that he who loveth good men must at the same time hate the bad; and he who hateth not bad men cannot love the good; because to love good men proceedeth from an aversion to evil, and to hate evil men from a tenderness to the good.' From this delicacy of the Muse arose the *little epic*, (more lively and choleric than her elder sister, whose bulk and complexion incline her to the phlegmatic), and for this some notorious vehicle of vice and folly was sought out, to make thereof an example. An early instance of which (nor could it escape the accurate Scriblerus) the father of epic poem himself affordeth us. From him the practice descended to the Greek dramatic poets, his offspring, who, in the composition of their *tetralogy*, or set of four pieces, were wont to make the last a *satiric tragedy*. Happily one of these ancient *Dunciads* (as we may well term it) is come down unto us amongst the tragedies of the poet Euripides. And what doth the reader suppose may be the subject thereof? Why, in truth, and it is worthy observation, the unequal contention of an *old, dull, debauched buffoon Cyclops*, with the heaven-directed favourite of Minerva; who, after having quietly borne all the monster's obscene and impious ribaldry, endeth the farce in punishing him with the mark of an indelible brand in his *forehead*. May we not then be excused, if for the future we consider the epics of Homer, Virgil, and Milton, together with this our poem, as a complete tetralogy, in which the last worthily holdeth the place or station of the *satiric* piece?

Proceed we therefore in our subject. It hath been long, and, alas for pity! still remaineth a question, whether the hero of the *greater epic* should be an *honest man*? or, as the French critics express it, un *honnête homme*: but it never admitted of any doubt, but that the hero of the *little epic* should *not* be so. Hence, to the advantage of our *Dunciad*, we may observe how much juster the *moral* of that poem must needs be, where so important a question is previously decided.

But then it is not every knave, nor (let me add) every fool, that is a fit subject for a *Dunciad*. There must still exist some analogy, if not resemblance of qualities, between the heroes of the two poems, and this in order to admit what neoteric critics call the *parody*, one of the liveliest graces of the little epic. Thus, it being agreed that the constituent qualities of the greater epic hero are *wisdom*, *bravery*, and *love*, from whence springeth *heroic virtue*; it followeth that those of the lesser epic hero should be *vanity*, *impudence*, and *debauchery*, from which happy assemblage resulteth *heroic dulness*, the never-dying subject of this our poem.

This being confessed, come we now to particulars. It is the character of true *wisdom* to seek its chief support and confidence within itself, and to place that support in the resources which proceed from a conscious rectitude of will.—And are the advantages of *vanity*, when arising to the heroic standard, at all short of this self-complacence? Nay, are they not, in the opinion of the enamoured owner, far beyond it? 'Let the world (will such an one say) impute to me what folly or weakness they please; but till *wisdom* can give me something that will make me more heartily happy, I am content to be GAZED AT.' This, we see, is *vanity* according to the *heroic* gauge or measure; not that low and ignoble species which pretendeth to *virtues* we *have not*, but the laudable ambition of being *gazed at* for glorying in those *vices* which everybody knows *we have*. 'The world may ask (says he) why I make my follies public? Why not? I have passed my time very pleasantly with them.' In short, there is no sort of vanity such a hero would scruple, but that which might go near to degrade him from his high station in this our *Dunciad*; namely, 'Whether it would not be *vanity* in him to take shame to himself for *not being a wise man?*'

Bravery, the second attribute of the true hero, is courage manifesting itself in every limb; while its correspondent virtue in the mock hero is that same courage all collected into the *face*. And as power when drawn together must needs have more force and spirit than when dispersed, we generally find this kind of courage in so high and heroic a degree, that it insults not only men, but gods. Mezentius is, without doubt, the bravest character in all the *Aeneis*; but how? His bravery, we know, was a high courage of blasphemy. And can we say less of this brave man's, who, having told us that he placed 'his *summum bonum* in those follies, which he was not content barely to possess, but would likewise glory in,' adds, '*If I am misguided*, 'TIS NATURE'S FAULT, *and I follow* HER.' Nor can we be mistaken in making this happy quality a species of *courage*, when we consider those illustrious marks of it which made his *face* 'more known' (as he justly boasteth) than most in the kingdom,' and his *language* to consist of what we must allow to be the most *daring* figure of speech, that which is taken from the *name of God*.

Gentle love, the next ingredient in the true hero's composition, is a mere bird of passage, or (as Shakespeare calls it) *summer-teeming lust*, and evaporates in the heat of *youth*; doubtless, by that refinement, it suffers in passing through those *certain strainers* which our poet somewhere speaketh of. But when it is let alone to work upon the *lees*, it acquireth strength by *old age*, and becometh a lasting ornament to the little epic. It is true, indeed, there is one objection to its fitness for such a use: for not only the ignorant may think it *common*, but it is admitted to be so, even by him who best knoweth its value. 'Don't you think,' argueth he, 'to say only *a man has his whore*, ought to go for little or nothing? Because *defendit numerus*; take the first ten thousand men you meet, and I believe you would be no loser if you betted ten to one that every single sinner of them, one with another, had been guilty of the same frailty.' But here he seemeth not to have done justice to himself: the man is sure enough a hero who hath his lady at fourscore. How doth his modesty herein lessen the merit of a *whole well-spent* life: not taking to himself the commendation (which Horace accounted the greatest in a theatrical character) of continuing to the very *dregs* the same he was from the beginning,

—*Servetur ad* IMUM
Qualis ab incepto processerat—

But let us farther remark, that the calling her *his* whore, implieth she was *his own*, and not his *neighbour's*. Truly a commendable continence! and such as Scipio himself must have applauded. For how much self-denial was necessary not to covet his neighbour's whore? and what disorders must the coveting her have occasioned, in that society, where (according to tin political calculator) *nine* in *ten* of all ages have their *concubines?*

We have now, as briefly as we could devise, gone through the three constituent qualities of either hero. But it is not in any, or all of these, that heroism properly or essentially resideth. It is a lucky result rather from the collision of these lively qualities against one another. Thus, as from wisdom, bravery, and love, ariseth *magnanimity*, the object of *admiration*, which is the aim of the greater epic; so from vanity, impudence, and debauchery, springeth *buffoonery*, the source of *ridicule*, that 'laughing ornament,' as he well termeth it, of the little epic.

He is not ashamed (God forbid he ever should be ashamed!) of this character; who deemeth, that not *reason* but *risibility* distinguisheth the human species from the brutal. 'As nature (saith this profound philosopher) distinguished our species from the mute creation by our risibility, her design MUST have been by *that faculty* as evidently to raise our HAPPINESS, as by OUR *os sublime* (OUR ERECTED FACES) to lift the dignity of our FORM above them.' All this considered, how complete a hero must he be, as well as how *happy* a man, whose risibility lieth not barely in his *muscles* as in the common sort, but (as himself informeth us) in his very *spirits?* And whose *os sublime* is not simply an *erect face*, but a brazen head, as should seem by his comparing it with one of iron, said to belong to the late king of Sweden!

But whatever personal qualities a hero may have, the examples of Achilles and Aeneas show us, that all those are of small avail, without the constant *assistance of the* GODS: for the subversion and erection of empires have never been judged the work of man. How greatly soever then we may esteem of his high talents, we can hardly conceive his personal prowess alone sufficient to restore the decayed empire of Dulness. So weighty an achievement must require the particular favour and protection of the GREAT; who being the natural patrons and supporters of *letters*, as the ancient gods were of Troy, must first be drawn off and engaged in another interest, before the total subversion of them can be accomplished. To surmount, therefore, this last and greatest difficulty, we have in this excellent man a professed favourite and intimado of the great. And look of what force ancient piety was to draw the gods into the party of Aeneas, that, and much stronger is modern incense, to engage the great in the party to Dulness.

Thus have we essayed to portray or shadow out this noble imp of fame. But now the impatient reader will be apt to say, if so many and various graces go to the making up a hero, what mortal shall suffice to bear this character I'll hath he read, who sees not in every trace of this picture, that *individual*, ALL-ACCOMPLISHED PERSON, in whom these rare virtues and lucky circumstances have agreed to meet and concentre with the strongest lustre and fullest harmony.

The good Scriblerus indeed, nay, the world itself, might be imposed on in the late spurious editions, by I can't tell what *sham-hero*, or *phantom*. But it was not so easy to impose on HIM whom this egregious error most of all concerned. For no sooner had the fourth book laid open the high and swelling scene, but he recognized his own heroic acts: And when he came to the words,

Soft on her lap her laureate son reclines,

(though *laureate* imply no more than *one crowned with laurel*, as befitteth any associate or consort in empire) he ROARED (like a lion) and VINDICATED HIS RIGHT OF FAME. Indeed not without cause, he being there represented as *fast asleep*; so unbeseeming the eye of empire, which, like that of Providence, should never slumber. 'Hah!' saith he, 'fast asleep it seems! that's a little too strong. Pert and dull at least you might have allowed me, but as seldom asleep as any fool.' However, the injured hero may comfort himself with this reflection, that though it be *sleep*, yet it is not the *sleep of death*, but of *immortality*. Here he will *live* at least, though not *awake*; and in no worse condition than many an enchanted warrior before him. The famous Durandarte, for instance, was, like him, cast into a long slumber by Merlin, the British bard and necromancer; and his example for submitting to it with so good a grace might be of use to our hero. For this disastrous knight being sorely pressed or driven to make his answer by several *persons of quality*, only replied with a sigh, '*Patience, and shuffle the cards*'.

But now, as nothing in this world, no not the most sacred or perfect things either of religion or government, can escape the teeth or tongue of envy, methinks I already hear these carpers objecting to the clear title of our hero.

'It would never' (say they) 'have been esteemed sufficient to make a hero for the *Iliad* or *Aeneis*, that Achilles was brave enough to overturn one empire, or Aeneas pious enough to raise another, had they not been goddess-born and princes bred. What then did this author mean by erecting a player instead of one of his patrons, (a person 'never a hero even on the stage,') to this dignity of colleague in the empire of Dulness, and achiever of a work that neither old Omar, Attila, nor John of Leiden could entirely compass.'

To all this we have, as we conceive, a sufficient answer from the Roman historian, *Fabrum esse suae quemque fortunae: Every man is the Smith of his own fortune.* The politic Florentine Nicholas Machiavel goeth still farther, and affirms that a man needs but to *believe himself a hero* to be one of the best. 'Let him,' saith he, 'but fancy himself capable of the highest things, and he will of course be able to achieve them.' Laying this down as a principle, it will certainly and incontestably follow, that, if ever hero *was* such a character, OURS *is*: for if ever man *thought* himself such, OURS *doth*. Hear how he constantly paragons himself, at one time to ALEXANDER The Great and CHARLES XII of SWEDEN, for the excess and delicacy of his ambition; to HENRY the IV of FRANCE, for honest policy; to the first BRUTUS for love of liberty; and to Sir ROBERT WALPOLE, for good government while in power: At another time, to the godlike Socrates, for his diversions and amusements; to HORACE, MONTAIGNE, and Sir WILLIAM TEMPLE, for an elegant vanity that makes them for ever read and admired; to TWO Lord CHANCELLORS, for law, from whom, when confederate against him at the bar, he carried away the prize of eloquence; and, to say all in a word, to the right reverend the Lord BISHOP Of LONDON himself, in the art of writing *pastoral letters*.

Nor did his *actions* fall short of the sublimity of his conceptions. In his early youth he *met the revolution* at Nottingham face to face, at a time when his betters contented themselves with *following* her. But he shone in his courts as well as camps: he was *called up* when *the nation fell in labor* of this *Revolution*: a gossip at her christening, with the Bishop and the ladies.

As to his *birth*, it is true he pretendeth no relation either to heathen god or goddess; but, what is as good, he was descended from a *maker* of both. And that he did not pass himself on the world for a hero, as well by birth as education, was his own fault; for his lineage he bringeth into his life as an anecdote, and is sensible he bad it in his power *to be thought nobody's son at all*: and what is that but coming into the world a hero?

There is in truth another objection of greater weight, namely. 'That this hero still existeth, and hath not yet finished his earthly course. For if Solon said well, that no man could be called happy till his death, surely much less can anyone, till then, be pronounced a hero: this species of men being far more subject than others to the caprices of fortune and humour.' But to this also we have an answer, that will be deemed (we hope) decisive. It cometh from *himself*, who, to cut this dispute short, hath solemnly protested that *he will never change or amend*.

With regard to his *vanity*, he declareth that nothing shall ever part them. 'Nature,' saith he, 'hath amply supplied me in vanity; a pleasure which neither the pertness of wit nor the gravity of wisdom will ever persuade me to part with.' Our poet had charitably endeavoured to administer a cure to it, but he telleth us plainly, 'My superiors perhaps may be mended by him, but for my part I own myself incorrigible. I look upon my follies as the best part of my fortune.' And with good reason: We see to what they have brought him!

Secondly, as to *buffoonery*, 'Is it,' saith he, 'a time of day for me to leave off these fooleries, and set up a new character? I can no more put off my follies than my skin; I have often tried, but they stick too close to me; nor am I sure my friends are displeased with them, for in this light I afford them frequent matter of mirth,' etc. etc. Having then so publicly declared himself *incorrigible*, he is become *dead in law*, (I mean the *law epopoeian*) and descendeth to the poet as his property: who may take him, and deal with him, as if he had been dead as long as an old Egyptian hero; that is to say, *embowel* and *embalm him for posterity*.

Nothing therefore (we conceive) remains to hinder his own prophecy of himself from taking immediate effect. A rare felicity! and what few prophets have had the satisfaction to see alive! Nor can we conclude better than with that extraordinary one of his, which is conceived in these oraculous words, 'MY DULNESS WILL FIND SOMEBODY TO DO IT RIGHT'.

ARGUMENT
TO
BOOK the FIRST

The proposition, the invocation, and the inscription. Then the original of the great empire of Dulness, and cause of the continuance thereof. The college of the Goddess in the City, with her private academy for poets in particular; the governors of it, and the four cardinal virtues. Then the poem hastes into the midst of things, presenting her, on the evening of a Lord Mayor's day, revolving the long succession of her sons, and the glories past and to come. She fixes her eye on Bays, to be the instrument of that great event which is the subject of the poem. He is described pensive among his books, giving up the cause, and apprehending the period of her empire. After debating whether to betake himself to the church, or to gaming, or to party-writing, he raises an altar of proper books, and (making first his solemn prayer and declaration) purposes thereon to sacrifice all his unsuccessful writings. As the pile is kindled, the Goddess, beholding the flame from her seat, flies and puts it out, by casting upon it the poem of Thule. She forthwith reveals herself to him, transports him to her temple, unfolds her arts, and initiates him into her mysteries; then announcing the death of Eusden the Poet Laureate, anoints him, carries him to court, and proclaims him successor.

THE
DUNCIAD
TO
Dr JONATHAN SWIFT
Book the First

The Mighty Mother, and her son who brings
The Smithfield muses to the ear of kings,
I sing. Say you, her instruments the great!
Called to this work by Dulness, Jove, and Fate;
You by whose care, in vain decried and cursed,
Still Dunce the second reigns like Dunce the first;

Say how the Goddess bade Britannia sleep,
And poured her spirit o'er the land and deep.

In eldest time, e'er mortals writ or read,
E'er Pallas issued from the Thunderer's head,
Dulness o'er all possessed her ancient right,
Daughter of Chaos and eternal Night:
Fate in their dotage this fair idiot gave,
Gross as her sire, and as her mother grave,
Laborious, heavy, busy, bold, and blind,
She ruled, in native anarchy, the mind.

Still her old empire to restore she tries,
For, born a goddess, Dulness never dies.

O thou! whatever title please thine ear,
Dean, Drapier, Bickerstaff, or Gulliver!
Whether thou choose Cervantes' serious air,
Or laugh and shake in Rabelais' easy chair,
Or praise the court, or magnify mankind,
Or thy grieved country's copper chains unbind;
From thy Boeotia though her power retires,
Mourn not, my SWIFT, at ought our realm acquires,
Here pleased behold her mighty wings out-spread
To hatch a new Saturnian age of lead.

Close to those walls where Folly holds her throne,
And laughs to think Monroe would take her down,
Where o'er the gates, by his famed by father's hand
Great Cibber's brazen, brainless brothers stand;
One cell there is, concealed from vulgar eye,
The cave of poverty and poetry.
Keen, hollow winds howl through the bleak recess,
Emblem of music caused by emptiness.
Hence bards, like Proteus long in vain tied down,
Escape in monsters, and amaze the town.
Hence miscellanies spring, the weekly boast
Of Curll's chaste press, and Lintot's rubric post:
Hence hymning Tyburn's elegiac lines,
Hence *Journals, Medleys, Merc'ries, Magazines*:
Sepulchral lies, our holy walls to grace,
And New Year odes, and all the Grub Street race.

In clouded majesty here Dulness shone;
Four guardian virtues, round, support her throne:
Fierce champion Fortitude, that knows no fears
Of hisses, blows, or want, or loss of ears:
Calm Temperance, whose blessings those partake
Who hunger, and who thirst for scribbling sake:
Prudence, whose glass presents th' approaching goal.
Poetic justice, with her lifted scale,
Where, in nice balance, truth with gold she weighs,
And solid pudding against empty praise.

Here she beholds the chaos dark and deep,
Where nameless somethings in their causes sleep,
Till genial Jacob, or a warm third day,
Call forth each mass, a poem, or a play:
How hints, like spawn, scarce quick in embryo lie,
How new-born nonsense first is taught to cry,
Maggots half-formed in rhyme exactly meet,
And learn to crawl upon poetic feet.
Here one poor word an hundred clenches makes,
And ductile dullness new meanders takes;
There motley images her fancy strike,
Figures ill paired, and similes unlike.
She sees a mob of metaphors advance,
Pleased with the madness of the mazy dance:
How tragedy and comedy embrace;
How farce and epic get a jumbled race;
How time himself stands still at her command,
Realms shift their place, and ocean turns to land.
Here gay description Egypt glads with showers,
Or gives to Zembla fruits, to Barca flowers;
Glittering with ice here hoary hills are seen,
There painted valleys of eternal green,
In cold December fragrant chaplets blow,
And heavy harvests nod beneath the snow.
    All these, and more, the cloud-compelling Queen
Beholds through fogs, that magnify the scene.
She, tinselled o'er in robes of varying hues,
With self-applause her wild creation views;
Sees momentary monsters rise and fall,
And with her own fools-colours gilds them all.
    'Twas on the day, when * * rich and grave,
Like Cimon, triumphed both on land and wave:
(Pomps without guilt, of bloodless swords and maces,
Glad chains, warm furs, broad banners, and broad faces)
Now night descending, the proud scene was o'er,
But lived, in Settle's numbers, one day more.
Now mayors and shrieves all hushed and satiate lay,
Yet eat, in dreams, the custard of the day;
While pensive poets painful vigils keep,
Sleepless themselves, to give their readers sleep.
Much to the mindful Queen the feast recalls
What city swans once sung within the walls;
Much she revolves their arts, their ancient praise,
And sure succession down from Heywood's days.
She saw, with joy, the line immortal run,
Each sire impressed and glaring in his son:
So watchful Bruin forms, with plastic care,
Each growing lump, and brings it to a bear.

She saw old Prynne in restless Daniel shine,
And Eusden eke out Blackmore's endless line;
She saw slow Philips creep like Tate's poor page,
And all the mighty mad in Dennis rage.
  In each she marks her image full expressed,
But chief in BAYS'S monster-breeding breast;
Bays, formed by nature stage and town to bless,
And act, and be, a coxcomb with success.
Dulness with transport eyes the lively dunce,
Remembering she herself was pertness once.
Now (shame to fortune!) an ill run at play
Blanked his bold visage, and a thin third day:
Swearing and supperless the hero sate,
Blasphemed his gods, the dice, and damned his fate.
Then gnawed his pen, then dashed it on the ground,
Sinking from thought to thought, a vast profound!
Plunged for his sense, but found no bottom there,
Yet wrote and floundered on, in mere despair.
Round him much embryo, much abortion lay,
Much future ode, and abdicated play;
Nonsense precipitate, like running lead,
That slipped through cracks and zigzags of the head;
All that on folly frenzy could beget,
Fruits of dull heat, and sooterkins of wit.
Next, o'er his books his eyes began to roll,
In pleasing memory of all he stole,
How here he sipped, how there he plundered snug
And sucked all o'er, like an industrious bug.
Here lay poor Fletcher's half-eat scenes, and here
The frippery of crucified Molière;
There hapless Shakespeare, yet of Tibbald sore,
Wished he had blotted for himself before.
The rest on outside merit but presume,
Or serve (like other fools) to fill a room;
Such with their shelves as due proportion hold,
Or their fond parents dressed in red and gold;
Or where the pictures for the page atone,
And Quarles is saved by beauties not his own.
Here swells the shelf with Ogilby the great;
There, stamped with arms, Newcastle shines complete:
Here all his suffering brotherhood retire,
And 'scape the martyrdom of jakes and fire:
A Gothic library! Of Greece and Rome
Well purged, and worthy Settle, Banks, and Broome.
  But, high above, more solid learning shone,
The classics of an age that heard of none;
There Caxton slept, with Wynkyn at his side,
One clasped in wood, and one in strong cow-hide;

There, saved by spice, like mummies, many a year,
Dry bodies of divinity appear:
De Lyra there a dreadful front extends,
And here the groaning shelves Philemon bends.
   Of these twelve volumes, twelve of amplest size,
Redeemed from tapers and defrauded pies,
Inspired he seizes: these an altar raise:
An hecatomb of pure, unsullied lays
That altar crowns: a folio commonplace
Founds the whole pile, of all his works the base:
Quartos, octavos, shape the lessening pyre;
A twisted birthday ode completes the spire.
   Then he: 'Great tamer of all human art!
First in my care, and ever at my heart;
Dulness! Whose good old cause I yet defend,
With whom my muse began, with whom shall end;
E'er since Sir Fopling's periwig was praise,
To the last honours of the butt and bays:
O thou! of business the directing soul!
To this our head like bias to the bowl,
Which, as more ponderous, made its aim more true,
Obliquely waddling to the mark in view:
O! ever gracias to perplexed mankind,
Still spread a healing mist before the mind;
And lest we err by wit's wild dancing light,
Secure us kindly in our native night.
Or, if to wit a coxcomb make pretence,
Guard the sure barrier between that and sense;
Or quite unravel all the reasoning thread,
And hang some curious cobweb in its stead!
As, forced from wind-guns, lead itself can fly,
And ponderous slugs cut swiftly through the sky;
As clocks to weight their nimble motion owe,
The wheels above urged by the load below:
Me emptiness, and Dulness could inspire,
And were my elasticity, and fire.
Some daemon stole my pen (forgive th'offence)
And once betrayed me into common sense:
Else all my prose and verse were much the same;
This, prose on stilts, that, poetry fallen lame.
Did on the stage my fops appear confined?
My life gave ampler lessons to mankind.
Did the dead letter unsuccessful prove?
The brisk example never failed to move.
Yet sure had heaven decreed to save the state,
Heaven had decreed these works a longer date.
Could Troy be saved by any single hand,
This grey-goose weapon must have made her stand.

What can I now? my Fletcher cast aside,
Take up the Bible, once my better guide?
Or tread the path by venturous heroes trod,
This box my thunder, this right hand my god?
Or chaired at White's amidst the doctors sit,
Teach oaths to gamesters, and to nobles wit?
Or bidst thou rather party to embrace?
(A friend to party thou, and all her race;
'Tis the same rope at different ends they twist;
To Dulness Ridpath is as dear as Mist.)
Shall I, like Curtius, desperate in my zeal,
O'er head and ears plunge for the commonweal?
Or rob Rome's ancient geese of all their glories,
And cackling save the monarchy of Tories?
Hold—to the minister I more incline;
To serve his cause, O Queen! is serving thine.
And see! Thy very gazetteers give o'er,
Even Ralph repents, and Henley writes no more.
What then remains? Ourself. Still, still remain
Cibberian forehead, and Cibberian brain.
This brazen brightness, to the 'squire so dear;
This polished hardness, that reflects the peer;
This arch absurd, that sit and fool delights;
This mess, tossed up of Hockley Hole and White's;
Where dukes and butchers join to wreathe my crown,
At once the bear and fiddle of the town.
    O born in sin, and forth in folly brought!
Works damned, or to be damned! (your father's fault)
Go, purified by flames ascend the sky,
My better and more Christian progeny!
Unstained, untouched, and yet in maiden sheets;
While all your smutty sisters walk the streets.
Ye shall not beg, like gratis-given Bland,
Sent with a pass, and vagrant through the land;
Not sail, with Ward, to ape-and-monkey climes,
Where vile mundungus trucks for viler rhymes;
Not sulphur-tipped, emblaze an alehouse fire;
Not wrap up oranges, to pelt your sire!
O! pass more innocent, in infant state,
To the mild limbo of our father Tate:
Or peaceably forgot, at once be blessed
In Shadwell's bosom with eternal rest!
Soon to that mass of nonsense to return,
Where things destroyed are swept to things unborn.'
    With that, a tear (portentous sign of grace!)
Stole from the master of the sevenfold face:
And thrice he lifted high the birthday brand,
And thrice he dropped it from his quivering hand;

Then lights the structure, with averted eyes:
The rolling smokes involve the sacrifice.
The opening clouds disclose each work by turns,
Now flames the *Cid*, and now *Perolla* burns;
Great *Caesar* roars, and hisses in the fires;
King John in silence modestly expires:
No merit now the dear *Nonjuror* claims,
Molière's old stubble in a moment flames.
Tears gushed again, as from pale Priam's eyes
When the last blaze sent Ilion to the skies.

    Roused by the light, old Dulness heaved the head;
Then snatched a sheet of Thulè from her bed,
Sudden she flies, and whelms it o'er the pyre;
Down sink the flames, and with a hiss expire.

    Her ample presence fills up all the place;
A veil of fogs dilates her awful face:
Great in her charms! as when on shrieves and mayors
She looks, and breathes herself into their airs.
She bids him wait her to her sacred dome:
Well pleased he entered, and confessed his home.
So spirits ending their terrestrial race,
Ascend, and recognize their native place.
This the Great Mother dearer held than all
The clubs of quidnuncs, or her own Guildhall:
Here stood her opium, here she nursed her owls,
And here she planned th' imperial seat of Fools.

    Here to her chosen all her works she shows;
Prose swelled to verse, verse loitering into prose:
How random thoughts now meaning chance to find,
Now leave all memory of sense behind:
How prologues into prefaces decay,
And these to notes are frittered quite away:
How index-learning turns no student pale,
Yet holds the eel of science by the tail:
How, with less reading than makes felons 'scape,
Less human genius than God gives an ape,
Small thanks to France, and none to Rome or Greece,
A past, vamped, future, old, revived, new piece,
'Twixt Plautus, Fletcher, Shakespeare, and Corneille,
Can make a Cibber, Tibbald, or Ozell.

    The Goddess then, o'er his anointed head,
With mystic words, the sacred opium shed.
And lo! her bird, (a monster of a fowl,
Something betwixt a Heidegger and owl,)
Perched on his crown: 'All hail! and hail again,
My son! The promised land expects thy reign.
Know, Eusden thirsts no more for sack or praise;
He sleeps among the dull of ancient days;

Safe, where no critics damn, no duns molest,
Where wretched Withers, Ward, and Gildon rest,
And high-born Howard, more majestic sire,
With fool of quality completes the quire.
Thou Cibber! thou, his laurel shalt support,
Folly, my son, has still a friend at court.
Lift up your gates, ye princes, see him come!
Sound, sound ye viols, be the catcall dumb!
Bring, bring the madding bay, the drunken vine;
The creeping, dirty, courtly ivy join.
And thou! his aide de camp, lead on my sons,
Light-armed with points, antitheses, and puns.
Let bawdry, Billingsgate, my daughters dear,
Support his front, and oaths bring up the rear:
And under his, and under Archer's wing,
Gaming and Grub Street skulk behind the king.
    O! when shall rise a monarch all our own,
And I, a nursing-mother, rock the throne,
'Twixt prince and people close the curtain draw,
Shade him from light, and cover him from law;
Fatten the courtier, starve the learned band,
And suckle armies, and dry-nurse the land:
Till senates nod to lullabies divine,
And all be asleep, as at an ode of thine.'

    She ceased. Then swells the Chapel Royal throat:
'God save King Cibber!' mounts in every note.
Familiar White's, 'God save king Colley!' cries;
'God save King Colley!' Drury Lane replies:
To Needham's quick the voice triumphal rode,
But pious Needham dropped the name of God;
Back to the Devil the last echoes roll,
And 'Coll!' each butcher roars at Hockley Hole.
    So when Jove's block descended from on high
(As sings thy great forefather Ogilby)
Loud thunder to its bottom shook the bog,
And the hoarse nation croaked, 'God save King Log!'

The End of the FIRST BOOK.

The
Dunciad
Book the Second

ARGUMENT

The King being proclaimed, the solemnity is graced with public games *and sports of various kinds; not instituted by the hero, as by Aeneas in Virgil, but for greater honour by the goddess in person (in like manner as the games Pythia, Isthmia, etc., were anciently said to be ordained by the gods, and as Thetis herself appearing, according to Homer,* Odyss. 24. *proposed the prizes in honour of her son Achilles). Hither flock the poets and critics, attended, as is but just, with their patrons and booksellers. The Goddess is first pleased, for her disport, to propose games to the* booksellers, *and setteth up the phantom of a poet, which they contend to overtake. The races described, with their divers accidents. Next, the game for a* poetess. *Then follow the exercises for the* poets, *of* tickling, vociferating, diving: *The first holds forth the arts and practices of* dedicators; *the second of* disputants *and* fustian poets; *the third of* profound, dark, *and* dirty party-writers. *Lastly, for the* critics, *the goddess proposes (with great propriety) an exercise, not of their parts, but their patience, in hearing the works of two voluminous authors, one in* verse, *and the other in* prose, *deliberately read, without sleeping. The various effects of which, with the several degrees and manners of their operation, are here set forth; till the whole number, not of critics only, but of spectators, actors, and all present, fall fast asleep; which naturally and necessarily ends the games.*

High on a gorgeous seat, that far out-shone
Henley's gilt tub, or Flecknoe's Irish throne,
Or that where on her Curlls the public pours,
All-bounteous, fragrant grains and golden showers,
Great Cibber sate: the proud Parnassian sneer,
The conscious simper, and the jealous leer,
Mix on his look: all eyes direct their rays
On him, and crowds turn coxcombs as they gaze.
His peers shine round him with reflected grace,
New edge their dulness, and new bronze their face.
So from the sun's broad beam, in shallow urns
Heaven's twinkling sparks draw light, and point their horns.
　　Not with more glee, by hands pontific crowned,
With scarlet hats wide-waving circled round,
Rome in her Capitol saw Querno sit,
Throned on seven hills, the Antichrist of wit.
　　And now the queen, to glad her sons, proclaims
By herald hawkers, high heroic games.
They summon all her race: an endless band
Pours forth, and leaves unpeopled half the land.
A motley mixture! in long wigs, in bags,
In silks, in crapes, in garters, and in rags,
From drawing-rooms, from colleges, from garrets,

On horse, on foot, in hacks, and gilded chariots:
All who true dunces in her cause appeared,
And all who knew those dunces to reward.
    Amid that area wide they took their stand,
Where the tall maypole once o'er-looked the Strand;
But now (so ANNE and piety ordain)
A church collects the saints of Drury Lane.
    With authors, stationers obeyed the call,
(The field of glory is a field for all).
Glory and gain the industrious tribe provoke;
And gentle Dulness ever loves a joke.
A poet's form she placed before their eyes,
And bade the nimblest racer seize the prize;
No meagre, muse-rid mope, adust and thin,
In a dun nightgown of his own loose skin;
But such a bulk as no twelve bards could raise,
Twelve starveling bards of these degenerate days.
All as a partridge plump, full-fed, and fair,
She formed this image of well-bodied air;
With pert flat eyes she windowed well its head;
A brain of feathers, and a heart of lead;
And empty words she gave, and sounding strain,
But senseless, lifeless! idol void and vain!
Never was dashed out, at one lucky hit,
A fool, so just a copy of a wit;
So like, that critics said, and courtiers swore,
A wit it was, and called the phantom More.
    All gaze with ardour: some a poet's name,
Others a sword-knot and laced suit inflame.
But lofty Lintot in the circle rose:
'This prize is mine; who tempt it are my foes;
With me began this genius, and shall end.'
He spoke: and who with Lintot shall contend?
    Fear held them mute. Alone, untaught to fear,
Stood dauntless Curll: 'Behold that rival here!
The race by vigour, not by vaunts is won;
So take the hindmost Hell.' He said, and run.
Swift as a bard the bailiff leaves behind,
He left huge Lintot, and out-stripped the wind.
As when a dab-chick waddles through the copse
On feet and wings, and flies, and wades, and hops;
So labouring on, with shoulders, hands, and head,
Wide as a wind-mill all his figure spread,
With arms expanded Bernard rows his state,
And left-legged Jacob seems to emulate:
Full in the middle way there stood a lake,
Which Curll's Corinna chanced that morn to make:
(Such was her wont, at early dawn to drop

Her evening cates before his neighbour's shop,)
Here fortuned Curll to slide; loud shout the band,
And 'Bernard! Bernard!' rings through all the Strand.
Obscene with filth the miscreant lies bewrayed,
Fallen in the plash his wickedness had laid:
Then first (if poets aught of truth declare)
The caitiff vaticide conceived a prayer.
'Hear Jove! whose name my bards and I adore,
As much at least as any god's, or more;
And him and his if more devotion warms,
Down with the Bible, up with the Pope's Arms.'
　　A place there is, betwixt earth, air, and seas,
Where, from Ambrosia, Jove retires for ease.
There in his seat two spacious vents appear,
On this he sits, to that he leans his ear.
And hears the various vows of fond mankind;
Some beg an eastern, some a western wind:
All vain petitions, mounting to the sky,
With reams abundant this abode supply;
Amused he reads, and then returns the bills
Signed with that Ichor which from gods distils.
　　In office here fair Cloacina stands,
And ministers to Jove with purest hands.
Forth from the heap she picked her votary's prayer,
And placed it next him, a distinction rare!
Oft had the goddess heard her servant's call,
From her black grottos near the Temple wall,
Listening delighted to the jest unclean
Of link-boys vile, and watermen obscene;
Where as he fished her nether realms for wit,
She oft had favoured him, and favours yet.
Renewed by ordure's sympathetic force,
As oiled with magic juices for the course,
Vigorous he rises; from the effluvia strong
Imbibes new life, and scours and stinks along;
Repasses Lintot, vindicates the race,
Nor heeds the brown dishonours of his face.
　　And now the victor stretched his eager hand
Where the tall nothing stood, or seemed to stand;
A shapeless shade, it melted from his sight,
Like forms in clouds, or visions of the night.
To seize his papers, Curll, was next thy care;
His papers light, fly diverse, tossed in air;
Songs, sonnets, epigrams the winds uplift,
And whisk them back to Evans, Young, and Swift.
The embroidered suit at least he deemed his prey;
That suit an unpaid tailor snatched away.
No rag, no scrap, of all the beau, or wit,

That once so fluttered, and that once so writ.
   Heaven rings with laughter: of the laughter vain,
Dulness, good Queen, repeats the jest again.
Three wicked imps, of her own Grub Street choir,
She decked like Congreve, Addison, and Prior;
Mears, Warner, Wilkins run: delusive thought!
Breval, Bond, Besaleel, the varlets caught.
Curll stretches after Gay, but Gay is gone,
He grasps an empty Joseph for a John:
So Proteus, hunted in a nobler shape,
Became, when seized, a puppy, or an ape.
   To him the Goddess: 'Son! thy grief lay down,
And turn this whole illusion on the town:
As the sage dame, experienced in her trade,
By names of toasts retails each battered jade;
(Whence hapless Monsieur much complains at Paris
Of wrongs from duchesses and Lady Maries);
Be thine, my stationer! this magic gift;
Cook shall be Prior, and Concanen, Swift:
So shall each hostile name become our own,
And we too boast our Garth and Addison.'
   With that she gave him (piteous of his case,
Yet smiling at his rueful length of face)
A shaggy tapestry, worthy to be spread
On Codrus' old, or Dunton's modern bed;
Instructive work! whose wry-mouthed portraiture
Displayed the fates her confessors endure.
Earless on high, stood unabashed Defoe,
And Tutchin flagrant from the scourge below.
There Ridpath, Roper, cudgelled might ye view,
The very worsted still looked black and blue.
Himself among the storied chiefs he spies,
As, from the blanket, high in air he flies,
'And oh!' (he cried) 'what street, what lane but knows,
Our purgings, pumpings, blankettings, and blows?
In every loom our labours shall be seen,
And the fresh vomit run for ever green!'
   See in the circle next, Eliza placed,
Two babes of love close clinging to her waist;
Fair as before her works she stands confessed,
In flowers and pearls by bounteous Kirkall dressed.
The Goddess then: 'Who best can send on high
The salient spout, far-streaming to the sky;
His be yon Juno of majestic size,
With cow-like udders, and with ox-like eyes.
This China jordan let the chief o'ercome
Replenish, not ingloriously, at home.'
Osborne and Curll accept the glorious strife,

(Though this his son dissuades, and that his wife.)
One on his manly confidence relies,
One on his vigour and superior size.
First Osborne leaned against his lettered post;
It rose, and laboured to a curve at most.
So Jove's bright bow displays its watery round,
(Sure sign, that no spectator shall be drowned).
A second effort brought but new disgrace,
The wild meander washed the artist's face:
Thus the small jet, which hasty hands unlock,
Spurts in the gardener's eyes who turns the cock.
Not so from shameless Curll; impetuous spread
The stream, and smoking flourished o'er his head.
So (famed like thee for turbulence and horns)
Eridanus his humble fountain scorns;
Through half the heavens he pours th' exalted urn;
His rapid waters in their passage burn.

    Swift as it mounts, all follow with their eyes:
Still happy impudence obtains the prize.
Thou triumph'st, victor of the high-wrought day,
And the pleased dame, soft-smiling, leadst away.
Osborne, through perfect modesty o'ercome,
Crowned with the jordan, walks contented home.

    But now for authors nobler palms remain;
Room for my Lord! three jockeys in his train;
Six huntsmen with a shout precede his chair:
He grins, and looks broad nonsense with a stare.
His honour's meaning Dulness thus expressed,
'He wins this patron, who can tickle best.'

    He chinks his purse, and takes his seat of state:
With ready quills the dedicators wait;
Now at his head the dexterous task commence,
And, instant, fancy feels the imputed sense;
Now gentle touches wanton o'er his face,
He struts Adonis, and affects grimace:
Rolli the feather to his ear conveys,
Then his nice taste directs our operas:
Bentley his mouth with classic flattery opes,
And the puffed orator bursts out in tropes.
But Welsted most the poet's healing balm
Strives to extract from his soft, giving palm;
Unlucky Welsted! thy unfeeling master,
The more thou ticklest, gripes his fist the faster.

    While thus each hand promotes the pleasing pain,
And quick sensations skip from vein to vein;
A youth unknown to Phoebus, in despair,
Puts his last refuge all in Heaven and prayer.
What force have pious vows! The Queen of Love

Her sister sends, her votress, from above.
As taught by Venus, Paris learnt the art
To touch Achilles' only tender part;
Secure, through her, the noble prize to carry,
He marches off, his Grace's secretary.
   'Now turn to different sports,' the Goddess cries,
'And learn, my sons, the wondrous power of noise.
To move, to raise, to ravish every heart,
With Shakespeare's nature, or with Jonson's art,
Let others aim: 'tis yours to shake the soul
With thunder rumbling from the mustard bowl,
With horns and trumpets now to madness swell,
Now sink in sorrows with a tolling bell;
Such happy arts attention can command,
When fancy flags, and sense is at a stand.
Improve we these. Three catcalls be the bribe
Of him whose chattering shames the monkey tribe:
And his this drum whose hoarse heroic bass
Drowns the loud clarion of the braying ass.'

   Now thousand tongues are heard in one loud din:
The monkey-mimics rush discordant in;
'Twas chattering, grinning, mouthing, jabbering all,
And noise and Norton, brangling and Breval,
Dennis and dissonance, and captious art,
And snipsnap short, and interruption smart,
And demonstration thin, and theses thick,
And major, minor, and conclusion quick.
'Hold' (cried the queen) 'a cat-call each shall win;
Equal your merits! equal is your din!
But that this well-disputed game may end,
Sound forth, nay brayers, and the welkin rend.'
   As when the long-eared milky mothers wait
At some sick miser's triple-bolted gate,
For their defrauded, absent foals they make
A moan so loud, that all the guild awake;
Sore sighs Sir Gilbert, starting at the bray,
From dreams of millions, and three groats to pay.
So swells each windpipe; ass intones to ass,
Harmonic twang! of leather, horn, and brass;
Such as from labouring lungs the enthusiast blows,
High sound, attempered to the vocal nose;
Or such as bellow from the deep divine;
There, Webster! pealed thy voice, and Whitfield! thine.
But far o'er all, sonorous Blackmore's strain;
Walls, steeples, skies, bray back to him again.
In Tottenham fields, the brethren, with amaze,
Prick all their ears up, and forget to graze;

Long Chancery Lane retentive rolls the sound,
And courts to courts return it round and round;
Thames wafts it thence to Rufus' roaring hall,
And Hungerford re-echoes bawl for bawl.
All hail him victor in both gifts of song,
Who sings so loudly, and who sings so long.

 This labour past, by Bridewell all descend,
(As morning prayer, and flagellation end)
To where Fleet Ditch with disemboguing streams
Rolls the large tribute of dead dogs to Thames,
The King of dykes! than whom no sluice of mud
With deeper sable blots the silver flood.
'Here strip, my children! here at once leap in,
Here prove who best can dash through thick and thin,
And who the most in love of dirt excel,
Or dark dexterity of groping well.
Who flings most filth, and wide pollutes around
The stream, be his the *Weekly Journals* bound;
A pig of lead to him who dives the best;
A peck of coals a-piece shall glad the rest.'

 In naked majesty Oldmixon stands,
And, Milo-like, surveys his arms and hands;
Then sighing, thus, 'And am I now threescore?
Ah why, ye gods! should two and two make four?'
He said, and climbed a stranded lighter's height,
Shot to the black abyss, and plunged downright.
The senior's judgment all the crowd admire,
Who but to sink the deeper, rose the higher.

 Next Smedley dived; slow circles dimpled o'er
The quaking mud, that closed, and oped no more.
All look, all sigh, and call on Smedley lost;
'Smedley!' in vain, resounds through all the coast.

 Then * essayed; scarce vanished out of sight,
He buoys up instant, and returns to light:
He bears no token of the sabler streams,
And mounts far off among the swans of Thames.

 True to the bottom, see Concanen creep,
A cold, long-winded, native of the deep:
If perseverance gain the diver's prize,
Not everlasting Blackmore this denies:
No noise, no stir, no motion canst thou make,
The unconscious stream sleeps o'er thee like a lake.

 Next plunged a feeble, but a desperate pack,
With each a sickly brother at his back:
Sons of a day! just buoyant on the flood,
Then numbered with the puppies in the mud.
Ask ye their names? I could as soon disclose
The names of these blind puppies as of those.

Fast by, like Niobe (her children gone)
Sits Mother Osborne, stupefied to stone!
And monumental brass this record bears,
'These are,—ah no! these were, the *Gazetteers*!'
  Not so bold Arnall; with a weight of skull,
Furious he dives, precipitately dull.
Whirlpools and storms his circling arm invest,
With all the might of gravitation blessed:
No crab more active in the dirty dance,
Downward to climb, and backward to advance.
He brings up half the bottom on his head,
And loudly claims the journals and the lead.
  The plunging Prelate, and his ponderous Grace,
With holy envy gave one layman place.
When, lo! a burst of thunder shook the flood.
Slow rose a form, in majesty of mud;
Shaking the horrors of his sable brows,
And each ferocious feature grim with ooze.
Greater he looks, and more than mortal stares:
Then thus the wonders of the deep declares.
  First he relates, how sinking to the chin,
Smit with his mien, the mud-nymphs sucked him in:
How young Lutetia, softer than the down,
Nigrina black, and Merdamante brown,
Vied for his love in jetty bowers below,
As Hylas fair was ravished long ago.
Then sung, how, shown him by the nut-brown maids;
A branch of Styx here rises from the shades,
That, tinctured as it runs with Lethe's streams,
And wafting vapours from the land of dreams,
(As under seas Alpheus' secret sluice
Bears Pisa's offerings to his Arethuse)
Pours into Thames: and hence the mingled wave
Intoxicates the pert, and lulls the grave:
Here brisker vapours o'er the Temple creep,
There, all from Paul's to Aldgate drink and sleep.
  Thence to the banks where reverend bards repose,
They led him soft; each reverend bard arose;
And Milbourne chief, deputed by the rest,
Gave him the cassock, surcingle, and vest.
'Receive', he said, 'these robes which once were mine,
Dulness is sacred in a sound divine.'
  He ceased, and spread the robe; the crowd confess,
The reverend Flamen in his lengthened dress.
Around him wide a sable army stand,
A low-born, cell-bred, selfish, servile band,
Prompt or to guard or stab, to saint or damn,
Heaven's Swiss, who fight for any god, or man.

Through Lud's famed gates, along the well-known Fleet
Rolls the black troop, and overshades the street,
Till showers of sermons, characters, essays,
In circling fleeces whiten all the ways:
So clouds replenished from some bog below,
Mount in dark volumes, and descend in snow.
Here stopped the goddess; and in pomp proclaims
A gentler exercise to close the games.
   'Ye critics! in whose heads, as equal scales,
I weigh what author's heaviness prevails,
Which most conduce to soothe the soul in slumbers,
My Henley's periods, or my Blackmore's numbers,
Attend the trial we propose to make:
If there be man, who o'er such works can wake,
Sleep's all-subduing charms who dares defy,
And boasts Ulysses' ear with Argus' eye;
To him we grant our amplest powers to sit
Judge of all present, past, and future wit;
To cavil, censure, dictate, right or wrong,
Full and eternal privilege of tongue.'
   Three college sophs, and three pert templars came,
The same their talents, and their tastes the same;
Each prompt to query, answer, and debate,
And smit with love of poesy and prate.
The ponderous books two gentle readers bring;
The heroes sit, the vulgar form a ring.
The clamorous crowd is hushed with mugs of mum,
Till all, tuned equal, send a general hum.
Then mount the clerks, and in one lazy tone
Through the long, heavy, painful page drawl on;
Soft creeping, words on words, the sense compose,
At every line they stretch, they yawn, they doze.
As to soft gales top-heavy pines bow low
Their heads, and lift them as they cease to blow:
Thus oft they rear, and oft the head decline,
As breathe, or pause, by fits, the airs divine.
And now to this side, now to that they nod,
As verse or prose infuse the drowsy god.
Thrice Budgell aimed to speak, but thrice suppressed
By potent Arthur, knocked his chin and breast.
Toland and Tindal, prompt at priests to jeer,
Yet silent bowed to Christ's no kingdom here.
Who sate the nearest, by the words o'ercome,
Slept first; the distant nodded to the hum.
Then down are rolled the books; stretched o'er 'em lies
Each gentle clerk, and, muttering, seals his eyes.
As what a Dutchman plumps into the lakes,
One circle first, and then a second makes;

What Dulness dropped among her sons impressed
Like motion from one circle to the rest;
So from the midmost the nutation spreads
Round and more round, o'er all the sea of heads.
At last Centlivre felt her voice to fail,
Motteux himself unfinished left his tale,
Boyer the state, and Law the stage gave o'er,
Morgan and Mandeville could prate no more;
Norton, from Daniel and Ostroea sprung,
Blessed with his father's front and mother's tongue,
Hung silent down his never-blushing head;
And all was hushed, as Polly's self lay dead.
    Thus the soft gifts of sleep conclude the day,
And stretched on bulks, as usual, poets lay.
Why should I sing what bards the nightly muse
Did slumbering visit, and convey to stews;
Who prouder marched, with magistrates in state,
To some famed round-house, ever open gate!
How Henley lay inspired beside a sink,
And to mere mortals seemed a priest in drink:
While others, timely, to the neighbouring Fleet
(Haunt of the muses!) made their safe retreat.

The End of the SECOND BOOK

THE
DUNCIAD
BOOK the THIRD

ARGUMENT

After the other persons are disposed in their proper places of rest, the Goddess transports the king to her temple, and there lays him to slumber with his head on her lap; a position of marvellous virtue, which causes all the visions of wild enthusiasts, projectors, politicians, inamoratos, castle-builders, chemists, and poets. He is immediately carried on the wings of fancy, and led by a mad poetical sibyl, to the Elysian shade; where, on the banks of Lethe, the souls of the dull are dipped by Bavius, before their entrance into this world. There he is met by the ghost of Settle, and by him made acquainted with the wonders of the place, and with those which he himself is destined to perform. He takes him to a mount of vision, from whence he shows him the past triumphs of the empire of Dulness, then the present, and lastly the future: how small a part of the world was ever conquered by science, how soon those conquests were stopped, and those very nations again reduced to her dominion: then distinguishing the island of Great Britain, shows by what aids, by what persons, and by what degrees it shall be brought to her empire. Some of the persons he causes to pass in review before his eyes, describing each by his proper figure, character, and qualifications. On a sudden the scene shifts, and a vast number of miracles and prodigies appear, utterly surprising and unknown to the King himself, till they are explained to be the wonders of his own reign now commencing. On this subject Settle breaks into a congratulation, yet not unmixed with concern, that his own times were but the types of these. He prophesies how first the nation shall be overrun with farces, operas, and shows; how the throne of Dulness shall be advanced over the theatres, and set up even at court: then how her sons shall preside in the seats of arts and sciences; giving a glimpse, or Pisgah-sight, of the future fullness of her glory, the accomplishment whereof is the subject of the fourth and last book.

> But in her temple's last recess enclosed,
> On Dulness' lap the anointed head reposed.
> Him close the curtains round with vapours blue,
> And soft besprinkles with Cimmerian dew.
> Then raptures high the seat of sense o'erflow,
> Which only heads refined from reason know.
> Hence, from the straw where Bedlam's prophet nods,
> He hears loud oracles, and talks with gods:
> Hence the fool's Paradise, the statesman's scheme,
> The air-built castle, and the golden dream,
> The maid's romantic wish, the chemist's flame,
> And poet's vision of eternal fame.
>   And now, on Fancy's easy wing conveyed,
> The King descending, views th' Elysian shade.
> A slip-shod sibyl led his steps along,
> In lofty madness meditating song;
> Her tresses staring from poetic dreams,
> And never washed, but in Castalia's streams.
> Taylor, their better Charon, lends an oar,
> (Once swan of Thames, though now he sings no more.)
> Benlowes, propitious still to blockheads, bows;
> And Shadwell nods the poppy on his brows.
> Here, in a dusky vale where Lethe rolls,
> Old Bavius sits, to dip poetic souls,
> And blunt the sense, and fit it for a skull
> Of solid proof, impenetrably dull:
> Instant, when dipped, away they wing their flight,
> Where Brown and Mears unbar the gates of Light,
> Demand new bodies, and in calf's array,
> Rush to the world, impatient for the day.
> Millions and millions on these banks he views,
> Thick as the stars of night, or morning dews,
> As thick as bees o'er vernal blossoms fly,
> As thick as eggs at Ward in pillory.
>   Wondering he gazed: when, lo! a sage appears,
> By his broad shoulders known, and length of ears,
> Known by the band and suit which Settle wore
> (His only suit) for twice three years before:
> All as the vest appeared the wearer's frame,
> Old in new state, another yet the same.
> Bland and familiar as in life, begun

Thus the great father to the greater son.
   'Oh born to see what none can see awake!
Behold the wonders of th' oblivious lake.
Thou, yet unborn, hast touched this sacred shore;
The hand of Bavius drenched thee o'er and o'er.
But blind to former as to future fate,
What mortal knows his pre-existent state?
Who knows how long thy transmigrating soul
Might from Boeotian to Boeotian roll?
How many Dutchmen she vouchsafed to thrid?
How many stages through old monks she rid?
And all who since, in mild benighted days,
Mixed the owl's ivy with the poet's bays.
As man's meanders to the vital spring
Roll all their tides, then back their circles bring;
Or whirligigs, twirled round by skilful swain,
Suck the thread in, then yield it out again:
All nonsense thus, of old or modern date,
Shall in thee centre, from thee circulate.
For this our queen unfolds to vision true
Thy mental eye, for thou hast much to view:
Old scenes of glory, times long cast behind,
Shall, first recalled, rush forward to thy mind:
Then stretch thy sight o'er all thy rising reign,
And let the past and future fire thy brain.
   Ascend this hill, whose cloudy point commands
Her boundless empire over seas and lands.
See, round the poles where keener spangles shine,
Where spices smoke beneath the burning line,
(Earth's wide extremes), her sable flag displayed,
And all the nations covered in her shade!
   Far eastward cast thine eye, from whence the sun
And orient science their bright course begun:
One godlike monarch all that pride confounds,
He whose long wall the wandering Tartar bounds;
Heavens! what a pile! whole ages perish there,
And one bright blaze turns learning into air.
   Thence to the south extend thy gladdened eyes;
There rival flames with equal glory rise,
From shelves to shelves see greedy Vulcan roll,
And lick up all their physic of the soul.
   How little, mark! that portion of the ball,
Where, faint at best, the beams of science fall:
Soon as they dawn, from Hyperborean skies
Embodied dark, what clouds of Vandals rise!
Lo! where Maeotis sleeps, and hardly flows
The freezing Tanais through a waste of snows,
The North by myriads pours her mighty sons,

Great nurse of Goths, of Alans, and of Huns!
See Alaric's stern port! the martial frame
Of Genseric! and Attila's dread name!
See the bold Ostrogoths on Latium fall;
See the fierce Visigoths on Spain and Gaul!
See, where the morning gilds the palmy shore,
(The soil that arts and infant letters bore)
His conquering tribes th' Arabian prophet draws,
And saving ignorance enthrones by laws.
See Christians, Jews, one heavy sabbath keep,
And all the western world believe and sleep.

Lo! Rome herself, proud mistress now no more
Of arts, but thundering against heathen lore;
Her gray-haired synods damning books unread,
And Bacon trembling for his brazen head.
Padua, with sighs, beholds her Livy burn,
And even the Antipodes Virgilius mourn.
See, the cirque falls, the unpillared temple nods,
Streets paved with heroes, Tiber choked with gods:
Till Peter's keys some christened Jove adorn,
And Pan to Moses lends his pagan horn;
See graceless Venus to a Virgin turned,
Or Phidias broken, and Apelles burned.

Behold yon isle, by palmers, pilgrims trod,
Men bearded, bald, cowled, uncowled, shod, unshod,
Peeled, patched, and piebald, linsey-woolsey brothers,
Grave mummers! sleeveless some, and shirtless others.
That once was Britain—Happy! had she seen
No fiercer sons, had Easter never been.
In peace, great goddess, ever be adored;
How keen the war, if Dulness draw the sword!
Thus visit not thy own! on this blessed age
Oh spread thy influence, but restrain thy rage.

And see, my son! the hour is on its way,
That lifts our Goddess to imperial sway;
This favourite isle, long severed from her reign,
Dovelike she gathers to her wings again.
Now look through fate! behold the scene she draws!
What aids, what armies to assert her cause!
See all her progeny, illustrious sight!
Behold, and count them, as they rise to light.
As Berecynthia, while her offspring vie
In homage to the mother of the sky,
Surveys around her, in the blessed abode,
An hundred sons, and every son a god:
Not with less glory mighty Dulness crowned,
Shall take through Grub Street her triumphant round;
And her Parnassus glancing o'er at once,

344

Behold an hundred sons, and each a Dunce.
   Mark first that youth who takes the foremost place,
And thrusts his person full into your face.
With all thy father's virtues blessed, be born!
And a new Cibber shall the stage adorn.
   A second see, by meeker manners known,
And modest as the maid that sips alone;
From the strong fate of drams if thou get free,
Another Durfey, Ward! shall sing in thee.
Thee shall each ale-house, thee each gillhouse mourn,
And answering gin-shops sourer sighs return.
   Jacob, the scourge of grammar, mark with awe,
Nor less revere him, blunderbuss of law.
Lo Popple's brow, tremendous to the town,
Horneck's fierce eye, and Roome's funereal frown.
Lo sneering Goode, half malice and half whim,
A fiend in glee, ridiculously grim.
Each cygnet sweet, of Bath and Tunbridge race,
Whose tuneful whistling makes the waters pass:
Each songster, riddler, every nameless name,
All crowd, who foremost shall be damned to fame.
Some strain in rhyme; the muses, on their racks,
Scream like the winding of ten thousand jacks:
Some free from rhyme or reason, rule or check,
Break Priscian's head and Pegasus's neck;
Down, down they larum, with impetuous whirl,
The Pindars, and the Miltons of a Curll.
   Silence, ye wolves! while Ralph to Cynthia howls,
And makes night hideous—Answer him, ye owls!
   Sense, speech, and measure, living tongues and dead,
Let all give way—and Morris may be read.
   Flow Welsted, flow! like thine inspirer, beer,
Though stale, not ripe; though thin, yet never clear;
So sweetly mawkish, and so smoothly dull;
Heady, not strong; o'erflowing, though not full.
   Ah Dennis! Gildon ah! what ill-starred rage
Divides a friendship long confirmed by age?
Blockheads with reason wicked wits abhor,
But fool with fool is barbarous civil war.
Embrace, embrace, my sons! be foes no more!
Nor glad vile poets with true critics' gore.
   Behold yon pair, in strict embraces joined;
How like in manners, and how like in mind!
Equal in wit, and equally polite,
Shall this a *Pasquin*, that a *Grumbler* write?
Like are their merits, like rewards they share,
That shines a consul, this commissioner.
   'But who is he, in closet close y-pent,

Of sober face, with learned dust besprent?'
Right well mine eyes arede the myster wight,
On parchment scraps y-fed, and Wormius hight.
To future ages may thy dulness last,
As thou preserv'st the dulness of the past!
   There, dim in clouds, the poring scholiasts mark,
Wits, who, like owls, see only in the dark,
A lumberhouse of books in every head,
For ever reading, never to be read!
   But where each science lifts its modern type,
History her pot, divinity her pipe,
While proud philosophy repines to show,
Dishonest sight! his breeches rent below;
Embrowned with native bronze, lo! Henley stands,
Tuning his voice, and balancing his hands.
How fluent nonsense trickles from his tongue!
How sweet the periods, neither said nor sung!
Still break the benches, Henley! with thy strain,
While Sherlock, Hare, and Gibson preach in vain.
O great restorer of the good old stage,
Preacher at once, and zany of thy age!
O worthy thou of Egypt's wise abodes,
A decent priest, where monkeys were the gods!
But fate with butchers placed thy priestly stall,
Meek modern faith to murder, hack, and maul;
And bade thee live to crown Britannia's praise,
In Toland's, Tindal's, and in Woolston's days.
   Yet oh, my sons! a father's words attend:
(So may the fates preserve the ears you lend)
'Tis yours, a Bacon or a Locke to blame,
A Newton's genius, or a Milton's flame:
But oh! with one, immortal one dispense,
The source of Newton's light, of Bacon's sense.
Content, each emanation of his fires
That beams on earth, each virtue he inspires,
Each art he prompts, each charm he can create,
Whate'er he gives, are given for you to hate.
Persist, by all divine in man unawed,
But, 'Learn, ye DUNCES! not to scorn your GOD'.'
   Thus he, for then a ray of reason stole
Half through the solid darkness of his soul;
But soon the cloud returned—and thus the sire:
'See now, what Dulness and her sons admire!
See what the charms that smite the simple heart
Not touched by nature, and not reached by art.'
   His never-blushing head he turned aside,
(Not half so pleased when Goodman prophesied),
And looked, and saw a sable sorcerer rise,

Swift to whose hand a winged volume flies:
All sudden, gorgons hiss, and dragons glare,
And ten-horned fiends and giants rush to war.
Hell rises, Heaven descends, and dance on earth:
Gods, imps, and monsters, music, rage, and mirth,
A fire, a jig, a battle, and a ball,
Till one wide conflagration swallows all.
   Thence a new world to Nature's laws unknown
Breaks out refulgent, with a heaven its own:
Another Cynthia her new journey runs,
And other planets circle other suns.
The forests dance, the rivers upward rise,
Whales sport in woods, and dolphins in the skies;
And last, to give the whole creation grace,
Lo! one vast egg produces human race.
   Joy fills his soul, joy innocent of thought;
'What power,' he cries, 'what power these wonders wrought?
Son; what thou seekst is in thee! Look, and find
Each monster meets his likeness in thy mind.
Yet wouldst thou more? In yonder cloud behold,
Whose sarsenet skirts are edged with flamey gold,
A matchless youth! his nod these worlds controls,
Wings the red lightning, and the thunder rolls.
Angel of Dulness, sent to scatter round
Her magic charms o'er all unclassic ground:
Yon stars, yon suns, he rears at pleasure higher,
Illumes their light, and sets their flames on fire.
Immortal Rich! how calm he sits at ease
'Mid snows of paper, and fierce hail of pease;
And proud his mistress' orders to perform,
Rides in the whirlwind, and directs the storm.
   But, lo! to dark encounter in mid air
New wizards rise; I see my Cibber there!
Booth in his cloudy tabernacle shrined,
On grinning dragons thou shalt mount the wind.
Dire is the conflict, dismal is the din,
Here shouts all Drury, there all Lincoln's Inn;
Contending theatres our empire raise,
Alike their labours, and alike their praise.
   And are these wonders, son, to thee unknown?
Unknown to thee? These wonders are thy own.
These Fate reserved to grace thy reign divine,
Foreseen by me, but ah! withheld from mine.
In Lud's old walls though long I ruled, renowned
Far as loud Bow's stupendous bells resound;
Though my own Aldermen conferred the bays,
To me committing their eternal praise,
Their full-fed heroes, their pacific mayors,

Their annual trophies, and their monthly wars:
Though long my party built on me their hopes,
For writing pamphlets, and for roasting popes;
Yet lo! in me what authors have to brag on!
Reduced at last to hiss in my own dragon.
Avert it, heaven! that thou, my Cibber, e'er
Shouldst wag a serpent-tail in Smithfield Fair!
Like the vile straw that's blown about the streets,
The needy poet sticks to all he meets,
Coached, carted, trod upon, now loose, now fast,
And carried off in some dog's tail at last.
Happier thy fortunes! like a rolling stone,
Thy giddy dulness still shall lumber on,
Safe in its heaviness, shall never stray,
But lick up every blockhead in the way.
Thee shall the patriot, thee the courtier taste,
And every year be duller than the last.
Till raised from booths, to theatre, to court,
Her seat imperial Dulness shall transport.
Already opera prepares the way,
The sure forerunner of her gentle sway:
Let her thy heart, next drabs and dice, engage,
The third mad passion of thy doting age.
Teach thou the warbling Polypheme to roar,
And scream thyself as none e'er screamed before!
To aid our cause, if Heaven thou canst not bend,
Hell thou shalt move; for Faustus is our friend:
Pluto with Cato thou for this shalt join,
And link the *Mourning Bride* to *Proserpine*.
Grub Street! thy fall should men and gods conspire,
Thy stage shall stand, ensure it but from fire.
Another Aeschylus appears! prepare
For new abortions, all ye pregnant fair!
In flames, like Semele's, be brought to bed,
While opening Hell spouts wild-fire at your head.
   Now Bavius take the poppy from thy brow,
And place it here! here, all ye heroes, bow!
This, this is he, foretold by ancient rhymes:
Th' Augustus born to bring Saturnian times.
Signs following signs lead on the mighty year!
See! the dull stars roll round and reappear.
See, see, our own true Phoebus wears the bays!
Our Midas sits Lord Chancellor of Plays!
On poets' tombs see Benson's titles writ!
Lo! Ambrose Philips is preferred for wit!
See under Ripley rise a new Whitehall,
While Jones' and Boyle's united labours fall:
While Wren with sorrow to the grave descends,

Gay dies unpensioned with a hundred friends.
Hibernian politics, O Swift! thy fate;
And Pope's, ten years to comment and translate.
 Proceed, great days! till Learning fly the shore,
Till Birch shall blush with noble blood no more,
Till Thames see Eton's sons for ever play,
Till Westminster's whole year be holiday,
Till Isis' elders reel, their pupils sport,
And alma mater lie dissolved in port!'
 'Enough! enough!' the raptured monarch cries;
And through the Ivory Gate the vision flies.

The End of the THIRD BOOK

THE
DUNCIAD
BOOK the FOURTH

ARGUMENT

The poet being, in this book, to declare the completion of the prophecies mentioned at the end of the former, makes a new invocation; as the greater poets are wont, when some high and worthy matter is to be sung. He shows the goddess coming in her majesty to destroy order and science, and to substitute the Kingdom of the Dull upon earth; how she leads captive the sciences, and silenceth the muses; and what they be who succeed in their stead. All her children, by a wonderful attraction, are drawn about her; and bear along with them divers others, who promote her empire by connivance, weak resistance, or discouragement of arts; such as half-wits, tasteless admirers, vain pretenders, the flatterers of dunces, or the patrons of them. All these crowd round her; one of them offering to approach her, is driven back by a rival, but she commends and encourages both. The first who speak in form are the genius's of the schools, who assure her of their care to advance her cause, by confining youth to words, and keeping them out of the way of real knowledge. Their address, and her gracious answer; with her charge to them and the universities. the universities appear by their proper deputies, and assure her that the same method is observed in the progress of education; the speech of Aristarchus on this subject. They are driven off by a band of young gentlemen returned from travel with their tutors; one of whom delivers to the goddess, in a polite oration, an account of the whole conduct and fruits of their travels: presenting to her at the same time a young nobleman perfectly accomplished. She receives him graciously, and indues him with the happy quality of want of shame. She sees loitering about her a number of indolent persons abandoning all business and duty, and dying with laziness: to these approaches the antiquary Annius, entreating her to make them virtuosos, and assign them over to him; but Mummius, another antiquary, complaining of his fraudulent proceeding, she finds a method to reconcile their difference. Then enter a troop of people fantastically adorned, offering her strange and exotic presents: amongst them, one stands forth and demands justice on another, who had deprived him of one of the greatest curiosities in nature; but he justifies himself so well, that the goddess gives them both her approbation. She recommends to them to find proper employment for the indolents before-mentioned, in the study of butterflies, shells, birds' nests, moss, etc. *but with particular caution not to proceed beyond* trifles, *to any useful or extensive views of nature, or of the author of* nature. *Against the last of these apprehensions, she is secured by a hearty address from the* minute philosophers *and* freethinkers, *one of whom speaks in the name of the rest. The youth thus instructed and principled, are delivered to her in a body, by the hands of Silenus; and then admitted to taste the cup of the* Magus *her high-priest, which causes a total oblivion of all obligations, divine, civil, moral, or rational. To these her adepts she sends* priests, attendants, *and* comforters, *of various kinds; confers on them* orders *and* degrees; *and then dismissing them with a speech, confirming to each his* privileges, *and telling what she expects from each, concludes with a* yawn *of extraordinary virtue: the progress and effects whereof on all orders of men, and the consummation of all, in the restoration of* Night *and* Chaos, *conclude the poem.*

> Yet, yet a moment, one dim ray of light
> Indulge, dread Chaos, and eternal Night!
> Of darkness visible so much be lent,
> As half to show, half veil the deep intent.
> Ye Powers! whose mysteries restored I sing,
> To whom time bears me on his rapid wing,
> Suspend a while your force inertly strong,
> Then take at once the poet and the song.
>   Now flamed the dog-star's unpropitious ray,
> Smote every brain, and withered every bay;
> Sick was the sun, the owl forsook his bower,
> The moon-struck prophet felt the madding hour:
> Then rose the seed of Chaos, and of Night,
> To blot out order, and extinguish light,
> Of dull and venal a new world to mould,
> And bring Saturnian days of lead and gold.
>   She mounts the throne: her head a cloud concealed,
> In broad effulgence all below revealed,
> ('Tis thus aspiring Dulness ever shines),
> Soft on her lap her laureate son reclines.
>   Beneath her foot-stool, Science groans in chains,
> And Wit dreads exile, penalties and pains.
> There foamed rebellious Logic, gagged and bound,
> There, stripped, fair Rhetoric languished on the ground;
> His blunted arms by Sophistry are borne,
> And shameless Billingsgate her robes adorn.
> Morality, by her false guardians drawn,
> Chicane in furs, and Casuistry in lawn,
> Gasps, as they straiten at each end the cord,
> And dies, when Dulness gives her Page the word.
> Mad Mathesis alone was unconfined,
> Too mad for mere material chains to bind,
> Now to pure space lifts her ecstatic stare,
> Now running round the circle, finds it square.
> But held in tenfold bonds the muses lie,

Watched both by envy's and by flattery's eye:
There to her heart sad Tragedy addressed
The dagger wont to pierce the tyrant's breast;
But sober History restrained her rage,
And promised vengeance on a barbarous age.
There sunk Thalia, nerveless, cold, and dead,
Had not her sister Satire held her head:
Nor couldst thou, CHESTERFIELD! a tear refuse,
Thou wept'st, and with thee wept each gentle muse.
    When, lo! a harlot form soft sliding by,
With mincing step, small voice, and languid eye;
Foreign her air, her robe's discordant pride
In patchwork fluttering, and her head aside:
By singing peers upheld on either hand,
She tripp'd and laugh'd, too pretty much to stand;
Cast on the prostrate Nine a scornful look,
Then thus in quaint recitative spoke.
    'O *Cara! Cara!* silence all that train:
Joy to great Chaos! let division reign:
Chromatic tortures soon shall drive them hence,
Break all their nerves, and fritter all their sense:
One trill shall harmonize joy, grief, and rage,
Wake the dull church, and lull the ranting stage;
To the same notes thy sons shall hum, or snore,
And all thy yawning daughters cry, *encore.*
Another Phoebus, thy own Phoebus, reigns,
Joys in my jigs, and dances in my chains.
But soon, ah soon rebellion will commence,
If music meanly borrows aid from sense:
Strong in new arms, lo! giant Handel stands,
Like bold Briareus, with a hundred hands;
To stir, to rouse, to shake the soul he comes,
And Jove's own thunders follow Mars's drums.
Arrest him, empress; or you sleep no more'—
She heard, and drove him to the Hibernian shore.
    And now had Fame's posterior trumpet blown,
And all the nations summoned to the throne.
The young, the old, who feel her inward sway,
One instinct seizes, and transports away.
None need a guide, by sure attraction led,
And strong impulsive gravity of head:
None want a place, for all their centre found,
Hung to the goddess, and cohered around.
Not closer, orb in orb, conglobed are seen
The buzzing bees about their dusky queen.
    The gathering number, as it moves along,
Involves a vast involuntary throng,
Who gently drawn, and struggling less and less,

Roll in her vortex, and her power confess.
Not those alone who passive own her laws,
But who, weak rebels, more advance her cause.
Whate'er of dunce in college or in town
Sneers at another, in toupee or gown;
Whate'er of mongrel no one class admits,
A wit with dunces, and a dunce with wits.
    Nor absent they, no members of her state,
Who pay her homage in her sons, the great;
Who false to Phoebus, bow the knee to Baal;
Or, impious, preach his word without a call.
Patrons, who sneak from living worth to dead,
Withhold the pension, and set up the head;
Or vest dull flattery in the sacred gown;
Or give from fool to fool the laurel crown.
And (last and worst) with all the cant of wit,
Without the soul, the muse's hypocrite.
There marched the bard and blockhead, side by side,
Who rhymed for hire, and patronized for pride.
Narcissus, praised with all a parson's power,
Looked a white lily sunk beneath a shower.
There moved Montalto with superior air;
His stretched-out arm displayed a volume fair;
Courtiers and patriots in two ranks divide,
Through both he passed, and bowed from side to side;
But as in graceful act, with awful eye
Composed he stood, bold Benson thrust him by:
On two unequal crutches propped he came,
Milton's on this, on that one Johnston's name.
The decent knight retired with sober rage,
Withdrew his hand, and closed the pompous page.
But (happy for him as the times went then)
Appeared Apollo's mayor and aldermen,
On whom three hundred gold-capped youths await,
To lug the ponderous volume off in state.
    When Dulness, smiling—'Thus revive the wits!
But murder first, and mince them all to bits;
As erst Medea (cruel, so to save!)
A new edition of old Aeson gave;
Let standard authors, thus, like trophies born,
Appear more glorious as more hacked and torn,
And you, my critics! in the chequered shade,
Admire new light through holes yourselves have made.
    Leave not a foot of verse, a foot of stone,
A page, a grave, that they can call their own;
But spread, my sons, your glory thin or thick,
On passive paper, or on solid brick.
So by each bard an alderman shall sit,

A heavy lord shall hang at every wit,
And while on Fame's triumphal car they ride,
Some slave of mine be pinioned to their side.'
   Now crowds on crowds around the Goddess press,
Each eager to present the first address.
Dunce scorning dunce beholds the next advance,
But fop shows fop superior complaisance.
When lo! a spectre rose, whose index-hand
Held forth the virtue of the dreadful wand;
His beavered brow a birchen garland wears,
Dropping with infants' blood and mothers' tears.
O'er every rein a shuddering horror runs;
Eton and Winton shake through all their sons.
All flesh is humbled, Westminster's bold race
Shrink, and confess the genius of the place:
The pale boy-senator yet tingling stands,
And holds his breeches close with both his hands.
   Then thus: 'Since man from beast by words is known,
Words are man's province, words we teach alone.
When reason doubtful, like the Samian letter,
Points him two ways, the narrower is the better.
Placed at the door of learning, youth to guide,
We never suffer it to stand too wide.
To ask, to guess, to know, as they commence,
As fancy opens the quick springs of sense,
We ply the memory, we load the brain,
Bind rebel wit, and double chain on chain,
Confine the thought, to exercise the breath;
And keep them in the pale of words till death.
Whate'er the talents, or howe'er designed,
We hang one jingling padlock on the mind:
A poet the first day he dips his quill;
And what the last? a very poet still.
Pity! the charm works only in our wall,
Lost, lost too soon in yonder house or hall.
There truant WYNDHAM every muse gave o'er,
There TALBOT sunk, and was a wit no more!
How sweet an Ovid, MURRAY was our boast!
How many Martials were in PULTENEY lost!
Else sure some bard, to our eternal praise,
In twice ten thousand rhyming nights and days,
Had reached the work, the all that mortal can;
And South beheld that master-piece of man.'
   'Oh,' cried the Goddess, 'for some pedant reign!
Some gentle JAMES, to bless the land again;
To stick the doctor's chair into the throne,
Give law to words, or war with words alone,
Senates and courts with Greek and Latin rule,

And turn the council to a grammar school!
For sure, if Dulness sees a grateful day,
'Tis in the shade of arbitrary sway.
Oh! if my sons may learn one earthly thing,
Teach but that one, sufficient for a king;
That which my priests, and mine alone, maintain,
Which as it dies or lives, we fall or reign:
May you, may Cam and Isis, preach it long!
The RIGHT DIVINE of kings to govern wrong.'
   Prompt at the call, around the Goddess roll
Broad hats, and hoods, and caps, a sable shoal:
Thick and more thick the black blockade extends,
A hundred head of Aristotle's friends.
Nor wert thou, Isis! wanting to the day,
[Though Christ-church long kept prudishly away.]
Each stanch polemic, stubborn as a rock,
Each fierce logician, still expelling Locke,
Came whip and spur, and dashed through thin and thick
On German Crousaz, and Dutch Burgersdyck.
As many quit the streams that murmuring fall
To lull the sons of Margaret and Clare Hall,
Where Bentley late tempestuous wont to sport
In troubled waters, but now sleeps in port.
Before them marched that awful aristarch!
Ploughed was his front with many a deep remark:
His hat, which never vailed to human pride,
Walker with reverence took, and laid aside.
Low bowed the rest: he, kingly, did but nod;
So upright Quakers please both man and God.
'Mistress! dismiss that rabble from your throne:
Avaunt——is Aristarchus yet unknown?
Thy mighty scholiast, whose unwearied pains
Made Horace dull, and humbled Milton's strains.
Turn what they will to verse, their toil is vain,
Critics like me shall make it prose again.
Roman and Greek grammarians! know your better,
Author of something yet more great than letter;
While towering o'er your alphabet, like Saul,
Stands our digamma, and o'ertops them all.
   'Tis true, on words is still our whole debate,
Disputes of *me* or *te*, of *aut* or *at*,
To sound or sink in *cano*, O or A,
Or give up Cicero to C or K.
Let Freind affect to speak as Terence spoke,
And Alsop never but like Horace joke:
For me, what Virgil, Pliny may deny,
Manilius or Solinus shall supply:
For Attic phrase in Plato let them seek,

354

I poach in Suidas for unlicensed Greek.
In ancient sense if any needs will deal,
Be sure I give them fragments, not a meal;
What Gellius or Stobaeus hashed before,
Or chewed by blind old scholiasts o'er and o'er,
The critic eye, that microscope of wit,
Sees hairs and pores, examines bit by bit:
How parts relate to parts, or they to whole,
The body's harmony, the beaming soul,
Are things which Kuster, Burman, Wasse shall see,
When man's whole frame is obvious to a *flea*.
    Ah, think not, mistress! more true Dulness lies
In Folly's cap, than Wisdom's grave disguise.
Like buoys, that never sink into the flood,
On Learning's surface we but lie and nod.
Thine is the genuine head of many a house,
And much divinity without a Νοῦς.
Nor could a BARROW work on every block,
Nor has one ATTERBURY spoiled the flock.
See! still thy own, the heavy cannon roll,
And metaphysic smokes involve the pole.
For thee we dim the eyes, and stuff the head
With all such reading as was never read:
For thee explain a thing till all men doubt it,
And write about it, goddess, and about it:
So spins the silk-worm small its slender store,
And labours till it clouds itself all o'er.
    What though we let some better sort of fool
Thrid every science, run through every school?
Never by tumbler through the hoops was shown
Such skill in passing all, and touching none.
He may indeed (if sober all this time)
Plague with dispute, or persecute with rhyme.
We only furnish what he cannot use,
Or wed to what he must divorce, a muse:
Full in the midst of Euclid dip at once,
And petrify a genius to a dunce:
Or, set on metaphysic ground to prance,
Show all his paces, not a step advance.
With the same cement, ever sure to bind,
We bring to one dead level every mind.
Then take him to develop, if you can,
And hew the block off, and get out the man.
But wherefore waste I words? I see advance
Whore, pupil, and laced governor from France.
Walker! our hat,'—nor more he deigned to say,
But, stern as Ajax' spectre, strode away.
    In flowed at once a gay embroidered race,

And tittering pushed the pedants off the place:
Some would have spoken, but the voice was drowned
By the French horn, or by the opening hound.
The first came forwards, with an easy mien,
As if he saw St James's and the Queen.
When thus the attendant orator begun:
'Receive, great empress! thy accomplished son:
Thine from the birth, and sacred from the rod,
A dauntless infant! never scared with God.
The sire saw, one by one, his virtues wake:
The mother begged the blessing of a rake.
Thou gavest that ripeness which so soon began,
And ceased so soon—he ne'er was boy nor man.
Through school and college, thy kind cloud o'ercast,
Safe and unseen the young Aeneas passed:
Thence bursting glorious, all at once let down,
Stunned with his giddy larum half the town.
Intrepid then, o'er seas and lands he flew:
Europe he saw, and Europe saw him too.
There all thy gifts and graces we display,
Thou, only thou, directing all our way!
To where the Seine, obsequious as she runs,
Pours at great Bourbon's feet her silken sons;
Or Tiber, now no longer Roman, rolls,
Vain of Italian arts, Italian souls:
To happy convents, bosomed deep in vines,
Where slumber abbots, purple as their wines:
To isles of fragrance, lily-silvered vales,
Diffusing languor in the panting gales:
To lands of singing or of dancing slaves,
Love-whispering woods, and lute-resounding waves.
But chief her shrine where naked Venus keeps,
And Cupids ride the lion of the deeps;
Where, eased of fleets, the Adriatic main
Wafts the smooth eunuch and enamoured swain.
Led by my hand, he sauntered Europe round,
And gathered every vice on Christian ground;
Saw every court, heard every king declare
His royal sense of operas or the fair;
The stews and palace equally explored,
Intrigued with glory, and with spirit whored;
Tried all *hors d'oeuvres*, all *liqueurs* defined,
Judicious drank, and greatly-daring dined;
Dropped the dull lumber of the Latin store,
Spoiled his own language, and acquired no more;
All classic learning lost on classic ground;
And last turned air, the echo of a sound!
See now, half-cured, and perfectly well-bred,

With nothing but a solo in his head;
As much estate, and principle, and wit,
As Jansen, Fleetwood, Cibber shall think fit;
Stolen from a duel, followed by a nun,
And, if a borough choose him, not undone;
See, to my country happy I restore
This glorious youth, and add one Venus more.
Her too receive (for her my soul adores),
So may the sons of sons of sons of whores
Prop thine, O empress! like each neighbour throne,
And make a long posterity thy own.'
    Pleased, she accepts the hero, and the dame,
Wraps in her veil, and frees from sense of shame.
    Then looked, and saw a lazy, lolling sort,
Unseen at church, at senate, or at court,
Of ever-listless loiterers that attend
No cause, no trust, no duty, and no friend.
Thee too, my Paridel! she marked thee there,
Stretched on the rack of a too easy chair,
And heard thy everlasting yawn confess
The pains and penalties of idleness.
She pitied! but her pity only shed
Benigner influence on thy nodding head.
    But Annius, crafty seer, with ebon wand,
And well-dissembled emerald on his hand,
False as his gems, and cankered as his coins,
Came, crammed with capon, from where Pollio dines.
Soft, as the wily fox is seen to creep,
Where bask on sunny banks the simple sheep,
Walk round and round, now prying here, now there;
So he; but pious, whispered first his prayer.
    'Grant, gracious goddess! grant me still to cheat,
Oh may thy cloud still cover the deceit!
Thy choicer mists on this assembly shed,
But pour them thickest on the noble head.
So shall each youth, assisted by our eyes,
See other Caesars, other Homers rise;
Through twilight ages hunt the Athenian fowl,
Which Chalcis gods, and mortals call an owl,
Now see an Attys, now a Cecrops clear,
Nay, Mahomet! the pigeon at thine ear;
Be rich in ancient brass, though not in gold,
And keep his Lares, though his house be sold;
To headless Phoebe his fair bride postpone,
Honour a Syrian prince above his own;
Lord of an Otho, if I vouch it true;
Blessed in one Niger, till he knows of two.'
    Mummius o'erheard him; Mummius, fool-renowned,

Who like his Cheops stinks above the ground,
Fierce as a startled adder, swelled, and said,
Rattling an ancient sistrum at his head:
　'Speakst thou of Syrian princes? Traitor base!
Mine, Goddess! mine is all the horned race.
True, he had wit to make their value rise;
From foolish Greeks to steal them, was as wise;
More glorious yet, from barbarous hands to keep,
When Sallee rovers chased him on the deep.
Then taught by Hermes, and divinely bold,
Down his own throat he risked the Grecian gold;
Received each demigod, with pious care,
Deep in his entrails—I revered them there,
I bought them, shrouded in that living shrine,
And, at their second birth, they issue mine.'
　'Witness, great Ammon! by whose horns I swore,'
Replied soft Annius, 'this our paunch before
Still bears them, faithful; and that thus I eat,
Is to refund the medals with the meat.
To prove me, Goddess! clear of all design,
Bid me with Pollio sup, as well as dine:
There all the learned shall at the labour stand,
And Douglas lend his soft, obstetric hand.'
　The Goddess smiling seemed to give consent;
So back to Pollio, hand in hand, they went.
　Then thick as locusts blackening all the ground,
A tribe, with weeds and shells fantastic crowned,
Each with some wondrous gift approached the power,
A nest, a toad, a fungus, or a flower.
But far the foremost, two, with earnest zeal,
And aspect ardent, to the throne appeal.
　The first thus opened: 'Hear thy suppliant's call,
Great Queen, and common Mother of us all!
Fair from its humble bed I reared this flower,
Suckled, and cheered, with air, and sun, and shower,
Soft on the paper ruff its leaves I spread,
Bright with the gilded button tipped its head;
Then throned in glass, and named it CAROLINE:
Each maid cried, charming! and each youth, 'Divine!'
Did nature's pencil ever blend such rays,
Such varied light in one promiscuous blaze?
Now prostrate! dead! behold that Caroline:
No maid cries, 'Charming!' and no youth, 'Divine!'
And lo the wretch! whose vile, whose insect lust
Laid this gay daughter of the spring in dust.
Oh, punish him, or to th' Elysian shades
Dismiss my soul, where no carnation fades.'
　He ceased, and wept. With innocence of mien,

Th' accused stood forth, and thus addressed the Queen:
  'Of all th' enamelled race, whose silvery wing
Waves to the tepid zephyrs of the spring,
Or swims along the fluid atmosphere,
Once brightest shined this child of heat and air.
I saw, and started, from its vernal bower
The rising game, and chased from flower to flower.
It fled, I followed; now in hope, now pain;
It stopped, I stopped; it moved, I moved again.
At last it fixed; 'twas on what plant it pleased,
And where it fixed, the beauteous bird I seized:
Rose or carnation was below my care;
I meddle, goddess! only in my sphere.
I tell the naked fact without disguise,
And, to excuse it, need but show the prize;
Whose spoils this paper offers to your eye,
Fair even in death! this peerless *butterfly*.'
  'My sons!', she answered, 'both have done your parts:
Live happy both, and long promote our arts.
But hear a mother, when she recommends
To your fraternal care our sleeping friends.
The common soul, of heaven's more frugal make,
Serves but to keep fools pert and knaves awake:
A drowsy watchman, that just gives a knock,
And breaks our rest, to tell us what's o'clock.
Yet by some object every brain is stirred;
The dull may waken to a humming bird;
The most recluse, discreetly opened, find
Congenial matter in the cockle-kind;
The mind in metaphysics at a loss,
May wander in a wilderness of moss;
The head that turns at super-lunar things,
Poised with a tail, may steer on Wilkins' wings.
  O! would the sons of men once think their eyes
And reason given them but to study *flies!*
See nature in some partial narrow shape,
And let the Author of the whole escape:
Learn but to trifle; or, who most observe,
To wonder at their maker, not to serve.'
  'Be that my task', replies a gloomy clerk,
Sworn foe to mystery, yet divinely dark;
Whose pious hope aspires to see the day
When moral evidence shall quite decay,
And damns implicit faith, and holy lies,
Prompt to impose, and fond to dogmatize:
'Let others creep by timid steps and slow,
On plain experience lay foundations low,
By common sense to common knowledge bred,

And last, to nature's cause through nature led.
All-seeing in thy mists, we want no guide,
Mother of arrogance, and source of pride!
We nobly take the high *priori* road,
And reason downward, till we doubt of God:
Make Nature still encroach upon his plan:
And shove him off as far as e'er we can:
Thrust some mechanic cause into his place;
Or bind in matter, or diffuse in space.
Or, at one bound o'er-leaping all his laws,
Make God man's image, man the final cause,
Find virtue local, all relation scorn,
See all in *self*, and but for self be born:
Of nought so certain as our *reason* still,
Of nought so doubtful as of *soul* and *will*.
Oh hide the God still more! and make us see
Such as Lucretius drew, a God like thee:
Wrapped up in self, a God without a thought,
Regardless of our merit or default.
Or that bright image to our fancy draw,
Which Theocles in raptured vision saw,
While through poetic scenes the genius roves,
Or wanders wild in academic groves;
That NATURE our society adores,
Where Tindal dictates, and Silenus snores.'
  Roused at his name, up rose the boozy sire,
And shook from out his pipe the seeds of fire;
Then snapped his box, and stroked his belly down:
Rosy and reverend, though without a gown.
Bland and familiar to the throne he came,
Led up the youth, and called the Goddess *Dame*.
Then thus: 'From priestcraft happily set free,
Lo! every finished son returns to thee:
First, slave to words, then vassal to a name,
Then dupe to party; child and man the same;
Bounded by nature, narrowed still by art,
A trifling head, and a contracted heart.
Thus bred, thus taught, how many have I seen,
Smiling on all, and smiled on by a queen.
Marked out for honours, honoured for their birth,
To thee the most rebellious things on earth:
Now to thy gentle shadow all are shrunk,
All melted down in pension or in punk!
So Kent, so Berkeley sneaked into the grave,
A monarch's half, and half a harlot's slave.
Poor Warwick nipped in folly's broadest bloom,
Who praises now? his chaplain on his tomb.
Then take them all, oh, take them to thy breast!

Thy *Magus*, Goddess! shall perform the rest.'
  With that, a WIZARD OLD his *cup* extends;
Which whoso tastes forgets his former friends,
Sire, ancestors, himself. One casts his eyes
Up to a *star*, and like Endymion dies:
A *feather* shooting from another's head,
Extracts his brain, and principle is fled,
Lost is his God, his country, everything;
And nothing left but homage to a king!
The vulgar herd turn off to roll with hogs,
To run with horses, or to hunt with dogs;
But, sad example! never to escape
Their infamy, still keep the human shape.
But she, good goddess, sent to every child
Firm impudence, or stupefaction mild;
And strait succeeded, leaving shame no room,
Cibberian forehead, or Cimmerian gloom.
  Kind self-conceit to some her glass applies,
Which no one looks in with another's eyes:
But as the flatterer or dependant paint,
Beholds himself a patriot, chief, or saint.
  On others interest her gay livery flings,
Interest, that waves on party-coloured wings:
Turned to the sun, she casts a thousand dyes,
And, as she turns, the colours fall or rise.
  Others the siren sisters warble round,
And empty heads console with empty sound.
No more, alas! the voice of Fame they hear,
The balm of Dulness trickling in their ear.
Great Cowper, Harcourt, Parker, Raymond, King,
Why all your toils? your sons have learned to sing.
How quick ambition hastes to ridicule!
The sire is made a peer, the son a fool.
  On some, a priest succinct in amice white
Attends; all flesh is nothing in his sight!
Beeves, at his touch, at once to jelly turn,
And the huge boar is shrunk into an urn:
The board with specious miracles he loads,
Turns hares to larks, and pigeons into toads.
Another (for in all what one can shine?)
Explains the *Séve* and *Verdeur* of the vine.
What cannot copious sacrifice atone?
Thy truffles, Perigord! thy hams, Bayonne!
With French libation, and Italian strain,
Wash Bladen white, and expiate Hays's stain.
Knight lifts the head; for what are crowds undone
To three essential partridges in one?
Gone every blush, and silent all reproach,

Contending princes mount them in their coach.
    Next bidding all draw near on bended knees,
The Queen confers her *titles* and *degrees*.
Her children first of more distinguished sort,
Who study Shakespeare at the Inns of Court,
Impale a glow-worm, or vertù profess,
Shine in the dignity of F.R.S.
Some, deep freemasons, join the silent race,
Worthy to fill Pythagoras's place:
Some botanists, or florists at the least,
Or issue members of an annual feast.
Nor passed the meanest unregarded, one
Rose a Gregorian, one a Gormogon.
The last, not least in honour or applause,
Isis and Cam made doctors of her laws.
    Then blessing all, 'Go children of my care!
To practice now from theory repair.
All my commands are easy, short, and full:
My sons! be proud, be selfish, and be dull.
Guard my prerogative, assert my throne:
This nod confirms each privilege your own.
The cap and switch be sacred to his Grace;
With staff and pumps the marquis lead the race;
From stage to stage the licensed Earl may run,
Paired with his fellow-charioteer the sun;
The learned baron butterflies design,
Or draw to silk Arachne's subtle line;
The judge to dance his brother sergeant call;
The senator at cricket urge the ball;
The bishop stow (pontific luxury!)
An hundred souls of turkeys in a pie;
The sturdy squire to Gallic masters stoop,
And drown his lands and manors in a soup.
Others import yet nobler arts from France,
Teach kings to fiddle, and make senates dance.
Perhaps more high some daring son may soar,
Proud to my list to add one monarch more;
And nobly conscious, princes are but things
Born for first ministers, as slaves for kings,
Tyrant supreme! shall three estates command,
And MAKE ONE MIGHTY DUNCIAD OF THE LAND!'
    More she had spoke, but yawned—all nature nods:
What mortal can resist the yawn of gods?
Churches and chapels instantly it reached;
(St James's first, for leaden Gilbert preached)
Then catched the schools; the Hall scarce kept awake;
The Convocation gaped, but could not speak:
Lost was the nation's sense, nor could be found,

While the long solemn unison went round:
Wide, and more wide, it spread o'er all the realm;
Even Palinurus nodded at the helm:
The vapour mild o'er each committee crept;
Unfinished treaties in each office slept;
And chiefless armies dozed out the campaign;
And navies yawned for orders on the main.
O Muse! relate (for you can tell alone,
Wits have short memories, and dunces none)
Relate, who first, who last resigned to rest;
Whose heads she partly, whose completely blest;
What charms could faction, what ambition lull,
The venal quiet, and entrance the dull;
Till drowned was sense, and shame, and right, and wrong—
O sing, and hush the nations with thy song!

*   *   *   *   *   *

In vain, in vain,—the all composing hour
Resistless falls: the Muse obeys the power.
She comes! she comes! the sable throne behold
Of *Night* primeval, and of *Chaos* old!
Before her, Fancy's gilded clouds decay,
And all its varying rainbows die away.
Wit shoots in vain its momentary fires,
The meteor drops, and in a flash expires.
As one by one, at dread Medea's strain,
The sickening stars fade off the ethereal plain;
As Argus' eyes, by Hermes' wand oppressed,
Closed one by one to everlasting rest;
Thus at her felt approach, and secret might,
Art after art goes out, and all is night.
See skulking Truth to her old cavern fled,
Mountains of casuistry heaped o'er her head!
Philosophy, that leaned on heaven before,
Shrinks to her second cause, and is no more.
Physic of Metaphysic begs defence,
And Metaphysic calls for aid on Sense!
See Mystery to Mathematics fly!
In vain! they gaze, turn giddy, rave, and die.
Religion, blushing, veils her sacred fires,
And unawares Morality expires.
Nor *public* flame, nor *private*, dares to shine;
Nor *human* spark is left, nor glimpse *divine!*
Lo! thy dread empire, CHAOS! is restored;
Light dies before thy uncreating word:
Thy hand, great Anarch! lets the curtain fall;
And universal darkness buries all.

FINIS

APPENDIX

I
PREFACE

Prefixed to the five first imperfect Editions of the DUNCIAD, in three books, printed at DUBLIN and LONDON, in octavo and duodecimo, 1727.

The PUBLISHER to the READER.

It will be found a true observation, though somewhat surprising, that when any scandal is vented against a man of the highest distinction and character, either in the state or in literature, the public in general afford it a most quiet reception; and the larger part accept it as favourably as if it were some kindness done to themselves: whereas, if a known scoundrel or blockhead but chance to be touched upon, a whole legion is up in arms, and it becomes the common cause of all scribblers, booksellers, and printers whatsoever.

Not to search too deeply into the reason hereof, I will only observe as a fact, that every week for these two months past, the town has been persecuted with pamphlets, advertisements, letters, and weekly essays, not only against the wit and writings, but against the character and person of Mr. Pope. And that of all those men who have received pleasure from his works, which by modest computation may be about a hundred thousand in these kingdoms of England and Ireland (not to mention Jersey, Guernsey, the Orcades, those in the new world, and foreigners who have translated him into their languages); of all this number not a man hath stood up to say one word in his defence.

The only exception is the author of the following poem, who, doubtless, had either a better insight into the grounds of this clamour, or a better opinion of Mr. Pope's integrity, joined with a greater personal love for him, than any other of his numerous friends and admirers.

Further, that he was in his peculiar intimacy, appears from the knowledge he manifests of the most private authors of all the anonymous pieces against him, and from his having in this poem attacked no man living, who had not before printed or published some scandal against this gentleman.

How I came possessed of it is no concern to the reader; but it would have been a wrong to him had I detained the publication, since those names which are its chief ornaments die off daily so fast, as must render it too soon unintelligible. If it provoke the author to give us a more perfect edition, I have my end.

Who he is I cannot say, and (which is a great pity) there is certainly nothing in his style and manner of writing which can distinguish or discover him: for if it bears any resemblance to that of Mr. Pope, 'tis not improbable but it might be done on purpose, with a view to have it pass for his. But by the frequency of his allusions to Virgil, and a laboured (not to say affected) *shortness* in imitation of him, I should think him more an admirer of the Roman poet than of the Grecian, and in that not of the same taste with his friend.

I have been well informed, that this work was the labour of full six years of his life, and that he wholly retired himself from all the avocations and pleasures of the world, to attend diligently to its correction and perfection; and six years more he intended t bestow upon it, as it should seem by this verse of Statius, which was cited at the head o his manuscript,

> Oh mihi bissenos multum vigilata per annos,
> Duncia!

Hence also we learn the true title of the poem; which, with the same certainty as w call that of Homer the *Iliad*, of Virgil the *Aeneid*, of Camoens the *Lusiad*, we ma pronounce, could have been, and can be no other than

The DUNCIAD

It is styled *heroic*, as being *doubly* so; not only with respect to its nature, which according to the best rules of the ancients, and strictest ideas of the moderns, is criticall such; but also with regard to the heroical disposition and high courage of the writer, wh dared to stir up such a formidable, irritable, and implacable race of mortals.

There may arise some obscurity in chronology from the *names* in the poem, by the inevitable removal of some authors, and insertion of others in their niches. For whoeve will consider the unity of the whole design, will be sensible that the *poem was not mad for these authors, but these authors for the poem.* I should judge that they were clapped in as they rose, fresh and fresh, and changed from day to day; in like manner as when the old boughs wither, we thrust new ones into a chimney.

I would not have the reader too much troubled or anxious, if he cannot deciphe them; since when he shall have found them out, he will probably know no more of the persons than before.

Yet we judged it better to preserve them as they are, than to change them fo fictitious names; by which the satire would only be multiplied, and applied to many instead of one. Had the hero, for instance, been called Codrus, how many would have affirmed him to have been Mr. T., Mr. E., Sir R. B., etc.; but now all that unjust scanda is saved by calling him by a name, which by good luck happens to be that of a rea person.

II

ADVERTISEMENT
To the FIRST EDITION with Notes, in Quarto, 1729

It will be sufficient to say of this edition, that the reader has here a much more correct and complete copy of the DUNCIAD than has hitherto appeared. I cannot answer but some mistakes may have slipped into it, but a vast number of others will be prevented by the names being now not only set at length, but justified by the authorities and reasons given. I make no doubt the author's own motive to use real rather than feigned names, was his care to preserve the innocent from any false application; whereas, in the former editions, which had no more than the initial letters, he was made, by Keys printed here, to hurt the inoffensive, and (what was worse) to abuse his friends, by an impression at Dublin.

The commentary which attends this poem was sent me from several hands, and consequently must be unequally written; yet will have one advantage over most commentaries, that it is not made upon conjectures, or at a remote distance of time: and the reader cannot but derive one pleasure from the very *obscurity* of the persons it treats of, that it partakes of the nature of a *secret*, which most people love to be let into, though the men or the things be ever so inconsiderable or trivial.

Of the *persons* it was judged proper to give some account; for since it is only in this monument that they must expect to survive (and here survive they will, as long as the English tongue shall remain such as it was in the reigns of Queen ANNE and King GEORGE,) it seemed but humanity to bestow a word or two upon each, just to tell what he was, what he writ, when he lived, and when he died.

If a word or two more are added upon the chief offenders, it is only as a paper pinned upon the breast, to mark the enormities for which they suffered; lest the correction only should be remembered, and the crime forgotten.

In some articles it was thought sufficient barely to transcribe from Jacob, Curll, and other writers of their own rank, who were much better acquainted with them than any of the authors of this comment can pretend to be. Most of them had drawn each other's characters on certain occasions; but the few here inserted are all that could be saved from the general destruction of such works.

Of the part of Scriblerus, I need say nothing; his manner is well enough known, and approved by all but those who are too much concerned to be judges.

The imitations of the ancients are added, to gratify those who either never read, or may have forgotten them; together with some of the parodies and allusions to the most excellent of the moderns. If, from the frequency of the former, any man think the poem too much a cento, our poet will but appear to have done the same thing in jest which Boileau did in earnest; and upon which Vida, Fracastorius, and many of the most eminent Latin poets, professedly valued themselves.

III

THE GUARDIAN.
Being a continuation of some former Papers on the
Subject of PASTORALS

Monday, April 27, 1713.

Compulerantque greges Corydon & Thyrsis in unum.—
Ex illo Corydon, Corydon est tempore nobis.

I designed to have troubled the reader with no farther discourse of pastoral; but being informed that I am taxed of partiality, in not mentioning an author whose Eclogues are published in the same volume with Mr. Philips's; I shall employ this paper in observations upon him, written in the free spirit of criticism, and without any apprehension of offending that gentleman, whose character it is, that he takes the greatest care of his works before they are published, and has the least concern for them afterwards.

I have laid it down as the first rule of pastoral, that its ideas should be taken from the manners of the Golden Age, and the moral formed upon the representation of innocence; 'tis therefore plain that any deviations from that design degrade a poem from being truly pastoral. In this view it will appear that Virgil can only have two of his *Eclogues* allowed to be such : his first and ninth must be rejected, because they describe the ravages of armies, and oppressions of the innocent; Corydon's criminal passion for Alexis throws oa the second; the calumny and railing in the third are not proper to that state of concord; the eighth represents unlawful ways of procuring love by enchantments, and introduces a shepherd whom an inviting precipice tempts to self-murder: as to the fourth, sixth, and truth, they are given up by Heinsius, Salmasius, Rapin, and the critics in general. They likewise observe that but eleven of all the *Idyllia* of Theocritus are to be admitted a pastorals; and even out of that number the greater part will be excluded for one or other of the reasons above mentioned. So that when I remarked in a former paper, that Virgil' *Eclogues*, taken altogether, are rather select poems than pastorals; I might have said the same thing, with no less truth, of Theocritus. The reason of this I take to be ye unobserved by the critics, viz., they never meant them all for pastorals.

Now it is plain Philips hath done this, and in that particular excelled both Theocritus and Virgil.

As simplicity is the distinguishing characteristic of pastoral, Virgil hath been thought guilty of too courtly a style; his language is perfectly pure, and he often forgets he is among peasants. I have frequently wondered that since he was so conversant in the writings of Ennius, he had not imitated the rusticity of the Doric, as well by the help of the old obsolete Roman language, as Philips hath by the antiquated English. For example, might not he have said *quoi* instead of *cui*, *quoijum* for *cujum*, *volt* for *vult*, etc. as well as our modern hath *welladay* for *alas*, *whilome* for *of old*, *make mock* for *deride*, and *witless younglings* for *simple lambs, etc.* by which means he had attained as much of the air of Theocritus, as Philips hath of Spenser.

Mr. Pope hath fallen into the same error with Virgil. His clowns do not converse in all the simplicity proper to the country; his names are borrowed from Theocritus and Virgil, which are improper to the scene of his pastorals. He introduces Daphnis, Alexis, and Thyrsis on British plains, as Virgil hath done before him on the Mantuan. Whereas Philips, who hath the strictest regard to propriety, makes choice of names peculiar to the country, and more agreeable to a reader of delicacy, such as Hobbinol, Lobbin, Cuddy and Colin-Clout.

So easy as pastoral writing may seem (in the simplicity we have described it) yet it requires great reading, both of the ancients and moderns, to be a master of it. Philips hath given us manifest proofs of his knowledge of books. It must be confessed his competitor hath imitated *some single thoughts* of the ancients well enough (if we consider he had not the happiness of an university education,) but he hath dispersed them, here and there, without that order and method which Mr. Philips observes, whose *whole* third pastoral is an instance bow well he hath studied the fifth of Virgil, and bow judiciously reduced Virgil's thoughts to the standard of pastoral; as his contention of Colin Clout and the nightingale shows with what exactness he hath imitated every line in Strada.

When I remarked it as a principal fault to introduce fruits and flowers of a foreign growth, in the descriptions where the scene lies in our own country, I did not design that observation should extend also to animals, or the sensitive life; for Mr. Philips hath with great judgment described wolves in England in his first pastoral. Nor would I have a poet slavishly confine himself (as Mr. Pope hath done) to one particular season of the year, one certain time of the day, and one unbroken scene in each eclogue. 'Tis plain Spenser neglected this pedantry, who in his pastoral of November mentions the mournful song of the nightingale.

Sad Philomel her song in tears doth sleep.

And Mr. Philips, by a poetical creation, hath raised up finer beds of flowers than the most industrious gardener; his roses, endives, lilies, kingcups, and daffodils blow all in the same season.

But the better to discover the merits of our two contemporary pastoral writers, I shall endeavour to draw a parallel of them, by setting several of their particular thoughts in the same light, whereby it will be obvious how much Philips hath the advantage. With what simplicity he introduces two shepherds singing alternately!

Hobb. *Come, Rosalind, O come, for without thee*
      What pleasure can the country have for me!
      Come, Rosalind, O come! my brinded kine,
      My snowy sheep, my farm, and all are thine,

Lanq. *Come, Rosalind, O come; here shady bowers,*
      Here are cool fountains, and here springing flowers,
      Come, Rosalind; here ever let us stay,
      And sweetly waste our live-long time away.

Our other pastoral writer, in expressing the same thought, deviates into downright poetry:

Streph. *In spring, the fields, in autumn, hills I love;*
      At morn the plains, at noon the shady grove;
      But Delia always; forced from Delia's sight,
      Nor plaint at morn, nor groves at noon delight.

Daph. *Sylvia's like autumn ripe, yet mild as May,*
      More bright than noon, yet fresh at early day;
      Ev'n spring displeases when she shines not here,
      But blessed with her 'tis spring throughout the year.

In the first of these authors, two shepherds thus innocently describe the behaviour of their mistresses:

Hobb. *As Marian bathed, by chance I passed by,*
      She blushed, and at me cast a side-long eye;
      Then swift beneath the crystal wave she tried
      Her beauteous form, but all in vain to hide.

Lanq. *As I to cool me bathed one sultry day,*
      Fond Lydia lurking in the sedges lay;
      The wanton laughed, and seemed in haste to fly;
      Yet often stopped, and often turned her eye.

The other modern (who, it must be confessed, hath a knack of versifying) hath it as follows:

Streph. *Me gentle Delia beckons from the plain,*
Then, hid in shades, eludes her eager swain;
But feigns a laugh, to see me search around,
And by that laugh the willing fair is found.

Daph. *The sprightly Sylvia trips along the green,*
She runs, but hopes she does not run unseen,
While a kind glance at her pursuer flies,
How much at variance are her feet and eyes!

There is nothing the writers of this kind of poetry are fonder of, than descriptions of pastoral presents. Philips says thus of a sheep-hook:

Of seasoned elm, where studs of brass appear,
To speak the giver's name, the month and year;
The hook of polished steel, the handle turned,
And richly by the graver's skill adorned.

The other of a bowl embossed with figures:

——where wanton ivy twines,
And swelling clusters bend the curling vines;
Four figures rising from the work appear,
The various seasons of the rolling year;
And what is that which binds the radiant sky,
Where twelve bright signs in beauteous order lie?

The simplicity of the swain in this place, who forgets the name of the zodiac, is no ill imitation of Virgil: but how much more plainly and unaffectedly would Philips have dressed this thought in his Doric?

And what that hight which girds the welkin sheen,
Where twelve gay signs in meet array are seen?

If the reader would indulge his curiosity any farther in the comparison of particulars, he may read the first pastoral of Philips with the second of his contemporary; and the fourth and sixth of the former with the fourth and first of the latter; whore several parallel places will occur to everyone.

Having now shown some parts in which these two writers may be compared, it is a justice I owe to Mr. Philips, to discover those in which no man can compare with him. First, that beautiful rusticity, of which I shall only produce two instances of an hundred not yet quoted:

O woeful day! O day of woe! quoth he;
And woeful I, who live the day to see!

The simplicity of the diction, the melancholy flowing of the numbers, the solemnity of the sound, and the easy turn of the words in this dirge (to make use of our author's expression) are extremely elegant.

In another of his pastorals, a shepherd utters a dirge not much inferior to the former, in the following lines:

> *Ah me, the while! ah me! the luckless day!*
> *Ah luckless lad! the rather might I say!*
> *Ah silly I! more silly than my sheep,*
> *Which on the flowery plain I once did keep.*

How he still charms the ear with these artful repetitions of the epithets; and how significant is the last verse! I defy the most common reader to repeat them without feeling some motions of compassion.

In the next place I shall rank his proverbs, in which I formerly observed he excels. For example:

> *A rolling stone is ever bare of moss;*
> *And, to their cost, green years old proverbs cross.*
>
> *—He that late lies down, as late will rise,*
> *And, sluggard-like, till noon-day snoring lies.*
>
> *—Against ill luck all cunning foresight fails;*
> *Whether we sleep or wake, it nought avails.*
>
> *—Nor fear, from upright sentence, wrong.*

Lastly, his elegant dialect, which alone might prove him the eldest born of Spenser, and our only true Arcadian. I should think it proper for the several writers of pastoral to confine themselves to their several counties. Spenser seems to have been of this opinion; for he hath laid the scene of one of his pastorals in Wales; where with all the simplicity natural to that part of our island, one shepherd bids the other good-morrow, in an unusual and elegant manner:

> *Diggon Davy, I bid hur God-day;*
> *Or Diggon hur is, or I mis-say.*

Diggon answers,

> *Hur was hur while it was day-light;*
> *But now hur is a most wretched wight, etc.*

But the most beautiful example of this kind that I ever met with, is in a very valuable piece which I chanced to find among some old manuscripts, entitled a *Pastoral Ballad;* which I think, for its nature and simplicity, may (notwithstanding the modesty of the title) be allowed a perfect pastoral. It is composed in the Somersetshire dialect, and the names such as arc proper to the country people. It may be observed, as a farther beauty of this pastoral, the words nymph, dryad, naiad, fawn, cupid, or satyr, are not once mentione throughout the whole. I shall make no apology for inserting some few lines of thi excellent piece. Cicily breaks thus into the subject as she is going a-milking:

Cicily. *Rager, go vetch tha kee, or else tha zun*
Will quite be go, bevore c'have half a don.

Roger. *Thou shouldst not ax ma tweece, but I've a bee*
To dreave our bull to bull tha parson's kee.

It is to be observed, that this whole dialogue is formed upon the passion of *jealousy*; an his mentioning the parson's kine naturally revives the jealousy of the shepherdess Cicily which she expresses as follows:

Cicily. *Ah Rager. Rager! ches was zore avraid*
When in yon vield you kissed the parson's maid;
Is this the love that once to me you zed,
When from the wake thou brought'st me ginger-bread!

Roger. *Cicily thou charg'st me valse,—I'll zwear to thee*
Tha parson's maid is still a maid for me.

In which answer of his are expressed at once that spirit of religion, and tha innocence of the Golden Age, so necessary to be observed by all writers of pastoral.

At the conclusion of this piece, the author reconciles the lovers, and ends the eclogue the most simply in the world:

So Rager parted, vor to vetch tha kee;
And vor her bucket in went Cicily.

I am loath to show my fondness for antiquity so far as to prefer this ancient British author to our present English writers of pastoral; but I cannot avoid making this obvious remark, that Philips hath hit into the same road with this old West Country bard of ours.

After all that hath been said, I hope none can think it any injustice to Mr. Pope, that I forbore to mention him as a Pastoral writer; since upon the whole, he is of the same class with Moschus and Bion, whom we have excluded that rank; and of whose eclogues, as well as some of Virgil's, it may be said, that (according to the description we have given of this sort of poetry) they are by no means pastorals, but something better.

IV
OF THE
POET LAUREATE
19 *November* 1729.

The time of the election of a Poet Laureate being now at hand, it may be proper to give some account of the *rites* and *ceremonies* anciently used at that solemnity, and only discontinued through the neglect and degeneracy of later times. These we have extracted from an historian of undoubted credit, a reverend bishop, the learned Paulus Jovius; and are the same that were practised under the pontificate of Leo X., the great restorer of learning.

As we now see an *age* and a *court*, that for the encouragement of poetry rivals, if not exceeds, that of this famous Pope, we cannot but wish a restoration of all its *honours* to *poesy*; the rather, since there are so many parallel circumstances in the *person* who was then honoured with the laurel, and in *him*, who (in all probability) is now to wear it.

I shall translate my author exactly as I find it in the 82nd chapter of his *Elogia Vir. Doct.* He begins with the character of the poet himself, who was the original and father of all Laureates, and called Camillo, He was a plain country-man of Apulia, whether a *shepherd* or *thresher*, is not material. 'This man', says Jovius, 'excited by the fame of the great encouragement given to poets at court, and the high honour in which they were held, came to the city, bringing with him a strange kind of lyre in his hand, and at least some *twenty thousand of verses*. All the wits and critics of the court flocked about him, delighted to see a *clown*, with a ruddy, hale complexion, and in his own long hair, so top full of poetry; and at the first sight of him all agreed he was born to be *Poet Laureate*. He had a most hearty welcome in an *island* of the river Tiber (an agreeable place, not unlike our Richmond) where he was first made to *eat* and *drink plentifully*, and to *repeat his verses to everybody*. Then they adorned him with a new and elegant garland, composed of *vine-leaves, laurel, and brassica* (a sort of cabbage) so composed, says my author, emblematically, *ut tam sales, quam lepida ejus temulentia, Brassicae remedio cohibenda, notaretur.* He was then saluted by common consent with the title of *archi-poeta*, or *arch-poet*, in the style of those days, in ours *Poet Laureate.* This honour the poor man received with the most sensible demonstrations of joy, his eyes drunk with tears and gladness. Next the public acclamation was expressed in a *canticle*, which is transmitted to us, as follows:

> *Salve, brassicea virens corona,*
> *Et lauro, archipoeta, pampinoque!*
> *Dignus principis auribus Leonis.*
> *All hail, arch-poet without peer!*
> *Vine, bay, or cabbage fit to wear,*
> *And worthy of the* prince's ear.

From hence he was conducted in pomp to the *Capitol* of Rome, mounted on an *elephant*, through the shouts of the populace, where the ceremony ended.

The historian tells us farther, 'That at his introduction to Leo, he not only poured forth verses innumerable, like a torrent, but also *sung* them with *open mouth.* Nor was he only *once* introduced, or on *stated* days (like our Laureates) but made a *companion* to his *master*, and entertained as one of the instruments of his *most elegant pleasures.* When the prince was at table, the poet had his place at the window. When the prince had half eaten his meat, he gave with his own hands the rest to the poet. When the poet drank, it was out of the prince's own flagon, insomuch (says the historian) that through so great good eating and drinking he contracted a most terrible gout.' Sorry I am to relate what follows, but that I cannot leave my reader's curiosity unsatisfied in the catastrophe of this extraordinary man. To use my author's words, which are remarkable, *mortuo Leone, profligatisque poetis etc.* 'When Leo died, and poets were no more' (for I would not understand *profligatis* literally, as if poets then were profligate) this unhappy Laureate was forthwith reduced to return to his country, where, oppressed with *old age* and *want* he miserably perished in a *common hospital.*

We see from this sad conclusion (which may be of example to the poets of our time that it were happier to meet with no encouragement at all, to remain at the plough, o other lawful occupation, than to be elevated above their condition, and taken out of the common means of life, without a surer support than the *temporary*, or, at best, *morta* favours of the great. It was doubtless for this consideration, that when the royal bounty was lately extended to a *rural genius*, care was taken to *settle it upon him for life.* And i hath been the practice of our Princes, never to remove from the station of Poet Laureate any man who hath once been chosen, though never so much greater geniuses might arise in his time. A noble instance, how much the *charity* of our monarchs hath exceeded their *love of fame.*

To come now to the intent of this paper. We have here the whole ancient *ceremonia* of the laureate. In the first place the crown is to be mixed with *vine-leaves*, as the vine is the plant of Bacchus, and full as essential to the honour, as the *butt of sack* to the salary.

Secondly, the *brassica* must be made use of as a qualifier of the former. It seems the *cabbage* was anciently accounted a remedy for *drunkenness*; a power the French now ascribe to the onion, and style a soup made of it, soupe d'Yvrogne. I would recommend a large mixture of the *brassica* if Mr. Dennis be chosen; but if Mr. Tibbald, it is not so necessary, unless the cabbage be supposed to signify the same thing with respect to *poets* as to *tailors*, viz. *stealing.* I should judge it not amiss to add another plant to this garland, to wit, *ivy*: not only as it anciently belonged to poets in general; but as it is emblematical of the three virtues of a court poet in particular; it is *creeping, dirty*, and *dangling.*

In the next place, a *canticle* must be composed and sung in laud and praise of the new poet. If Mr. CIBBER be laureated, it is my opinion no man can *write* this but himself: and no man, I am sure, can *sing* it so affectingly. But what this canticle should be, either in his or the other candidate's case, 1 shall not pretend to determine.

Thirdly, there ought to be a *public show*, or entry of the poet: to settle the order or procession of which, Mr. Anstis and Mr. DENNIS ought to have a conference. I apprehend here two difficulties : one, of procuring an *elephant*; the other of teaching the poet to ride him: therefore I should imagine the next animal in size or dignity would do best; either a *mule* or a large *ass*; particularly if that noble one could be had, whose portraiture makes so great an ornament of the *Dunciad*, and which (unless I am misinformed) is yet in the park of a nobleman near this city—unless Mr. CIBBER be the man; who may, with great propriety and beauty, ride on a *dragon*, if he goes by land; or if he choose the water, upon one of his own *swans* from *Caesar in Egypt.*

We have spoken sufficiently of the *ceremony*; let us now speak of the *qualifications* and *privileges* of the laureate. First, we see he must be able to make verses *extempore*, and to pour forth innumerable, if required. In this I doubt Mr. TIBBALD. Secondly, he ought to *sing*, and intrepidly, *patulo ore*: here, I confess the excellency of Mr. CIBBER. Thirdly, he ought to carry a *lyre* about with him: if a large one be thought too cumbersome, a small one may be contrived to hang about the neck, like an order, and be very much a grace to the person. Fourthly, he ought to have a good *stomach*, to eat and drink whatever his betters think fit; and therefore it is in this high office as in many others, no puny constitution can discharge it. I do not think CIBBER or TIBBALD here so happy: but rather a staunch, vigorous, seasoned, and dry *old gentleman*, whom I have in my eye.

I could also wish at this juncture, such a person as is truly jealous of the *honour* and *dignity* of *poetry*; no joker, or trifler; but a bard in *good earnest*; nay, not amiss if a critic, and the better if a little *obstinate*. For when we consider what great privileges have been lost from this office (as we see from the forecited authentic record of Jovius) namely those of *feeding* from the *prince's table*, *drinking* out of his *own flagon*, becoming even his *domestic* and *companion*; it requires a man warm and resolute, to be able to claim and obtain the restoring of these high honours. I have cause to fear the most of the candidates would be liable, either through the influence of ministers, or for rewards or favours, to give up the glorious rights of the laureate: yet I am not without hopes, there is *one*, from whom a *serious* and *steady* assertion of these privileges may be expected; and, if there be such a one, I must do him the justice to say, it is Mr. DENNIS, the worthy president of our society.

EPITAPH ON BOUNCE

Ah Bounce! ah gentle beast! why wouldst thou die,
When thou hadst meat enough, and Orrery?

CONVERSATIONS WITH JOSEPH SPENCE

(a) When I had done with my priests, I took to reading by myself, for which I had a very great eagerness and enthusiasm, especially for poetry: and in a few years I had dipped into a great number of the English, French, Italian, Latin, and Greek poets. This I did without any design, but that of pleasing myself: and got the languages, by hunting after the stories in the several poets I read; rather than read the books to get the languages. I followed everywhere as my fancy led me, and was like a boy gathering flowers in the fields and woods, just as they fall in his way. These five or six years I still look upon as the happiest part of my life.

(June 1739)

(b) I learned versification wholly from Dryden's works; who had improved it much beyond any of our former poets, and would probably have brought it to perfection, had not he been unhappily obliged to write so often in haste.

(March 1743)

(c) The great matter to write well is, 'to know thoroughly what one writes about,' and 'not to be affected.'

(December 1743)

(d) A poem on a slight subject, requires the greater care to make it considerable enough to be read. [Just after speaking of his *Dunciad*.]

(1728?)

(e) After writing a poem, one should correct it all over, with one single view at a time. Thus for language, if an elegy: 'these lines are very good, but are not they of too heroical a strain?' and so vice versa. It appears very plainly, from comparing parallel passages touched both in the *Iliad* and *Odyssey*, that Homer did this, and it is yet plainer that Virgil did so, from the distinct styles he uses in his three sorts of poems. It always answers in him, and so constant an effect could not be the effect of chance.

(May 1730)

(f) I have nothing to say for rhyme, but that I doubt whether a poem can support itself without it in our language, unless it be stiffened with such strange words as are likely to destroy our language itself.

The high style that is affected so much in blank verse would not have been borne, even in Milton, had not his subject turned so much on such strange out-of-the-world things as it does.

(June 1739)

(g) 'T is easy to mark out the general course of our poetry. Chaucer, Spenser, Milton, and Dryden, are the great landmarks for it.

(1736)

(h) Donne had no imagination, but as much wit, I think, as any writer can possibly have.

(1734?)

(i) All the rules of gardening are reducible to three heads: the contrasts, the management of surprises, and the concealment of the bounds.

(1742)

(j) A tree is a nobler object than a prince in his coronation robes.

(1728?)

(k) I *must* make a perfect edition of my works, and then shall have nothing to do but to die.

(January 1744)

(l) On the fifteenth, on Mr. Lyttelton's coming in to see him, he said, 'Here am I, dying of a hundred good symptoms.'

(15 May 1744)

THE END

CPSIA information can be obtained at www.ICGtesting.com
Printed in the USA
LVOW111715070612

285124LV00008B/33/P